U.S. FOREIGN POLIC[illegible]

THE COLD WAR

Pitt Series in Policy and Institutional Studies

U.S. FOREIGN POLICY AFTER THE COLD WAR

Edited by Randall B. Ripley

and James M. Lindsay

University of Pittsburgh Press

Published by the University of Pittsburgh Press, Pittsburgh, Pa. 15261

Manufactured in the United States of America

Printed on acid-free paper

10 9 8 7 6 5 4 3 2 1

CATALOGING-IN-PUBLICATION-DATA

U.S. foreign policy after the Cold War / edited by Randall B. Ripley and James M. Lindsay.

p. cm. — (Pitt series in policy and institutional studies)

Includes bibliogaphical references and index.

ISBN 0-8229-3981-9 (acid-free paper). — ISBN 0-8229-5625-X (pbk. : acid-free paper)

1. United States—Foreign relations—1989– 2. Cold War. I. Ripley, Randall B. II. Lindsay, James M., 1959– . III. Series.

E840.U1715 1997

327.73—dc21 97-4569

CIP

A CIP catalog record for this book is available from the British Library.

Contents

Preface

The cold war came to a grinding halt during the astounding developments of 1989–1991. The Berlin Wall fell, the eastern European Soviet satellites freed themselves from Soviet domination, and the Soviet Union itself disintegrated after witnessing a failed coup presumably aimed at restoring a communist dictatorship. Suddenly, the "evil empire" was no more and the raison d'être for most post–World War II U.S. foreign policy vanished.

What has happened to the content of U.S. foreign policy and to the bureaucratic structures and processes responsible for making that policy in the years since these momentous events? Have there been significant changes in content or in the bureaucracy? If so, what has been the nature and effect of that change? If not, why not? Have George Bush and Bill Clinton—the two presidents who served during and after the events of 1989–1991—provided leadership designed to produce meaningful change?

These are the most general questions addressed in this volume. The authors of the individual chapters examine a wide variety of bureaucratic institutions and some major substantive policy areas in providing partial answers to these questions. In the last chapter we seek to aggregate these partial answers to provide more general responses to the questions.

All the chapters in this volume are published here for the first time. The authors presented first drafts at a May 1994 conference in Columbus, Ohio, sponsored jointly by the Mershon Center at Ohio State University and the Midwest Consortium for International Security Studies. The authors subsequently revised these papers many times. This was a collective enterprise in which all of us were involved for several years.

From inception, our intent was to generate a set of individually interesting papers that would also have a cumulative impact. To this end, the first drafts and the conference were organized around questions posed in a paper by the coeditors. All the authors participated in intensive discussions of all the papers. This initial interchange, coupled with subsequent revisions by the authors and by the interaction of the coeditors and authors has, we think, resulted in a degree of coherence too often missing in edited volumes of original papers.

We are grateful to the two financial sponsors of this project—the Mershon Center at Ohio State University and the Midwest Consortium for International Security Studies. Reviewers for the University of Pittsburgh Press provided insightful comments. A large number of other colleagues commented usefully on individual chapters. Two able graduate students in the Ohio State Department of Political Science—Eric Heberlig and Lisa Campoli—performed numerous important tasks with care, talent, and admirable spirit. The personnel at the University of Pittsburgh Press have been helpful throughout. Above all, we are indebted to the authors of the individual chapters. They freely entered into the spirit of working together to generate a book that was more than the sum of its parts.

Randall B. Ripley, Columbus, Ohio
James M. Lindsay, Washington, D.C.

PART I

INTRODUCTION

James M. Lindsay and Randall B. Ripley

1. U.S. Foreign Policy in a Changing World

The end of the cold war has stimulated a vigorous debate on the nature of America's role in the world. That debate has focused in part on whether to restructure a foreign policy bureaucracy born in the wake of World War II and forged in the fires of the cold war. It has also focused on how to reorient the content of a foreign policy predicated for more than four decades on the goal of containing Soviet expansion. At the heart of the debate, then, lies a simple question: Are the structures and policies of U.S. foreign policy appropriate to meet the needs of the United States as it heads into the twenty-first century?

To judge by the outpouring of proposals for restructuring the many departments and agencies that make up the foreign policy bureaucracy and for reorienting the content of U.S. foreign policy, the answer is no. Scholars, lobbyists, practitioners, and pundits have all rushed forward with their pet proposals to shrink the Defense Department, revitalize the State Department, promote trade, and advance human rights. Now that these debates have been under way for more than five years, it is time to step back and ask if the dramatic changes in structure and policy that seemed inevitable in 1991 have in fact taken place.

The chapters in this book attempt to provide just such an assessment. Taken together, they address two major questions. First, how are individual foreign policy agencies responding to the pressure to reorient themselves to the new realities of the post–cold war era? Second, how is the content of U.S. foreign policy changing in response to the end of the cold war?

Answers to these questions will help us understand how U.S. foreign policy is adapting to the end of the cold war. They will also help us better understand how U.S. foreign policy is made, and particularly, how bureaucracies and decision makers adapt to periods of dramatic change in the international environment. Much of the seminal literature on foreign policy making in the United States was written in the late 1960s and early 1970s, a time when a consensus existed on both the rationale for individual agencies and the purpose of U.S. foreign policy. The changes that did occur tended to be small and incremental. Yet what the United States faces in the international environment in the 1990s is discontinuous, or revolutionary, change. Do such monumental changes lead to equally dramatic changes in the structure and outcomes of U.S. foreign policy?

Context

The debate over how U.S. foreign policy should adapt to the end of the cold war typically invokes the need for change. Yet what precisely that change should look like varies with the observer. Most discussions implicitly or explicitly assume that the collapse of the Soviet Union has ushered in a period of retrenchment. According to this view, the task facing the United States is to decide which agencies can be eliminated or streamlined and which policies can be jettisoned or deemphasized. On the other hand, a minority argues that the post–cold war world presents the United States not with fewer threats but with new dangers and new opportunities. In this view, the United States needs to reorient, if not expand, its existing foreign policy agencies and to assume a more active role in world affairs.

A World of Retrenchment

As talk about the "peace dividend" and articles with titles such as "The Orphaned Agency," "Does the CIA Still Have a Role?" and "Back to the Womb?" all attest, much of the debate over the future of U.S. foreign policy assumes that the task facing the United States is retrenchment. The popularity of the retrenchment theme clearly rests on the belief that the collapse of the Soviet Union has led to *problem depletion*—a decrease in the number and severity of foreign policy problems facing the United States. (On problem depletion generally, see Levine 1978.) With the Soviet Union no longer threatening the security of western Europe and with the appearance of democracies throughout eastern Europe, the rationale for containment, the bedrock principle guiding U.S. foreign policy for forty years, ceased to exist.

The impact of problem depletion on a foreign policy bureaucracy is perhaps clearest with respect to the Defense Department. The central problem that generated political support for massive defense spending—aggressive world communism—has largely gone away, except for a few vestigial remains, such as the government of North Korea. Although other threats have moved to the forefront of the foreign policy debate—nuclear proliferation, state-sponsored terrorism, and ethnic rivalries come to mind—these threats are not new, nor do they seem to be as severe as the formal global confrontation with "the evil empire." Moreover, traditional military forces may not be equipped to respond to such problems. The result has been repeated calls to downsize the Defense Department or what Lawrence Korb (1996) has called "our overstuffed armed forces."

The assumption of problem depletion also explains the widespread belief that the post–cold war world requires less of the United States in foreign affairs. The belief that the United States should now pay more attention to matters at home is most visible in the writings and speeches of neoisolationists such as Pat Buchanan, but it also can be seen even among committed internationalists. Thus, during the 1992 presidential election Bill Clinton made the slogan, "It's the economy, stupid," the theme of his campaign, and George Bush downplayed his interest in foreign affairs. The belief that the United States can now pay more attention to its domestic needs has clearly taken hold of the American public. During most of the cold war era, when asked to identify the most important problem facing the United States, 10 to 20 percent of those polled volunteered a foreign policy issue. In contrast, by 1996, polls found that less than 2 percent of those polled named a foreign policy issue as posing a major challenge to the United States (Rosner 1996, 124).

Although a belief in problem depletion explains why the debate over the future of U.S. foreign policy typically speaks in terms of retrenchment, *environmental entropy* also plays a role. Environmental entropy arises when the capacity of the government to support a public agency at existing levels of activity erodes. As Levine argues (1978, 318), "The capacity of a government is as much a function of the willingness of taxpayers to be taxed as it is of the economic base of the taxing region." In the years since the fall of the Berlin Wall, and especially since the collapse of the Soviet Union, public enthusiasm in the United States for defense spending has declined, as has public enthusiasm for spending on foreign affairs, which was never high to begin with (see, e.g., "Foreign Aid: Under Siege in the Budget Wars" 1995). This environmental entropy has its roots in the public's perception of problem depletion in foreign affairs and its growing unease about the government's indebtedness and the future of the American economy.

A World of New Dangers and New Opportunities

Although much of the current debate over the future of U.S. foreign policy proceeds from the assumption that the main task faced by American officials is retrenchment, some people argue (again, either explicitly or implicitly) that the United States now confronts not problem depletion but *problem expansion.* For some, the roots of problem expansion lie in the rise of new dangers to U.S. national security. The passing of the Soviet Union has meant less order in the international arena and with it a surge in problems such as nuclear proliferation and ethnic conflict. For others, the roots of problem expansion lie in the new opportunities for U.S. foreign policy. As the lone remaining superpower, the United States has a singular opportunity to promote its interests and values abroad.

The assumption that the United States faces a situation of problem expansion can be seen in calls for increased spending and for giving some foreign policy agencies more responsibilities. The House Republicans' Contract with America called for passing a National Security Revitalization Act that, among other things, promised to spend more on defense (see Gillespie and Schellhas 1994). In 1996, House Republicans voted to increase funding on intelligence activities by nearly 5 percent to enable the intelligence community to handle the new threats facing the country (Kehoe 1996b). Meanwhile, some executive branch officials complain that the end of the cold war has given them more rather than less to do. For example, State Department officials often note that since 1989 the department has opened embassies in twenty new nations (Kirschten 1993c, 2369).

Although the Clinton administration came to office promising to focus its energies on domestic issues, some of its foreign policy initiatives sought to expand the U.S. role in world affairs (see Hendrickson 1994). This is perhaps clearest in the case of peacekeeping, where the administration sought to increase American contributions to UN peacekeeping operations (see Daalder 1994). In Somalia, for example, the Clinton administration expanded the Bush administration's humanitarian relief mission into an "assertive multilateralism" that sought to rebuild the Somali political system (see Bolton 1994). In addition to the Clinton administration's own inclination to expand the U.S. role overseas, interest groups dealing with the environment, human rights, international development, and nuclear proliferation all pressured the White House to move their issue to the forefront of the foreign policy agenda.

Contrary to claims of an isolationist public, polling data provide some evidence that the Americans support a continued, and perhaps even expanded, American role in world affairs. According to polls sponsored by the Chicago Council on Foreign Relations, in 1994, 65 percent of the American public favored an active role for the United States in world affairs, compared to 54 percent in 1982 (Rielly 1995b). A poll conducted in 1993 by the Program on International Policy Attitudes at the University of Maryland found that 88 percent agreed with the statement that "because the world is so interconnected today it is important for the U.S. to participate, together with other countries, in efforts to maintain peace and protect human rights" (Kull 1995–1996). Although these poll results should be treated with caution—as we noted earlier, other polls show rising isolationist sentiment in the United States—they suggest that if properly framed, proposals to expand America's role in the world can resonate with the American public.

Competing Visions

Academic discussions of what change in the international arena entails for state behavior often assume that the linkage is straightforward. Yet the debate in the United States in the first half of the 1990s suggests that how a state responds to external change is a subjective and not an objective matter. While many Americans believe the international environment now requires less of the United States, a minority argues that it demands more. The outcome of this debate will shape the evolution of both the structure and content of U.S. foreign policy into the twenty-first century.

Which vision ultimately prevails depends in part on developments in the international arena. If the trend toward market democracy continues around the world and fears of nuclear terrorism and environmental degradation prove overblown, the sense that the United States can afford to do less overseas is likely to grow. Conversely, if Russia's experiment with democracy fails, if China attacks Taiwan, or if terrorists steal a nuclear weapon—to mention only a few possibilities—the perception that the United States faces renewed external threats will grow and with it the belief the United States needs to do more in world affairs.

At the same time, politics will also drive the debate over the future of U.S. foreign policy. As the polling data show, Americans harbor conflicting beliefs about the United States' role in world affairs. As a result, which proposals win public support may depend on less on the merits than on which groups succeed in framing their proposals in ways that resonate with core American values. Moreover, because both problem depletion *and* environmental entropy are driving the calls for retrenchment in U.S. foreign policy, what the United States does in foreign affairs will inevitably be tied to domestic politics. So long as the American public opposes paying higher taxes, demands greater domestic services, and insists that the federal government reduce its deficit, the pressure to downsize individual foreign policy agencies and to reduce foreign commitments will be felt for years to come.

Change and the Foreign Policy Bureaucracy

Although the U.S. foreign policy bureaucracy clearly faces pressure to change in the wake of the end of the cold war, it is less clear what kind of change we are likely to see. Part of the reason is that scholars, practitioners, and pundits have offered a dizzying array of reform proposals. Another part of the reason is that the scholarly literature has not adequately addressed the question of how foreign policy bureaucracies react to revolutionary changes in the international environment.

Proposals for Change

Proposals to restructure the Agency for International Development (AID) run the gamut from greatly expanding its duties to abolishing it entirely (e.g., Madison 1992a, 1992b). Likewise, some critics dismiss the Central Intelligence Agency (CIA) as a historical relic and call for its abolition (e.g., Hersh 1994, 5; Moynihan 1991). Others recommend rejuvenating the agency and giving its director greater powers to lead the intelligence community (see, e.g., Kehoe 1996a).

One task the chapters in Part II attempt to accomplish is to describe the major proposals for restructuring the U.S. foreign policy bureaucracy. Part of this task involves making clear which interests, both inside and outside government, favor what kinds of changes. Although calls for structural reforms are typically cast in value-neutral terms, they often have clear consequences for the substance of policy. To take one example, calls for rejuvenating the Arms Control and Disarmament Agency (ACDA) have been strongest within the arms control community, which believes that a properly structured ACDA can make arms control a major U.S. priority and can link it to foreign policy in general, a linkage ACDA has never succeeded in forging.

Organizational Interests and Bureaucratic Change

The agencies that make up the U.S. foreign policy bureaucracy face tremendous pressure to adapt to the end of the cold war. Given these pressures, how would we expect individual agencies to respond? Here previous research provides only limited guidance.

The general literature on government bureaucracies has paid much greater attention to how organizations respond to incremental changes in their external environments than to revolutionary changes. Yet U.S. foreign policy agencies now face revolutionary changes in their external environment.

Research on the foreign policy bureaucracy also provides little direct guidance to answering the question of how individual agencies will adapt to the end of the cold war. Allison (1969, 1971), Allison and Halperin (1972), Armacost (1969), Art (1968), and Halperin (1974), among others, explored bureaucratic decision making in a relatively stable political environment. For example, Halperin (1974, 11) begins his seminal work by noting, "From the onset of the cold war until quite recently, a majority of American officials (as well as the American public) have *[sic]* held a set of widely shared images." And while Halperin acknowledges that "dramatic changes in the outside world, either at home or abroad, may become so sharp that they . . . [lead] to changes in shared images" (ibid., 14), his analysis of bureaucratic decision making never explicitly addresses how a bureaucracy might respond to a period of revolutionary change.

Although neither the general literature on public bureaucracies nor the more narrow literature on the foreign policy bureaucracy developed a well-articulated theory about how agencies respond to revolutionary changes in their external environments, they do provide a solid basis for developing hypotheses about how agencies might respond. Much of the literature on bureaucratic politics, both foreign and domestic, devotes considerable attention to how the interests and cultures of individual organizations drive their decision making. Since organizational interests and cultures are deep-seated—to the point that organizations frequently resist external pressure to change—it seems reasonable to assume, at least as a starting point for discussion, that an agency's interests and culture will persist even in the face of revolutionary changes in its environment.

In this regard, Halperin's comments on organizational interests are instructive. He argues that each agency has its own culture or *essence,* that is, "the view held by the dominant group in the organization of what the missions and capabilities should be" (1974, 28). Halperin further argues that an organization's essence manifests itself in several ways:

> 1. An organization favors policies and strategies which its members believe will make the organization as they define it more important. . . .
>
> 2. An organization struggles hardest for the capabilities which it views as necessary to the essence of the organization. . . .
>
> 3. An organization resists efforts to take away from it those functions viewed as part of its essence. . . .

> 4. An organization is indifferent to functions not seen as part of its essence or necessary to protect its essence. . . .
>
> 5. Sometimes an organization attempts to push a growing function out of its domain entirely. (1974, 39–40)

Elsewhere in the book, Halperin makes two other critical points about organizational essence in the foreign policy bureaucracy:

> 6. . . . There are often conflicts among subgroups within a single career structure to define the essence of the organization.
>
> 7. In order to keep open promotions to top positions, an organization resists efforts to contract the size of the organization (unless the contraction is necessary to protect the essence of its activities.) (1974, 28, 54–55)

Taken together, these seven claims about organizational essence produce three broad hypotheses about how foreign policy agencies should react to revolutionary change in their external political environments:

> H_1. Organizations will resist changes that require them to forfeit missions and to accept smaller budgets (claims 1, 2, 3, and 7).
>
> H_2. If an organization lacks the political power needed to maintain the status quo, the dominant groups in the organization will respond to the push for change by protecting the organization's core functions (claims 1, 2, 3, 7) and jettisoning those functions it doesn't consider to be crucial (claims 4 and 5).
>
> H_3. Subordinate groups within an organization may attempt to use external change to push their preferred core functions to the top of the heap (claims 1, 2, and 6).

Of course, none of these three hypotheses is terribly surprising. After all, tales of bureaucratic resistance to change are legion. Yet these hypotheses do suggest four sets of questions that have considerable practical and theoretical importance for our understanding of how the U.S. foreign policy bureaucracy will adjust to the end of the cold war. These questions involve the depth and pervasiveness of change, the role of leadership, the nature of bureaucratic resistance to change, and the success bureaucracies have in resisting change.

The Depth and Pervasiveness of Change

Bill Clinton made *change* the watchword of his 1992 presidential campaign. It is not surprising, then, that his many cabinet and subcabinet appointees went to great pains in their early public appearances to stress that their agencies were changing to meet the needs of a new world. But change can come in many forms. What kinds of change are we witnessing in the U.S. foreign policy bureaucracy?

At a minimum we need to understand the precise reforms and innovations that individual agencies are now proposing and undertaking. We also need to understand the nature of the change that is taking place. Some change within bureaucracies is relatively deep and pervasive, whereas other change is not (Levy 1986; Mohrman et al. 1989). Deep change affects many aspects of an organization: organizational structure; management practices and style; decision-making processes; distribution of rewards; dominant beliefs, values, and norms; and organizational mission, strategy, and policy choices. Pervasive change affects a high proportion of the subsystems in an organization. This change is difficult to achieve, but it lasts longer than change that affects fewer subsystems.

The depth and pervasiveness of change are crucial because an agency's organizational essence typically inclines it to embrace the rhetoric but not the reality of change. In turn, changes that are shallow and limited in all likelihood will turn out to be ephemeral.

Have specific agencies begun to alter their structures and procedures or are their plans for change still mired in the proposal stage? Are agencies responding to budgetary pressures by cutting peripheral missions, or are they distributing budgetary cuts across the board? Do the changes that are occurring now represent a significant shift from the kinds of reorganization proposals individual agencies were advocating before the end of the cold war? The answers to these questions would give us a much better understanding of what precisely is happening within the foreign policy bureaucracy.

Leadership and Bureaucratic Change

High-ranking officials would seem to have the best opportunity to change the missions and operations of their agency during periods of great change in the external environment. When the outside world is in flux, high-level officials can use the power of initiative to set the agency's agenda. In contrast, during quieter periods in the outside world high-level officials presumably find it more difficult to reorient the missions and procedures of the agency. Instead, middle-level officials should call most of the shots.

Although the claim that high-ranking officials are better able to redirect their agencies during times of flux is plausible, it remains to be seen whether it is true. The experience of Secretary of Defense Les Aspin provides some reason for caution on this point. While serving as chair of the House Armed Services Committee, Aspin criticized the Bush administration for failing to recognize that the collapse of the Soviet Union necessitated a fundamental restructuring of the Pentagon (see Stockton 1993). He repeatedly called for a bottom-up review of U.S. security needs in order to achieve a radical reorganization of the armed services. Yet during his one-year tenure as secretary of defense, Aspin failed to revolutionize the Defense Department. Despite his insistence on the need for a bottom-up review, he made at most modest changes to U.S. force structure. By the time Aspin stepped down as secretary, President Clinton was insisting in his State of the Union Address (1994, 197): "We must not cut defense further."

The demise of Aspin's career as secretary of defense points to the importance of context in trying to understand organizational adaptation. What precisely are the conditions under which an agency's leadership can redirect its functions? Can a leadership successfully redirect an agency's functions if it has only external and not internal support? Conversely, can high-ranking officials protect the core essence of the agency in face of concerted external pressure? And, finally, given that Aspin's tenure at Defense was undercut by President Clinton's retreat from his campaign pledges to revolutionize the Pentagon, to what extent does entrepreneurial leadership at the agency level depend on presidential support?

Bureaucratic Resistance to Change

Both the general literature on organizations and the literature on bureaucratic politics within the foreign policy establishment discuss the many strategies that agencies use to resist change (e.g., Aspin 1973; Fox 1974; Halperin 1974; Levine 1980; Smith 1988). In general, these strategies fall into two categories: stonewalling and cooptation. When an agency pursues a strategy of stonewalling, it explicitly rejects calls for change in its missions and operations. In contrast, when an agency pursues a strategy of cooptation, it seeks to redefine the external environment in ways that justify existing missions and operations.

To make the distinction between stonewalling and cooptation concrete, consider the Defense Department. Many critics argue that Defense has pursued a mix of both strategies (see, e.g., Korb 1994). On the one hand, military leaders consistently have blocked efforts to reopen the 1948 agreement by which the four armed services agreed to allocate missions among themselves, even though many criticize the agreement for allowing the services to duplicate each other's functions. On the other hand, since the collapse of the Soviet Union, U.S. military leaders have argued that countries such as Iraq and North Korea pose considerable threats to U.S. national interests. Perhaps not surprisingly, military officials argue that defeating these regional threats to U.S. interests requires a force structure remarkably similar to the one developed during the cold war.

Of course, different agencies may respond to calls for change in different ways. If so, are their responses determined by their structure, history, and personnel, or are they essentially random? (see Meyer, Goes, and Brooks 1993). If agencies deliberately choose different strategies for reacting to change, do they do so primarily to make "good" policies that best serve the interests of the United States, or rather to enhance their own standing in the bureaucracy by protecting jurisdictional turf and maximizing budget and personnel? Or do their strategies stem from a mix of policy and nonpolicy motivations?

Success in Resisting Change

Although the agencies that make up the U.S. foreign policy bureaucracy are now all under pressure to adapt to the end of the cold war, there is no reason to believe that change is, or will be, felt to the same degree throughout the foreign policy establishment. Changes in the external environment that make the core duties of one agency potentially obsolete may make the core duties of another more important. Likewise, each agency has its own history, structure, and leadership, which, in turn, may lead it to pursue its own particular mix of resistance strategies with different records for success.

A key question for study, then, is how has change varied across agencies and why? In the abstract, a number of different factors may explain why some agencies change more than others. One possibility is that agencies with large domestic constituencies are better able to resist change because they have more political allies. Another is that agencies in which there is widespread agreement about the core duties will fare better in resisting change than agencies in which no such consensus exists. Still a third possible explanation is that the degree of change correlates with size; large agencies may simply be more difficult to restructure than small ones. Only systematic empirical analysis can shed light on the validity of these (and other) explanations of variations in bureaucratic change.

Policy Change

Systematic analysis of how individual bureaucracies are responding to the end of the cold war offers to improve our understanding of how foreign policy is now made in the United States. An equally important question is how the content of U.S. foreign policy has changed since the fall of the Berlin Wall. Put simply, are the means, ends, and priorities of U.S. foreign policy much different in 1997 compared to 1987 or 1977? And what accounts for the changes we are witnessing in the substance of policy?

The Substance of Policy

Since the collapse of the Soviet bloc in 1989, discussions of U.S. foreign policy have been rife with claims of "new thinking." Executive branch officials, members of Congress, interest groups, and think tanks have all weighed in with their ideas on how to redirect U.S. foreign policy now that the Soviet Union is on the "ash heap of history." Yet for all the talk of new thinking, it is by no means clear that the substance of policy has changed much since the 1980s. Is the substance of U.S. foreign policy changing, or only the rhetoric with which we discuss it?

One major task that part III attempts to accomplish is to trace the evolution of U.S. foreign policy in specific areas. Part of this task involves identifying which policy areas have seen changes in substance—as measured, say, by increased spending or a higher priority—and which have seen only changes in rhetoric. It also involves distinguishing between revolutionary change and the routine changes that occur as a new administration takes office. After all, even during the cold war the substance of specific policies sometimes changed from one administration to the next, as a comparison of the different approaches the Carter and Reagan administrations took to arms control suggests.

The Sources of Policy Change

We have good reason to believe that changing the structure or mission of a bureaucracy can change the kinds of policies it produces. In recent years, so-called new institutionalists have emphasized the idea that structures and procedures profoundly affect the outcome of the decision making process (see, e.g., Calvert, McCubbins, and Weingast 1989; Fiorina 1986; McCubbins, Noll, and Weingast 1987, 1989). These scholars make a simple point: "Alterations in procedures will change the expected policy outcomes of administrative agencies by affecting the relative influence of people who are affected by the policy" (McCubbins, Noll, and Weingast 1987, 254).

In emphasizing that procedures affect policy, new institutionalists highlight a lesson already well known to government reformers: policies that do not have a champion in the bureaucracy are doomed. For example, Congress created ACDA in 1961 in an effort to push the executive branch into integrating arms control concerns with military objectives. Likewise, in 1986, Congress passed the Goldwater-Nichols Act, which sought to curtail the problem of interservice squabbling over combat missions in wartime by streamlining the chain of command and enhancing the authority of theater commanders. In both instances, proponents believed that imposing new structures and procedures on the executive branch would improve its performance.

Although changes in the structure and procedures of the U.S. foreign policy bureaucracy can affect the substance of policy, few foreign policy scholars have explored the link between process and policy (for exceptions, see Forsythe 1987, 1988; Lindsay 1994b). What we do know suggests that the impact of bureaucratic change on policy varies greatly. In the case of Goldwater-Nichols, for example, many observers credit the act with helping to dampen interservice disagreements during the Gulf War. Secretary of Defense Dick Cheney went so far as to describe Goldwater-Nichols as "the most far-reaching piece of legislation affecting the [Defense] Department since the original National Security Act of 1947. . . . Clearly, it made a major contribution to our recent military successes" (quoted in U.S. Congress, House Committee on Armed Services 1992a, 41). In contrast, despite hopes that ACDA would integrate arms control concerns with military objectives, it "has always been either wholly or substantially excluded from that [weapons acquisition] process" (Clarke 1979, 97).

The example of ACDA provides a useful reminder that bureaucratic change does not always lead to policy change. By the same token, however, the fact that a policy changes is not definitive evidence that bureaucratic change is responsible. Another possible (and perhaps even more important) source of policy change is a change in personnel. For example, Halperin notes (1974, 13) that even in a stable political environment personnel changes can produce major changes in the content of policy as new decision makers bring new ideas and assumptions to their posts. The wisdom of Halperin's insight can be seen in the dramatic ways that some foreign policies changed during the cold war, as one administration gave way to another. To take the most obvious example, U.S. policy toward the Soviet Union varied significantly over the twenty-year period from the Nixon administration through the Reagan administration, even though the structure of the foreign policy establishment for the most part did not change.

Conclusion

In the aftermath of World War II, the United States developed a foreign affairs bureaucracy and a set of substantive policies predicated on the central task of containing world communism. With the abrupt end of the cold war, many agencies lost their central mission and many policies lost their rationale. Candidates and commentators of all ideological stripes now argue that the United States needs to restructure its foreign affairs bureaucracy and reorient the substance of its foreign policies.

While the pressure for change is obvious, whether and how individual agencies and policies are changing is not. The well-known ability of bureaucracies to resist or coopt change and the difficulty inherent in rethinking the fundamental premises of policy make it imperative that scholars assess how structure and policies are changing.

The chapters in this volume attempt to provide this assessment. Part II examines the institutions of U.S. foreign policy. In chapter 2, Bert Rockman discusses the nature of the presidential-bureaucratic relationship in foreign policy and the obstacles presidents face in generating change. In chapter 3, Vincent Auger analyzes how Bill Clinton structured the National Security Council (NSC) during his first term and how he sought to create a National Economic Council that in many ways would emulate the NSC and thereby give economics greater prominence in foreign policy. In chapter 4, James Lindsay explores the many proposals to restructure the organization of the State Department, and especially the proposal made by Sen. Jesse Helms (R-N.C.) to merge the Agency for International Development, the Arms Control and Disarmament Agency, and the United States Information Agency into a "Super State Department."

Chapters 5, 6, and 7 continue the focus on institutional change by examining the defense and intelligence agencies. In chapter 5, Paul Stockton reviews the changes the Bush and Clinton administrations made to defense budgeting and the military. In chapter 6, Loch Johnson explores how the leadership of the Central Intelligence Agency (CIA) sought to remake the agency in the midst of a political environment that emphasized budget cutting and downsizing. In chapter 7, Kimberly Zisk analyzes the differences between how the Joint Chiefs of Staff and the Directorate of Intelligence at the CIA reacted to the demise of the Soviet Union and the emergence of an independent Russia.

Part III examines the changing nature of U.S. policy in specific issue areas. In chapter 8, Peter Hahn compares the evolution of grand strategy since the end of the cold war with its evolution in the first decade after World War II. In chapter 9, Duncan Clarke and Daniel O'Connor discuss how the emergence of democracies in eastern Europe affected the allocation of U.S. security assistance. In chapter 10, Pietro Nivola analyzes the Clinton administration's much trumpeted effort to push commercial and trade policy to the forefront of the foreign policy agenda. In chapter 11, David Forsythe discusses whether the diminished East-West struggle has enabled the United States to concentrate more energy on promoting human rights around the world. In chapter 12, Richard Herrmann and Shannon Peterson review public opinion data and ask whether public attitudes toward the use of force have changed with the end of the cold war.

Part IV presents the conclusion of the volume. In chapter 13, we return to the basic questions that motivated the book. What kinds of reform proposals have been made and which groups and interests have made them? How have individual agencies and policies changed in response to changes in the international environment? What role does leadership play in making change happen? To what extent have the structural and procedural changes we are witnessing in U.S. foreign policy bureaucracy affected the substance of foreign policy? In revisiting these and other questions, we try to weave the diverse threads of the preceding twelve chapters into a coherent picture of where U.S. foreign policy stands a half decade into the post–cold war era.

PART II

INSTITUTIONS

Bert A. Rockman

2. The Presidency and Bureaucratic Change After the Cold War

In the equation of factors that contribute to U.S. foreign policy, presidents and situations vary while the foreign policy bureaucracy tends to remain more or less constant. Presidents' foreign policy ideas and levels of interest differ. Presidents differ too in their style of engaging foreign policy issues, and they differ strikingly in what they define as a foreign policy issue and in which issues they select as a priority.

Bureaucracies for the most part provide ballast. They represent continuity and constancy. While the president generalizes, the bureaucracy in its various parts specializes. Over time, each of the vast departments and, even more, each of their specialized agencies develops distinctive habits, particular ways of defining the essence of a problem (Halperin and Kanter 1973), and particular methods and techniques for coping with problems. Each agency touches on a part of the amorphous concept called foreign policy. The part it touches on helps define its distinctive set of priorities. An agency's mission (the rationale behind its creation) tends to define how it will cope with these priorities.

The bureaucracy reflects constancy and yet, taken as a whole, it reflects diversity as well. The president's problem is to harness horses inclined to take off in different directions while also availing himself of the advantages of specialization and expert knowledge. The problem is inherent in Max Weber's classic theory of organizations; namely, how is specialized jurisdiction to be made compatible with the chain of command?

Situations are a third element in the foreign policy equation. Situations provide both constraints and opportunities. They may become so determinative that they force decision makers, even those of different inclinations, to respond in remarkably similar ways. The cold war, at least until disenchantment with the military engagement in Vietnam set in (partially coinciding with détente with both China and the Soviet Union), provided such a paradigm of constraint upon policy options. Only when the price of responding to that paradigm began to be regarded as excessive and when contradictions developed in it did significant variations in response to the cold war become legitimate. For example, how could there be an international communist threat in Southeast Asia or elsewhere when détente was being pursued with the supposed sources of that threat? By constraining choice, however, the cold war brought a certain predictability to policy and provided an undertone to operations (Rockman 1994a).

A dramatic shift in the prevailing paradigm, such as that which occurred in 1989 with the fall of the Berlin Wall and the crumbling of the remnants of the Soviet empire, or with the end of the Soviet Union itself in 1991, also provides opportunities for choice. How will these opportunities for choice be interpreted? And who will do the interpreting? Since bureaucracies are based upon a prevailing modality of problem definition and response, they will certainly find adjustments difficult, at least initially, to the extent that the past has been organizationally institutionalized.

The end of the cold war, of course, has provided a historic moment of readjustment. It has also provided numerous new opportunities for dangerous entanglements. Yet the existence of opportunity has also provided at least two presidents, Bush and Clinton, with a chance to give the U.S. foreign policy apparatus a new direction.

I seek in this chapter to disentangle various pieces of the presidential-bureaucratic relationship in foreign policy, especially with respect to the problem of generating change. First, I examine the problematic relationship that presidents have with bureaucracy generally, a relationship that keeps them distant from each other. Second, I look at the variable in this relationship, namely, the presidents themselves, by examining how their style of engagement (or disengagement) influences the capacity to create institutional change. Third, I look at the relationship between careerists and appointees in the foreign policy bureaucracy and the sometimes unpredictable relationship between them and between the appointees and the White House. In the end, whatever change a president wants to create in the bureaucracy has to be performed by the appointees. They are the emissaries of the presidential message—if there is to be a message. Next, I look at how the cold war's end has affected policy priorities, and thus the changing importance of various institutional players. Finally, I look at the incumbent president, Bill Clinton, and his style of foreign policy decision making. The central matter here is what that style tells us about the nature of the relationship between the president and the foreign policy apparatus.

Presidents and the Bureaucracy

The relationship between the presidency and the bureaucracy in U.S. foreign policy after the cold war can be divided into parts. The first part has to do with how much attention presidents are likely to give the bureaucratic machinery. This issue involves the problematics of attention (March and Olsen 1984), by which I mean the following: (1) What can the president know? (2) What is the president interested in knowing? and (3) Can the president share a framework of feasible operations, which must necessarily exist within a bureaucracy charged with carrying out policy?

The answers to these three questions will vary to some extent depending on who is president. Presidents vary a great deal in their interests and especially in their interest in, and perhaps even capacity for, knowing. This especially affects the answer to the second of the three questions posed above. I will focus more exclusively on variability among presidents a bit later in the chapter. For now, however, I want to focus on the first and third of the questions related to the problematics of presidential attention—what can a president know, and can he share a discourse that is relevant to the bureaucracy?

The role of the chief executive is virtually never hands-on. In large and complex organizations, the top leader is distanced from the organizational apparatus that carries out policies made in the CEO's name. Distance, complexity, and delegation deter hands-on activity from the top (at least on a regular basis) even if there is a powerful motive to intervene. The deterrent effect is that much greater when the motivation for presidential involvement is weak. From the president's vantage point, more important matters beckon. Choices that cannot be made elsewhere in the system come to the president. The opportunities to think strategically about the management of policy and consequent implications for bureaucratic change are limited, whatever the inclinations of the person at the top.

In addition, the president is first and foremost a politician concerned with his own political fate, the prospects of his party, and, if sufficiently astute, the implications of foreign policy actions for other policy and political choices likely to come down the road (Neustadt 1990). This means that presidents are likely to invest little time in organizational matters unless these are obviously connected to political or policy purposes they deem essential. Usually such interventions are highly episodic and particularistic. Nixon's threats to send some bureaucrat off to Guam (Aberbach and Rockman 1976) or Carter's concerns about leaks he concluded were coming from the State Department (Rockman 1981) are examples of the episodic and particularistic nature of presidential concerns with the implementing agencies.

In short, the problematics of attention for presidents are such that presidents are unlikely to engage what Colin Campbell has called the "gearbox problem" of government, how to move from grand presidential desires to operational choices and professional appraisals (1991, 207–10). Presidents tend to see little reason to invest much time or effort in such engagement because they believe the yield is low in relation to other matters that have to be dealt with. Presidents tend to have less a love-hate affair with the bureaucracy than a hate-indifference relationship to it. Those who distrust it will want to de-bureaucratize operations and bring them directly into the White House with all the consequences that entails. Those (most) who are indifferent to the bureaucracy will only episodically, and often inconsistently, engage the apparatus, primarily through their principal appointees.

A problem characteristic of American presidents, in contrast to their counterparts in parliamentary systems, is that they must create a government when they come into office. A U.S. president has many more discretionary appointments available to him than would exist in parliamentary democracies, where civil servants or foreign service officers fill roles that are typically occupied in the U.S. by political appointees. There are implications for both policy substance and policy process that derive from this difference. From a substantive point of view, the good news for American presidents is that they are less likely to be captives of the institutionalized past; they have the discretion to change it if they have will, persistence, and strategy. That, of course, is also the bad news. The inertia of past policy is inherently neither good nor bad. The past can be helpful to understanding the present.

In terms of policy process, however, American presidents are singularly disadvantaged by the absence of an institutionalized personnel system. They have to start from scratch and frequently have more positions to fill than individuals they can vouch for. Above all, they have difficulty getting a feel for the chemistry of the team they will eventually put into place—and the appointment process tends to take longer at subcabinet levels with each succeeding administration. Added to this instability is the fact that presidents invest little time in personnel management. They are typically uninterested in how people are likely to relate to one another until major problems created by personnel discord arise and threaten their administration's appearance of competence.

The pervasive lack of interest that most presidents have in the mechanics of government gives them few means for thinking in organizational or staffing terms. Only rarely have presidents had experience in large organizational settings. They are instead generalists who have attained their positions through a variety of means—by advancing ideas that resonate with popular opinion or with particular constituencies—but certainly rarely by making allocative or managerial decisions. Politicians excel in a positive-sum world, or at least, they excel at acting as though the world were positive-sum, by promising more goods than exist. There is little that prepares a politician for the operational realities of implementation—a decidedly nonpositive-sum world. What politicians sometimes, if rarely, have the ability to excel at is directional leadership. Such leadership, if clear, can give ample guidance to agencies within certain discretionary boundaries. Nonetheless, the Margaret Thatchers and Ronald Reagans of this world are a rare breed of the species *homo politicus.*

It is notable that, in France, many leading politicians have themselves come from the civil service. About 25 percent of cabinet ministers, for example, have had such career backgrounds (Dogan 1989). In the United States, however, it is rare for American politicians to have had civil or foreign service careers. While there is a tiny smattering of former foreign service officers (FSOs) in Congress (Barone and Ujifusa 1993), no American president has emerged from such a background. (The closest in this regard may have been George Bush, who was a political appointee to several foreign policy positions and organizations.) Indeed, given the penchant for candidates to identify themselves as outsiders, this is not likely to change. One consequence is that U.S. presidents are especially unlikely to be on the same wavelength as the denizens of the agencies responsible for interpreting and carrying out U.S. policy. The language they speak is not the same. The concerns likely to be foremost in their minds will differ. The gap between symbolic utterance and realistic choice is likely to be great. Thus, another aspect of the problematics of attention is that presidents and bureaucrats do not generally share a common discourse.

The problematics of attention are to some degree affected by what it is that presidents are interested in knowing. Interest inevitably directs attentiveness, and knowledge helps connect means to ends. Presidents, in other words, are themselves a source of variability in the foreign policy–making equation. Whatever their perspectives, interest, knowledge, or experience, all presidents are ultimately forced to grapple with the constriction of operational realities imbedded in the process of making choices.

The President as Variable

There are several ways in which presidents differ as foreign policy decision makers. Some of these influence the way they will relate to the foreign policy apparatus. One is the extent to which their priorities lie in domestic or foreign policy.

Interest and Priority

Although all presidents must do foreign policy and all appear especially presidential when they are visiting abroad or hosting foreign dignitaries at home, some clearly relish this sphere of activity while others merely tolerate it as a necessary part of their job. It is reasonable to operate on the assumption that presidents, like all other people, have finite attention spans. Therefore, they will tend to give greatest attention to those agendas they are most interested in pursuing, barring unexpected events.

Given the complicated structure of the American political system and the difficulties of constructing issue majorities within it, U.S. presidents have a natural inclination to escape the frustrations and controversies of domestic policy making by seeking opportunities to strut their stuff in the realm of foreign and national security policy. No doubt the existence of the cold war made this option more attractive. Equally, its absence creates bewilderment and frequently makes foreign policy decision making merely a subset—in fact an especially contentious subset—of domestic politics. The end of the cold war has made it harder to reach a consensus on most matters of foreign policy, except that whatever is going on, American troops should stay out. It may well be, however, that dissensus has been with us ever since the U.S. intervention in Vietnam weakened the consensual underpinnings of the cold war.

For the most part, Democratic and Republican presidents enter office expecting to do different things. Democrats usually feel committed to a domestic policy agenda. They believe in domestic policy making, and their party and interest constituencies demand it. Democratic presidents who are reluctant to press a domestic policy agenda forcefully, such as Jimmy Carter, are likely to get into trouble with their party and its constituencies. More important, this difference means that Democrats more than Republicans see foreign policy as something that can get them into trouble and deflect them from the purpose of domestic social reform. One account, for example, of why Lyndon Johnson escalated the involvement of U.S. military forces in Vietnam was that he wanted to protect his domestic agenda (Berman 1982). While it is not possible for Democratic presidents to avoid paying attention to foreign policy matters, it would seem to follow that Democrats are more likely to see foreign affairs as something they must attend to, whereas Republican presidents are more likely to see foreign affairs as the central aspect of the job. The simple fact is that Democrats want to do something other than foreign policy even when they must do foreign policy.

In contrast, Republican presidents are generally a great deal more skeptical than Democrats about the uses of public policy. They prefer a lower government profile in social and economic matters. Thus, they generally prefer to devote their energies to foreign policy since they are likely to see it as a legitimate function of government. Republican presidents tend to be aficionados of foreign policy, often claiming it as their special domain of expertise—Eisenhower (especially on matters of defense), Nixon, and Bush in particular come to mind.

The clear implication of this argument is that Republicans give a higher priority to foreign policy than do Democrats, to the extent that they have a choice. Notably, the Democrats used Bush's propensity to travel abroad as a campaign weapon against him, beginning with the deepening of the recession in 1991. The party connection, however, may be less clear than it seems, if only because foreign policy involvement is rarely a matter of choice. Regardless of how presidents may wish to spend their time, they will be called upon to respond to matters they had not anticipated. That is the fate of being a leader of a country with great power status. The expectations of others frequently consume a president's freedom, regardless of how he wished to exercise it and regardless of policy predilection. Furthermore, at least one Republican president did come to office with a strong interest in a domestic policy agenda (Reagan), while another (Ford) came to office with a primary need to assure the country that all was quiet on the West Wing front.

What are the implications, if any, of different levels of presidential interest in foreign policy making for the style of presidential involvement, particularly with respect to his engagement with the foreign policy apparatus? Ironically, there may not be an unambiguous relationship between foreign policy interest and style of involvement on the part of a president. While Eisenhower and Bush were foreign policy aficionados who found it useful to delegate direct responsibility, Nixon, and to some degree on the Democrat's side, Kennedy, found it more convenient to centralize decision making through the White House. In their roles as foreign policy decision makers, presidents also vary in the certainty or complexity of their ideology and in the centralization or delegation of their decision making.

Ideology and Complexity

Some presidents are more confident than others that they know what they need to know. When certainty reigns, there is little need to tap experts for answers, except to legitimize the answers already arrived at. Ronald Reagan was a president untroubled by doubts. He had the answers he needed in connection with the world as he knew it. Because his presidency had no need to entertain doubt, it was set up to do, rather than to know. On the domestic front that largely meant undoing—deregulating the economy, lowering tax rates, and decreasing the activities of government (except for the regulation of social behavior). These were Reagan's main passions. The foreign policy front, however, presented him primarily with the opportunity to force-feed the Pentagon and confront the Soviet Union and its real and illusionary allies.

Ideological passion and certainty fueled policy. With enough energy and certainty imparted by the chief's ideological directions, delegation was characteristic of the Reagan style (Wildavsky 1988). It is hard to imagine that Reagan could have been intimately involved with matters whose complexity he denied. His attentiveness, it is fair to say, was likewise very limited. The fact is, it is hard to imagine an active verb following Reagan's name. That said, the point is that powerful ideological gusts move many objects. Ideological certainty can work by means of a combination of centralized personnel selection and delegated authority. Caspar Weinberger was anxious to spend money at the Department of Defense (DOD) and Reagan was pleased to give it to him. William Casey was anxious to involve the CIA in a variety of subterranean schemes and low-level military interventions, and Reagan was more than willing to oblige him.

In essence, Reagan turned the agenda of U.S. foreign policy on its head, and he began doing so as a candidate in 1976, well before he became president. The cold war was waning until Reagan's candidacy in 1976. Reagan's political agenda was to reinvigorate it, a task at which he proved quite successful, both as a prepresidential presence and as president. From Reagan's perspective, simplicity worked—at least up to a point. The point at which it stopped working was when it proved hard to impose a cold war framework on a persistent but localized problem such as the civil war in

Lebanon and the unfortunate U.S. intervention there. The obvious asset of a clear ideological lens is that it makes following directions easier; the obvious liability is that it produces errors of overinclusiveness, since one interprets all events in terms of the ideological framework.

By its nature, foreign policy is not highly predictable. Events rapidly overtake the best-laid plans. Even so, two of the more unpredictable U.S. presidents in regard to foreign policy in the modern era may have been Jimmy Carter and Bill Clinton. Carter had few preconceptions other than a belief he brought to the office that the cold war was a distraction from more pressing long-term global problems between the northern and southern hemispheres. Unlike Reagan, Carter read and listened voraciously before making a decision. In the absence of a clear framework—or perhaps with two distinctly different frameworks competing for his attention—his message was garbled. His administration, for example, was for human rights, unless raising the issue offended a crucial ally (Cottam and Rockman 1984). Carter set up his administration to create competing voices, because he wanted information from diverse perspectives so that he might ultimately arrive at rational decisions. In consequence, the overall appearance of decision making in the Carter administration was that diverse perspectives were the order of the day. Volatility was the result. Carter came into office inclined to change the cold war fixation of U.S. foreign policy and to focus instead on global collective goods. It is fair to say he left office having reinforced the cold war fixation. Events often overpower intentions, and the Soviet invasion of Afghanistan at the end of 1979 heightened cold war tensions, marking the end of whatever remained of Carter's original interests.

Clinton too has prided himself on his pragmatism. Unlike Carter, there appears to have been no guiding set of ideas about how his administration should be arranged. The early take on Clinton is that on matters of foreign policy he is a quick study when he chooses to be a student. Foreign policy seems less attractive to Clinton than it did to Carter, in part because the end of the cold war, by lessening the sense of direct threat, has impaired the political capacity for action (Rockman 1994a). The more foreign policy can be directly connected to social and economic change in the United States, however, the more Clinton's interests are aroused. Thus, trade and international economic issues have been central to Clinton's foreign policy agenda, and represent its most consistent features. Both Carter and Clinton appear to have had relatively complex, but also inconsistent, views on foreign policy. As easy as it would be to hum Reagan's foreign policy tune, therefore, it would be extremely difficult to do the same for Carter or Clinton. Simplicity, by definition, is easy to grasp; complexity is not. Thus, a complex policy requires great care and attention in order to be linked to the foreign policy apparatus. It is impossible to expect organizations built on inertia to generate a head of steam when the direction is not clearly communicated.

Centralization and Delegation

Presidents have different styles in how they choose to organize and conduct foreign policy. Presidents with seemingly equal commitments to foreign policy have organized foreign policy making in remarkably different ways. At first glance, this is rather surprising, since the greater the level of presidential interest, the more one would think presidents might wish to intervene directly and centralize operations as much as possible. The cases of three foreign policy presidents—Eisenhower, Nixon, and Bush—are perversely instructive about how little presidential foreign policy interest predicts style of organization. Nixon was intent on operating foreign policy as much as possible from the White House, with his national security adviser, Henry Kissinger. Eisenhower, on the other hand, was fond of formalized arrangements in which cabinet secretaries and agency heads met with one another collectively in the presence of the president. Bush was less formal but inclined for the most part to delegate to his principals.

Despite his spotty knowledge and interest in foreign policy, Lyndon Johnson, ironically, often turned out to be a policy micromanager. His hands-on targeting of U.S. bombing during the Vietnam War was a classic and repeated episode of micromanagerial intervention. Less widely known is a case illustrated by Paul Hammond (1992, 83–89): Johnson's direct intervention in food famine relief to India in 1966. According to Hammond's account, Johnson decided to avoid committing U.S. resources to a long-term food aid program, first, because he was dismayed by what he perceived as the foreign aid bureaucracy's reflexive support of Indian government claims and demands, and second, because he was displeased by the Indian government's overt criticisms of U.S. policy in Southeast Asia. Johnson may not have been wholly on top of the intricacies of the Indian food relief request but, as things turned out, he was very much on top of the politics of it. Signals from Congress and criticisms by the Indian government of U.S. policy gave Johnson sufficient reason to oversee the foreign aid bureaucracy and cast doubt on its policy inclinations. A president with an eye for politics should be able to ask good questions of the bureaucracy as it purportedly carries out the policies of the elected politicians. In Neustadt's view (1990), this, after all, is what Franklin Roosevelt would have done.

On the face of it, the extent to which presidents centralize or decentralize appears to be little related to their interest in or commitment to foreign policy. Styles vary, and, as Terry Moe (1993) poignantly asks, so what? Moe's very good question unfortunately remains unanswerable in this respect, at least for the time being. The null hypothesis of no patterned differences across presidencies seems to prevail.

The problem for presidents in foreign policy is that organizing to remedy some matters complicates others. For a president to deal effectively with the foreign policy apparatus, to change its tendency toward inertia, yet also to take advantage of its expertise requires the attentiveness and interest to listen and the skepticism to inquire. It also requires a commitment to a policy direction and a willingness to render that direction clearly and persistently and to adjust it tactically. Above all, it requires political savvy on the part of presidents, so that they do not foreclose their options. All these virtues could have been lifted from the Book of Platitudes for Presidents. The sad but inevitable fact is that not all these virtues can be practiced at once. In particular, doing and knowing are often in conflict. Reagan did because he knew what he thought he had to know and was not very interested in adding nuances to matters he perceived as uncomplicated.

Presidents stand apart from the bureaucracy itself. Their dealings are primarily with the principal leaders of the departments. But what is the relationship between those leaders and the career officers who serve them?

Inside the Bureaucracy: Appointees and Careerists

Just as every president varies in leadership style, so too do the heads of the foreign policy agencies. Opposing styles immediately come to mind. Henry Kissinger was a secretary of state who disdained his own department's corps of career officials and the whole concept of moving anything through a sluggish bureaucracy. James Baker similarly gave the careerists short shrift. Alternatively, Secretaries of State Dean Acheson and George Schultz were regarded as closely connected to and respected by the careerists at the State Department.

Although the array of foreign policy agencies is large, it has typically been in the State Department and the CIA that tensions between the White House and the agencies—and between appointees and careerists—are greatest.

The problem at the State Department has been long-standing, and is often attributed to the tendency of foreign service officers to be more attuned to the politics of, say, Katmandu, than to that of Washington (Destler 1972). Whatever the reasons, foreign service officers, unlike many of their counterparts at the Defense Department or the National Security Agency or even the Treasury, are typically operating with a soft technology (diplomacy) and often appear to their political subordinates to be skeptical of bold courses of action—though this skepticism now seems most deeply centered within the senior military officer corps. In some administrations, the national security adviser and NSC staff have displaced the State Department in policy-making prominence (Rockman 1981).

The one thing that is clear about the relationship between political appointees and careerists is that it follows no single model. Nixon wanted foreign policy close to him and was reluctant to give Kissinger the secretary of state role, a position Kissinger came to (in addition to his role as national security adviser) when Nixon's political troubles began to mount. Kissinger also wanted foreign policy close to him and was, in any event, skeptical of bureaucracy. Therefore, the relationship between the foreign service and Kissinger was hardly intimate. On the other hand, another former professor, George Schultz, had a collegial operating style in the department, often holding seminars with senior foreign service officers. Reagan, of course, granted much leeway to his appointees as long as they were on the right ideological track. But both the Defense Department and the CIA were more important instruments of Reagan's foreign policy than was the State Department. As a consequence, Schultz's own style (he replaced the contentious and somewhat paranoid Alexander Haig) was given more latitude. Both George Bush and James Baker liked to do things quietly and to keep as few participants in the circle as possible. Whatever Bush's views about the foreign service, Baker early on concluded that the department would be run through an intimate circle of advisers. The larger the number of participants, the greater the opportunity for an uncontrollable process—not exactly Baker's style.

Under Reagan, the more important organizational actors were Defense and the CIA. Weinberger and the military professionals at Defense were as one—bring in the money, keep the hardware shiny, get the preparation for its use up to speed, and then don't use it unless the chances of success are overwhelming. There were naturally other types of tensions at Defense, but these were often between Reagan's own appointees. Conflicts between organizational leaders, such as Secretary of the Navy John Lehman and DOD Assistant Secretary for Manpower Lawrence Korb became the stuff of news stories. Here the conflict between broadly stipulated hardware-related goals (such as the six hundred–ship fleet) and available support resources (such as personnel) to meet those goals came into play. Such conflicts are not unusual when leaders commit to very broad goals at the top of the organization, as Reagan and Weinberger did, and leave the messy details to be cleaned up below deck.

In the Clinton administration, two careerist/administration tensions were notable in the early phases. One was in the State Department, where a number of upper middle–level FSOs left, voicing criticism of the Clinton administration's unclear posture in the civil war in the Balkans. The FSOs sought a stronger commitment by the U.S. to an interventionist strategy, whereas the secretary of state and the Clinton administration initially took a far more cautious approach toward involvement in that triangulated conflict.

The other and more prominent early tension was with the senior military officer staff. Here, the interaction between conditions and the presidential incumbent was important. The conditions after the demise of the Soviet Union meant that the military apparatus would be downsized while the opportunities (and pundits' demands) for policelike military intervention, or the ever seductive "surgical air strikes," would grow. Reduced resources, however, made the military even more reluctant to get involved in potentially costly expeditions than it had been under Reagan. The Gulf War success did little to alleviate the military's reluctance, inasmuch as that success was based on nearly optimal conditions for the use of American military power, conditions not replicated in any current circumstance into which the U.S. might be drawn. Military downsizing under a president who was politically vulnerable on military matters limited Clinton's latitude on the conditions under which American military power could be committed (Rockman 1996). It has certainly been difficult for President Clinton to call upon others to make sacrifices he himself avoided. Thus, while external resistance in the form of a competing great power no longer impeded military intervention, the desire of both the military and the public to avoid costly entanglements with indigenous forces or irregulars in unfriendly places initially overwhelmed the opportunities created by the disappearance of great power competition.

Eventually, events, especially in Haiti and Bosnia, lured the Clinton administration into military policing arrangements under the cover of multilateral sponsorship. The relative success of these operations enabled Clinton simultaneously to take credit for them and to distance himself from his past. Certainly, too, as the administration settled into office, more of the senior command owed its rise to the Clinton administration. And notably the Clinton chair of the Joint Chiefs of Staff (JCS), General John Shalikashvili, was less reluctant than his predecessor, General Powell, to commit U.S. forces to policing activity.

Nevertheless, should American combat fatalities occur, as in Somalia, Clinton will come under heavy fire (of the political variety) and the political cost of further operations will be likely to rise. Like most politicians, but probably more than most, Clinton is a highly adaptable creature. Adaptability is made especially easy when commitments are weak, minds are uncertain, and costs are high. So far, the costs of involvement have been lower than expected, but it remains to be seen to what extent Clinton's commitments have grown firmer and his mind more certain.

In the end, tensions between career professionals and the presidential administration and its appointees are not always predictable. To the extent that presidents centralize operations, the conflict is more likely to be between the White House and the departments, not simply between appointees and career professionals. To the extent that authority is delegated, much depends on the chemistry and relationship between particular sets of appointees in particular departments. For example, while Schultz and the foreign service officers seemed to have had a good relationship, Elliot Abrams, the assistant secretary for inter-American affairs, controlled a critical choke point for the Reagan administration's policies in Central America. Abrams knew the answers—those that resonated at the White House—so he was not very interested in the advice of the foreign service officers.

Generally, however, conflicts are more often between parts of organizations struggling to be given the lead in policy than between appointees and careerists per se. The careerists frequently look to the appointees to be effective advocates for their side of the organization and to carry the day for them (Allison 1969). Since functional divisions are usually at least as important as those between political appointees and professional careerists, we turn now to the influence of changing priorities on organizational winners and losers.

Changing Policy Priorities: Winners and Losers

Two presidents have been in office in the post–cold war era—George Bush and Bill Clinton. With exceptions for global environmental and population control matters, their policies have differed relatively little, in spite of some rhetorical flourishes. In broad terms, each president has had to downsize the military and focus more attention on trade and commercial issues. Clinton's defense budget reductions were only moderately larger than those Bush had proposed, and, since the 1994 midterm elections, the Clinton administration has proposed a $25 billion increase in the defense budget, anticipating that larger increases would be proposed by the new Republican congressional majorities. The major cuts in both the Bush and Clinton administrations were in strategic weapons systems and warheads and in theater weapons systems. Reductions in force, especially in Europe, have also followed. To a considerable extent, under both presidents attention has been given to high-technology conventional weapons systems and mobile forces. On the whole, the new posture is a sort of defense lite—mobile, conventionally armed, but high-tech forces.

Beyond internal changes affecting the Pentagon and its relative decline in the configuration of U.S. foreign policy actors, the agencies that have come to greater prominence are those dealing with international trade and commercial issues. There is no doubt that the economic side of the State Department, the International Trade Administration in the Commerce Department, the Special Trade Representative's office, and the Treasury have all become more important players, compared to an arms-obsessed past that was part and parcel of the cold war. The shift often seems remarkably radical, but the altered influence of organizational actors derives primarily from what is, after all, a radical shift in the world situation within a decade. The Reagan administration, which was firmly fixated on the cold war, did its utmost to limit U.S. commerce with the Soviet Union and its allies. Now the U.S. is looking for ways to exploit commercial opportunities.

The end of the cold war has also meant a reduction in cultural and informational activity, especially in Europe. The consolidation of USIA outlets reflects the lessening importance of U.S. cultural contacts in Europe in the post–cold war climate. It also reflects a tightened discretionary budget under which more and more trade-offs must be made about where resources are to go.

In general, the changing priorities are a reasonably realistic reflection of the changing environment and goals of U.S. foreign policy. In my estimation, these overpower differences between presidents and their constituencies. No one is going to be building more ICBMs or investing in strategic weapons systems for now. But presidents of both parties are going to be paying more attention to opening markets for American products abroad.

Presidents and their political constituencies do count somewhat, however. Clinton sees trade issues as the extension of domestic policy abroad, and so this is one area that attracts his enthusiasm and attention. Clinton is clearly attracted to global economic perspectives, as evidenced by his championing of NAFTA and GATT. Yet, because Clinton is a Democrat and because Democrats have trade unions as a major constituency, it is natural for a Democratic president to act tough, at least symbolically, on imports from countries running large trade imbalances with the U.S. or from countries with lower wage rates. At the same time, Clinton's political constituencies dwell on human rights concerns more than was traditionally the case under Republican administrations, and trade has become a weapon for dealing with human rights problems. To be sure, human rights pressures used to stem from a Congress controlled by Democrats. But a president from the same party as the congressional majority had to pay greater heed to human rights than Clinton's Republican predecessors were inclined to do. With the isolationist Jesse Helms now occupying the chair of the Senate Foreign Relations Committee in the new Republican-dominated Washington order, however, the Clinton administration is under no major pressure on the human rights front, except with regard to Cuba. In spite of occasional annoyances, such as the Helms-Burton amendment forced on the administration and the obvious limitations that an opposition Congress will seek to impose on an incumbent president of the other political party, Clinton has virtually flourished as a foreign policy maker since the Republican majority arrived in Congress. This could well be a consequence of how the Republican majority has altered Clinton's own priorities, putting him in a more defensive posture regarding his domestic policy agenda and, by default, giving him a greater degree of freedom to explore and take initiatives in international affairs.

Nonetheless, in broad contours, despite some differences in rhetoric and emphasis across presidencies, the post–cold war environment has changed the nature of policy priorities and has required organizational adaptation and refocusing. Formerly peripheral organizational players are now at the core. The central players of the past no longer exclusively determine the agenda. Trade, commercial, financial, economic, and even regulatory issues now play a much larger independent role in U.S. policy than they did in the bipolarized world of the cold war.

But what of Bill Clinton's attachment to foreign policy and its apparatus? How closely involved is he? What sort of leadership has he provided, if any? The particular style and interests of this fully post–cold war president are likely to be relevant to his ability to change the course of the foreign policy machinery.

The Clinton Foreign Policy Style—Leave It to the Bureaucracy

Bill Clinton's principal foreign policy interest when he came to the White House was to stay out of trouble. As a Democrat, Clinton began with powerful domestic policy interests. In the view of many Democrats, the end of the cold war and its reputed peace dividend should have allowed room for policies to deal with the country's most pressing domestic problems. The 1994 elections dramatically altered Clinton's domestic policy options and seem consequently to have increased his attentiveness to and persistence in foreign policy.

Despite the end of the cold war, the world Bill Clinton inherited was not so tranquil, and the only choices available were often tragic. Clinton did not want to get involved in any matters that would threaten the priority of his domestic agenda of deficit reduction, health care, and welfare reform. Difficult choices abounded—Bosnia, Haiti, Somalia, the Korean peninsula, numerous ethnic hostilities in the former Soviet Union, and so on. Capability for intervention was low, primarily because there was virtually no political or public support for it and because the military made clear its misgivings well in advance. In any event, military involvements appear to have been the farthest thing from Clinton's mind. The absence of an international consensus on how to deal with these issues—even in Korea and Haiti where there were resolutions—made Clinton look indecisive and unprepared to handle foreign policy, especially in contrast to his predecessor's experience, which, of course, became more idealized after his departure from office.

From Clinton's standpoint, the foreign policy apparatus was there to keep him out of trouble, not get him into it. (A Bush administration appointee in a domestic agency asserted in confidence that his job was to keep Bush out of trouble on matters affecting his agency. It is striking that Bush's and Clinton's areas of interest and lack of interest are mirror images of each other.) Except for Clinton's first defense secretary, Les Aspin, the administration's first-term appointees were, to say the least, figures known for their cautious competence, exactly the right team for a president with limited interest in the classic presidential concerns of foreign policy. The competence of the president's team would later be called into question, as indecisiveness and inconsistency, bluff and lack of follow-through, became its hallmarks.

Indeed, the one clear guidepost of the Clinton years, though not meant to be publicized, is the Tarnoff doctrine. While the Tarnoff doctrine was officially disowned by the Clinton administration shortly after it was leaked to the news media following a confidential background briefing by Undersecretary of State Peter Tarnoff in May 1993, it remains the only real guide the administration has developed. The essence of the Tarnoff doctrine is that the United States has limited leadership resources to commit to a world that suddenly has much call for them. Those resources, therefore, will be used sparingly. The postscript to the Tarnoff doctrine could be stated as follows: Please take care of your own problems.

Yet, as Clinton discovered, the United States was perceived to be part of the solution to nearly every problem. For much of the first years of the Clinton presidency, the administration wrestled with finding an acceptable balance between responding to the call for American involvement and avoiding entanglements in costly or interminable arrangements. The erosion of Clinton's domestic policy prospects have coincided with an apparent willingness to adjust somewhat the point of equilibrium in risk taking. Clinton's persistence in support of risk—not a notable Clinton trait—has so far been largely untested, however.

When presidents combine a lack of interest with a lack of clear ideological guideposts, policy making shifts to the bureaucracy—or, more accurately, bureaucracies. Such was the case with trade issues—the principal exception to Clinton's lack of interest in foreign policy—at least during the first half of the first Clinton administration. The foreign policy decision makers in the Clinton administration were put together to keep the president from getting bogged down elsewhere and being derailed from his principal concerns. The fate of Lyndon Johnson and his misadventure in Vietnam, which helped destroy his presidency, looms large in Clinton's mind. In these terms, the apparatus created to keep Clinton out of big trouble has for the most part succeeded. But it also succeeded too often in making the president look weak and indecisive, not, of course, a difficult feat in view of Clinton's inconsistency. Thus, when press coverage turned negative or events seemed to make the United States look weak and helpless, Clinton would assert himself, only to withdraw once again. None of this is to say that Clinton failed to make the right decisions; that is not a scientifically knowable matter. But the pattern of "talking the talk without walking the walk" was not kind to Clinton's image as a leader. In particular, one of the costs was to make the president look bad before the pundits, who themselves are rarely short on opinions self-righteously arrived at.

The Clinton style of decision making on foreign policy—if not its content—has been largely accommodating toward the bureaucracy, where much of the action has occurred. While Richard Nixon wanted to concentrate foreign policy in his own hands at the White House, Bill Clinton has wanted to keep it as far away from himself as possible. If Nixon was the ultimate risk taker, Clinton has been primarily a risk avoider. His game is elsewhere. Accordingly, his guidance is neither strategic nor tactical. It is not designed to change the bureaucracy. Instead, it is designed to make use of bureaucratic prudence. Simply put, the policy is: Do not get into anything you cannot get out of.

Clinton's on-again, off-again style of foreign policy engagement weakened his credibility both internationally and domestically. During most of the first two years of the Clinton presidency, it was difficult for other governments or intermediaries to place much store in the administration's foreign policy pronouncements, because their shelf life was so brief. While the American public was hardly aware of the details of Clinton's wavering courses of action, the image of vacillation lingered. On the whole, Clinton was awarded low midterm marks on foreign policy in opinion polls. Between March 1994 and the election of that year, public disapproval of Clinton's handling of foreign affairs consistently outweighed approval in the Gallup surveys. Clinton's first-half foreign policy performance contributed to his image as an inept president of shallow convictions.

Clinton's notorious lack of self-discipline weakens him in foreign policy, where it is often best to leave thoughts unarticulated until they can face some reality testing. In addition, his lack of attentiveness to organizational and personnel matters frequently results in a public display of the administration's varying perspectives. Ironically, the first purged victim of the administration's frontline players, former defense secretary Les Aspin, was a personality who exhibited many of Clinton's own traits—too many for his own good. As with most presidencies, however, there is a learning curve. The disorganization of the foreign policy process has been contained, and in addition, Clinton has benefited from better luck than he had earlier in his presidency. Moreover, for good or ill, and by design or not, Clinton's second-term appointments to key foreign policy and national security positions suggest more adventurous possibilities. Specifically, there may be less reluctance to use American force on behalf of peacekeeping missions, although in the end these decisions are the president's and the Congress's to make, not the advisers.

In the end, however, Clinton's fundamental problem in foreign policy is that he has no underlying theory about what he should want and what it is possible for him to get. That problem is not uniquely Clinton's in the post–cold war era by any stretch of the imagination. But it is Clinton from whom guidance is being sought, which makes it his problem as well as our own.

Conclusion

Presidents are distant from the foreign policy apparatus. They can, however, convey direction and must in the end make decisions that simply cannot be made elsewhere. But only on rare occasions do they have an nterest in micromanaging foreign policy. Nor is foreign policy so easily micromanaged by presidential organizations such as the Office of Management and Budget (OMB). The issues here are not dollars or even specific management procedures, but judgments about unpredictable events. Presidents who do not send clear and consistent signals send confusing ones by default. Yet diplomacy is the art of ambiguity.

It seems that a president has three options to be effective in foreign policy. The first is directional clarity; Ronald Reagan is an example of this. But once clarity runs its course, what next? The second option is centralized control over foreign policy, à la Nixon and Kissinger. Here subtlety is possible even if directional clarity is lacking. The problem here lies in the secrecy in operational details, since those in the apparatus may have a need to know. The third option is delegation to officials who can be trusted to implement presidential wishes. The third solution is inconsistent with the second and can work only in conjunction with the first. Reagan delegated to people who fully shared his perspective in the areas of foreign policy with which he was most concerned. There was naturally some slack in areas with which he was less deeply concerned. The problems arise when presidents are uncertain of what they want, or are at least certain of what they do not want, namely trouble. Then delegation becomes problematic because all actors may justly claim to be speaking for a president whose wishes may have to be divined. It is possible, if not highly probable, that bureaucratic leadership will work harmoniously even when the president is distanced from the foreign policy process. In order for that to happen, a president would have to have a high degree of sensitivity to organizational dynamics, interests, and staffing. The foregoing analysis suggests that prospect is fairly dim.

Presidential agendas, to the extent that they exist, are as much a product of change as a determinant of it. Changing conditions, once the magnitude and depth of change becomes apparent, also change presidential minds and organizational incentives. The end of the cold war did not spell the end of a need for diplomacy, intelligence gathering, or defense, though it may change the way these activities are to be organized. The end of bipolarity makes diplomacy more complicated, not less. The cold war's demise means that intelligence functions will be refocused and defense postures reconfigured. In the face of powerful change, organizational readjustments are made because organizational leaders want their organizations to survive and prosper.

I began this chapter by arguing that presidents and situations vary, whereas bureaucracy tends to be constant. A better way of stating this is that bureaucratic change is a function of the joint impact of situational and presidential change. Ultimately, when situations are obvious enough, everything changes. The collapse of the Soviet Union at the end of 1991 fully confirmed changes that had already advanced across the foreign policy apparatus. So far, change has been more clearly demarcated *from* a prior state than *to* a future state. In plainer language, the old order has gone and the new order, if there is to be any, remains uncertain. Clinton, like the rest of us, is still groping his way toward it.

Vincent A. Auger

3. The National Security Council System After the Cold War

The Clinton administration came to office in January 1993 proclaiming "the challenge of shaping an entirely new foreign policy for a world that has fundamentally changed" and the need to "adapt our foreign policy goals and institutions" to meet those changes (Christopher 1993c, 45–46). The end of the cold war demanded a reformulation of American priorities, with economic issues singled out as having paramount importance. Bill Clinton declared during the 1992 campaign that "the currency of national strength in this new era will be denominated not only in ships, tanks and planes, but also in diplomas, patents and paychecks" (quoted in Wessel 1992). He promised to create an "economic security council," modeled after the National Security Council, to ensure sufficient attention to U.S. economic interests in his administration's foreign policy.

Clinton's choice of the template for his new economic council was understandable but ironic, since the National Security Council (NSC) is the quintessential cold war institution in the U.S. foreign policy structure. By 1992, however, some experts were questioning the adequacy of the NSC system (comprised of the council and its interagency committee process, the assistant to the president for national security affairs—also called the national security adviser, or NSA—and the NSC staff of foreign policy analysts, which reports to the NSA) for formulating a post–cold war U.S. foreign policy. Those questions were prompted by two related developments. The first was what Lindsay and Ripley earlier in this volume) call "problem depletion": The dominant threat to U.S. security, which justified the centralization of foreign policy making in a council that emphasized the military component of national security concerns, no longer existed. The second development was the increasing salience of "new issues" on the foreign policy agenda, especially economic and ecological interdependence, which the NSC as traditionally constituted was poorly suited to manage (see Garten 1992b; May 1992, 228; Shoemaker 1991, 82–83).[1]

It was somewhat surprising, therefore, when Presidential Decision Directive 2 (PDD 2) was issued on January 20, 1993, outlining an NSC structure and process extremely similar to that the Bush administration had used since January 1989 (see Clinton 1993b). While several factors influenced this choice, the most important were the incoming administration's own evaluation of the Bush NSC system and the expectation that foreign policy would not be among the president's highest priorities. Clinton and several of his top advisers were impressed with the efficient operation of their predecessor's NSC system; they hoped to achieve the same results by simply plugging their own personnel into the existing structure and process. Several administration officials also mentioned in interviews that the president and his political advisers saw such continuity as attractive because they intended to devote relatively little time to foreign policy issues. According to one former NSC staffer, "This administration wanted to put foreign policy on autopilot, and the Clinton people consciously chose the Bush model to do that."[2]

In doing so, the incoming administration fell into the trap of believing that choosing the "correct" NSC organization and process was the key to producing a successful foreign policy. This belief is only partially correct, however. Rational organization and coherent processes in the NSC system can reduce the number of mistakes an administration will make in foreign policy, but those structures and procedures ensure neither consistency in policy making nor successful policy outcomes. The level of criticism concerning the consistency and coherence of the Clinton foreign policy is evidence that the Bush NSC system had no talismanic qualities.

I argue in this chapter that the interests and abilities of the individuals who serve in the NSC system, and the level and nature of presidential involvement in that system, are the crucial variables in explaining NSC behavior. That is, the *people* filling the organizational slots and their skill in making the process work are the key to understanding both the strengths and weaknesses of the NSC system and its role in shaping Clinton's foreign policy. This insight is especially relevant in the case of the National Security Council, because of the unique nature of the NSC system, when compared to typical bureaucracies involved in making foreign policy.

The NSC as a Foreign Policy Bureaucracy

The National Security Act of 1947 established the National Security Council to "advise the President with respect to the integration of domestic, foreign, and military policies relating to the national security." Unlike almost every other executive branch agency dealing with foreign policy and national security issues, the NSC and its staff are extremely malleable. As the Tower Commission Report (1987, 4) states, the NSC system "is properly the President's creature. It must be left flexible to be molded by the President into the form most useful to him."

This flexibility is evident in several ways. The National Security Council itself has only four statutory members—the president, vice president, and the secretaries of state and of defense—and two statutory advisers—the chairman of the Joint Chiefs of Staff and the director of central intelligence. The president may add other government officials to the NSC at his discretion, and most presidents have included other cabinet officials and White House advisers in NSC deliberations. The formal processes by which the NSC system functions are set by presidential directive. The only staff position specifically mandated by the National Security Act of 1947 is that of a civilian executive secretary (a position that is now primarily administrative rather than policy oriented), so that the size, structure, and responsibilities of the NSC staff also reflect presidential preferences and requirements.[3]

This adaptability is also enhanced by the fact that the NSA and the NSC staff have no distinct set of "organizational interests," missions, or capabilities of the type Halperin (1974) identifies as likely obstacles to reorganization efforts. There are no enduring substantive or budgetary agendas to be pursued and protected. The small size and the transient nature of the NSC staff guarantee there is neither time, interest, nor capacity to build a unique set of "organizational interests" within the NSC system that might hinder the restructuring of that organization in response to a changing international context or a new set of presidential preferences. Although detailees to the NSC staff from line departments such as State and Defense sometimes use their position on the NSC staff to advance the preferences of their "home agencies," this influence is felt primarily in the way specific issues are managed, rather than in any continuity in the basic structure and priorities of the NSC system.

Indeed, the NSC system has been in a constant state of change from its very inception. The role of the NSA and NSC staff in shaping U.S. foreign policy has expanded significantly over time, and NSC structures and processes have varied considerably across different administrations (see Inderfurth and Johnson 1988; Shoemaker 1991).

Despite these variations, however, officials and analysts have identified several functions that the NSA and NSC staff must perform adequately to facilitate the achievement of any administration's foreign policy goals (see Hunter 1982; Odeen 1985; Shoemaker 1991). The first is its function as the president's personal staff for foreign policy issues: to anticipate which issues will require presidential review and decision, keep the president informed about those issues, and communicate presidential preferences concerning those issues to the relevant departments in the foreign policy bureaucracy. A second role is crisis management and contingency planning: The proximity and responsiveness of the NSA and NSC staff make them indispensable in helping the president respond to fast-breaking events (Shoemaker 1991, 35–38).

A third and crucial role is the management of the interagency process. This includes coordinating policy reviews in the bureaucracy; providing a policy framework and a sense of priorities to guide decision making across departments; integrating the various aspects of national security policy into coherent programs; sharpening the options and choices available to the president when an issue requires a presidential decision; bringing the president into the process in a timely fashion; and forcing decisions on issues rather than allowing them to linger unresolved. If the NSA is not interested in performing this process management task, then the adviser's deputy must be a skilled manager (Hunter 1982, 28).

A fourth task, closely related to the management of the interagency decision process, is the monitoring of implementation of presidential decisions by the departments. This might include adjudicating among different interpretations of what the decision requires, and what Shoemaker (1991, 111) has called being willing "to crack the whip" to ensure that implementation occurs and that officials who break ranks are disciplined in an appropriate manner.

These are "functions that need to be performed in some way for any President" (Tower Commission 1987, 4). Acknowledgment of this fact still leaves a great deal of room for debate over, first, the prominence of the NSA and NSC staff in the foreign policy process and, second, the appropriate scope of the NSC's coordinating and monitoring activities. While debate over the first of these had largely come to a close by the time the cold war ended, the demise of the Soviet empire reopened the second subject and produced several proposals for reorganizing the NSC system, as the Clinton administration prepared to take office.

Reforming the NSC System: Indictments and Prescriptions

Calls to reform the NSC system are hardly new. In 1959 and 1960, Sen. Henry Jackson criticized and investigated the operations of the NSC under Eisenhower. The dominance of the foreign policy process by National Security Advisers Henry Kissinger and Zbigniew Brzezinski in the 1970s produced a torrent of debate over the NSC system and their particular roles within it. The nature of the criticism has changed significantly in the last few years, however. While most of the earlier debates focused on the struggle between the NSA and the secretary of state for control over the policy-making process, more recent critiques have emphasized the inadequacies of that process itself in the post–cold war environment.

The Proper Role for the NSA and NSC Staff

Since the early 1970s, the appropriate role for the national security adviser and the NSC staff had been one of the most controversial issues in U.S. foreign policy. It is neither necessary nor germane to detail the extensive debate over the virtues of a "presidential" versus a "secretarial" system of policy making (Brzezinski 1987–1988) in this chapter, since the basic outlines of that debate are well known and have been discussed at length elsewhere (Destler, Gelb, and Lake 1984; Inderfurth and Johnson 1988; Rockman 1981; Shoemaker 1991). Suggested remedies to the problem of competition between the NSA and secretary of state, and to the confusion in U.S. policy that often resulted, ranged from upgrading the NSA to the "director of national security affairs" (Brzezinski 1983a) to eliminating the position of national security adviser altogether (Destler 1980).

However, the often poor performance of the NSC system during the first six years of the Reagan administration (see Shoemaker 1991, 57–73 for a detailed analysis) culminated in the Iran-contra debacle and the reality of an NSC staff run amok. In an effort to control the political damage done by that affair and to preempt calls that the NSC be brought under tighter congressional supervision, Reagan appointed a commission to study NSC operations. This produced at least a temporary resolution to this debate concerning the appropriate role for the NSA and the NSC staff. The report of the President's Special Review Board, and its specific recommendations concerning the components and operation of the NSC system (Tower Commission 1987, 87–99), was praised by many members of Congress and analysts outside the government. Other observers viewed the report as flawed because it affirmed a requirement for a strong NSC-centered system without imposing any new controls over the operations of the national security adviser or the NSC staff.

Several of the Tower Commission's conclusions regarding the NSC system are worth noting. The commission validated the basic "structure and operation of the NSC system," but more important, placed the national security adviser at the center of that system. It also stated that while the secretary of state should be the primary spokesperson for U.S. foreign policy, the NSA should play two roles that are essential to an effective policy process. The first is as manager of the national security process. The NSA should coordinate information from the executive branch agencies, prepare the agenda and decision papers for NSC meetings, and act as an "honest broker" in representing the views of other officials and departments in the government to the president.

The Tower Commission (1987, 90) was quick to indicate that this managerial role is not the NSA's only function, however:

> But the National Security Advisor does not simply manage the national security process. He is himself an important source of advice on national security matters to the President. He is not the President's only source of advice, but he is perhaps the one most able to see things from the President's perspective. He is unburdened by departmental responsibilities. The President is his only master.

While fully aware of the potential abuse of such a role by an unscrupulous national security adviser, the commission concluded that "performing both these roles well is an essential, if not easy, task."[4]

The centrality of the NSA in the policy process was further enhanced by the Tower Commission's recommendation that the adviser chair all senior-level committees in the NSC system. After reviewing the struggle for control of these interagency committees in previous administrations, the commission concluded that "the system generally operates better when the committees are chaired by the individual with the greatest stake in making the NSC system work," the national security adviser (1987, 95–96).

The other crucial set of recommendations concerning the operation of the NSC system pertained to the role of the president, "who bears a special responsibility for the effective performance of the NSC system" (Tower Commission 1987, 88). The president must provide clear instructions to the principal foreign policy officials concerning the structure and operation of the policy process, and their specific roles in that process. The president must also monitor the performance of the system, especially the activities of the NSA, and intervene if necessary to resolve disputes or correct malfunctions in the process.

Despite objections and resistance from Secretary of State George Shultz, the Reagan White House moved quickly to adopt many of the

Tower Commission's recommendations (Gordon 1987; "Tower Report Assumes Biblical Status at NSC" 1987). When the Bush administration took office in 1989, Brent Scowcroft (a member of the Tower Commission and former national security adviser during the Ford administration) was named as the president's assistant for national security affairs. Not surprisingly, the structure and operations of the Bush NSC system resembled the Tower Commission recommendations quite closely, with Scowcroft and his deputy, Robert Gates, chairing the two principal NSC committees and tightly controlling the policy process (Callahan 1992; Snow and Brown 1994, 149–52). According to officials who served on the Bush NSC staff, this influence was facilitated by a clear division of labor between Scowcroft and Gates: Gates was the primary manager of the paper flow and interagency process, while Scowcroft devoted most of his attention to advising the president on foreign policy issues. Given the widely held view that the Bush NSC machinery worked fairly well, a broad consensus concerning a central but "low-profile" role for the national security adviser and his staff had firmly taken root by 1992.

The Scope of the NSC's Competence

Concern about the ability of the NSC to manage the expanding range of foreign policy issues is not completely new with the demise of the cold war. In the mid-1970s, for example, Allison and Szanton (1976, 76) argued that "the intertwining of foreign and domestic issues and the politicization of foreign policy" made "reliance on a body as narrow as the NSC for the coordination and decision of central issues of our international relations . . . an anachronism."

More recent critiques have echoed that theme, while emphasizing the changes produced by the end of the cold war. Jeffrey Garten (1992b, 45) has argued that the NSC's "structure and its mission are outdated. . . . Its focus is exclusively on yesterday's preoccupations such as NATO, missiles, and troop deployments." Ernest May (1992, 228) has suggested that the "NSC is an odd mechanism for framing policy options regarding trade resources, the environment, population, hunger, or disease." The Commission on Government Renewal, a bipartisan group of former officials sponsored by the Carnegie Endowment for International Peace and the Institute for International Economics, asserted in 1992: "The present system, by failing to integrate economic and other global concerns, makes it virtually impossible to develop a coherent and effective national strategy for the post–cold war era" (Carnegie Endowment 1992–1993, 175). The commission's report goes on to state that the NSC system "should be modernized and better integrated with the economic and domestic portions of government, enabling it to deal more effectively with the 'new' economic and global issues." I. M. Destler (1994), a member of that commission, offers similar reasons why the post–cold war environment requires an integration of what he calls the "security complex" and the "economic complex" within the U.S. government. Finally, the report of the State Department's Management Task Force argues that while the NSC process served the nation's needs well in the past, "we must . . . forge a new balance between overseas political-military imperatives and international economic and global needs" (U.S. Department of State 1992, 19).

Allison and Szanton's original proposal to correct this deficiency (1976, 78) by replacing the National Security Council with "an executive committee of the Cabinet" (or ExCab), which would include officials in foreign, domestic, and economic policy, was obviously never adopted. While recent analyses of the traditional NSC system's ability to manage a broader foreign policy agenda mirror Allison and Szanton's skepticism, none call for dismantling that system. Instead, their recommendations fall into one of two general categories: the expansion of the NSC system's responsibilities beyond its conventional political-military focus; and the creation of a parallel advisory and coordinating system (explicitly modeled on the NSC) to manage economic issues.

The most sweeping suggestions for NSC reform came from Jeffrey Garten (later named undersecretary of commerce for international trade by Clinton), who argued that the mandate of the council should "be broadened to include our most pressing economic and social priorities," including workforce training, defense industrial base conversion, and treatment for drug addiction (1992b, 45–46). The NSC membership would also be expanded to include most cabinet departments and additional advisers such as the chair of the Federal Reserve. Garten noted that for his proposal to work, however, significant reorganization of the executive branch bureaucracies and of the congressional committee system would probably be necessary.

The report of the State Department's Management Task Force also argued that the NSC system should be strengthened and expanded in competence. It urged the creation of "a single foreign policy forum" to consider "political-military imperatives and international economic and global needs" (U.S. Department of State 1992, 19).[5] While not recommending the addition of statutory members to the NSC, the State Department report suggested that officials from Treasury, Commerce, the U.S. Trade Representative's office, and the Office of Management and Budget should be mandatory participants "in various NSC fora." Whatever the exact form of reorganization, "under no circumstances should the NSC be allowed to remain in its political-security shell" (U.S. Department of State 1992, 20).

The State Department report also advocated changes at the level of the national security adviser and the NSC staff. The NSA should have some background in economic and "global" issues, and should have two deputy NSAs—one for political-security issues and another for economic and global affairs. This division of responsibilities would also be reflected in the staff's structure and expertise. In addition, the report advocated establishing a "small policy planning unit" in the NSC staff as the "locus for longer-term strategic planning . . . particularly important for consideration of global issues" (U.S. Department of State 1992, 182; another advocate of this idea is Shoemaker 1991, 122).

Both Garten and the State Department report explicitly rejected a "parallel" solution to the problem of integrating foreign policy issues:

> There are those who will call for a separate council alongside the traditional NSC, in order not to water down the security mission. But these critics misread the need to mesh domestic and foreign policy with greater intensity than has ever been tried before. . . . They also ignore past Presidential failures to set up an effective economic and social counterpart to the NSC. (Garten 1992b, 47)

The State Department report (1992, 19) warned that the creation of a separate process for each set of issues would eventually force the president "to establish yet another forum to forge consensus" (see also Wessel 1992).

The most prominent proponents of the creation of a parallel advisory system were the members of the Commission on Government Renewal (another important advocate of this approach was Robert Reich, a close friend of Clinton and his future secretary of labor: see Walker 1992–1993, 89). The commission rejected the expansion of the NSC system to fully cover international economic and "global" issues in a single advisory and staff system as impractical on several grounds. The large domestic content of many foreign economic policy decisions would involve the NSC in a wide range of domestic political disputes that would divert it from its primary functions (Destler 1994, 143; for a similar argument, see Clarke 1989, 25–26). According to Destler, several members of the commission also contended that in a unified advisory system, "the aura of urgency" that surrounds traditional security issues would crowd out less glamorous economic policy.

Rather than expand the NSC system, the commission's report recommended some minor modifications of the NSC staff and the creation of an economic council and a domestic council, each headed by an assistant to the president equivalent to the national security adviser in rank and responsibility.[6] These three "coequal councils" would be responsible for "all policy coordination" and would therefore have to work very closely together (Carnegie Endowment 1992–1993, 179). As a demonstration of a "determination to break down the barriers between the national security world and the rest of the White House," the commission suggested that all three assistants for policy participate in the president's morning briefing, which has traditionally been the domain of the national security adviser.

Focusing on the economic council, the commission report stated (181) that it should be the "instrument for assuring that economic policy *gets attention equal to* national security" (emphasis added). Other advocates of the "parallel" solution described its function in similar terms: the council would "coordinate domestic and international economic policy much as the [NSC] balances competing diplomatic and military concerns" (Stokes 1992–1993, 44).

"Equal attention" is not necessarily the same as "fuller integration," however. Building parallel but distinct advisory systems may equalize the level of attention that issues in each realm receive and may also be effective in fostering integration between domestic and foreign *economic* policy, but it would *not* ensure that political, military, and economic factors are all considered together in a single foreign policy process. This solution also raised the specter of competition between those parallel structures: Brzezinski, a critic of the proposal, suggested that such an approach "will simply enhance the turf struggles which already take too much time" (quoted in Wessel 1992).

Proponents of the idea recognized some of these dangers. The Commission on Government Renewal's report acknowledged that if the three assistants for policy fail to work well together, "turf battles would be immensely costly" (1992–1993, 179). Destler notes that a parallel structure "risks institutionalizing the security-economics divide" (1994, 144). He suggests that either the president or the White House chief of staff would have to play a very active role in "coordinating the coordinators" to ensure an effective integration of policy (see also Carnegie Endowment 1992–1993, 181–83).

The Clinton System: Structure and Process

Within a week of the 1992 election, it became clear which models the new administration planned to use. The Clinton transition office announced that the new president would create an "economic security council" (later changed to the National Economic Council, or NEC), following the model presented by the Commission on Government Renewal (Ifill 1992; Wessel 1992). Several of the commission's members had been foreign policy advisers to the Clinton campaign, and they were subsequently selected to fill policy positions in the new administration. Clinton himself was favorably impressed by the operation of the Bush NSC system, and wished to create a similar structure that would produce powerful initiatives in the area of economic policy (Ifill 1993a).

Clinton's directive establishing his NSC system did expand the formal scope of NSC activities, compared to the language of the National Security Act of 1947:

> The NSC shall advise and assist me in integrating all aspects of national security policy as it affects the United States—domestic, foreign, military, *intelligence and economic (in conjunction with the National Economic Council).* (Clinton 1993a, emphasis added)

This clearly indicated that the NSC was to be the forum where the integration of the economic and noneconomic aspects of foreign policy would occur.

The basic structure of the NSC itself and the interagency committee system, as well as the role of the national security adviser and the NSC staff, all remained very similar to the Bush NSC system, even though some changes were made to accommodate the incoming administration's new priorities. In addition to the reasons already mentioned, Clinton's national security adviser, Anthony Lake, had a conception of the NSA's role that was close to that held by Brent Scowcroft. Lake had also warned previously (Destler, Gelb, and Lake 1984, 279) that a new administration should not precipitously dismantle the policy process inherited from its predecessor, however strong the political temptation to do so: "Just take the existing mechanism, use it for a while, see how things really work, and then formalize the relationships [the president] finds effective." Under these conditions, substantial continuity rather than dramatic change was to be expected in the Clinton NSC system, despite the end of the cold war.

Advisory System Organization: The NSC

The Clinton administration made only minor changes in the composition of the NSC itself and no significant changes in the interagency committee structure. The membership of the National Security Council proper was expanded by presidential order to include the secretary of the treasury; the U.S. representative to the United Nations; the assistants to the president for national security affairs and for economic policy; and the White House chief of staff. This change was intended to facilitate the consideration of economic policy concerns in the discussion of traditional national security issues, and to reflect the increased importance of multilateralism in the administration's approach to foreign policy.

Subordinate to the NSC is a hierarchy of committees. The Principals Committee (NSC/PC) is "the senior interagency forum . . . available for Cabinet-level officials to meet to discuss and resolve issues not requiring the President's participation" (Clinton 1993b, 2). The members of the NSC/PC are the secretaries of state and defense (or their designated representatives), the U.S. representative to the UN, the chairman of the JCS, the director of central intelligence, and the national security adviser (who serves as chair).

One rung below the NSC/PC is the Deputies Committee (NSC/DC). It is at this level that the great bulk of the NSC's work is done. The primary functions of the NSC/DC are to monitor the NSC interagency process and to resolve policy disputes that resisted resolution at earlier stages in the process, especially in the interagency working groups (to be discussed later). The Deputies Committee is expected to "focus significant attention on policy implementation," including reviews of existing policy directives. The NSC/DC is also charged with ensuring the adequacy of issue papers to be considered by the NSC/PC or the NSC. Finally, the Deputies Committee is responsible for "day-to-day crisis management" as well as crisis prevention and contingency planning (Clinton 1993b, 2–3).

Mirroring the membership of the NSC/PC, the Deputies Committee is composed of the deputy national security adviser (chair), the deputy secretary of defense, the deputy secretary of state, the deputy director of central intelligence, the vice chairman of the JCS, and the deputy U.S. representative to the United Nations. The vice president's assistant for national security affairs is also a member of this body.

The Deputies Committee is also authorized to establish and oversee a system of interagency working groups (IWGs, pronounced "I-wigs"), to prepare preliminary studies of foreign policy options, and to coordinate the implementation of presidential decisions. These IWGs are chaired by an assistant secretary of state, defense, or treasury, or by NEC or NSC staff, as appropriate to the policy area under consideration and as determined by the Deputies Committee. Several IWGs are specifically earmarked as the NSC staff's responsibility: intelligence, nonproliferation, arms control, and crisis management (Clinton 1993b, 4).

The IWGs are supplemented and backstopped by a large number of ad hoc working alliances among officials, alliances that cut across agencies. According to NSC and State Department staffers, these informal groups of four to six officials are very useful for generating ideas, building consensus across organizations, and hashing out some policy differences before a formal IWG or NSC/DC meeting on an issue.

Several aspects of this system are worth noting. One of the most striking, in light of the administration's rhetoric, is the relatively small role for economic officials in the formal structure of the NSC system. While both the assistant to the president for economic policy and the secretary of the treasury are members of the full NSC, their agencies are not automatically represented on either the Principals or Deputies Committees. NEC and Treasury officials are to be invited to meetings of those committees "as appropriate" or "as needed" (Clinton 1993a, 2–3). There is a stipulation that the assistant to the president for economic policy "shall be informed of [NSC/PC] meetings and be invited to attend all those with international economic considerations" (Clinton 1993a, 2), but this still leaves considerable discretion for the national security adviser in defining when those "considerations" warrant an invitation to his counterpart at the NEC. Interviews with NSC and NEC officials indicate there have been relatively few instances where this power of invitation has been manipulated in an attempt to exclude NEC people from NSC-sponsored meetings, but all agree that this is due primarily to the cordial and scrupulous working relationship established by Lake and Robert Rubin, when he was the assistant to the president for economic policy and director of the NEC staff. As an example, early in the administration, Rubin and some of his staff complained to Lake that they felt they were out of the policy loop on some issues the NSC was handling; Lake responded by instructing the NSC staff to route their memos to the NEC to ensure their inclusion in the process.

Another noteworthy feature of this organization is the dominance of the national security adviser and his deputy in the process. The NSA chairs the Principals Committee, the deputy NSA chairs the Deputies Committee: in each instance, the chair is responsible for calling meetings of the committee, inviting participants in addition to those who are core members of the committee, setting the agenda, and preparing the necessary paperwork. Only at the level of the interagency working groups do representatives of other agencies chair meetings, and even here (as noted previously) several of the most important IWGs are chaired by NSC staffers. This central role for the NSA is highly consistent with the prescriptions of the Tower Commission Report, and it is extremely similar to the system the Bush administration used (Snow and Brown 1994, 149–52).

Organization of the NSC Staff

The administration did modify the NSC staff structure it inherited from the Bush administration somewhat (U.S. Congress, House Committee on Appropriations 1993, 759–60). Initially, three new offices were created to account for the new political geography of the post–cold war era (the Office of European Affairs was divided into an Office for Western European Affairs and an Office for Russia, Ukraine and Eurasian Affairs) or to focus attention on issues whose relative importance has increased since the end of the cold war (the offices for Non-Proliferation Policy and for Environmental Affairs). The Office of Global Issues and Multilateral Affairs (formerly International Programs) was expanded and reorganized in recognition of the "increasing emphasis on multilateral approaches to regional problems" (U.S. Congress, House Committee on Appropriations 1993, 779). A new position of staff director, who was supposed to serve as a "policy coordinator," was created (U.S. Congress, House Committee on Appropriations 1993, 779). Two additional offices were created in 1994: the Office of Democracy Affairs and (through a new division of the Office for Western European Affairs) the Office for Central and Eastern European Affairs (U.S. Congress, House Committee on Appropriations 1994b, 373–74).[7] Additional staff were also assigned to the Office of Legislative Affairs and the Press Office (Kamen 1994a).

Even while the administration increased the number of offices within the NSC staff, however, the overall size of the staff was reduced significantly. As a result of Clinton's pledge to reduce White House staff by 25 percent, the NSC staff was cut in 1993 from 179 to 147 positions (60 of these are professional and staff slots funded directly through the NSC staff budget; the remainder are detailees from executive branch departments). Finding they had cut too deeply, administration officials restored four positions in 1994, bringing the authorized staff to 151 (U.S. Congress, House Committee on Appropriations 1994b, 366–68), but budget pressures forced the number back down to 145 by January 1995 (U.S. Congress, House Committee on Appropriations 1995, 231).

This meant that some NSC offices shrank considerably from their size during the Bush administration. The Defense Policy and Arms Control Office, for example, was reduced by 50 percent after the Clinton administration took office. Other offices were asked to handle more issues without any additional resources or staff.

In an attempt to ensure policy coordination between the parallel advisory structures of the NSC and NEC, two levels of interaction were built into the policy-making system. The national security adviser is a member of the NEC, and the economic policy adviser sits on the NSC. At the staff level, "the management, direction and coordination" of U.S. foreign economic policy was institutionalized in the form of the Office of Trade and International Economic Policy, jointly funded and staffed by the NSC and NEC (according to administration officials, this arrangement resulted from a conversation between Lake and Rubin during the transition, as they discussed how to coordinate their operations and cope with anticipated staff shortages). The "Sherpa function" of preparing for the annual G-7 economic summits was moved from the State Department's Office of the Undersecretary for Economic Affairs (which had performed this task during the Reagan and Bush administrations) to this joint NSC/NEC office (U.S. Congress, House Committee on Appropriations 1993, 768–69).

Advisory System Organization: The NEC

Although the structure and function of the National Economic Council is not a primary concern of this study, a brief examination is in order, given the role the NEC was expected to play in shaping administration policy and in elevating the level and quality of attention devoted to economic issues in foreign policy.

The NEC was established by executive order in January 1993 (Clinton 1993a); two years later, Clinton proclaimed it was "one of the most significant organizational changes we . . . have made, and one that I predict all future administrations will follow" (quoted in Harris and Pearlstein 1995). Given the fact that the NSC supposedly provided the inspiration for its economic counterpart, the contrasts between the NEC and the NSC are as notable as the similarities. The council itself has eighteen members, six of whom (the president, vice president, secretaries of state and treasury, and the assistants to the president for national security affairs and for economic policy) also sit on the NSC (interviews and press reports indicated that it was Lake's deputy, Samuel R. Berger, who usually attended NEC meetings: see Ifill 1993a). This makes the formal NEC twice as large as the NSC, encompassing a much broader array of agencies and interests. Provisions were made for the creation of committees and working groups; unlike the very detailed hierarchy of NSC committees, these were left unspecified in the executive order creating the NEC.

Like the NSA, the assistant for economic policy is charged with managing the interagency coordination process and is provided with a staff. Due to tight budget restrictions and Clinton's pledge concerning staff cuts, however, the NEC staff remained extremely small. In 1994, there were twenty-two professional staff at the NEC, seven of whom had international policies or programs as their primary responsibility (this number included those "dual-hatters" who serve both the NSC and NEC).

The NEC was given several specific functions, the first of which was "to coordinate the economic policy-making process with respect to domestic and international economic issues" (Clinton 1993a, 95). Other functions involved ensuring the implementation and consistency of the administration's economic policies. Notably absent from the description of functions was any responsibility for integrating economic with noneconomic facets of foreign policy decisions.

There is a final characteristic of the NSC/NEC advisory and staff system created by Clinton and his aides that must be mentioned. In opting for an NSC system modeled on the Tower Commission's recommendations, and in embracing the Commission for Government Renewal's preference for a parallel advisory and staff system for economic policy, Clinton chose two models which (in the eyes of their proponents) demanded sustained and forceful presidential involvement in the foreign policy process. The adoption of both placed an enormous burden on the incoming president and his White House chief of staff to ensure that the various pieces of the foreign policy machinery meshed smoothly. However, given Clinton's clear desire to focus on domestic issues and to relegate foreign policy to the "back burner" as much as possible (Drew 1994, 138), the responsibility for the successful operation of the system was delegated primarily to the national security adviser and his top aides. The ability of these officials to manage this system, especially absent any sustained presidential interest, was therefore crucial to the effectiveness of the interagency process.

The Clinton NSC System: Operation

In evaluating the strengths and weaknesses of the Clinton NSC system, I will examine four salient issues that analysts or administration officials themselves have identified as central to the functioning of that system: the NSA/NSC role as "honest broker" and coordinator among the foreign policy bureaucracies; the management of the interagency process; the coordination and integration of the economic and noneconomic aspects of the administration's foreign policy; and the role of the president in leading and overseeing the system.

The NSA/NSC as "Honest Broker"

By all accounts, Lake was remarkably evenhanded in representing other agencies and principals fairly to the president, in ceding the spotlight to the secretary of state, and in minimizing the open disharmony and competition that characterized NSC relations with the line agencies in previous administrations. Officials interviewed at the NSC, NEC, and State Department were unanimous in their view that the relatively smooth working relationship among those agencies was primarily due to the commitment by all the principals—but especially Lake—to the idea that differences over policy would not be permitted to erupt into "bloodletting" among administration officials. Even when such sniping occurred—for example, concerning the U.S. military intervention in Haiti in September 1994—Lake and Christopher were quick to rebuke their subordinates and they swiftly brought an end to the public recriminations (Kirschten 1994b; Sciolino 1994d).

Lake's desire to maintain a low profile as NSA was also increasingly seen as a source of difficulties, however. The president's unwillingness to articulate a clear foreign policy strategy, and the inability of Secretary of State Warren Christopher to do so effectively, left a glaring gap in the domestic support for the administration's foreign policy initiatives. Indeed, Lake argued near the end of his first year as NSA that this was the main foreign policy failure of the administration: "Tell me of another Administration that has gotten so much done on so many issues in its first 10 months. The failure has been in explaining our policy adequately to the public" (quoted in Sciolino 1993a). Lake vowed to play a more public role in educating Congress and the American people about the administration's foreign policy.

His first notable attempt at public explication came in September 1993, when he outlined the "strategy of enlargement" as "the successor to a doctrine of containment" (Lake 1993, 659). This and a handful of subsequent forays by Lake into the public arena during the next nine months were not very well received, however; in June 1994 Lake conceded he was still not playing a very visible role in building support for administration policy, admitting, "I may have made a mistake in how I conceived of my own job" (quoted on C-SPAN 1994). The administration's continuing concern over this issue was demonstrated by the attendance of communications adviser David Gergen at meetings of the NSC/PC during the last half of 1994, in an effort to ensure that the public presentation of policy be considered during the decision-making process (Kirschten 1994b).

Lake did take a more public role beginning in 1995, largely in reaction to the new political difficulties the administration was encountering as a result of the 1994 elections, when the Republicans gained control of Congress. His speeches emphasized the dangers of "backdoor isolationism" and outlined the parameters for using U.S. military forces in the post–cold

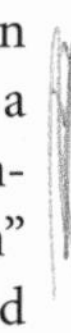

war era (Lake 1995b, 1996), and Lake led a delegation to Europe in August 1995 in an attempt to make progress in negotiating a solution to the war in Bosnia. Lake's more prominent public role and forceful assertion of his own policy preferences raised questions, however, about his ability to play the "honest broker role" effectively, especially in the State Department (DeParle 1995).

Management of the Interagency Process

Discussions with administration officials clearly indicate that poor management has seriously hampered the Clinton NSC committee system and interagency process. Participants identify several reasons why this was the case.

The NSC staff structure, and the division of labor among the staff, constituted one set of factors. The expansion of the number of offices within the NSC staff, combined with constraints on staff hiring, reduced the size of many individual NSC offices and produced a situation where the workload sometimes overwhelmed the staff. Attention to many issues was sporadic, and the paper flow slowed to a crawl; one State Department official remarked that an important cable to U.S. embassies in Europe, providing instructions for consultations and negotiations in the wake of the G-7 summit in June 1994, took two weeks to receive routine clearance from the NSC staff.

Contrary to the initial guidelines of PDD-2, reports from both State and NSC officials indicated that NSC staffers chaired the vast majority of IWGs. Veteran officials attributed this to what they viewed as the mistaken belief by new NSC staffers that the only way they could stay on top of policy was to chair as many working groups as possible.[8] This was an enormous administrative burden for the small NSC staff and further slowed the decision process on many issues.

This problem was also compounded by the fact that several individual "shops" in the NSC were forced to confront multiple crises during the first eighteen months of the administration. The Office for Global Issues and Multilateral Affairs, for example, had primary responsibility for policy coordination on Somalia, Haiti, and Rwanda during this period. According to several NSC sources, the tendency of beleaguered offices was to "circle the wagons" rather than ask for help from other NSC offices. Several staffers criticized the staff director, who could have assisted in a redistribution of staff/workload, for her inattention to this problem and unwillingness to take corrective action.[9]

A related problem administration officials identified was the apparent lack of interest of the national security adviser and his deputy in managing the NSC staff and the interagency process. Unlike the Bush NSC system, in which Scowcroft primarily advised the president on foreign policy substance and Gates managed and oversaw the process, Lake and Berger divided the substantive issues between them. Berger, for example, was said by NSC staffers to take the lead on Haiti and economic issues; one staffer, when discussing Haiti policy (in early July 1994), said: "Lake doesn't touch it" (see also Kirschten 1994c, 2973). Neither Lake nor Berger took primary responsibility for oversight of the process.

This resulted in the ineffective coordination of interagency working groups and the often poor quality of their recommendations to the Deputies Committee. The IWGs quickly became very large and unwieldy; different IWGs with overlapping responsibilities disagreed on policy options, and senior NSC officials were reluctant "to butt heads" to resolve the differences. As a result, in many cases the problem was merely bucked up the organizational hierarchy to the NSC/DC, where the issue would be reworked almost from scratch. This also slowed the decision process enormously, creating a backlog of issues that needed resolution and a pattern of postponed and rescheduled NSC/DC meetings.

One public glimpse of this difficulty occurred regarding the administration's policy in Somalia. Secretary of State Christopher publicly criticized the Deputies Committee, which Berger chaired, for failing to conduct a review of Somalia policy after several American troops were killed in June 1993. Lake defended the work of the NSC/DC, arguing that the committee's schedule was overloaded and that the interagency working group the State Department chaired should have done more preparatory work for a high-level review (Robbins 1993b; Sciolino 1993a). NSC staffers said that the performance of the Deputies Committee in this instance was not unusual and that the problem continued well into 1994.

Another example of this problem of interagency coordination was the delay in the completion of the administration's National Security Strategy paper. This document, a report to Congress required by law, has usually been a bland statement of an administration's general national security policy goals. In 1993, however, the drafting of the document was complicated by questions concerning U.S. foreign policy priorities after the cold war and the budget implications of those choices. Initially, the NSC staff—viewing this as a routine reporting requirement—delegated responsibility for drafting the document to the Defense Department. The DOD draft focused primarily on military strategy, with little comment about economic or other "global issues," and the IWG led by Defense Department officials cleared the document and passed it up the staff ladder to the NSC/DC level. However, at the State Department, officials from the Office of Policy Planning complained that the narrow definition of national security was "totally inadequate," and they pushed within the department for a much broader definition of foreign policy and national security. Secretary Christopher refused to concur with the Defense Department draft, and the Policy Planning staff wrote their own version, which Christopher sent to Lake at the NSC. Lake preferred the State draft and, after insisting that the concept of "enlargement" be worked into the document, sent the State-based draft back through the interagency process for approval. The document was finally issued in July 1994 (Clinton 1994).

Defense Department officials and some NSC staffers were very upset by what they viewed as the State Department's ability to hijack the process and be rewarded for it. These officials implied that State's actions were motivated primarily by a desire to raid the Defense Department's budget by expanding the definition of national security to include issues in which the State Department would take the lead (see also Holmes 1993). State Department officials insist that the budget issue was separate and coincidental to the debate over the national security strategy document, and they were disturbed that the White House did little to curb press leaks from the Pentagon that attacked State's actions on this issue. Congress and the press criticized the administration for its seeming inability to accomplish even routine tasks in foreign policy making (see also Lancaster and Gellman 1994; Pine 1994a).

Finally, a major management and leadership difficulty that almost every NSC, NEC, and State official interviewed identified was what one NSC staffer called a "fetish for consensus building" among the administration's foreign policy principals. In his attempt to ensure a collegial relationship among administration officials, Lake (who advised Clinton in this matter during the transition) created a policy-making environment in which there were few major differences among the top officials. When differences on policy did exist, the first priority was to find a solution that every principal could support. Lake himself seemed to recognize that this could lead to problems when he remarked in October 1993: "I think there is a danger that when people work well together, you can take the edge off the options" (quoted in Friedman 1993c; also see Sciolino 1993a).

According to some administration officials, however, the consequences of this attitude went beyond a lack of creative tension among the foreign policy leadership. They identified two additional problems: a failure to maintain discipline within the decision process and a failure to "sharpen the options" available to the president.

The failure to maintain discipline within the decision process had two components. The desire by top NSC officials to maintain cordial relations among the agencies paradoxically encouraged individuals in those agencies to attempt "end runs" around the NSC-based policy coordinating mechanisms. Few penalties or sanctions were imposed on those who deviated from agreed policy or circumvented the prescribed channels for policy coordination. On many issues, according to several clearly frustrated NSC staffers, Lake and Berger were obviously unwilling to confront State or Defense Department officials in order to resolve such problems.

The second failure of discipline within the process was the absence of a clear mechanism for forcing decisions on issues. Several NSC staff members related tales of lengthy meetings, especially at the working group and Deputies Committee levels, where no decisions were taken. Several days later, the participants would reconvene and rehash the issue. This sequence was sometimes repeated for months; two NSC staffers specifically mentioned the IWG on Bosnia as a case where this occurred, and Elizabeth Drew (1994, 150) reports that one administration official commented that policy discussions of Bosnia during 1993 were "group therapy—an existential debate over what is the role of America, etc."

This indecisiveness was also directly linked to the second facet of the pursuit of consensus: the failure to "sharpen the options" presented to the president. Indeed, Lake and Berger preferred to reach an agreed *recommendation* among the foreign policy principals for presentation to the president. When a consensus was not found, they tended to "walk the issue back" to a point where everyone could agree. This was not only a very time-consuming process, it tended to produce a "least common denominator" solution to policy problems. One veteran government official likened the process to that of the Eisenhower NSC system, which emphasized compromise recommendations and "agreement by exhaustion," as Dean Acheson once remarked (in Falk 1988, 75; for a different view of the Eisenhower NSC, see Henderson 1988, chap. 4). Eventually, Lake seemed to recognize that this was a problem, and he began to assert his own preferences more forcefully "because it helps to move issues to a resolution" (quoted in DeParle 1995, 37).

Most officials who discussed this problem saw it as a reflection of the personalities of the foreign policy principals and their goal of smoothing over internal administration disputes.[10] One former NSC official also suggested that this reflected a broader "cultural" context in the Democratic

Party, which emphasized consensus building and increased the reluctance of administration officials to take decisions in the face of open dissent (for a related argument, see Ignatius 1994). However, this desire to smooth differences and present a consensus recommendation may have also reflected their recognition that the president preferred to rely on the advice of his "wise men" as a way of limiting his own direct involvement in foreign policy. One of Lake's jobs was to "keep foreign policy submerged" and to prevent foreign policy concerns from interfering with domestic policy (Drew 1994, 138). In this case, the search for an elusive consensus may have been an appropriate response to the president's own preference to be told what needed to be done on foreign policy issues, rather than devoting the energy and time to decide this himself.

Integration of Political-Military and Economic Issues

A major question about the advisory structure Clinton chose was whether it would provide an effective method of integrating political-military and economic facets of a post–cold war foreign policy. In two areas where both these factors were very important, China and Japan, the answer would have to be no, though for different reasons.

In the case of China, the problem was the administration's inability to maintain a clear set of priorities concerning diverse U.S. goals regarding human rights, security issues, and economic interests (see Auger 1995). Policy toward China was initially dominated by Assistant Secretary of State Winston Lord and guided by Clinton's own campaign statements. Human rights considerations were given a very high priority, especially in declaratory policy, despite growing concern among the business community and the members of the NEC that economic interests were being slighted.

Clinton did renew China's most-favored nation (MFN) trade status in May 1993, but with a list of specific human rights conditions that the Chinese government would have to meet before that status could be renewed in 1994. Lord and Deputy NSA Berger wrote the executive order that announced this shift in U.S. policy, in close consultation with Democratic leaders in the Congress (Greenberger 1994). The economic agencies in the executive branch had virtually no role in drafting that initial policy statement, despite the rapidly expanding trade and investment relationship between the United States and China.

Within weeks of the May 1993 announcement, however, the administration's official policy was challenged from within. An interagency review completed in September recommended a policy of engagement rather than confrontation with China. Treasury and Commerce Department officials visited China, stressing the U.S. desire to expand trade and investment, even as officials from State were threatening to revoke MFN status because of Beijing's continuing human rights violations. One State Department official complained, "It's irritating. We seem to do the Chinese work for them. If they need someone to argue against revoking MFN, they only have to get hold of some guy from the economic branch of [the U.S.] government" (quoted in Williams 1994a).

This tension within the administration came to a head with the perceived failure of Secretary of State Christopher's visit to China in March 1994, when the Chinese government brusquely rejected his message about human rights. Officials in the Treasury and Commerce Departments began to call publicly for eliminating the linkage between China's human rights policies and U.S.-China economic relations. At a joint meeting of the NSC and NEC principals (which the president did not attend) after Christopher's return to Washington, the State Department and the NSC staff regained control over the debate by reaffirming MFN conditionality as administration policy, with one State Department official arguing, "It's not tenable to have the economic agencies in open revolt against the policy" (quoted in Sciolino 1994f). However, in return for their agreement to support the official policy, the NEC officials insisted that the policy-making process regarding China be changed to give greater weight to the economic aspect of U.S.-China relations. Ultimately, in May 1994, Clinton sided with his economic advisers, declaring that China had done the bare minimum to meet his May 1993 conditions and was therefore eligible for MFN status. He also eliminated any further linkage between the Chinese government's human rights practices and its trade status with the United States.

After May 1994, the administration's China policy continued to be hampered by an inability to integrate the economic and noneconomic components of policy, though the officials from the economic agencies were now playing a much larger role in shaping that policy. In early 1996, for example, Clinton's trade officials began to push for economic sanctions against China for violation of intellectual property rights, even as the State Department and White House attempted to persuade China to relax its pressure on Taiwan in the period before Taiwan's presidential elections (Sanger and Erlanger 1996). In May, on the advice of his economic advisers, Clinton announced sharp increases on the tariffs for more than $2 billion in Chinese exports to the United States as punishment for those violations, just five days after the State Department had declined to impose sanctions on China for the export of nuclear weapons–related equipment to Pakistan (Erlanger 1996d; Sanger 1996b). During all the administration discussions leading up to these decisions, the focus was on the tactical details of the sanctions. Despite growing recognition and concern within the administration that the various components of its policy toward China were at odds, in the words of one report, "There was little discussion of a grander plan for dealing with China" (Sanger 1996a).

A very different problem characterized the administration's Japan policy. Many officials and analysts have argued that during the cold war, American foreign economic policy was subordinated to the political and military concerns of the Defense and State Departments, especially in Asia (Fallows 1989; Harrison and Prestowitz 1990). From the start of the Clinton administration, that balance was almost completely reversed, with concerns about the stability of the broader U.S.-Japanese relationship receiving much less attention than U.S. economic interests. This was a deliberate decision, fully consistent with Clinton's emphasis during the campaign on "economic security" and with statements by Secretary Christopher that foreign economic policy would no longer be the poor relation of traditional foreign policy issues (Christopher 1993c).

According to NSC and NEC staffers, the NEC and officials from Treasury, Commerce, and the U.S. Trade Representative's office (USTR) dominated policy concerning Japan from the outset. These officials emphasized confrontation with Japan, in the belief that only sustained and substantial pressure would produce acceptable changes in Japanese economic policy (see also Chandler 1994). The political consequences of that pressure were dismissed as irrelevant or of secondary importance. One American official stated that "the politics are obviously delicate. . . . Our business is with Japan, and their political problems are their problem" (quoted in Bradsher 1993). U.S. officials also appeared willing to hold the broader political relationship hostage until Japanese economic policies met American demands. Deputy U.S. Trade Representative Charlene Barshefsky declared: "The political climate between the United States and Japan will be determined by economics. If the economics aren't right, the political climate isn't going to be right. To the extent the Japanese are concerned about the political climate, they have it in their power to ensure that the political climate is positive" (Stokes 1994). Even the collapse of what U.S. officials considered a "reformist" Japanese government in April 1994 elicited no immediate signs that the administration was reconsidering its strident approach (Davis 1994). By May 1995, U.S. Trade Representative Mickey Kantor had convinced the president to levy heavy sanctions on Japanese luxury auto exports to the United States in retaliation for what Clinton administration officials declared were restrictive Japanese trade practices (Chandler 1995). Six weeks of brinkmanship followed, and the imposition of sanctions was avoided by a last-minute compromise in which the Clinton administration settled for considerably fewer, and less specific, Japanese concessions than it had originally sought.

This close call did have the effect of beginning the process of rethinking the balance between economic and political-strategic issues in U.S. policy toward Japan. In explaining why the administration ultimately settled for a vague compromise, one senior official said, "We all looked over the precipice and discovered we couldn't see the bottom. The sanctions were a big risk. So we took what we had in hand" (quoted in Sanger 1995a). Shortly after this, Undersecretary of Commerce Garten suggested that the United States and Japan needed to place their trade disputes in a larger political context, saying that the constant conflict "seems as anachronistic as the old gunboat diplomacy" (quoted in Pollack 1995). Although the administration quickly repudiated Garten's statement, other forces at work in the U.S.-Japanese relationship during the next nine months (including the outrage in Japan over the rape of an Okinawan girl by American military personnel based there, the growing aggressiveness of China, and a drop in Japan's trade surplus with the United States) did lead to more attention to the political-strategic aspects of the U.S.-Japan relationship. By the time Clinton visited Japan in April 1996, trade issues had lost their priority on the bilateral agenda and the economic agencies were no longer so dominant in shaping U.S. policy toward Japan (WuDunn 1996). This was due primarily to the changing international context, however, and was not attributable to the NSC/NEC system's ability to integrate and coordinate the various components of the administration's policy toward Japan.

One of Clinton's senior economic advisers said in July 1995: "Everyone acknowledges that economics now plays a central role in foreign policy—that battle is over. What no one has really grappled with is what happens when commercial interests push out other concerns" (quoted in Sanger 1995b). The trade-offs and coordination of policy with political-strategic goals are inherently difficult when economic priorities clash, but this is *exactly* the area in which the NSC/NEC arrangement should have a comparative advantage over alternative organizational arrangements, according to its proponents. The fact that the economic and noneconomic components of foreign policy toward China and Japan remained uncoordinated or in open competition for so long suggests that the NSC/NEC system has failed a crucial test as an effective mechanism for integrating those aspects of policy.

Inconsistent Presidential Leadership

For all the attention justifiably devoted to understanding the formal structure and process of the NSC system, it is crucial to remember that, ultimately, that system is an extension of the president's own concerns and interests. Robert Hunter (1982, 92) has argued that while a well-ordered NSC system can facilitate coherent policy making, "the president's own behavior in operating the system will speak more loudly than formal structures."

A striking aspect of the Clinton administration's foreign policy process, given the advisory and staff structures it selected, has been what one State Department official termed the president's "selective interest" in foreign policy. On certain topics, such as Russia or trade ("economic security"), the president has evinced enthusiasm, sustained interest, and a certain consistency in policy pronouncements. On most foreign policy issues, however, Clinton has taken an active role only when confronted by a crisis. In these cases, the president became intensely engaged for a brief period, and officials who attended NSC meetings where Clinton was present attested to his ability to assimilate information and quickly identify the crux of the matter. However, as the immediate crisis faded, the president would return to a general lack of interest in the subject, rarely following up the decisions made or the general line of policy established.

This pattern was established beginning in January 1993. Clinton reportedly did not hold a meeting of the NSC during his first three weeks in office; one foreign policy official commented, concerning Clinton's participation in foreign policy discussions early in his term, "He is there to do things when asked. But that is the extent of it" (quoted in Friedman 1993a).

According to several NSC officials, this reduced the effectiveness and morale of the NSC staff, and produced puzzlement among the executive branch agencies concerning the direction of policy. For example, in mid-May 1993—less than three weeks before the initial deadline on MFN status—the president had yet to look over an interdepartment review of options on China policy prepared weeks earlier (Kristof 1993). The disengagement of the president from policy discussions on Bosnia and Somalia in 1993 produced uncertainty and inaction among foreign policy officials, who had no clear lead to follow. This distance also meant that at times, it was clear that the president was unaware of activities his officials were undertaking in his name (Devroy 1994; Gigot 1993; Robbins 1993a; Sciolino 1993a).

Clinton rarely attended meetings of his top NSC officials, even when China's MFN status or (until mid-1995) policy concerning Bosnia was the subject (on Bosnia, see Engelberg 1995; Gordon 1994b). This in itself is not unusual; most presidents have relied more heavily on informal advisory systems for information and options rather than attend formal NSC meetings (see Rosati 1993, 90–103). In Clinton's case, however, he also rarely participated in the informal advisory process during his first two years in office. Persistent efforts by Lake and Christopher to get the president to commit to weekly meetings with his foreign policy advisers were repeatedly rebuffed. Even Lake's daily morning briefing of the president was often shortened or canceled (Drew 1994, 144; Robbins 1993b; Sciolino 1994a).

Lake's expressed wish to draw the president into "larger contemplative discussions" (quoted in Friedman 1993c) with his advisers about foreign policy goals and strategies was rarely fulfilled, according to NSC and State Department officials. As with every president, there was great competition between the domestic and foreign policy staffs for Clinton's time and attention. Given Clinton's professed priorities, the domestic aides had a clear advantage; Lake constantly had to fight to get foreign policy issues on the president's agenda.

The selective and crisis-driven nature of presidential attention to foreign policy was compounded by a chaotic White House staff operation, in part the result of the president's personal style and in part due to the managerial weakness of Clinton's first chief of staff, Thomas McLarty (for an early diagnosis of this problem, see Frisby 1993a). As one official complained, the president encouraged "deliberate disorganization" within the White House and easy access to the Oval Office for the staff. While this allowed Lake access to the president for brief discussions, there was rarely the follow-up by Clinton or his aides that might have been expected from lengthier, more structured meetings.

By late 1993, it was clear to some administration officials that the coordination across policy arenas needed improvement; as one White House aide complained, "Policy decisions aren't getting closed and don't necessarily hang together" (quoted in Drew 1994, 188). An attempt was made to move Deputy NSA Berger to a broader policy coordination role within the White House, but he successfully resisted the change ("Washington Wire" 1993b). In early December, a new deputy chief of staff was appointed with the explicit responsibility of coordinating the work of the NSC, the NEC, and the Domestic Policy Council (Devroy 1993). Finally, in June 1994, the overall inadequacy of White House management was acknowledged, with the appointment of Leon Panetta as chief of staff. One of Panetta's first moves was to limit access to the Oval Office by most senior officials, including Lake (Solomon 1994). Panetta's arrival eventually improved policy coordination and discipline somewhat (Mitchell 1995), but it still could not substitute for sustained and consistent presidential attention to foreign policy substance and process. Warren Christopher noted this in early 1996, in a comment that could be read as veiled criticism of most of the first three years of Clinton's administration: "One of the lessons of my three years is how essential presidential leadership is. . . . You can't do without presidential leadership" (quoted in Erlanger 1996b).

It is instructive on this point to note that those few areas of foreign policy where Clinton has evidenced sustained attention and commitment are those that reflect what Berman and Goldman call Clinton's "domestic national-purpose orientation," which "locates the chief threats to U.S. interests in the domestic and social condition of the nation" (1996, 297). For example, Clinton's commitment to free trade principles, born of his conviction that U.S. economic prosperity can only be maintained in a liberal global economic system, was responsible for the sustained efforts on NAFTA and GATT (though even in these cases the president was accused by his allies in Congress of waiting until the hour was very late before throwing his personal political capital into the ratification fights).

Similarly, the remarkable turnabout in presidential attention to, and administration policy concerning, Bosnia after June 1995 can be attributed largely to domestic political concerns. After the failure of NATO attacks in May (when the Bosnian Serbs seized hundreds of UN peacekeepers as hostages) and the embarrassing confusion of early June (when Clinton first stated that U.S. troops might be sent to Bosnia shortly and then quickly backed away from that position; see Engelberg and Mitchell 1995), the president pressed his advisers to develop a much more active and forceful U.S. approach to the problem. Given the likelihood that the U.S. would have to send troops to Bosnia to help with the withdrawal of the UN peacekeepers if the war in Bosnia continued to escalate, Clinton told his advisers that "the status quo is not acceptable." Administration officials clearly understood the president's concerns; according to one senior aide, "I don't think the President relishes going into the 1996 election hostage to fortune in the Balkans, with the Bosnian Serbs able to bring us deeper into a war" (quoted in Engelberg 1995). The president was also faced with the embarrassing possibility that the Republican Congress might override his veto of a bill ending U.S. participation in the UN-sponsored arms embargo on Bosnia if the prospects for peace did not improve.

The dramatic U.S. diplomatic effort that eventually led to the Dayton Peace Accords and the deployment of U.S. troops to Bosnia under very controlled conditions did result from sustained presidential attention (and from the changed conditions on the ground, where a joint Croatian-Bosnian offensive in August and September succeeded in retaking much of the territory held by the Bosnian Serbs). However, it was a turnaround driven more by the lurking danger to Clinton's reelection prospects than by a broader commitment to remain involved in foreign policy.

Conclusion

I have analyzed the structure and operations of the Clinton NSC system, but two tasks remain: to evaluate the effects of the end of the cold war on the organization and functioning of that system, and to weigh the relative importance of structure and process versus personnel in understanding NSC behavior and performance.

In thinking about how the end of the cold war affected the National Security Council system, we should distinguish between two types of effects: *direct* (where the NSC structure or process was deliberately changed to conform to the "new realities" of the post–cold war era), and *indirect* (where new political and economic pressures, constraints, and incentives influenced the environment in which the NSC operates). We can then identify the influence of each of these effects, first, on the structure of the NSC/NEC advisory system and, second, on the interagency process.

At the structural level, the direct effect of the end of the cold war was the creation of several new offices within the NSC staff and (in combination with the domestically motivated pledge to cut the White House staff) a "thinning out" of the available staff across a larger number of offices. This resulted in high-level attention to a larger variety of issues, at the risk of straining the very limited resources of the NSC staff.

The indirect structural effects were much more significant. The cold war's conclusion was clearly instrumental in the sharp shift of national priorities toward domestic rather than foreign policy, and within foreign policy toward economic rather than political-military issues. As Bert Rockman notes in chapter 2, presidents take an interest in organizational matters only to the extent that those issues affect their core political agenda. Since the NSC was much more closely identified with the traditional foreign policy agenda than with economic issues, the creation of the NEC as a parallel—and potentially competing—advisory system reflected Clinton's priorities and his feeling that the NSC system alone would be substantively and politically inadequate to address those priorities. The unusual sharing of staff by the NEC and NSC was also an innovative (and generally successful) structural adaptation to coordinate this parallel advisory system.

Ironically, these indirect effects also played a role in the incoming administration's willingness to adopt much of the Bush/Scowcroft NSC model. Since Clinton did not wish to devote very much time to most traditional foreign policy issues, the lure of using a proven structure and process to handle those issues in a low-profile manner was very powerful.

The direct effects of the end of the cold war on the NSC process are more subtle. In some ways, the process was characterized by a significant degree of continuity with the last cold war variant of the NSC system. The formal system of interagency committees, and the role of the national security adviser and NSC staff at the center of the policy-making process, were very similar to both the Bush administration's approach and to the recommendations of the Tower Commission.

Yet officials at the NSC and the State Department pointed to other ways in which the demise of the cold war directly altered the process. Most frequently mentioned was the absence of a clear focus and sense of priorities among the staff. One State Department official who had previously served on the NSC staff said he had been able to devote most of his attention to two or three crucial issues related to the U.S.-Soviet competition; he would periodically check on other issues in his area of responsibility, but felt no need to monitor them constantly. The loss of "the Soviet prism," through which events were interpreted and priorities established, left the NSC staff working on a larger number of issues of seemingly equal importance. This diffusion of effort has slowed the policy process and has left the staff scrambling to catch up with events even more than had normally been the case for previous NSC staffs.

The indirect effect of the conclusion of the cold war on the NSC process is closely related to this point. The collapse of the Soviet Union left the United States without a clear foreign policy "doctrine" to replace the idea of containment. It is widely recognized that such doctrines play a useful function in declaring U.S. intentions to allies and adversaries abroad, and in explaining (however simplistically) the rationale for U.S. involvement overseas to a skeptical American public. What is not so often recognized is that such doctrines—clear statements of general foreign policy goals and purposes—also play a crucial role in focusing internal planning and providing guidance to foreign policy officials throughout the government. Despite the need for such guidance from the top, the Clinton administration has not clearly articulated such a purpose. The president rarely tries to do so, and Lake and Christopher were not effective in this role.

In the absence of such a statement, it is more difficult for the NSC to define and guide policy and get cooperation from the agencies; as one administration official put it, "The NSC doesn't control the strands of policy as much as they used to." Not only does this produce less coherent policy, it also increases the level of frustration and dissatisfaction among NSC staffers.

The direct effects of the end of the cold war on the structure and process of the NSC system have therefore been fairly modest. Given the nature of the NSC system, even those structural changes the Clinton administration has made could be reversed or modified easily by subsequent presidents. The indirect effects are likely to be much longer lasting and pervasive; a new administration will not be able to sweep away the different priorities, expectations, and constraints that the end of the cold war has generated. These effects will therefore continue to pose considerable challenges to any NSC system operating in the post–cold war environment.

Analysts who have served on the NSC have long warned against overemphasizing the impact of NSC structure on the effectiveness of that system. Morton Halperin (1974, 105) cautions that "the attention focused on alternate NSC systems because they are visible tends to obscure the fact that most business is conducted outside of those systems." Robert Hunter adds that "procedure is only as good as the people administering it and the quality of their relationships. This is at the heart of foreign policymaking, once the formal lines of authority and action are established" (1982, 39). Christopher Shoemaker suggests that "more than any other organization in Washington, the NSC staff depends on its people. There are no insulating layers to screen the system [from poor personnel performance]" (1991, 130–31; see also Odeen 1985, 38).

These insights certainly find validation in the history of the Clinton NSC system. The very fact that the Clinton NSC system is so similar to that of its predecessor in design, but is seen by most analysts *and* a significant number of Clinton NSC and State Department officials as so different in its effectiveness, would support the conclusion that the *people* in the process constitute the crucial variable in explaining that result.[11] Both the strengths (the degree of coordination between the NSC and NEC, the success of the NSC's role as an "honest broker" among the executive branch foreign policy agencies) and the weaknesses (mismanagement both at the NSC staff and White House levels, confused policy pronouncements, the inability to expedite decision making or to discipline those who undermine established procedures) of the Clinton NSC system can be traced primarily to the personnel who lead and manage that system.

This is particularly true concerning those at the apex of the decision process: the president and his top advisers. As Colin Campbell has noted (1996, 53–54), weaknesses in the relationship among these principals—which Campbell calls the second "gearbox" of the institutional presidency—have been a major problem for several recent administrations, not just Clinton's (though the foreign policy consequences may be more severe than in any administration since Carter). The president must play an active role in giving what Rockman calls "directional clarity" and in overseeing his subordinates' management of the NSC system and the larger foreign policy process, *especially* if a White House–centered system is chosen. The value that the Tower Commission and others saw in having the NSA and NSC staff at the center of the process declines immensely if it becomes clear that the national security adviser does not have the ear or the confidence of the president, or if the NSA and the NSC staff are unable to use that central position effectively.

Many of the foreign policy problems the Clinton administration has faced would be difficult to solve even with a well-organized and efficiently managed NSC process (after all, the Bush administration had made little progress on Haiti or Bosnia when it handed those issues to the incoming administration). Conceptual lacunae, tactical errors, or plain bad luck may also explain many of the administration's foreign policy difficulties. No process ensures correct decisions; however, a well-organized and carefully staffed NSC system, adequately supported by the president, can help an administration avoid the perception of confusion or incompetence which is so damaging politically, both at home and abroad. It can also provide high-quality options and information for decision makers and help to ensure that decisions are made in a timely manner. The difficult nature of the foreign policy problems facing the United States after the cold war is precisely the strongest argument for getting the NSC process—and the personnel who lead and manage that process—right. Only then will any administration have at least a fighting chance of coping successfully with the myriad international challenges facing the United States in the years ahead.

James M. Lindsay

4. The State Department Complex After the Cold War

The State Department as we know it, the U.S. Agency for International Development (USAID), the U.S. Information Agency (USIA), [and] the Arms Control and Disarmament Agency (ACDA) are all creatures of the Cold War period. They evolved during an era when our nation was facing a single, overwhelming challenge—that is, the challenge of containing the communist threat. With the demise of communism, that threat also died. Containment has served its purpose, and it's taken its rightful place in our history.

And yet our foreign policy institutions continue in large measure to mirror the Cold War imperatives. Maps have changed considerably faster than mind-sets. Budgets and bureaucracies still reflect the reality of a world that's passed. For our institutions, including the State Department, it may be that it was easier to deal in an earlier time when almost any program could be justified in terms of the global struggle against communism. That struggle is passed, and that easy rationale of the past is also a thing of the past.

—Secretary of State Warren Christopher (1993a, 137)

The Clinton administration came to office in January 1993 pledging to revamp the State Department Complex—the State Department and its three affiliated agencies, the Agency for International Development (AID), the Arms Control and Disarmament Agency (ACDA), and the U.S. Information Agency (USIA)—to reflect the realities of the post–cold war era. Four years later, however, the State Department Complex continued to reflect "the reality of a world that's passed." Although the Clinton administration did make some structural and procedural changes during its first two years in office, the changes fell well short of fundamentally altering the structure, operation, or culture of the State Department, AID, ACDA, or USIA. Moreover, by mid-1995 the administration had abandoned its push for reform and had begun resisting Republican efforts to merge AID, ACDA, and USIA into the State Department.

The Clinton administration's failure to restructure the State Department Complex and its eventual embrace of the status quo stemmed from a combination of bureaucratic opposition, congressional intransigence, the administration's indifference to its own proposals, and the lack of a consensus between Democrats and Republicans about the direction of U.S. foreign policy. The State Department, AID, ACDA, and USIA all recognized early on that the demise of the Soviet Union threatened to render their core missions obsolete. But whereas critics saw the end of the cold war producing "problem depletion," to borrow the terminology from chapter 1, agency officials saw it as presenting them with entirely new, and in some ways more demanding, challenges. Thus, the State Department argued that the demise of the Soviet Union complicated diplomacy by ending old political alignments and creating new states; AID argued that the need to help democracy take root in the former Soviet Union and elsewhere made its work essential; ACDA argued that the dissolution of the Soviet Union into four nuclear powers made the fight against nuclear proliferation more pressing than ever; and USIA argued that its public diplomacy was needed to shore up popular support in eastern Europe and elsewhere for democratic government. In redefining what others took to be problem depletion as problem expansion, each of the agencies reflected its organizational essence, which defined its mission as both critical and likely to be ignored by other parts of the State Department Complex.

Career officials in the State Department Complex frequently found political support for their claims that the end of the cold war had made their agencies more rather than less essential to U.S. foreign policy. Sometimes that support came from past and present White House officials, sometimes from political interest groups, and at times even from foreign heads of state. But in 1993 and 1994 particular support came from Capitol Hill, where sympathetic members of Congress, many of whom had nurtured and protected AID, ACDA, and USIA when they had come under assault for different reasons during the Reagan and Bush administrations, rallied to protect their progeny. Although the number of legislators who resisted the proposed changes was always small, they had considerable clout in 1993 and 1994 because of their seniority and because very few of their colleagues took an interest in what the Clinton administration was trying to accomplish.

The Clinton administration might have overcome congressional resistance to its reform proposals if it had been willing to pay a political price to restructure the State Department Complex. But it was not. While President Clinton and Secretary of State Christopher frequently invoked the rhetoric of "reinventing government," neither displayed much interest in forcing such changes through Congress. Thus, the administration regularly floated proposals in 1993 and 1994 to "downsize" various aspects of the State Department Complex, and they just as regularly retracted the proposals when they encountered bureaucratic or congressional resistance. The inability to translate the rhetoric of change into reality no doubt stemmed in part from Clinton's well-known and often criticized lack of passion for foreign policy. But it also reflected sympathy within the White House for the arguments the State Department and its affiliated agencies made on their behalf as well as an inability to make tough choices among competing priorities.

Of course, the 1994 congressional midterm elections brought to Capitol Hill a Republican majority intent on reducing the size of the federal government in general and the State Department Complex in particular. Leading Republicans, including the chairs of the Senate Foreign Relations Committee and the Senate Foreign Operations Subcommittee, denounced wasteful overseas programs and embraced proposals to fold AID, ACDA, and USIA into the State Department. Yet rather than create an opportunity for a bipartisan reconstruction of the State Department Complex, the Republican victory exposed deep-seated differences between the two parties over the means and ends of foreign policy. Without any consensus over what the United States should seek to accomplish overseas and how it should set out to do it, the question of how best to restructure the State Department Complex became hopelessly entangled in partisan wrangling.

The State Department

The State Department is the oldest executive agency in the U.S. government, tracing its history back to its original incarnation under the Articles of Confederation as the Department of Foreign Affairs. The State Department may also be the most heavily studied and criticized executive agency. Between 1946 and 1995, for example, it was the subject of ninety different studies (Krebsbach 1995, 45). These studies have charged the State Department with numerous failings, including weak leadership, poor internal management, inadequate policy planning, excessive caution, lack of innovation, and ineffective policy coordination (see, e.g., Clarke 1987, 1989;

Horan 1993; Pringle 1977–1978; Rockman 1981; Rubin 1987; Sorenson 1987–1988).

The end of the cold war prompted the Bush administration to undertake yet another appraisal of the State Department. In 1991, Secretary of State James Baker appointed an eighteen-member task force "to analyze the likely future foreign affairs policy and operating environment and propose appropriate changes in the organization and management of the Department of State" (U.S. Department of State 1992, 19). The task force, which finished its work under Baker's successor, Lawrence Eagleburger, reviewed studies of the department dating back to World War II and conducted more than one thousand interviews with State Department and other government employees, and with private citizens (U.S. Department of State 1992, 99). In December 1992, the task force published its findings and recommendations in a 99-page executive summary entitled *State 2000: A New Model for Managing Foreign Affairs.* (The main report was accompanied by a 357-page annex that examined sixteen specialized topics.)

The recommendations contained in the *State 2000* report were extensive, touching on nearly every aspect of the State Department and its relations with affiliated agencies. For example, the task force recommended that undersecretaries be put in charge of overseeing the line bureaus. It further recommended streamlining the operations of the department by drastically reducing the number of bureaus and independent offices within the agency. To some extent this could be accomplished by consolidating programs dealing with global problems such as drugs, terrorism, and refugees under the authority of the new post of undersecretary for global programs. The task force concluded that both AID and USIA should continue to operate independently but that ACDA should be merged with the State Department (U.S. Department of State 1992, 3–15).

Although the Bush administration did not act on the recommendations found in the *State 2000* report before leaving office, the report greatly influenced the Clinton foreign policy team. In February 1993, after only two weeks in office, Secretary of State Christopher unveiled his plan for reorganizing the State Department. The centerpiece was his proposal to create the post of undersecretary for global affairs. Much as the *State 2000* report had envisioned, the undersecretary for global affairs would oversee programs dealing with democracy, the environment, human rights, narcotics, scientific affairs, and terrorism (see, e.g., Callahan 1993). At the same time, Christopher's plan called for organizing the State Department's other bureaus, offices, and programs into four broad groups, each of which would be headed by one of the four existing undersecretaries—political affairs, arms control and international affairs, management, and economic affairs. The new alignment would put the undersecretaries in charge of the various line bureaus (Christopher 1993b; Goshko 1993; Newsom 1993).

Christopher's reorganization proposal also called for abolishing many of the small, independent offices and bureaus that had grown up over the years within the State Department. For example, he accepted the recommendation in the *State 2000* report that the work of the International Communications and Information Policy Office be consolidated under a newly strengthened Bureau of Economic, Business, and Agricultural Affairs. Likewise, he accepted the recommendation in the *State 2000* report that the offices dealing with narcotics and counterterrorism be abolished and their duties transferred to a new Bureau for Narcotics, Terrorism, and Crime. Finally, to help streamline decision making in the State Department, Christopher recommended eliminating forty of the roughly one hundred deputy assistant secretary of state positions (Christopher 1993b; Goshko 1993; Newsom 1993).

Most of the changes Secretary Christopher proposed in his reorganization plan required congressional approval, and the necessary legislation was promptly attached to the biennial State Department authorization bill. Despite initial concerns that the proposal to create the position of undersecretary of global affairs would encounter opposition on Capitol Hill because it promised to give higher visibility to controversial programs such as population control, the reorganization provisions prompted remarkably little debate. Although disputes over other provisions in the State Department authorization bill delayed final congressional approval until April 1994, Congress eventually approved most of the elements of Christopher's reorganization plan.

The one aspect of Christopher's reorganization plan that did not survive the legislative journey was his proposal to merge the State Department's narcotics and counterterrorism units into a new Bureau for Narcotics, Terrorism, and Crime. Members of the House denounced the proposal, arguing that it effectively de-emphasized terrorism as an issue. Whereas the existing Office of the Coordinator for Counterterrorism reported directly to the secretary of state, under Christopher's reorganization proposal it would report to the assistant secretary in charge of the Bureau for Narcotics, Terrorism, and Crime. In July 1993, the House accepted on a voice vote a motion by Rep. Benjamin Gilman (R-N.Y.), the ranking member of the House Foreign Affairs Committee, to maintain the Office of the Coordinator for Counterterrorism as a separate unit. After the Senate finally passed its version of the State Department authorization bill in February 1994 without a provision protecting the independent status of the Office of the Coordinator for Counterterrorism, the House voted 357 to 2 to instruct its conferees to insist that the office be maintained as a separate unit within the State Department and that it report directly to the secretary of state. In light of the House vote, the conferees agreed to protect the independent status of the counterterrorism office for at least one year (Doherty 1994a; Lippman 1994a; U.S. Congress, House 1994, 178). Three years later the office was still operating as an independent unit at State.

Although Secretary Christopher succeeded in persuading Congress to approve most of his proposed changes in the structure of the State Department, he met with much less success in persuading the White House and Congress to appropriate the funds needed to breathe life into the plan for a reinvigorated State Department. In September 1993, the Office of Management and Budget (OMB) tentatively set funding in fiscal year 1995 for international affairs—which covers spending by the entire State Department Complex—at $19.6 billion, nearly a billion dollars less than in fiscal year 1994. State Department officials subsequently conducted their own budgetary review and concluded that to meet OMB's target figure, spending on global affairs programs would have to be cut (Holmes 1993; Lippman 1993a).

In response to the State Department's budgetary review, Secretary Christopher and his chief aides launched an unusually public campaign to persuade the White House and Congress to endorse the so-called Big Pie proposal, a plan to add $3 billion to the foreign affairs budget. To counter the impression that the foreign affairs budget had no constituency, State Department officials encouraged private relief agencies, environmental groups, and other charitable organizations to ask the White House and Congress for more spending on foreign affairs. In October, nearly two hundred such groups signed a letter to President Clinton urging him to protect foreign affairs programs from the budget ax (Bacchus 1994, 105; Holmes 1993; Lippman 1993a).

The State Department's lobbying effort, which also included private meetings with the president and OMB officials, produced only modest results. When the Clinton administration's budget was formally unveiled in February 1994, it requested $20.8 billion for all international affairs programs. This represented a $44 million increase over fiscal year 1994, an increase that fell below what was needed to keep pace with inflation. Moreover, a substantial portion of the monies added to OMB's original target figure was designed to pay off arrearages that had accumulated over the years because the United States had fallen behind on its financial commitments to the United Nations and international financial institutions. As a result, the Clinton budget for fiscal year 1995 contained little funding for new policy initiatives (Doherty 1994c; Lippman 1994b).

The Agency for International Development

AID was established by the Foreign Assistance Act of 1961 to implement U.S. economic assistance policies overseas. In its early years, AID sought to promote economic development by financing capital-intensive projects such as steel mills and to counter communist insurgencies by promoting popular support for pro-Western governments. In the 1970s, Congress substantially revised AID's authorizing legislation, directing the agency to focus greater attention on using foreign aid to solve basic human needs (Hellinger, Hellinger, and O'Regan 1988, 13–31; Posz, Janigian, and Jun 1994). Over the next two decades, Congress mandated thirty-three separate policy objectives for AID, ranging from promoting human rights to protecting forests to encouraging the use of appropriate technology. In turn, the agency itself identified seventy-five different priority areas in development assistance (Callahan 1994; Jentleson 1990; U.S. General Accounting Office 1992).

Given AID's hodgepodge of different policy objectives and priority areas, it is not surprising that the agency became a target of criticism. In February 1989, for example, the House Committee on Foreign Affairs released a report lambasting AID's management of foreign assistance programs. The report urged that the Foreign Assistance Act be rewritten and that AID be replaced with a new Economic Cooperation Agency (U.S. Congress, House Committee on Foreign Affairs 1989b). The Foreign Affairs Committee tried in 1989 and again in 1991 to rewrite the Foreign Assistance Act and to restructure AID, but both efforts failed for lack of support in both the Senate and the executive branch (U.S. Congress, House 1993a, 2).

AID again became the target of criticism in 1992. In January, AID and the Office of Management and Budget formed a joint "SWAT Team" to investigate "significant management problems" at AID (Bacchus 1994, 36; Oberdorfer and McAllister 1992). Although the investigation did not examine the long-term future of AID, it criticized "almost everything from the agency's 'poor' employee training to its 'inadequate' oversight and auditing of overseas development projects" (Wagner 1992). The General Accounting Office echoed many of these criticisms in its report on AID, concluding that "the agency has no clear priorities or meaningful direction. Without a clear vision of what AID should be doing and why, [agency] efforts to reorganize, . . . focus, plan . . . may be futile" (quoted in Madison 1992a, 2669). An even more pessimistic conclusion about AID's future was reached by the President's Commission on the Management of AID Programs, known informally as the Ferris Commission, after its chairman, George Ferris. Established in 1991 at the request of Congress to investigate the management of AID, the five-member commission concluded in April 1992 that the agency's job "is basically impossible" and that "AID should be fully merged into the State Department" (quoted in Oberdorfer 1992; see also Bacchus 1994, 35–36; Madison 1992b; Priest 1992b).

The proposal to merge AID into the State Department met with little enthusiasm at Foggy Bottom. The *State 2000* report carefully distinguished the differing roles of the two organizations, noting that State is a policy agency that traditionally leaves the implementation of specific programs to agencies such as AID. Moreover, in a diplomatic reference to the many criticisms being leveled against the agency, the report warned that "in the case of AID especially, fundamental rethinking of its role and objectives must precede any organizational decisions" (U.S. Department of State 1992, 10). The State Department's argument against absorbing AID was put bluntly by John Rogers, the undersecretary for management who directed the writing of *State 2000:* incorporating AID into State "would bring nothing to the doorstep of the Secretary of State other than problems" (quoted in Kirschten 1995c, 197).

Against this backdrop, the Clinton administration sought to refashion AID to meet the demands of the post–cold war era. One of Warren Christopher's first decisions as secretary of state was to direct his deputy, Clifford R. Wharton, to chair a review of AID programs and foreign assistance in general. Wharton's task force consulted with officials from eighteen agencies, and with members of Congress and their staffs, before forwarding a draft report to Capitol Hill in June 1993 (Callahan 1994, 20–22; Doherty 1993a, 1892; Kirschten 1993a, 1167).

The Wharton report rejected calls to abolish AID or to merge it with State. It instead endorsed retaining the agency as a semiautonomous entity while reorganizing many of its procedures. The report repeated the complaints of previous studies that AID had too many statutory goals and objectives, had too few employees administering too many programs, and had no clear vision of how to advance U.S. national interests in the post–

cold war era. As Wharton (1993, 528) summarized the problem in testimony before the Senate Foreign Relations Committee, AID's "problems stem less from where its functions are than from an unfocused mandate, over-regulation and poor management." But despite setting out a broad framework for reform, the Wharton Report presented little in terms of detail. As a result of an internal dispute with the staff of the National Security Council, which was conducting its own review of foreign assistance programs, it was decided that the Wharton Report would be released "with nothing on specific responsibilities of who is going to do what" (Kamen and Lippman 1993).

The responsibility of breathing life into the Wharton Report's vague recommendation to focus the work of AID fell to J. Brian Atwood. (Atwood had originally been nominated and confirmed as undersecretary of state for management, and he assumed the post of administrator for AID only after the Clinton White House failed to agree on someone else to hold the post.) After conducting his own review of AID, Atwood concluded that the agency was grossly overextended relative to its resources. While it maintained field offices in ninety-nine countries and operated programs in twenty-six others, AID actually had "enough money to do a full-scale sustainable development program in only about 50 countries" (quoted in Kirschten 1993c, 2370).

In the summer of 1993, Atwood made a series of organizational changes at AID in the hope of streamlining the agency's decision making. He also took steps to reduce the size of the agency's 3,800-strong professional staff. In August, he broke with a long-standing agency practice of automatically renewing the contracts of agency officials who had been passed over for promotion, and fired fifty career employees. Not surprisingly, Atwood's decision alienated many members of AID's professional staff (Kamen 1993b; Kirschten 1993c, 2371–72). Atwood subsequently committed the agency to reducing its professional staff by 10 percent by year-end 1994, a goal the agency met (Greenhouse 1995a).

Atwood's commitment to paring back AID's operations was reinforced by developments elsewhere in government. In September 1993, Vice President Al Gore's National Performance Review recommended that AID reduce the number of its overseas missions from one hundred and five to as few as fifty. One month later, the final version of the 1994 foreign operations appropriations bill prohibited AID from spending any funds after March 31, 1994, "unless the Administration has acted to implement those recommendations of the Report of the National Performance Review which can be accomplished without legislation" and has submitted legislation outlining "a planned reduction of a specific number of Agency for

International Development missions during the next three years, of which at least twelve are to be terminated during the first year" (U.S. Congress, House 1993b, 23).

In November 1993 Atwood provided just the evidence House members were looking for when he announced that the agency would close twenty-one field offices and phase out development programs in thirty-five countries by year-end 1996. Closing the offices was estimated to eliminate more than eleven hundred jobs, most of them held by foreign citizens, and to save $26 million over three years. The decision marked the first time since the Truman administration unveiled the Marshall Plan that the United States had cut the number of countries receiving U.S. assistance (Horne 1993).

In addition to restructuring and streamlining AID's operations, Atwood lobbied on behalf of an administration proposal to reduce and rationalize the agency's objectives. In November, the staffs of the National Security Council and National Economic Council released a draft proposal recommending that the Foreign Assistance Act of 1961 be rewritten. Instead of appropriating foreign aid on a country-by-country basis or by specific program, the administration called on Congress to appropriate foreign assistance according to six general goals: promoting democracy, promoting peace, providing humanitarian aid, promoting growth through trade and investment, advancing diplomacy, and promoting sustainable development. The draft report argued that rewriting the Foreign Assistance Act in this fashion would empower "the president to use the resources authorized under this act with flexibility to respond decisively to new opportunities and unforeseen dangers" (quoted in Doherty 1994d, 74).

The Peace, Development, and Democracy Act was introduced when Congress returned to session in 1994. Despite the hopes of its supporters, however, the House and Senate failed to act on the bill. Part of the problem lay in congressional objections to specific provisions in the bill, especially those proposing to end the earmarking of funds for specific countries. Although frequently derided by administration officials for hamstringing U.S. aid programs, many earmarks, particularly those for Israel, enjoyed widespread congressional support. Rep. David Obey (D-Wis.), chair of the House Appropriations Subcommittee on Foreign Operations, summarized the views of his colleagues bluntly: "We will not give to an unelected bureaucracy federal authority to spend dollars any way they want, so long as they call it 'pursuit of democracy' or 'expanding economic development'" (quoted in Doherty 1994d, 74).

The bigger obstacle to passage of the Peace, Development, and Democracy Act, however, was procedural wrangling on Capitol Hill. Congress had not passed a foreign aid authorization bill since 1985, largely because the subject of foreign aid touched off lengthy and bitter debate. Mindful that several previous foreign aid authorization bills had cleared the House only to die in the Senate, House Democratic leaders refused to schedule debate on the bill until they received assurances that it would be considered on the floor of the Senate. Senate Majority Leader George Mitchell (D-Maine) declined to provide such assurances, however, fearing that any aid authorization bill would trigger a lengthy floor fight (Doherty 1994e, 808). With President Clinton unwilling to lobby for the administration's proposal, the 103d Congress adjourned without passing the Peace, Development, and Democracy Act.

With the failure of the Peace, Development, and Democracy Act, the Clinton administration's hopes for "reinventing" AID dimmed. Although some progress had been made at reorganizing the agency's internal procedures and at eliminating two dozen field missions, at the beginning of 1995 AID did not look much different than it had a decade earlier. Its structures and policy objectives remained those developed during the cold war, and the bulk of its spending was still concentrated in a few countries, most notably Israel and Egypt. Despite Director Atwood's admission that "AID's relevancy in the post–Cold War period will be [determined by] its effectiveness in dealing with the new strategic threats to the United States," by the end of 1994 the Clinton foreign policy team had failed to build a bipartisan consensus on the agency's proper role in the post–cold war era (quoted in Kirschten 1993c, 2369).

Arms Control and Disarmament Agency

ACDA was created in 1961 at the height of the cold war to provide the president and the secretary of state with an independent source of advice on arms control matters. In practice, however, the agency never became the bureaucratic heavyweight that its sponsors had envisioned. Throughout the cold war era, the agency was "either wholly or substantially excluded from the [weapons acquisition] process" (Clarke 1979, 97), and its own supporters described its history as one of "continued decline, marginalization, and exclusion" (Krepon, Smithson, and Schear 1992, 75).

Like AID and the State Department itself, ACDA was the subject of several studies released in 1992. While all the studies described ACDA as an agency in trouble, they disagreed on the appropriate solution. The *State 2000* report explicitly argued that ACDA was a prototypical example of an agency rendered obsolete by events:

> The era of prolonged, painful, and highly politicized arms negotiations with a superpower adversary are [*sic*] over. The bureaucratic resources needed for such negotiations have markedly diminished. Nonproliferation and arms control policies are increasingly converging. . . . The Departments of Energy and Defense, as well as the CIA, have large divisions with hundreds of skilled specialists working exclusively on these problems. (U.S. Department of State 1992, 43)

Not surprisingly, given this pessimistic description of ACDA's potential contributions, the *State 2000* report recommended abolishing the agency and transferring its "functions, including technical support, elsewhere, chiefly to the Department's proposed Bureau for Proliferation and Arms Control Affairs" (U.S. Department of State 1992, 43).

The State Department's position was echoed in a report released in November 1992 by a commission sponsored by the Carnegie Endowment for International Peace and the Institute for International Economics. The report, entitled "Memorandum to the President-Elect," dealt with ACDA only in passing. But its brief reference to the agency urged that the State Department's Bureau of Political-Military Affairs "take responsibility for the residual functions of the Arms Control and Disarmament Agency, which we recommend be abolished" (quoted in Mendelsohn 1992, 29).

Whereas the *State 2000* and the Carnegie/IIE reports held that the end of the cold war had rendered ACDA obsolete, two other studies released in late 1992 reached the opposite conclusion. The first was a report prepared under the auspices of the Henry L. Stimson Center. While acknowledging ACDA's historical weakness, the Stimson Center report argued that "in the aftermath of the demise of the Soviet Union, there is even more need, and more opportunity, for the government to focus on the issues of non-proliferation, regional arms control, export controls, and treaty implementation, each of which tends to be displaced from the top of the U.S. national security agenda by the competing priorities of other executive branch agencies" (Krepon, Smithson, and Schear 1992, 60).

The second study affirming the continued need for ACDA had been mandated by Congress in December 1991 and conducted under the direction of Sherman M. Funk, inspector general of ACDA (and the State Department). Funk appointed a panel chaired by retired ambassador James E. Goodby, a former chief U.S. delegate to the Conference on Disarmament. Goodby's panel concluded that ACDA should either be rejuvenated or abolished.

> The choice between the two options for ACDA's future is a close call. On balance, the panel concludes that it remains important to the nation to have a specialized and technically competent arms control institution providing its

> independent perspective on arms control issues under the direction of the Secretary of State. A separate agency is the more promising solution to retaining continuity, enhancing technical expertise, and fostering innovation. The panel, therefore, favors retaining an independent ACDA, but one which is reshaped and rejuvenated. (U.S. Arms Control and Disarmament Agency 1992, iii)

Among other steps aimed at rejuvenation, the Funk report urged that ACDA establish a new bureau dedicated specifically to nonproliferation matters.

The Clinton administration's foreign policy team assumed office in January 1993, split over the merits of ACDA. Several senior administration officials, including Undersecretary of State for Management J. Brian Atwood and Undersecretary of State for Arms Control and International Security Affairs Lynn Davis, argued in favor of killing the agency (Kamen 1993a, 1994a; Kirschten 1993d, 1016). Other officials argued that any effort to abolish ACDA would only serve to antagonize the agency's supporters on Capitol Hill and in the arms control community. A far better strategy in their view would be "to let the agency languish until congressional support for retaining it dissipates" (Kamen 1993a).

Well aware that key members of the Clinton State Department favored abolishing ACDA, the agency's supporters rallied to its side. In April, seventeen different arms control groups sent a letter to National Security Adviser Anthony Lake contending that if the State Department assumed the duties of ACDA "the voice that argues for . . . arms control, confidence-building measures and negotiation will be stifled at the bottom of the bureaucratic heap" (quoted in Kirschten 1993d, 1016). The agency's supporters also wrote letters to the editor extolling its virtues and organized former government officials to speak publicly of the need to revitalize ACDA ("ACDA on the Line" 1993; Smith and Krepon 1993). At the same time, ACDA's supporters on Capitol Hill moved to protect the agency. In particular, staff members for Sen. Claiborne Pell (D-R.I.), the chair of the Foreign Relations Committee, and Sen. Paul Simon (D-Ill.), a senior member of the committee, began to draft legislation designed to rejuvenate ACDA by designating it the government's primary arms control and nonproliferation agency and by giving it stature equal to that of the State and Defense departments at arms control talks.

The legislative and lobbying efforts on behalf of ACDA eventually worked. In late May, Secretary of State Christopher abandoned the proposal to absorb ACDA into the State Department. Christopher then informed Senator Pell privately that the administration would support legislation to rejuvenate and strengthen ACDA as an independent agency (Kirschten 1994a, 235).

The decision to abandon the proposal to abolish ACDA did not signal an increased respect for the agency on the part of administration officials. President Clinton did not formally announce the decision to retain ACDA until July 3, and he did not nominate anyone to serve as director of ACDA until October. The administration was even slower filling other agency positions; in May 1994 several of the most senior posts at the 250-person agency remained to be filled (Kamen 1993c, 1994c).

The administration also quickly found itself battling with members of Congress over how much ACDA should be strengthened. Especially controversial was a provision in the Pell-Simon bill to give the director of ACDA power to block the export of so-called dual-use technologies, products that can be used for military as well commercial ends. Under the proposed law, only the president could overrule a decision by the director of ACDA to block the export of dual-use technology. Although administration officials agreed that ACDA should have a say in decisions over the export of dual-use products, they argued that the provisions in the Pell-Simon bill gave the director of ACDA too much power at the expense of the secretaries of state, commerce, and defense (U.S. Congress, Senate 1993, 28–35).

In September 1993, the Senate Foreign Relations Committee agreed to strip the dual-use provision from the Pell-Simon bill. In turn, the administration threw its support behind the bill. Scheduling concerns kept the bill from coming to a floor vote before the Senate adjourned for the year, however, and its main provisions were attached to the FY 1994–1995 State Department authorization bill on a voice vote when the Senate returned for business in January 1994. The House had included similar provisions strengthening ACDA in the version of the authorization bill it had passed in June 1993.

The final version of the State Department authorization bill, which emerged from conference in late April, delineated the respective roles of the State Department and ACDA in the areas of arms control and nonproliferation. "The legislation makes clear that the Director [of ACDA] shall have primary responsibility within the government for matters relating to arms control and disarmament and, whenever directed by the President, primary responsibility for matters relating to nonproliferation" (U.S. Congress, House 1994, 256). Although the authorization bill gave the president authority to bypass ACDA on nonproliferation matters, the report accompanying the bill emphasized that "the committee of conference is united in its belief that . . . the presumption should be, unless there are compelling reasons to believe otherwise, that ACDA will, indeed, receive the President's direction to have the primary responsibility" (U.S. Congress, House 1994, 256). And the authors of the bill, no doubt leery of the administration's commitment to a genuine revitalization of ACDA, inserted a provision in the bill instructing the director of ACDA to prepare a report detailing the steps taken to revitalize the agency (U.S. Congress, House 1994, 124).

Congress's concern about whether ACDA would be successfully revitalized was justified. Despite its avowed objectives of strengthening ACDA, the legislation did little (and in fact could do little) about the fundamental structural and environmental problems facing the agency. With the end of the cold war, arms control issues slipped from prominence, and ACDA continued to operate at a huge disadvantage relative to the armed services in terms of size, technical expertise, and constituency support. In the realm of nonproliferation, President Clinton gave ACDA the lead U.S. role in handling the issue in multilateral negotiations, such as the ongoing talks over the extension of the Nonproliferation Treaty. Yet as the disputes in 1993 and 1994 over the nuclear programs of Iran, North Korea, and Pakistan attested, the administration's efforts to prevent proliferation rested largely on bilateral diplomatic efforts spearheaded by State Department officials and special envoys. And with the resounding Republican victory in the 1994 midterm elections, ACDA faced a much more hostile political environment.

U.S. Information Agency

Created in 1953, USIA is responsible for trying "to strengthen foreign understanding of American society, obtain greater support of U.S. policies, and increase understanding between the United States and other countries" (*United States Government Manual 1994–1995* 1994, 742; see also Hansen 1989). By the end of the cold war, USIA had come to encompass a wide range of agencies and programs. Besides administering a variety of publication services and cultural exchange programs, USIA administered many (though not all) of the U.S. government's overseas broadcast services. Of these, the most visible were the Voice of America, the official voice of the U.S. government, and Radio Marti and TV Marti, programs begun under the Reagan and Bush administrations to weaken the government of Fidel Castro.

Because a primary aim of USIA's activities had always been to undermine support for communist governments, the end of the cold war inevitably prompted debate over whether the agency had outlived its usefulness. Indeed, in May 1990, USIA's own oversight committee, the Advisory

Commission on Public Diplomacy, criticized the agency for its "disappointingly slow" response to the collapse of the Soviet empire in eastern Europe (quoted in Havemann 1990). Further fueling debate over the future of USIA were budgetary constraints. The Bush administration's budget proposal for fiscal year 1991 did not provide USIA with funds sufficient to meet its existing level of services, thereby necessitating some cutbacks in programs (Havemann and Devroy 1990).

The debate in 1993 and 1994 over the future of USIA frequently turned on questions regarding the effectiveness of TV Marti and the need for a new Radio Free Asia. But the major point of contention was the nature of the relationship between USIA and Radio Free Europe and Radio Liberty. Created and run by the Central Intelligence Agency for more than two decades, Radio Free Europe (which broadcast to eastern Europe) and Radio Liberty (which broadcast to the Soviet Union) were placed under the independent Board for International Broadcasting in 1973. Supporters of the radio services historically defended their independence from USIA on the grounds that as a government agency USIA faced pressure from the State Department not to offend strategically important countries. In contrast, the status of Radio Free Europe and Radio Liberty as independent corporations enabled them to broadcast without fear or favor.

The first major salvo in the debate over the future of USIA came in June 1991, when the Advisory Commission on Public Diplomacy released a fifty-six-page report criticizing several USIA programs. The commission held that the Voice of America was broadcasting in more languages (forty-four) than its budget allowed and that some of the broadcasts should be dropped. The commission also questioned the effectiveness of TV Marti—treaty obligations and technical problems limited the broadcasts to between 3:30 A.M. and 6 A.M., and the Cuban government had successfully jammed these broadcasts. Likewise, the advisory commission called the proposal for a Radio Free Asia unnecessary in light of the Voice of America's capabilities in the region. Finally, in perhaps its most important move, the advisory commission concluded that Radio Free Europe's broadcasts to Czechoslovakia, Hungary, and Poland were no longer needed and should be dropped (McAllister 1991).

The advisory commission issued its report on the same day that another government panel, the Task Force on U.S. Government International Broadcasting, met for the first time. The Bush administration had established the eleven-member task force the previous April to review the status of the government's various overseas broadcast services. President Bush (1991c, 444) charged the task force with telling him "when and how" all U.S. government broadcast operations "eventually would be consolidated, in steps and over time, under a single U.S. government broadcasting entity." The expectation was that the task force would suggest how to consolidate the Voice of America, Radio and TV Marti, Radio Free Europe, Radio Liberty, and other overseas broadcast services under one organizational roof (McAllister 1991).

Contrary to expectations, however, the task force declined to offer a plan for consolidation when it released its report in December. Instead, it concluded that the demands of the post–cold war era made it essential that the U.S. government expand rather than contract its overseas broadcast services. The task force called for expanding the Voice of America's programming, continuing Radio Free Europe and Radio Liberty as independent radio services, and creating a separate Radio Free Asia to beam Western news and cultural programs into China (Korologos 1992; Priest 1992a; Smith 1991). In proposing to create Radio Free Asia, the task force rejected a proposal to expand the Voice of America's existing operations in Asia and the State Department's recommendation that a new radio service would be too costly and too easy to jam (Smith 1991).

The task force's recommendations did not sit well with members of the Advisory Commission on Public Diplomacy. Whether from conviction or from a desire to defend its role as overseer of USIA, the advisory commission released a report in August 1992 criticizing many of the task force's proposals. In particular, the advisory commission recommended shutting down Radio Free Europe and Radio Liberty while maintaining Voice of America, terminating TV Marti, and abandoning plans to create Radio Free Asia. Tom Korologos, the chair of the advisory commission, defended the commission's recommendation that Radio Free Europe and Radio Liberty be abolished, arguing that "the world has changed; their goals have been achieved, they have succeeded" (quoted in Rudavsky 1992).

Consumed with the 1992 presidential election campaign, the Bush administration never worked out the contradictory recommendations made by the Advisory Commission on Public Diplomacy and the Task Force on U.S. Government International Broadcasting. When the Clinton administration took office in January 1993, it initially adopted a posture close to that advocated by the advisory commission. In its budget proposal for fiscal year 1994, the administration proposed creating Radio Free Asia—a proposal Clinton had endorsed during the election campaign—but it also called for saving $644 million over four years by consolidating and reorganizing programs within USIA. Although the budget documents announced that "specific measures to effect consolidation are the subject of an Administration review to be completed shortly" (U.S. Office of Management and Budget 1993, 1042), it was widely expected that the administration would recommend closing down both Radio Free Europe and Radio Liberty ("Europe Freed, Radio Signs Off?" 1993; Fisher 1993; Kirschten 1993b, 865).

Supporters of Radio Free Europe and Radio Liberty lost little time mobilizing to save both radio services. In mid-March, the human rights organization Freedom House took out a full page ad in *Roll Call,* a twice-weekly newspaper widely read on Capitol Hill, trumpeting the virtues of Radio Free Europe and Radio Liberty. (Penn Kemble, a senior associate at Freedom House, was subsequently named to the number two position at USIA.) The ad was signed by more than three dozen prominent Washington insiders, including Zbigniew Brzezinski, Geraldine A. Ferraro, and Jeane Kirkpatrick (Kirschten 1993b, 866). Kirkpatrick (1993) also wrote an op-ed article for the *Washington Post* arguing that Radio Free Europe and Radio Liberty were "needed now while democratic media take root in the countries they have served for four decades." Other conservative news commentators attacked the proposal to close down the radio services on similar grounds (Forbes 1993a, 1993b; Laqueur 1994; Novak 1993a, 1993b).

Officials at Radio Free Europe and Radio Liberty also looked overseas for political support. Mikhail Gorbachev, Vaclav Havel, Lech Walesa, and other leading political figures in eastern Europe provided testimonials praising the crucial role the radio services played in undermining communism and hailing them as key instruments for nurturing the fragile democracies born following the collapse of the Soviet Union. And officials with Radio Free Europe trumpeted the results of a survey conducted by the European Community showing that its programs were far more popular than those of either the British Broadcasting Corporation or Voice of America (Fisher 1993; Kirkpatrick 1993).

Such high-level opposition helped to persuade the Clinton administration to abandon proposals to close down Radio Free Europe and Radio Liberty. In its formal reorganization plan unveiled in June 1993, the administration proposed to keep Voice of America, Radio Free Europe, and Radio Liberty as separate services. The proposal also called for the creation of Radio Free Asia. The Board for International Broadcasting, however, would be abolished, and responsibility for overseeing Radio Free Europe and Radio Liberty would be transferred to a new presidentially appointed board that would report to USIA. In defending his decision not to terminate either Radio Free Europe or Radio Liberty, President Clinton argued that people living in the democracies emerging from the ruins of the Soviet empire needed "a source of news that is reliably free from the manipulation of their own government" (quoted in "Plan Would Shuffle Broadcast Services" 1993, 1588).

The Clinton administration's reorganization proposal for USIA drew the support of many in Congress. An especially vocal supporter was first-term senator Russ Feingold (D-Wis.). Feingold, whose very first piece of legislation as a senator was a bill proposing to slash funding for the government's overseas radio services, repeatedly pointed out that the plan would save taxpayers an estimated $240 million over three years (Doherty 1993b, 1890; Kirschten 1993b, 865). But not all members of Congress were supportive. Feingold's senior colleague, Sen. Joseph Biden (D-Del.), denounced the reorganization proposal. In a hearing before the Senate Foreign Relations Committee in July, Biden complained that bringing Radio Free Europe and Radio Liberty under the auspices of USIA and terminating their status as an independent corporation under the auspices of the Board for International Broadcasting would make them organs of the U.S. government and thereby fundamentally compromise their journalistic integrity. As he put it: "If it ain't broke, why fix it?" (quoted in Doherty 1993b, 1890).

Although Biden lacked the votes needed to reverse the reorganization proposal, his threat to filibuster any legislation affecting Radio Free Europe and Radio Liberty effectively blocked the plan from reaching the Senate floor for six months. Finally, in January 1994, Biden and Feingold announced they had reached a compromise. In a victory for Senator Biden, Radio Free Europe and Radio Liberty were allowed to remain as an independent corporation rather than be made part of the U.S. government. And in a victory for Senator Feingold and the Clinton administration, the compromise retained the original proposal to do away with the Board for International Broadcasting and to create a new Broadcasting Board of Governors to oversee all U.S.-funded overseas broadcast services, including the newly created Radio Free Asia. The board, whose six members would be nominated by the president and confirmed by the Senate, would in turn report to USIA. In a further victory for Senator Feingold, the compromise cut funding for Radio Free Europe and Radio Liberty from $210 million to $75 million annually over three years (Palmer 1994, 127–29). Congress subsequently enacted the compromise proposal into law when it passed the FY 1994–95 State Department authorization bill.

One issue not settled by the Biden-Feingold compromise was the future of government broadcast operations aimed at Cuba. In 1993, Congress had made part of the 1994 funding for Radio and TV Marti conditional on the completion of a review of their broadcast operations (U.S. Congress, House 1993c, 100). The funding restriction had come in response to serious turmoil within USIA's Office of Cuba Broadcasting, over charges that senior officials were engaged in Red-baiting against nearly a dozen employees (Gugliotta 1994). The review panel completed its work in April 1994. The panel's report essentially sidestepped the question of whether Red-baiting had occurred, and strongly recommended that the U.S. government continue to operate both broadcast services. The panel did recommend, however, that TV Marti's signal be changed from VHF to UHF to make it harder to jam and that its broadcast hours be cut to save money (Goshko 1994b). Joseph Duffey, the director of USIA, subsequently rejected both recommendations, arguing that conversion was too costly and that a full programming schedule should be pursued for symbolic reasons: "By continuing Radio and TV Marti despite Castro's jamming, we send the people of Cuba a clear message, that this country is prepared to make reasonable efforts to insure that the people of this hemisphere have access to basic human rights" (quoted in Williams 1994c).

The Republican Revolution and State Department Consolidation

The Clinton administration's efforts in 1993 and 1994 to restructure the State Department Complex took place while fellow Democrats controlled Congress. But in November 1994, Republicans took control of both houses of Congress for the first time in forty years. Almost immediately, Republican leaders began to call for smaller government, especially in the area of foreign affairs. In mid-November, Sen. Jesse Helms (R-N.C.), the incoming chair of the Senate Foreign Relations Committee, likened foreign aid to throwing "money down foreign rat holes," and a month later, Sen. Mitch McConnell (R-Ky.), the incoming chair of the Senate Foreign Operations Appropriations Subcommittee, proposed abolishing AID and slashing all overseas assistance by 20 percent (quoted in Doherty 1994b; see also Greenhouse 1994a; Kirschten 1994d). The Clinton administration suddenly found itself no longer championing change but rather defending the status quo against changes far more radical than those it had proposed.

The White House and the State Department responded quickly to Republican pressure to shrink the size of government. On January 3, 1995, Vice President Al Gore, who was in charge of the administration's "Reinventing Government" project, sent a two-page directive to all federal agencies asking for proposals to make government more efficient. Two days later, at a meeting at the White House, Secretary of State Christopher presented the vice president with a plan to reorganize the State Department Complex. The plan, which ran fifteen single-spaced pages, argued that "the current organizational structures and activities of the department and other foreign affairs agencies . . . are cumbersome and hierarchical, and often seem designed more to err on the side of caution, thus preventing quick action, rather than expediting responses to rapidly changing circumstances." The solution to these problems lay in "designing a new foreign affairs complex from the ground up" (quoted in Lippman 1995; see also Sciolino 1995c). To that end, the proposal called for merging AID, ACDA, and USIA into the State Department. Officials estimated that the administrative savings from the merger would total $300 to $500 million per year (Sciolino 1995c).

Christopher's proposal to create a "super State Department" touched off what one official called "a very bitter fight, very intense and personal" within the administration (quoted in Lippman 1995). The directors of AID, ACDA, and USIA—each of whom had close political or personal ties to the White House—denounced the merger proposal as a "power grab" by the State Department that would save the federal government little money and would compromise the ability of the United States to manage foreign affairs wisely. To increase the political heat on the White House, officials from AID, ACDA, and USIA faxed articles and studies trumpeting the virtues of their agencies to major newspapers, and they urged their friends outside government to write letters and columns criticizing the merger. For example, former president Jimmy Carter (1995) wrote a letter to the editor of the *Washington Post* dismissing the merger proposal as "a bad idea whose time has not come." Finally, Atwood reportedly threatened to resign as director of AID if the administration decided to accept the State Department proposal (Lippman 1995).

The intensity of the political infighting over Christopher's proposal ultimately worked against it. In late January, Vice President Gore announced that AID, ACDA, and USIA would remain independent agencies under the overall policy guidance of the secretary of state. The vice president and his advisers reportedly concluded that the merger would distract the administration from pressing foreign policy problems and that much of the proposed savings could be generated without major restructuring (Greenhouse 1995c; Lippman 1995). Yet in announcing that the three agencies would remain independent, Gore committed the administration to continuing to find ways to shrink spending on international affairs. The vice president's office estimated that "the overall review of international affairs programs and agencies will result in savings of at least $5 billion over five years" (quoted in *Congressional Record* 1995, S18633).

If the Clinton administration recoiled from Christopher's proposal to consolidate the State Department Complex, Republicans on Capitol Hill embraced it. In mid-February, Senator Helms (1995) wrote an op-ed piece for the *Washington Post* with the self-explanatory title, "Christopher Is Right." A month later, Helms held a press conference on Capitol Hill to announce his plan to introduce legislation merging AID, ACDA, and USIA into the State Department. Flanked by moderate Republicans such as Representative Gilman, chair of the House International Relations Committee, and Sen. Olympia Snowe (R-Maine), a junior member of the Senate Foreign Relations Committee, Helms declared that "our foreign policy institutions are a complete mess . . . a constellation of money-aborbing, incoherent satellites, each with its own entrenched, growing bureaucracies" (quoted in Greenhouse 1995d).

Helms's proposed legislation incorporated many of the features of Christopher's proposal, but it also went beyond it in several respects (see Doherty 1995a, 1995b, 1995e; Greenhouse 1995a; Harris 1995a; Kirschten 1995d; Krebsbach 1995; Morrison 1995). As Christopher had done, Helms called for merging AID, ACDA, and USIA into State. But whereas Christopher's proposal would have left much of the organizational structure of all three agencies intact, Helms proposed abolishing AID entirely—by giving some of its duties to existing bureaus within the State Department and by giving its primary mission of long-term development assistance to a new nongovernment international development foundation. (Ironically, Atwood had endorsed just such a plan before he joined AID [Kirschten 1995d]). Helms also proposed transferring responsibility for foreign trade promotion activities from the Agriculture and Commerce departments to the State Department. Finally, Helms's plan also included provisions designed to ensure that the bulk of savings would come from personnel cuts rather than from cuts in programs. In all, it was estimated that Helms's plan would cut the work force by 50 percent at AID; by 25 percent at USIA; and by at least 9 percent at State—leading to an estimated savings of $3.5 billion over five years (Doherty 1995c, 1437–39; Harris 1995b).

Senator Helms's consolidation plan won high praise from luminaries in the Republican foreign policy establishment (see *Congressional Record* 1995, S18623; Kirschten 1995a). Five former Republican secretaries of state, including George Shultz, James Baker, and Lawrence Eagleburger, endorsed the legislation, as did Gen. Brent Scowcroft, George Bush's national security adviser. (Baker and Eagleburger's praise for Helms's proposal was surprising given that they had presided over the drafting of *State 2000*, which explicitly argued against proposals to "throw out the current structure and start over, creating a mega-foreign ministry" [U.S. Department of State 1992, 10].) Such support ensured that moderate Republicans on the Senate Foreign Relations Committee would support Helms's bill. Still, to maintain a majority, Helms was eventually forced to soften the bill in several respects, most notably by dropping the provisions that would have created an international development fund and transferred foreign trade promotion activities to the State Department.

For their part, House Republicans offered a less sweeping consolidation proposal (Doherty 1995f, 1995g). The House International Relations Committee drafted a State Department authorization bill that called for merging AID, ACDA, and USIA into the State Department by March 1, 1997. But fearful that Helms's bill specified the State Department's new structure in excessive detail, the committee gave the administration considerable latitude in deciding how to integrate the three agencies into the State Department. Moreover, unlike Helms's bill, which was eventually folded into the Senate's version of the State Department authorization bill, the bill drafted by the House International Relations Committee did not mandate staff cuts.

Although the House plan gave the executive branch considerable flexibility to restructure the State Department, it had few supporters in the executive branch. In late May, Secretary of State Christopher argued that the House bill "wages an extraordinary assault on this and every future president's constitutional authority to manage foreign policy," and President Clinton denounced both the House and Senate plans as "the most isolationist proposals to come before Congress in the last 50 years" (quoted in Doherty 1995d). Clinton pledged to veto the final State Department authorization bill unless the consolidation proposal and other objectionable provisions were dropped.

Emboldened by such criticisms, congressional Democrats sought to derail the merger legislation. In June 1995, House Democrats offered an amendment to the State Department authorization bill that would have stopped consolidation from proceeding until both OMB and the Congressional Budget Office had studied its merits. The Republican-dominated House rejected the amendment on a party-line vote and passed the State Department authorization bill. Senate Democrats had more success. They launched a filibuster that prevented the State Department authorization bill from coming to the floor for a vote.

Senator Helms responded to the filibuster by refusing to call business meetings of the Senate Foreign Relations Committee and by invoking a traditional courtesy that allows any senator to place a hold on, and thereby delay indefinitely, a floor vote on ambassadorial and other government nominations. By exercising his prerogatives, Helms blocked Senate consideration of more than a dozen treaties—including the second Strategic Arms Reduction Treaty (START II) and the Chemical Weapons Convention—as well as thirty ambassadorial nominees (see, e.g., Doherty 1995c; "Holding Up the Process" 1995; Sciolino 1995a, 1995b). The point of such "hostage taking," which was unprecedented in its scope if not in its logic, was simple. As Helms put it on the floor of the Senate, "Let me have a vote and you will have your ambassadors" (*Congressional Record* 1995, S18617).

Senator Helms's work stoppage at the Senate Foreign Relations Committee lasted for four months, and it left nearly a fifth of U.S. embassies without ambassadors (Lewis 1995). In December, Senator Helms and Sen. John Kerry (D-Mass.) announced a compromise that required the administration to cut $1.7 billion from the budget of the State Department Complex over five years. The bill further directed the president to send to Congress within six months of passage a plan to restructure the State Department Complex. If the president failed to issue such a report, AID, ACDA, and USIA would be abolished. Finally, the Helms-Kerry compromise also contained a variety of provisions designed to ensure that no more than 30 percent of the $1.7 billion in savings would come from cuts in programs; the bulk of savings would have to come from cuts in salaries and other administrative expenses. Moreover, at the behest of Secretary of State Christopher, the provisions stipulated that no more than 15 percent of the savings could come from cuts in the State Department's operating budget. These provisions shifted much of the brunt of the cost-cutting exercise to the operating budgets of AID, ACDA, and USIA (*Congressional Record* 1995, S18617–20; Doherty 1995h).

Although the Helms-Kerry compromise did not mandate the abolition of any agencies, Helms and his supporters argued that the magnitude of the required cuts would make it likely that one or more of these agencies would have to be eliminated (see Lewis 1995). Helms's critics agreed. Senator Biden criticized the compromise on the floor of the Senate, arguing that AID, ACDA, and USIA would "be emasculated by this bill" (*Congressional Record* 1995, S18621). Despite such claims, however, the compromise was more a loss than a victory for Helms. Seven months earlier he and his fellow Republicans had rejected Kerry's proposal to require the administration to cut $2.5 billion from the budget for the State Department Complex and to eliminate at least one of the three agencies Helms had targeted (Doherty 1995e).

The full Senate accepted the Helms-Kerry compromise in mid-December. Three months later, House-Senate conferees approved a final version of the State Department authorization bill, including a revised plan for agency consolidation (Doherty 1996a, 1996b). The bill retained the requirement that the administration cut the budget for the State Department Complex by $1.7 billion over five years. But in a step back in the direction favored by congressional Republicans, the bill added a provision directing the president to abolish ACDA, AID, and USIA. If he so chose, the president could waive the closure requirement in the case of any two of the agencies, meaning that just one of the agencies would have to be closed. By the end of March 1996, both the House and Senate had approved the conference report.

Throughout the consolidation debate, administration officials vowed that the president would veto the State Department authorization bill if it abolished ACDA, AID, or USIA. In April, President Clinton made good on his subordinates' claim, arguing that the consolidation plan "would seriously impede the president's authority to organize and administer foreign affairs agencies to best serve the nation's interests and the administration's foreign policy priorities" (quoted in Doherty 1996c; see also Gray 1996). (Clinton's decision to veto the State Department authorization bill also reflected his opposition to a variety of policy prescriptions embedded in the bill.) A House effort to override Clinton's veto fell far short of the necessary two-thirds majority.

In standing fast against the final version of the State Department authorization bill, President Clinton blocked a consolidation plan that in many respects was more modest than changes envisioned by the *State 2000* report, by Secretary of State Christopher's January 1995 proposal, or by Vice President Gore's pledge to find $5 billion in savings in the foreign affairs bureaucracy. Nor did the Clinton administration seek to counter Republican efforts with a consolidation plan of its own. Although Gore pledged in his September 1995 report on reinventing government to issue a plan for reorganizing the State Department later that fall, a year later no such plan had yet appeared (Gore 1995, 261, 263). The administration that had come to office promising change found itself the prime defender of the status quo.

The State Department Complex and Organizational Change

The Clinton administration came to office in January 1993 pledging to remake the State Department and its affiliated agencies to reflect the new realities of the post–cold war era. Over the next four years the administration imposed numerous changes on the State Department Complex. In a bid to save money and to streamline management, the State Department, AID, and USIA all cut and reorganized staff positions. To take but one example, USIA implemented plans to reduce its personnel by more than 11 percent by the end of 1996, and it cut the number of staff in Washington handling its informational and cultural programs by roughly 40 percent (Goshko 1995; Kirschten 1995b, 977). The Clinton administration also shut down a number of marginal programs. USIA again provides a case in point. It closed several of its libraries in western Europe and halted publication of its four-decades-old journal *Problems of Communism* as well as four other glossy foreign-language magazines (Goshko 1994c, 1995). Finally, the administration succeeded in creating several new positions and programs, perhaps the most visible being the post of undersecretary of state for global affairs.

Although the Clinton administration trumpeted many of these changes as part of its bid to reinvent government, none of them fundamentally altered the operation of the State Department Complex. To borrow the terms introduced in chapter 1, the changes made to the State Department Complex in 1993 and 1994 were neither deep (affecting organizational mission, strategy, and policy choices) nor pervasive (affecting a high proportion of the subsystems in the organization). The Clinton administration failed to win legislative approval of its proposal to rewrite the authorizing legislation for AID, saw its initial proposal for merging ACDA into the State Department transformed into legislation expanding ACDA's mandate, and found itself forced to abandoned its proposal to abolish Radio Free Europe and Radio Liberty. Moreover, in 1995 the Clinton administration found itself fighting off congressional proposals to consolidate the State Department Complex, even though the State Department's own reorganization proposal argued that the foreign affairs bureaucracy was "a set of organizations which are increasingly redundant, bloated and unresponsive to policy makers" (quoted in Lippman 1995).

Why did the State Department Complex fail to undergo fundamental change between 1993 and 1996, despite considerable public rhetoric about the need to adapt to the new realities of the post–cold war era? There are four reasons. The first is bureaucratic resistance. The State Department, AID, ACDA, and USIA all reacted to calls for change much as the hypotheses set forth in chapter 1 suggest: they fought to survive. They did so in part by trying to stonewall efforts aimed at change. Nowhere was this clearer than in the 1995 battle over congressional proposals to consolidate the State Department Complex. As a top official at AID put it in an internal memorandum that was leaked to the news media, the agency's (and administration's) strategy was to "delay, postpone, obfuscate, derail" the Republican proposals (quoted in Pear 1995). Affected agencies resisted change both by fighting bureaucratic battles within the executive branch and by appealing for support from their allies on Capitol Hill and in the private sector. For example, AID officials sought to maintain the agency's continued independence by mobilizing political support from interest groups as diverse as Bread for the World, the National Wildlife Federation, and the Bankers' Association for Foreign Trade (see *Congressional Record* 1995, S18626–27).

In addition to trying to resist change, the State Department, AID, ACDA, and USIA also sought to co-opt change in their favor. Rather than agreeing with their critics that the end of the cold war had made them less relevant, all four agencies argued that the cold war had made them more relevant. Thus, the State Department argued that it needed more resources and new authorities to handle relations with the newly independent nations of the former Soviet Union; AID and USIA argued that their work was essential to promoting democratization in the former Soviet Union; and ACDA argued that nuclear proliferation had become an even greater threat to the United States. What made these arguments particularly effective in the political arena was that none of the agencies was grasping at straws in making them; each argument had a good deal of plausibility. The State Department did find itself confronted with more demands on its resources, the United States did have a stake in promoting democracy in the former Soviet Union, and the demise of the Soviet Union did increase the threat of nuclear proliferation.

The resistance within the State Department Complex to proposals for change clearly reflected the organizational culture of the agencies involved. As noted in chapter 1, each agency has its own organizational essence or culture, the sense that its mission is important and that other agencies are not likely to give that mission the care and attention it deserves. Thus, it is not surprising that, when confronted with the prospect of being merged into the State Department, officials at AID would see State as uninterested in economic development, officials at ACDA would see it as inclined to subordinate arms control issues to other matters, and officials at USIA would see it as too willing to censor international broadcasting if that would placate a strategically important country. Nor is it surprising that many career officials in the State Department disliked the idea of absorbing AID, ACDA, and USIA. From their perspective, consolidation would saddle them with the burden of administering programs, thereby diverting them from their core mission of formulating foreign policy and managing diplomatic relations.

Organizational culture also explains the great irony of the debate over Republican plans to consolidate the State Department Complex. While the administration fought the State Department authorization bill tooth and nail in 1995 and 1996, it accepted the foreign operations appropriations bill, which cut funding for foreign aid by more than 10 percent ("Foreign Aid Spending" 1995a, 1995b). Moreover, at the same time it was seeking to derail consolidation proposals, the administration proposed a balanced budget plan that called for cutting spending on international affairs, excluding aid to Israel and Egypt, by 17 percent by fiscal year 2002 (Harris 1995b, 1995c). While the decision to give a higher priority to organizational structure than to programs might not make much sense in policy terms, it makes great sense in terms of organizational culture. Although each agency suffered sharp budget cuts, in the end each emerged with its independence still intact.

Bureaucratic opposition alone does not explain the lack of fundamental change in the State Department Complex between 1993 and 1996. The second reason the State Department, AID, ACDA, and USIA escaped major change was congressional intransigence. In 1993 and 1994, the Clinton administration saw a number of its legislative proposals derailed by fellow Democrats and it abandoned others in anticipation of congressional opposition. In most cases, the problem was less the membership of Congress as a whole than a few key members, especially in the Senate, who saw their job as protecting a threatened agency. Thus, Senators Pell and Simon used their positions as chair and senior member of the Senate Foreign Relations Committee to force the administration to accept legislation that strengthened the mandate of ACDA, and Senator Biden used the threat of a filibuster to force the administration to maintain the independent status of Radio Free Europe and Radio Liberty. With strong administration leadership, such opposition in all likelihood could have been overcome. But once it became clear that neither the president nor the secretary of state would expend political capital on behalf of the administration's proposals, the prospects for reorganization dimmed considerably.

Legislative intransigence remained a problem even when the Republicans took control of Congress and impetus for organizational change shifted from the White House to Capitol Hill. Senate Democrats forced the Republicans to water down their reorganization proposal and blocked the possibility of a veto override, thereby providing a powerful example of why reorganization of the State Department Complex is nearly impossible to achieve without the administration's cooperation. But opposition to reorganization also came from within Republican ranks. The chairs of the Senate Agriculture Committee and the Senate Banking, Housing, and Urban Affairs Committee forced Helms to drop his proposal to transfer the foreign trade promotion activities from the Agriculture and Commerce departments to the State Department. If the original reorganization proposal had proceeded, the Agriculture and Banking committees would have lost jurisdiction over the programs to the Foreign Relations Committee (Kirschten 1995d, 742; Krebsbach 1995, 37).

The third reason for the failure to impose fundamental change on the State Department Complex was that the most senior members of the Clinton administration had little interest in organizational matters. As other contributions to this volume attest, President Clinton's interest in foreign policy was fitful. He made no effort to secure congressional support for his administration's Peace, Development, and Democracy Act, and he did not play an active role in the debate over how to reorganize the State Department Complex. Of course, government reorganization is a low priority with most presidents, but Clinton's absence from the debate is notable, given his oft-stated public pledge to reinvent government. Much of the responsibility for reinventing government instead fell to Al Gore, but he too failed to make a mark on the process. Despite public promises that his review of the foreign affairs agencies would yield $5 billion in savings over five years, the vice president failed to produce a plan for restructuring the State Department Complex. As for Secretary of State Christopher, he gave organizational matters a low priority. Both the Peace, Development, and Democracy Act and his January 1995 reorganization proposal were drafted and pushed by subordinates with little input from Christopher himself (Greenhouse 1995c; Kirschten 1995d).

With the president, vice president, and secretary of state unwilling to push for major changes in the structure of the State Department Complex, much of the pressure within the administration for change came from undersecretaries of state (see, e.g., Greenhouse 1995c; Lippman 1995). For example, Timothy Wirth, undersecretary of state for global affairs, lobbied hard for merging AID into the State Department, largely because the latter theoretically controlled development policy while AID controlled the programs (and funds) needed to implement that policy. Likewise, Lynn Davis, undersecretary of state for arms control and international security affairs, pushed to fold ACDA into State. Whatever the merits of what Wirth and Davis sought to accomplish, they and other senior State Department officials seeking to restructure the foreign affairs bureaucracy faced a key obstacle: they were seeking to abolish agencies headed by officials of equal rank whose personal and political ties within the administration were as good if not better than their own. (For example, Atwood had close ties to both Hillary Rodham Clinton and Al Gore, while the director of ACDA had formerly practiced law with Christopher.) Without support from the most senior levels of the administration, proponents of structural change within the executive branch were unlikely to prevail either within the administration or on Capitol Hill.

The fourth and in many ways most important reason why the State Department Complex did not experience fundamental change was the absence of a consensus, both in Washington and in the country as a whole, about the future direction of U.S. foreign policy. Foreign policy structures and procedures during the cold war were conceived and directed toward one positive end—containing communist expansion. The demise of the Soviet Union, however, produced considerable disagreement over the means and ends of U.S. foreign policy. Indeed, as the very term "post–cold war era" suggests, U.S. foreign policy in the first half of the 1990s was defined not so much by what it was but by what it was not. Yet in the absence of agreement about what the United States hoped to accomplish in foreign policy and how it should rank its priorities, it became very difficult to build the sort of executive-legislative-bureaucratic coalitions that are needed to fundamentally alter the operations of the State Department Complex.

The lack of a consensus over the future direction of U.S. foreign policy explains why the battle over Senator Helms's consolidation proposal became so bitter. With no consensus on what the United States should seek to accomplish overseas or how it might best go about accomplishing it, debate over consolidation quickly degenerated into partisan wrangling. Senator Helms and his supporters pointed to a welter of studies critical of the operations of the State Department Complex, including studies generated by administration officials themselves; but opponents seized on Senator Helms's long-standing distaste for foreign aid to argue that his reorganization proposal was probably a stalking horse for an effort "to cut and gut" foreign aid programs (see Kirschten 1995d). Thus, while Democrats and Republicans traded charges of "mindless isolationism" and "reckless internationalism," the opportunity to find common ground for reorganizing the State Department Complex—which by almost all accounts desperately needs it—was missed.

Conclusion

The Clinton foreign policy team assumed office in 1993 hoping to "reinvent" the State Department and its associated agencies to meet the demands of the post–cold war world. Yet four years later, despite much talk both inside and outside the administration that the State Department, AID, USIA, and ACDA "reflect the reality of a world that's passed," the State Department Complex looked remarkably as it had twenty years earlier.

Of course, reinventing a bureaucracy can take time, and the future may well see dramatic changes in the structure of the State Department Complex. Yet the fights that took place between 1993 and 1996 over restructuring suggest that major organizational changes are unlikely to occur unless there is some degree of consensus between the two major parties over the direction of U.S. foreign policy and unless there is a willingness on the part of the administration to expend political capital to push its reforms through both the executive branch and Congress. Without both policy consensus and political will, proposals to restructure the State Department Complex are likely to founder over bureaucratic and congressional resistance.

If Congress and the administration do agree to change the formal structure of the State Department Complex, it remains an open question what the changes will accomplish. To reformers hoping to make a sizable dent in the federal deficit, State Department reform is likely to prove disappointing. In fiscal year 1997, spending on international affairs ($18.3 billion) accounted for less than 1.2 percent of total government spending ($1.6 trillion). Moreover, many of the agencies and programs within the State Department Complex consume relatively little in the way of federal funds. For example, ACDA received only $42 million in fiscal year 1997. In contrast, many of the big-ticket items in the international affairs budget, such as aid to Israel and Egypt ($5.1 billion in fiscal year 1997), are politically sacrosanct. Finally, after a decade of tight budgets, most of the easy cost savings have been squeezed out of the international affairs budget. For example, spending on international affairs programs fell by 50 percent in real terms between fiscal years 1985 and 1997, and in fiscal year 1997 USIA had suffered through seven consecutive years of funding reductions.

It also remains an open question whether a fundamental restructuring of the State Department Complex will actually improve the substance of U.S. foreign policy. As Secretary of State Christopher noted early in his tenure, the primary aim of restructuring the operations of the State Department "is quicker policy-making, more open policy-making, and better policy-making" (1993a, 140). While structural reforms can improve the quality of decision making, it is by no means guaranteed that they will. Indeed, the cold war era is replete with examples of structural and procedural reforms that failed to produce the policy improvements claimed for them (Lindsay 1994b). The potential for empty reforms is particularly high in the State Department Complex because much of the work of all four agencies is interrelated. For instance, because AID is housed in the State Department and many of its employees are foreign service officers, abolishing the agency might in practice amount to little more than changing nameplates on doors and shuffling around boxes on organization flowcharts.

Structural reforms will produce noticeable improvements in how U.S. foreign policy is made and what kinds of policy decisions are made only if the changes are both deep and pervasive. This in turn requires that fundamental changes be made in the organizational cultures within the State Department Complex. As the *State 2000* report noted in its closing pages, successful reforms put a premium on leadership that "is open to new ideas and that promotes a new culture in the institution. . . . We must change a culture that often breeds caution and constrains the very creativity vital to change" (U.S. Department of State 1992, 79–80). Whether such leadership is on the horizon remains an open question. Yet to ask structural reforms to substitute for the political will and vision needed to override bureaucratic resistance is to court failure and disappointment.

Paul N. Stockton

5. When the Bear Leaves the Woods

Department of Defense Reorganization in the Post–Cold War Era

The Department of Defense offers an especially crucial and contentious example of U.S. organizational change in the post–cold war era. For forty years, the Soviet Union provided the principal focus of U.S. decisions on defense budgeting and force structure. The Soviet Union has disintegrated. Despite this revolution in the security environment, however, many analysts and policy makers argue that remarkably little has changed in U.S. forces and defense spending (Korb 1994; Krepinevich 1994; Quinn-Judge 1993). Other critics charge that the United States has responded to the Soviet breakup all too drastically, slashing the military in a precipitous and dangerous fashion (see Weiner 1996b). How much change has actually occurred in U.S. defense budgets and forces? What accounts for the successes, and failures, of initiatives to cut and restructure the U.S. military for the post–cold war era?

I argue that the reductions in spending and force level adopted by the Bush administration, while smaller than those advocated by some congressional Democrats, overcame the entrenched preferences of the armed services. The administration's success in advancing these cuts depended on two underlying factors, both of which will be crucial for future efforts to restructure the military. First, the Goldwater-Nichols Defense Reorganization Act of 1986 redistributed power within the Pentagon, giving the chairman of the Joint Chiefs of Staff (JCS) unprecedented authority to propose changes in defense policy. Gen. Colin Powell exploited that authority to develop the base force proposal for defense cutbacks, and (despite the opposition of the armed services) built a winning coalition with Bush administration officials in support of those reductions. Second, Congress was vital to the implementation of the base force. In the Goldwater-Nichols Act, Congress preserved the right of service officers to make "end runs" around the president and to ask legislators to reject any cutbacks the administration proposed. With the collapse of the Soviet threat, however, legislators were in no mood to protect the services from deep overall reductions in budget and force levels. On the contrary: spurred by legislators such as Rep. Les Aspin (D-Wis.), chair of the House Armed Services Committee, Congress imposed budget and force level cuts beyond those endorsed by the Bush administration.

The Clinton administration's drive to impose still greater change on the military casts a different light on the role of the JCS chairman and Congress, and on the ability of the armed services to shape their own destiny. In the Bush administration's "Base Force" proposal for military cuts, General Powell proved that Goldwater-Nichols empowered the chairman to take the lead in defense restructuring. But a chairman can also use that influence to limit change. When Les Aspin became secretary of defense in 1993, he wanted to slash U.S. forces below the levels Powell endorsed. Aspin faced the risk, however, that Powell would use his position to attack such cuts and intensify the political crisis that President Clinton already faced with the U.S. military (and its allies in Congress) over allowing gays and lesbians to serve openly in the armed forces. Aspin's staff responded to this danger by grafting a new objective onto their bottom-up review (BUR) of U.S. forces: winning Powell's approval. The resulting force structure responded to the end of the cold war in new ways, but reflected the policy preferences—and political power—of the chairman. The Goldwater-Nichols Act did not determine whether Powell's successors would be friends or foes of defense restructuring. Rather, the act ensured that whenever a chairman weighs in on the subject and uses his preeminent military status to gain the ear of the president (or of Congress, when the chairman opposes an administration initiative), he will be an extraordinarily powerful player.

The behavior of the Republican-controlled Congress in 1995–1996 also had important implications for defense restructuring. During the Bush administration, Congress offered a generally hostile environment for end runs by the services, slashing budget and force levels below those the executive branch proposed. The election of a Republican majority in both houses of Congress created a very different dynamic. In terms of overall defense spending levels, Republican legislators blunted the post–cold war drawdown, adding $7 billion to Clinton's defense budget request for fiscal year 1996 and calling for an additional $13 billion in fiscal year 1997 (Graham 1996). Moreover, Republican leaders explicitly requested that the armed services offer their own proposals on how the additional money should be spent—proposals that turned out to conflict with administration planning (Weiner 1996b). General Powell cut the services out of the first phase of post–cold war defense restructuring. Congress invited them back in, altering the patterns of coalition building that have both facilitated and constrained U.S. responses to the Soviet breakup.

Lindsay and Ripley argue in chapter 1 that, in response to the end of the cold war, organizations are likely to vary in the depth and pervasiveness of the changes they adopt. In the Department of Defense, these variations also occur across "issue areas"—that is, across different policies and organizational arrangements called into question by the disappearance of the Soviet threat. Some areas of potential DOD change would show only minor departures from cold war era arrangements. In the formal allocation of service roles and missions, for example, two reform initiatives (first under General Powell and then Undersecretary of Defense William Perry) produced far less change than many critics deemed necessary (Powell 1993a; *Directions for Defense* 1995; Lancaster 1993c). By other measures, more dramatic developments have occurred. The navy's elimination of its entrenched warfare "baronies" and other organizational changes within the services mark especially sharp departures from the cold war era (Steigman 1993). Rather than attempt to survey all such aspects of change in the Pentagon—an impossible task in such a short chapter—I focus on shifts in defense budgets and force structure. These shifts will help determine the kind of military the United States will possess in the next century, and they will affect an especially high percentage of DOD suborganizations. Decisions to cut and reorient the defense budget can also jeopardize the core institutional interests of the armed services, and therefore offer an especially stringent measure of change in the Pentagon.

When the Wall Tumbled Down

The post–cold war Pentagon offers a classic case of problem depletion. In 1993, Les Aspin argued that the breakup of the Soviet Union shattered the Pentagon's long-standing reason to exist and the rationale for its force structure and budget:

> For decades this building has focused almost all of its planning—budgets, force structures, the way we organize our forces—everything has been focused against the Soviet threat. . . . There is no more Soviet Union. So how do we size

> and shape our defense budgets now? How do you know whether you need a \$100 billion defense budget or a \$300 billion or what kind of defense budget? (ASD/Public Affairs 1993, 2)

Aspin was not the first Pentagon official to recognize this problem. In 1990, General Powell argued that the "absolute, total demise of the Cold War" justified drastic changes in U.S. forces and defense spending (1990, 13). Powell and Secretary of Defense Dick Cheney responded by crafting the Bush administration's base force proposal, which was designed to cut U.S. forces by 25 percent and restructure them for the post–cold war era. Les Aspin—who was then chair of the House Armed Services Committee—blasted Powell's proposal as woefully inadequate. He charged that the base force "did not represent a new conceptual approach for a new security era but was essentially 'less of the same,' that is, a downsized force largely shaped by Cold War priorities" (Aspin 1992d, 1). Aspin's attacks helped earn him his nomination as Bill Clinton's secretary of defense and gave him the opportunity to launch his own bottom-up review of U.S. forces. Within a year, Aspin was driven from office and critics attacked his bottom-up force structure for offering only marginal changes from the base force (Korb 1994; Krepinevich 1994; Quinn-Judge 1993).

While there is more than a little irony in Aspin's fate, this pattern of criticism suggests a broader possibility: that regardless of party affiliation or commitment to reform, a president and his secretary of defense cannot impose fundamental change on the U.S. armed services. Many scholars argue that during the cold war, the armed services grew so resistant to reform, and so politically effective in resisting outside initiatives for change, that restructuring the U.S. military has become inherently difficult (Allard 1990; Blechman et al. 1993; Builder 1989; Davis 1967, 1985, 150–58; Fox 1974; Halperin 1974; Hendrickson 1988; Hilsman 1971; Jones 1984; Komer 1985; Stubbing 1986; Tupfer 1984; U.S. Congress, Senate Committee on Armed Services 1985; Wilson 1989). Gen. David Jones, while serving as chairman of the Joint Chiefs of Staff, offered a classic explanation for this service resistance to change. He argued that the armed services

> find it difficult to adapt to changing conditions because of understandable attachments to the past. The very foundation of each service rests on imbuing its members with pride in its missions, its doctrine and its customs and discipline—all of which are steeped in traditions. While these deep-seated service distinctions are important in fostering a fighting spirit, cultivating them engenders tendencies to look inward and to insulate the institutions against outside challenges. (U.S. Congress, Senate Committee on Armed Services 1985, 624–25)

Scholars also argue that defense restructuring is difficult because the services have retained considerable autonomy from centralized military and civilian control, and they can often defend their interests and preferred force structures against outside pressures for change. Since the National Security Act of 1947 established a national military establishment to impose greater unification on the U.S. military, DOD has undergone repeated reorganization designed to limit the autonomy of the armed services and centralize control over defense planning, budgeting, and the command of forces. Yet, from the moment of DOD's creation, the armed services preserved remarkable independence within the department. Robert Art argues that the Department of Defense "began as a system of halfway measures, representing a compromise between a highly centralized tightly integrated army plan, on the one hand, and the loosely coordinated, navy-like plan on the other. The separate services were housed in one governmental department, but they remained distinct and autonomous organizations" (Art 1992, 16; see also Caraley 1962; Hammond 1961, 187–228; Lowi 1967). And while repeated DOD reorganization initiatives attempted to increase centralized control over the services, "the military services retained considerable autonomy to develop war plans, to train and equip the forces, and to allocate resources in ways each judged best for their own interests" (Art 1992, 16; see also Allard 1990, 7–24, 243–48; Art 1985c, 111; Blackwell and Blechman 1990b, 1–4; Huntington 1988, 412–15, 417–20; Komer 1985; Lucas and Dawson 1974).

Part of this persistent service autonomy stemmed from the weakness of the Joint Chiefs of Staff. The National Security Act of 1947 established the JCS to provide at least a modicum of centralized military coordination and leadership of the services. In drafting that legislation, however, Congress explicitly rejected proposals that it establish a "Prussian-style" general staff to exercise tight control over the military, in large part because of fears that a united military would be more difficult for civilians to control (Hammond 1961, 220–28, 382). The chiefs were left free to promote the interests of their respective services; the chairman of the JCS could only attempt to override the opinions of his colleagues by appealing to the secretary of defense. Moreover, by the early 1960s, the chiefs had settled into a pattern of collusion to help preserve service autonomy in the face of civilian authority, and they adopted "lowest common denominator" policy decisions that reflected logrolling and compromising between individual service preferences (Art 1974a, 433–37; Cushman 1990, 105–07; Davis 1985, 158–60; Gorman 1984; Hammond 1961; Huntington 1988, 415–20; Kanter 1979, 25–30; Komer 1985, 214–15).

Repeated efforts to strengthen civilian control over the services also failed to eliminate their autonomy. Robert Art, Barry Blechman, and others argue that, despite repeated legislative and administrative changes during the cold war, those initiatives almost always failed to produce meaningful change, especially in terms of reducing the ability of the services to pursue their own organizational interests (Art 1985c, xiii; Blackwell and Blechman 1990b, 1–4; Komer 1985). Vincent Davis and Samuel P. Huntington agree with that assessment, arguing that while many cold war era reforms centralized and strengthened the power of the secretary of defense over other civilian DOD officials, the power and autonomy of the services to allocate their own budgets and determine their primary missions continued to grow, long after the reforms adopted in the 1960s by Defense Secretary Robert S. McNamara (Davis 1985, 150–58; Huntington 1988, 410–13).

The persistence of this service autonomy was reinforced by the ability of service leaders to seek support from Congress to block policy initiatives by DOD civilians. In theory, because the secretary of defense oversees the drafting of DOD's annual budget request, he can use that request to help impose force structure changes on the armed services. But the president decides how much of DOD's proposal to include in his own budget request, and Congress decides whether to enact that budget into law. Military officers who oppose the budget cuts recommended by a defense secretary can make an end run around him and lobby the president or Congress to reject those cuts. Military end runs to Congress are particularly common: for example, when Cheney attempted to cancel the V-22 aircraft, marine corps lobbying helped congressional advocates of the program preserve its funding (Scarborough 1991). To avoid such embarrassing, highly visible defeats, civilian officials often seek to anticipate and accommodate the concerns of the military and their allies on Capitol Hill, thus giving the military bargaining leverage over civilian initiatives on weapons and force levels.

Even before the end of the cold war, the services sometimes failed in their efforts to resist civilian initiatives for change, as when the Eisenhower administration drove significant shifts in force structure and defense spending under the New Look strategy (Kanter 1979; Murdock 1974). Two events in the late 1980s posed more fundamental threats to service power and budgets. First, Congress enacted the Goldwater-Nichols Department of Defense Reorganization Act of 1986 (PL 99-433, 99th Cong., Oct. 1, 1986.) This act made the chairman the principal military adviser to the defense secretary and president, gave him all the power over strategic planning and the unified commands that the chiefs had previously exercised as a group, and gave him authority to review service budget proposals and spending priorities (with the support of a greatly strengthened Joint Staff that reported directly to him). Together with the other changes mandated by Goldwater-Nichols, this legislation enabled the chairman to exercise unprecedented influence over defense policy (Art 1992; Cushman 1990, 107–10; Davis 1991, 159–68).

By itself, of course, Goldwater-Nichols did not guarantee that the chairman would challenge the services' budgets and force preferences, particularly while the Soviet Union provided a stable basis for U.S. defense planning. The tumbling of the Berlin Wall in 1989 shattered the foundations of U.S. military policy and undermined the rationale used by the services to defend their existing force structures. The response of Gen. Colin Powell to that event highlights the impact of Goldwater-Nichols (GWN) on the defense policy–making process, and the consequences for the initial U.S. effort to devise a post–cold war military.

Chairman Powell, Congress, and the Base Force

Powell began revising his view of the Soviet threat before he became chairman of the JCS in October 1989. In May of that year, while still serving in an army billet, he told a group of senior army leaders that the security environment was undergoing a radical change. While the Soviet Union had long been the bear in the woods, "our bear is now wearing a Smoky hat and carries a shovel to put out fires. Our bear is now benign" (Powell 1995, 402). However, when he suggested that this shift in the threat should drive reductions in army force levels, many of his colleagues (including Army Chief of Staff Carl E. Vuono) resisted that argument. According to an internal JCS history of the base force, which was based on interviews with Powell and other military and civilian leaders of the Bush-era Pentagon, service opposition to force cuts grew stronger after Powell became chairman (Jaffe 1993, 12). Powell argued that with the decline of the Soviet threat, the United States no longer needed the ability to fight a global-scale, short-warning conflict (Powell 1990, 13). His proposal for a reduced force structure—the base force—called for a 25 percent reduction in U.S. forces by 1994, cutting active duty personnel from 2.1 million to 1.6 million, and reducing the number of navy ships, air force fighter wings, and army divisions accordingly (Jaffe 1993, 17, 21).

That Powell could draft the base force plan at all testifies to the changes wrought by Goldwater-Nichols. Prior to GWN, the services possessed the largest and most capable analytic staffs within the military, and they used those capabilities to justify and promote their own force structure and budget requests. Goldwater-Nichols gave the chairman his own source of analysis by putting the Joint Staff under his authority and significantly increasing its size and quality. This independent staff allowed Powell to examine force structure issues without relying on the services, and thereby minimized the risk that the services would be able to blunt or skew the recommendations of the base force. Indeed, the Joint Staff's initial reassessment of the U.S. force structure was called the "Quiet Study"; it was closely held within the Joint Staff and set the pattern for keeping the services at arm's length during the base force's development.

When Powell finally briefed the chiefs of the armed services on his proposal in November 1989, their opposition to force reductions solidified. The service chiefs rejected Powell's initiative as a threat to their existing force structures and budget preferences, and initially refused to even discuss his restructuring proposals (Jaffe 1993, 18–23, 27, 32–34, 38). Powell also encountered opposition from the civilian leadership of the Pentagon. When he first approached Secretary of Defense Cheney in late 1989 with his agenda for change, Cheney told him he disagreed with Powell's beliefs that the Soviet threat had plummeted and that the United States should make deep cuts in its force structure (Jaffe 1993, 16–18, 20). Thus, although Powell was able to draft the base force without interference from its potential opponents, he still faced the challenge of overcoming that opposition and transforming his initiative into official administration policy.

Goldwater-Nichols did not grant the chairman the power to dictate his force structure preferences to the armed services. Rather, it made the chairman the principal military adviser to the defense secretary and president on force structure and budgeting issues, gave him the authority to review service budget requests, and enabled him to propose changes in service budgets through his chairman's program assessment. The power of the chairman lies ultimately in the power to persuade. The secretary of defense and president do not have to accept his recommendations; and while the chairman can recommend changes in service budget requests, it is up to the president and his secretary of defense (and ultimately Congress) to decide whether to accept those changes or to follow the recommendations made by the services themselves. Given these limits on the chairman's power, how was Powell able to advance a plan to restructure the military that was initially opposed by both the services and the secretary of defense?

Powell decided to concentrate first on winning over the civilian leaders of the Pentagon, who could then use their power to help Powell overcome the resistance of the armed services. The secretary of defense has sources of influence over the services that the chairman lacks, including his power to dictate the defense planning guidance (DPG) for service budget requests and to enforce his preferences in the final DOD budget request he submits to the president. Moreover, while Cheney told Powell in 1989 that he disagreed with Powell's assessment of the declining Soviet threat, Cheney also encouraged Powell to continue his force structure review and suggested that Powell eventually brief the president on his recommendations (Jaffe 1993, 16–18, 20). In spring 1990 Powell focused on gaining Cheney's support for the base force and worked with other civilian officials (including Paul Wolfowitz, undersecretary of defense for policy) to refine the proposal and build a persuasive case for defense restructuring. As Wolfowitz and other civilian officials developed their "regional strategy" framework to help address such issues, Powell and Cheney built a consensus on force requirements and established the basis for Bush's August 1990 speech, which explained the administration's overall security approach to the post–cold war era.

Prior to the base force and the end of the cold war, however, the armed services always had an opportunity to fight an administration's proposed cutbacks: they could ask their allies in Congress to reject the proposal. Congress can modify the president's budget request and legislate changes in U.S. force structure. During the cold war, the services often made end runs around the secretary of defense and president, and appealed to Congress to protect their forces and budgets. Indeed, the ability to make such end runs was a key underpinning of service autonomy. Given the intensity of service opposition to the base force, why did the service chiefs not turn to their allies on Capitol Hill and seek to block what had become Bush administration policy?

One factor that may have discouraged an end run was Powell's own status as an officer. During the cold war, the services won congressional support against Pentagon civilians by arguing that civilians lacked the specialized, professional expertise of the uniformed military. General Powell was invulnerable to such accusations, and he capitalized on the military preeminence that Goldwater-Nichols attached to the chairmanship. More decisive, however, was the political climate in Congress when the base force evolved. To say that Capitol Hill was inhospitable to service concerns is like saying the ocean is wet. In spring 1990, when Powell began his campaign within the Pentagon to win support for his proposal, legislators were howling for defense cutbacks. Senate Armed Services Committee

Chair Sam Nunn (D-Ga.) gave a series of speeches on the Senate floor attacking the president's fiscal year 1991 request (which did not incorporate the base force cutbacks), and he called for a total rethinking of the U.S. force structure (Nunn 1990a, 1990b, 1990c). Representative Aspin followed suit and began crafting his own version of the defense budget to help restructure U.S. forces for the post–cold war era. Even Republican legislators such as Sens. John McCain (R-Ariz.) and William Cohen (R-Maine) castigated the Pentagon for failing to respond to reductions in the Soviet threat and called for deep cuts in defense spending (Dewar 1990).

While this congressional drive for defense cuts imperiled the Bush administration's 1991 defense budget, Powell did not create the base force merely to co-opt legislative critics and regain control over defense budgeting. His interest in restructuring U.S. forces predated the 1990 calls by Nunn and Aspin for change. However, while Powell was careful not to reveal the base force to Congress until Cheney endorsed it, he was concerned with the congressional drive to cut defense spending and force structure. Powell worried that unless DOD offered a sufficiently far-reaching plan of its own, Congress would reduce U.S. forces far below the level he deemed safe. Indeed, Powell adopted the term "base force" to convey the notion that his recommended force levels were the absolute minimum that the United States had to retain, and that any further reductions would endanger U.S. security (Jaffe 1993, 21 29, 32–34). Powell also tried to forestall deeper congressional cutbacks by accelerating his schedule for force reductions, moving up the date for completion of the base force cuts from 1997 to 1994 (Jaffe 1993, 34).

More important, congressional enthusiasm for cutting defense helped Powell win support for the base force within the Pentagon. Through spring 1990, Cheney continued to believe that Powell was exaggerating the decline of the Soviet threat. However, legislators were attacking Cheney for failing to propose changes in defense policy, and Cheney shared Powell's concern that without a plan such as the base force, Congress would impose unacceptably deep cuts. These concerns (and some substantive modifications in the base force) helped convince Cheney to endorse Powell's proposal (Jaffe 1993, 35). Powell also raised the specter of congressional budget cutting in his efforts to overcome service opposition. By August 1990, House and Senate action on the defense authorization bill convinced the service chiefs that Congress was certain to slash their budget requests, and this recognition helped convince them to accept the base force (Jaffee 1993, 34, 39–44). Congressional behavior not only discouraged an end run by the services; Powell was also able to use Congress as a tacit ally within the Pentagon by raising the specter of congressional cuts to overcome civilian and service opposition.

The fate of the base force highlights a further source of congressional influence over defense reform. While Powell hoped that his initiative would help forestall deeper congressional cuts, legislators began attacking the base force as inadequate soon after it was unveiled. Aspin was especially critical. He denigrated Powell's force structure as nothing more than a downsized cold war military and called instead for a wholly redesigned force structure based on post–cold war threats (Aspin 1992d, 10–23; Stockton 1993). In particular, Aspin criticized the "top-down" process that the Pentagon had used to devise the final base force proposal. Aspin argued that Powell and Cheney simply took successive cuts out of the existing budget and force structure, leaving the United States with "a smaller version of the force we built up for the Cold War." Instead of following this process of subtraction, Aspin argued that the United States needed a fundamental reexamination of the threats to U.S. security and of U.S. defense requirements, which would then provide the basis for restructuring U.S. forces. What the United States required was "a bottom-up review of our forces" (Aspin 1992a, 1–3).

Aspin's staff of policy analysts on the House Armed Services Committee outlined the basis for this review in *An Approach to Sizing American Conventional Forces for the Post–Cold War Era: Four Illustrative Options.* Their study described the methodology that the bottom-up review ought to follow and offered a preliminary assessment of post–cold war threats and four force structure options to deal with them. Aspin and his staff then produced a series of studies that presented the findings of a more detailed bottom-up review and recommended a force structure ("Option C") that Aspin cited as the basis for his alternative to the president's proposed fiscal year 1993 defense budget (Aspin 1992b, 1992c, 1992e). Moreover, Aspin used this force structure analysis to help draft and promote his own version of the defense budget. Emphasizing the differences between his proposal and the one the administration submitted, Aspin told his colleagues: "We have been working for months on a new bottom-up threat-based methodology for sizing and shaping the forces of the future," and that this bottom-up review "is at the very heart of our bill" (1992b, 2). Other factors helped shape the final defense budgets Congress enacted for fiscal years 1991 and 1992—including the desire by legislators to protect defense production jobs in their districts. Nevertheless, in terms of overall defense spending, specific force levels (especially for the reserves), and funding of major programs such as the B-2 bomber and the strategic defense initiative, Congress imposed major changes on the defense restructuring efforts of Powell and the administration (Stockton 1993).

Goldwater-Nichols and the New Politics of Defense Restructuring

Goldwater-Nichols has shifted the distribution of power within the Pentagon and enabled the chairman of the Joint Chiefs of Staff to play a decisive role in U.S. efforts to adapt to the end of the cold war. Rep. Ike Skelton (D-Mo.), one of the principal authors of Goldwater-Nichols, argues that Congress enacted the legislation to "reduce the influence of the service chiefs" and create a powerful chairman of the Joint Chiefs (Skelton 1992, 16). Congress scored knockouts on both counts. General Powell exercised enormous influence over defense policy during the Bush administration, shaping the thrust of post–cold war defense planning against bitter service resistance. Powell was able to use the enhanced analytic capabilities of the Joint Staff to craft the base force, without relying on the services. Moreover, because Goldwater-Nichols made the chairman the principal military adviser to the secretary of defense and the president, Powell was in a stronger position to win administration support for imposing his plan on the services.

Goldwater-Nichols has also created the opportunity for new patterns of civil-military conflict and cooperation in defense reform. During the cold war, the services usually made their end runs around the secretary of defense, appealing to Congress to overturn his proposed cutbacks in service programs. In the immediate post–cold war era, however, it was a military officer—the chairman of the Joint Chiefs of Staff—who proposed slashing service forces by 25 percent. And it was a civilian official—the secretary of defense—who initially agreed with the services that Powell's cutbacks were unwarranted and dangerous to U.S. security. Powell moved to split this civilian service opposition by persuading Dick Cheney and his civilian subordinates that the services' position was wrong. Doing so helped ensure that President Bush would accept the base force.

Congress also played an important (if inadvertent) role in Powell's victory within the Pentagon, by reinforcing his argument that unless the Pentagon offered a plan for defense cuts, Congress was likely to impose a plan more radical than Powell's. The history of the base force suggests that Congress affects post–cold war defense reform in four ways. First, fear of congressional activism can encourage Pentagon officials to adjust their proposals to forestall or co-opt congressional efforts to change U.S. defense spending and force structure. Second, Congress can shape the patterns of conflict and coalition building within the Pentagon, rewarding end runs by the services or (as in the base force) serving as the tacit ally of Pentagon reformers. Third, Congress can use its power of the purse to legislate changes in force structure and modify efforts by military or civilian officials to reshape the armed services. Fourth, by enacting legislation such as Goldwater-Nichols, Congress can alter the authorities granted to defense policy makers and shift the power relationships between them.

But Congress did not guarantee that the chairman of the JCS would always lead the charge on defense reform. Although Goldwater-Nichols grants the chairman enormous authority, the individual holding that office decides how much of that authority to use and how much planning autonomy to leave to the services. The personal skills and policy preferences of a chairman play a decisive role in determining whether—and how effectively—he will seek to restructure U.S. forces. Moreover, even a chairman as dynamic as Powell may not pursue the kind of fundamental changes deemed necessary by civilian officials or legislators. When Powell issued his December 1992 report suggesting changes in service roles and missions—a key issue for post–cold war reform—many legislators and incoming Clinton administration officials were disappointed by what they considered the modest scope of those proposals (Blechman et al. 1993, 1–4; Gellman 1993a; Gordon 1992a; Lancaster 1993c). Goldwater-Nichols makes the characteristics of individual chairmen a key independent variable in defense reform.

Patterns of civil-military conflict will also vary with the role the chairman chooses to play. During the Bush administration, General Powell pushed for defense cuts deeper than those Secretary of Defense Cheney initially preferred. When president-elect Clinton named Les Aspin secretary of defense, Aspin called for changes far beyond those in Powell's base force, thereby reversing the Bush-era relationship between the chairman and DOD civilians on military restructuring. How did Aspin deal with the danger that Powell would use his considerable power not to promote defense reform, but to block it? How far-reaching were the changes in force structure and defense priorities that Aspin (and his successor, William Perry) ultimately proposed? What new patterns of civil-military conflict and cooperation emerged in DOD and the Congress, and how will these relationships affect defense reform in the Clinton administration and beyond?

The Bottom-Up Review

When Aspin arrived at the Pentagon, he had good reason to fear that Powell would unite with the services to oppose deep cuts in the force structure. In his House version of the bottom-up review, Aspin attacked Powell for proposing far too modest changes in U.S. force structure. Powell returned the compliment. He declared that Aspin's House study was "overly simplistic and relie[d] on static measures in a way that ignores actors such as technology, terrain, location, leadership, coalitions, and the introduction of . . . unconventional weapons" (quoted in Grossman 1992, 10). The rest of the Pentagon allied quickly with Powell in this attack. Cheney testified that adopting Aspin's preferred force structure (Option C) could lead to "a hell of a lot of casualties" in future wars ("Stick With Pentagon Plan" 1992, 370). Gen. Merrill McPeak, air force chief of staff, attacked the proposal as "kind of senseless" and claimed that if it were adopted, "What you'll have to do is close down the Air Force" (quoted in "Huge Defense Cut" 1992, B-5; Maze 1992). Army Chief of Staff Gen. Gordon Sullivan testified that Option C would "break the institution" of the American military (quoted in "Aspin Plan" 1992). Navy leaders offered similarly dire predictions and called on the House to reject Aspin's force structure and the analysis behind it ("Another Top Navy Official" 1992).

Aspin's relationship with Powell and the services was complicated by a defense reform initiative separate from the force structure issue allowing gays and lesbians to serve openly in the military. Clinton's proposal on gays provoked bitter opposition from the uniformed military. While Aspin had to deal with the resulting firestorm within the Pentagon, he also incurred the wrath of White House officials for publicly noting that if Congress were to vote on Clinton's proposal, legislators would be "overwhelmingly against it" (quoted in Gertz 1993a). Clinton also had broader problems with the military that undermined Aspin's position in the Pentagon. Already suspicious of Clinton because he had never served in the armed forces, U.S. officers launched repeated and highly publicized criticisms of their new commander in chief (Bacevich 1993). Richard Kohn argues that the resulting tensions between the military and civilian officials have escalated to the point that the United States faces a "crisis" in civil-military relations. The roots of this crisis "go back to the beginning of the Cold War, when the creation of a large, 'peacetime' standing military establishment overloaded the traditional process by which civilian control was exercised" (1994, 4). Kohn and others argue that the resulting power of the military has expanded under Goldwater-Nichols, and that the military exercises great influence over issues such as U.S. force structure—especially when civilians threaten to impose cuts (Kohn 1994, 7–13; Bacevich 1993; Holzer and LeSueur 1994a; Lehman 1994).

Under these circumstances, it is not surprising that, as a number of analysts argue, Aspin and the Clinton administration backed away from their commitment to restructure the U.S. military, and they ended up proposing a force structure that was little more than "Bush Lite" (Korb 1994). Aspin launched his reassessment of the force structure shortly after arriving at the Pentagon. This bottom-up review (BUR), which borrowed both its title and its analytic starting point from Aspin's House Armed Services Committee studies, was supposed to provide "the direction for shifting America's focus away from a strategy designed to meet a global threat to one oriented toward the new dangers of the post–Cold War era" (Aspin 1993, iii). The resulting *Report on the Bottom-Up Review,* published in October 1993, described the threats likely to confront the United States in the post–cold war era, Aspin's strategy to counter them, and the conventional forces required to implement that strategy. In particular, the review argued that the United States needed to meet four "new dangers": (1) the proliferation of nuclear weapons and other weapons of mass destruction; (2) aggression by major regional powers or ethnic and religious conflict; (3) the potential failure of democratic reform in the former Soviet Union and elsewhere; and (4) the potential failure to build a strong and growing U.S. economy. The review concluded that the United States had to field forces that, in concert with its allies, were capable of fighting and winning two major regional conflicts that occur nearly simultaneously. The review also identified a number of new initiatives for DOD to pursue, including the promotion of democracy in the former Soviet Union and elsewhere, programs for counterproliferation, and environmental initiatives (Aspin 1993, iii–12).

A number of critics charge that the BUR force structure is nothing more than a marginally downsized version of Bush's base force. Although Aspin claimed that the bottom-up review marked a sharp departure from Bush administration policies, particularly in assessing post–cold war security requirements, the BUR shared some important similarities with Bush-era planning assumptions. In particular, the BUR accepted the Bush administration's requirement that the United States be able to wage two major regional conflicts at the same time—or in the case of the BUR, "nearly simultaneously" (Krepinevich 1994). Larry Korb argues that the review was "bottom-up in name only," and that it resulted in a "barely changed military force" that retained twelve navy aircraft carriers and other forces no longer required in the post–cold war world (Korb 1994). Andrew Krepenevitch agrees that "the BUR maintains the U.S. planning perspective that existed during the Cold War: it focuses on the near-term future, and on the most familiar threats, as opposed to the greatest or most likely threats to national security" beyond the next decade (1994, i). And in terms of the BUR's recommended force structure, Elliot Cohen argues that the BUR "is essentially the Bush Base Force with some interesting if not inexplicable tweaks" (quoted in Quinn-Judge 1993).

Nevertheless, for the armed services that are the target of these tweaks, the BUR recommended a number of significant and often unwelcome changes. The BUR proposed that the army be cut to ten active duty divisions by the end of fiscal year 1999, down from the twelve proposed for the base force and far below the eighteen active divisions maintained by the army in fiscal year 1990. Although the BUR follows the base force in allowing the navy to retain 12 carriers, the total number of navy ships would decline under the BUR to 330, instead of the 450 called for under the base force (and 40 percent below the fiscal year 1990 total of 546 ships). Combined with the reductions slated for the air force, total active duty personnel would decline to 1.45 million by fiscal year 1999, in contrast to 1.6 million under the base force and over 2 million in fiscal year 1990 (U.S. Congress, Congressional Budget Office 1994, 8–10; Jaffe 1993, 21). Table 5.1 presents a comparison of the force structures proposed for base force and in the bottom-up review.

The Clinton administration has made even more dramatic cuts in weapons procurement, especially for the types of weapons most essential to the core missions of the armed services for the past forty years. Under

Table 5.1 Comparison of Force Structure Plan

	Cold War Force	*Base Force*	*Bottom-Up Review*
Active duty personnel (in millions)	2.1	1.6	1.45
Army divisions			
Active	18	12	10
Reserve	10	8	5+
Major navy ships	546	450	330
Air force fighter wings			
Active	24	16	13
Reserve	12	12	7

Sources: CBO 1994, 8–10; Jaffe 1993, 21; Aspin 1993, 28.

Clinton's fiscal year 1995 defense budget request, which was structured to help implement the bottom-up review, the army was not given the money to buy a single tank. The air force was denied all funds to buy fighter aircraft. The navy was allocated enough money to build only six ships—a decline of 80 percent from the ship construction levels of the mid-1980s (Finnegan 1994; Ricks 1994). Total defense procurement fell from $94 billion in fiscal year 1990 to $43 billion in the fiscal year 1995 request, a cut of 54 percent (U.S. Congress, Congressional Budget Office 1994, 7). And while the BUR proposed that procurement spending rise slightly after 1995, the administration estimates that total procurement spending from fiscal year 1995 through 1999 will drop by $32 billion below the Bush administration's programs for that period. The Clinton administration also plans to slash spending on ballistic missile defenses by $21 billion below the estimated Bush spending plans for fiscal years 1995–1999 (Aspin 1993, 108).

At the same time, the Clinton administration launched some new spending initiatives, reflecting the bottom-up review's emphasis on post–cold war threats. The BUR called for allocating a five-year total of $5 billion for new defense programs, including global initiatives to promote democracy and peacekeeping operations (Aspin 1993, 71–76, 108). The administration also increased the share of the defense budget devoted to environmental cleanup and other nontraditional defense programs; indeed, in the fiscal year 1995 request, Clinton proposed spending as much on environmental cleanup as on the army's entire acquisition plan, and more on peacekeeping than the marines spend on weapons and ammunition (Ricks 1994). In keeping with the BUR's emphasis on maintaining the readiness of U.S. forces, the administration's fiscal year 1995 request also called for a $5 billion increase in operation and maintenance funding. Yet, despite these increases, the BUR called for cuts in overall defense spending not only below the Bush administration's plans, but lower than the target adopted by the Clinton administration in April 1994. The total estimated cost of the Bush administration's proposed defense program for fiscal years 1995–1999 was $1,325 billion. The Clinton administration's April 1993 defense budget target for that same period was $1,221 billion, a cut of $104 billion below projected Bush spending. In September 1993, the bottom-up review nearly doubled that initial cut, calling for an additional $91 billion in reductions for the five-year period (Aspin 1993, 108).

These cuts in spending and force structure go well beyond the base force—which, according to Powell, was the absolute minimum force the United States needed to maintain for the post–cold war era. On some issues, including the number of aircraft carriers, the bottom-up review did back away from the reductions Clinton proposed as a presidential candidate, and it adopted recommendations similar either to the base force or to the Bush administration's subsequent defense plans. Moreover, in the 1994 State of the Union address, Clinton declared he would "draw the line against further defense cuts" (*Fiscal Year 1995* 1994, 1). Nevertheless, the defense budget he submitted that year marked a sharp departure from Bush-era planning, and—especially in defense procurement—ran roughshod over entrenched military spending priorities. What accounts for this record of defense restructuring? How was the Clinton administration able to accomplish as much as it did, given the power Chairman Powell demonstrated during the Bush administration, and given the risk that he would ally himself with the services—and perhaps Congress—to block more radical force reductions?

Powell and the Politics of Civil-Military Cooperation

When Les Aspin was still in the House, he used his initial version of the bottom-up review to serve two related purposes. The review provided the reassessment of U.S. defense requirements and forces that created a basis for Aspin to craft his own version of the defense budget. The review also helped Aspin sell that budget to his colleagues. Aspin and his staff made a concerted effort to gain support by providing legislators with preliminary drafts of committee studies and by soliciting their input and participation in further bottom-up review efforts. Even as members were voting on the defense bill on the floor of the House, Aspin's staff continued to hand them study summaries that made the analytic case for his proposed force structure (U.S. Congress, House Committee on Armed Services 1992b; see also Stockton 1993).

When Aspin arrived at the Pentagon, his staffers hoped that the new version of the bottom-up review would serve a similar mix of substantive and political purposes in DOD. Frank Wisner, the undersecretary of defense for policy, issued a memorandum to Aspin describing the substantive and political objectives that the review was designed to achieve. Wisner pointed out that the BUR was supposed to meet two related objectives. The first was to guide the analytic basis for drafting a post–cold war force structure and defense budget. The second goal was to build a political consensus for that budget, despite the potential opposition of General Powell and the services. Wisner told Aspin that the BUR needed "to establish a broad, stable political consensus on the transition to an eventual steady state for the defense budget, the overall structure of our forces, and selected defense programs that are big spenders and/or important symbols of your agenda." Wisner also emphasized that the BUR was structured "to give you presentational material and analytical backup that you can use to persuade various audiences to support the Clinton-Aspin defense program. This would involve first the administration (President, NSC, NEC) and later the Hill and public." However, winning the support of General Powell was especially vital: "We will need you and the Chairman standing shoulder-to-shoulder on basic positions" (Wisner 1993, 1).

The goal of co-opting Aspin's potential opponents helped drive the methodology and output of the bottom-up review; Aspin had previously co-opted other legislators through his committee studies on new security dangers and post–cold war force options. Wisner noted that the review "will follow the same construct you used with the Democratic caucus last year. But it will use the analytical expertise in OSD and the Joint Staff to update that effort by 1) providing more thorough and compelling descriptions of the New Dangers; 2) firming up the rationale for the force structures need for Building Blocks based on analytical methods of the Joint Staff" (Wisner 1993, 2). Accordingly, from the outset of the bottom-up review, Aspin ensured that the members of the Joint Staff and other officers had considerable input into the study, thereby helping to elicit their support for the final product. The BUR was directed by a steering group chaired by John Deutch, undersecretary of defense for acquisition, and included representatives from OSD, the Joint Staff, and the services. Aspin argued: "It couldn't be any other way. The process has brought the civilian and military communities closer together. We've established a working relationship over the last five months that would have taken a year or two to develop with this review" (ASD/Public Affairs 1993, 1). This underlying political and managerial purpose of the BUR guaranteed that its results would be more akin to a Pentagon consensus than a radical, anti-Pentagon revolution. This process of co-optation also stands in marked contrast to the way Powell and Cheney drafted strategy during the Bush era, reflecting the very different political problems facing the two administrations.

Measured by Powell's public response to the BUR, the review was a resounding political success. At the press conference at which Aspin and Powell announced the study's findings, Powell praised the BUR as "a good, sound military strategy" (quoted in ASD/Public Affairs 1993, 37–38). He emphasized that the review "was a very, very collaborative effort. The Joint Chiefs of Staff, the Joint Staff, and the services worked very closely with the new appointees in Mr. Aspin's organization—on his team—and we have been in sync with them step by step throughout this entire, almost seven-month process, and I'm very, very pleased at the level of collaboration that existed" (ibid., 6). This collaboration accounts for the continuities between the base force and the bottom-up review. Aspin acknowledged that the "BUR builds on the Base Force," relying on studies of military transportation and other analytic efforts that Powell and the Joint Staff had begun while Aspin was still in the House. Powell noted that the BUR is "the successor to the Base Force, and builds on some of the work we did during the Base Force because the strategy underpinning is quite similar, and it ought to be quite similar because the world looks the same to us, whether you were wearing Base Force eyes or Bottom-Up Review eyes. . . . You have those two major regional contingencies that it is prudent for us to be able to deal with" (ibid., 45, 55–57).

Yet, the BUR's planning assumption of two regional contingencies highlights the difficulty Aspin faced in compromising between the need to win military support and the desire for deeper force reductions. In June 1993, while the review was still under way, Aspin announced that he might abandon the Bush-era requirement to be able to fight and win two major regional contingencies simultaneously. Aspin proposed instead that the United States adopt a "win-hold-win" strategy: that is, that it be able to defeat one adversary while holding the other at bay, until forces from the initial conflict could be brought to bear against the second adversary. This shift in strategy would permit deeper reductions in U.S. forces and was consistent with the overall thrust of Aspin's reform agenda and assessment of post–cold war threats. However, Aspin's announcement provoked immediate criticism by military leaders. One four-star general termed the proposed strategy "win-lose-lose" (quoted in Lancaster 1993b). Aspin quickly reversed himself and announced: "We've come to the conclusion that our forces must be able to fight and win two major regional conflicts, and nearly simultaneously." Aspin and his team augmented the BUR's force structure with "force enhancements" to meet this additional requirement, and increased Clinton's proposed five-year defense plan by $13 billion to pay for the enhancements (quoted in Gertz 1993b).

General Powell also confronted a potential conflict between his preferences on force structure and political considerations. When Aspin offered his congressional bottom-up review in 1991–1992, Powell attacked its methodology as "overly simplistic," and the service chiefs attacked its force and spending recommendations as a threat to U.S. security. The 1993 BUR called for cuts equal to (and in some cases exceeding) those of Aspin's earlier congressional recommendation, and much greater than those Powell proposed as the absolute minimum in the base force. And while the 1993 BUR did include some last-minute force enhancements, critics outside government were quick to attack them as totally inadequate to meet the two-war criteria that Powell endorsed ("Capability Enhancements" 1993). Yet, instead of joining that criticism and insisting on further increases, Powell held a press conference to praise the 1993 BUR and declare that "the force structure we have arrived at is a solid one" (quoted in ASD/Public Affairs 1993, 37–38). Why did Powell offer such strong support for Aspin's bottom-up review?

One possible explanation is that Powell felt constrained by the principle of civilian control over the Pentagon. Criticized during his JCS chairmanship for exercising inordinate influence over defense policy making, Powell argued in 1993 that "Presidents Bush and Clinton, and Secretaries Cheney and Aspin, exercised solid, unmistakable civilian control over the Armed Forces and especially me" (Powell et al. 1994, 23). Powell also noted that he fought against Aspin's force recommendations when Aspin was in the House. However, in accepting Aspin's 1993 BUR, Powell noted, "[Aspin is] now my boss" and "he wins the debates now" (quoted in ASD/Public Affairs 1993, 45). But Powell's belief in civilian control did not prevent him from openly attacking Clinton's proposal on gays in the military, and—in a classic example of an end run—building a tacit alliance with legislators who threatened to overturn the Clinton initiative.

Another more plausible explanation for Powell's support of the BUR is that he participated so closely in its analysis that he could endorse its findings, even where the BUR called for cuts below the base force. Powell emphasized he was "very, very pleased at the level of collaboration" between his Joint Staff officers and Aspin's study team. Noting the cuts imposed by the BUR, Powell admitted that "as a conservative military officer, I always like to have more" forces. However, "looking at this strategy carefully with the chiefs and with the Joint Staff and running a lot of war games and examining the changes that have taken place in the world, we are comfortable that we can move from our previous plan down to this level that came out of the bottom-up review" (ibid., 6, 37). Aspin's strategy of coopting Chairman Powell was a resounding success, but came at the price of negotiating a force structure that Powell would support. Yet Powell was willing to support force reductions below those envisioned in the base force, in large part because the international security environment had changed since 1990. Powell noted that in devising the base force, "we anticipated a fundamental change in the nature of the Soviet Union . . . but we didn't predict its absolute collapse the way it happened." Since then, "with a little more time passing, with another review of the strategy, I think the Base Force served its purpose as a transitional concept coming out of the cold war period" (ibid., 45). In the final year of the Bush administration, Powell reassessed the U.S. force requirements and began planning for deeper cuts under a "Base Force II" initiative. When Aspin arrived in office and incorporated some of the base force II analysis in the bottom-up review, Powell came to view the BUR as "the successor" to the base force, and declared that the BUR's cuts do not impose "any additional risk" to U.S. security (ibid., 45–46).

Another reason Powell supported the BUR was the unattractive nature of the alternative: reject collaboration with Aspin and ask Congress to overturn the review's force reductions. Although Goldwater-Nichols gave Powell the authority to make defense budget recommendations to the secretary, the chairman has no independent authority to impose his suggestions or countermand civilian-proposed force reductions. He can only affect the budget indirectly, by persuading the defense secretary (and ultimately the president) to incorporate his recommendations in the administration's budget request, or by persuading Congress to act on his proposals. And while Goldwater-Nichols enhanced the status and military preeminence of the chairman, his ability to influence Congress depends on the larger political circumstances that shape members' attitudes toward defense. During the Bush administration, legislators were pressing for defense cuts when Powell created the base force; congressional sentiment discouraged end runs by the service leaders and helped Powell win support from Secretary of Defense Cheney. Indeed, partly because of Aspin's efforts in the House Armed Services Committee, Congress imposed cuts beyond those proposed by the chairman and rejected base force recommendations on reserve levels and other issues.

Powell and Aspin faced very different political circumstances when Aspin launched his Pentagon BUR in early 1993. In the aftermath of the controversy over gays in the military, Powell had a receptive bipartisan audience in Congress on that issue and enjoyed especially strong support from Senator Nunn. On the question of defense budget reductions and military restructuring, the situation in early 1993 was less clear-cut. Nunn continued to press for changes in the defense budget and attacked Powell for not going far enough to restructure service roles and missions. In the House, Aspin was replaced as chairman of the Armed Services Committee by Ron Dellums (D-Calif.), who called for much deeper cuts in defense than Clinton had endorsed during the campaign. Support for such cuts extended beyond the Democrats: Rep. John Kasich (R-Ohio) led growing numbers of conservative Republicans who supported defense reductions, not to free up funds for domestic spending but to cut the federal budget deficit. Powell crafted the base force to put a floor on defense cuts and to devise a politically sustainable budget. In accepting the bottom-up review, Powell argued that BUR also offered a force structure that "is achievable with the dollars that I suspect will be available to the Department" (ibid., 37–38).

Congress initially sustained this defense restructuring plan and the political circumstances that facilitated it, even after Aspin and Powell left office. Secretary of Defense William Perry emphasized that the administration's defense budget request for fiscal year 1995 was tailored to implement the bottom-up review. Congress adopted that request with very few modifications, particularly in comparison to the changes imposed on the base force–oriented budgets during the Bush administration. But the Republican takeover of the House and Senate in November 1994 shifted the political circumstances under which the administration had to pursue its defense agenda. How have the changes in Congress affected the prospects for military restructuring and the power relationships between military and civilian authorities?

Defense Restructuring Beyond the Bottom-Up Review

Even before the Republicans gained control of Congress, some legislators were arguing that the Clinton administration had cut defense too deeply. Sen. Robert Dole (R-Kans.) attacked Clinton's defense budget as "dangerous and inadequate," and representatives such as Jim Talent (R-Mo.) and Curtis Weldon (R-Pa.) charged that Clinton's budget cuts had transformed the U.S. military into a "hollow force" (quoted in Gellman 1993a; "GOP Lawmakers" 1994). The drive to increase defense spending gained new impetus from the 1994 Republican triumph on Capitol Hill. In the Contract with America, which Rep. Newt Gingrich (R-Ga.) and his allies offered as their congressional campaign platform, Republicans pledged to increase defense spending. So long as a more supportive congressional environment exists for funding increases, the armed services will also have stronger incentives to make end runs around the administration and seek relief from BUR-imposed force reductions. This shift could even lead to a recurrence of cold war patterns of defense politics, with executive branch civilians proposing cuts in service programs, and the services turning to Congress to defend their programs from attack.

The defense budgets for fiscal years 1996 and 1997 reflected growing legislative support for service priorities. Floyd Spence (R-S.C.), chair of the House National Security Committee (which, in slightly modified form, replaced the Armed Services Committee), led a charge to halt the post–cold war decline in defense spending. Spence and other Republicans attacked the Clinton administration's budget request for fiscal year 1996 as dangerously inadequate. Congress ended up adding $7 billion of unrequested spending to the president's proposal, authorizing a total of $265 billion for defense for fiscal year 1996. While legislators earmarked some of that additional money for the accelerated purchase of weapons already approved under the BUR, other funds (including $494 million for unrequested B-2 bomber procurement) marked a stark rejection of administration plans and budget priorities (Cassata 1995; Towell 1996).

In the debate over the fiscal year 1997 budget, congressional leaders broke still further from the administration and strengthened their reliance on the services as an alternative source of policy guidance. During hearings on defense spending in March 1996, Spence asked each of the service chiefs what they would do with up to $3 billion in additional money for the next fiscal year and invited them to submit written proposals for inclusion in the chairman's mark (i.e., Spence's draft of the budget). The services responded quickly: the army proposed more than $7 billion in additional spending for itself, the navy and air force about $3 billion each, and the marines more than $2 billion (Weiner 1996b). The ensuing authorization bills adopted by the House National Security and Senate Armed Services committees called for a total of $267.3 billion for fiscal year 1997, an increase of $12.9 billion over the president's request. Within that higher ceiling, the committees departed even more sharply from the president's defense priorities than they did in the fiscal year 1996 budget, with a reported 40 percent of the items on the service wish lists excluded from the administration's long-term defense plan (Graham 1996).

But it is too soon to conclude that Congress will put a lasting clamp on defense restructuring. Increases in defense spending do not necessarily reflect a failure to respond to the end of the cold war; Spence and other legislators argued that in funding unrequested weapons (and in calling for more rapid deployment of ballistic missile defenses), they were meeting the new security threats of the post–cold war era. The willingness of Congress to ally itself with the services against administration-sponsored cuts could also erode. Even before the Berlin Wall fell, pressures to cut the federal deficit encouraged legislators to impose repeated reductions in defense after 1985. Barring the rise of a new large-scale threat to U.S. security, service programs could again become a tempting source of cuts in discretionary spending.

More enduring changes have occurred within the Pentagon. Before the enactment of Goldwater-Nichols, the Joint Chiefs of Staff rarely infringed on service autonomy and preferences, adopting "lowest common denominator" policy recommendations hammered out by the services themselves. General Powell's creation of the base force demonstrates just how radically these roles and relationships have changed. Against persistent service opposition, Powell exploited the new authority and military preeminence that Goldwater-Nichols granted him to propose far-reaching force reductions, and he seized a leading role in the Bush administration's effort to create a post–cold war military. And while Powell's successor, Gen. John Shalikashvili, did not play such a politically dominant, visible role during the Clinton administration, he and Vice Chairman Adm. William Owens (who retired in 1996) launched quieter—but potentially momentous—drives to extend their dominance of the military.

Most significant is the effort by Admiral Owens undertook to gain additional control over defense budgeting at the expense of the services. Under Goldwater-Nichols, the vice chairman chairs the Joint Requirements Oversight Council (JROC), which was given the authority to assess joint war-fighting requirements and recommend budget changes to meet them. The JROC did not exploit this potential authority until Admiral Owens took it over. He used the JROC process to make "resolute changes" in defense priorities and to propose shifts in service budget requests to Chairman Shalikashvili (who incorporated those proposals into his own Chairman's Program Assessment) (Holzer and LeSueur 1994b; "The Jane's Interview" 1993; Owens 1994). Owens argued that this process will "provide the Secretary of Defense with a single, authoritative military view of key issues," and "represents the corporate advice of the Nation's military leaders (as distinguished from a compilation of programs advanced by each service)" (Owens 1994, 56–57).

With this growth of joint control over the services and the rise in power of the chairman, the structural problems of defense reform have changed. Prior to Goldwater-Nichols, reform was impeded by the autonomy of the armed services and their ability to defend their entrenched preferences. Today, there is no doubt that a chairman can defeat service interests in pursuit of his overall defense restructuring plan—General Powell proved this was possible. But Goldwater-Nichols does not guarantee that the chairman will take the lead in defense reform. That legislation only ensures he will have a much more powerful voice in defense policy making. What if a future chairman were to use his heightened powers not to promote military restructuring, but to resist it—especially with the assistance of a Republican-controlled Congress?

The history of the bottom-up review demonstrates that even when the chairman and civilian reformers disagree over force reductions, both have political incentives to craft a mutually acceptable compromise. When Aspin arrived at the Pentagon from the House, he brought not only plans for defense cuts beyond those of the base force but a history of political conflict with Powell and the services. Aspin's political relationship with the military worsened even further when he had to deal with Clinton's proposal on gays in the military. Facing the risk that Powell would attack the bottom-up review and encourage Congress to reject its force reductions, Aspin made the goal of winning Powell's support a top priority of the BUR and incorporated the Joint Staff's analytical efforts, which grew out of the base force. That effort was a resounding success: Powell went out of his way to praise the bottom-up review and endorse its cuts, which went beyond his base force recommendations. In return, Powell and the Joint Staff gained significant influence over the BUR and its preservation of the base force's two-war planning assumption.

But Congress has an important influence over these political incentives for cooperation, and over the broader prospects for post–cold war defense reform. As in the Bush and Clinton administrations, Congress will continue to shape the patterns of conflict within the Pentagon, by either rewarding end runs by the services or by acting as the ally of Pentagon reformers. Congress can also continue to use its power of the purse to modify efforts by military or civilian officials to reshape the armed services. Moreover, by enacting legislation such as Goldwater-Nichols, Congress can alter the authority granted to defense policy makers and shift power relationships among them. Congress can also change its own authority over defense budgeting, as it has done by giving the president a line-item veto (which may enable him to obviate end runs by the services). Already, however, Congress has broken the cold war mold of defense politics. The successes, and limitations, of military restructuring reflect the new patterns of conflict and coalition building that Goldwater-Nichols put in place. As the United States grapples with the security threats of the next century, these domestic power relationships—and the pivotal role of Congress in shaping them—will remain critical to defense budget and force structure decision making.

Loch K. Johnson

6. Reinventing the CIA

Strategic Intelligence and the End of the Cold War

Rare are the global sea changes that disrupt the fundamental patterns of world politics. Such a change took place between 1989 and 1991, when the Berlin Wall fell and the Soviet Union came tumbling after. The cold war rivalry between the USSR and the United States, waged with intensity since the close of World War II, had—quite unexpectedly—come to an end.

In this chapter I explore the effects of this upheaval on the Central Intelligence Agency, a secret bureaucracy that engaged in espionage and clandestine warfare against the Soviet empire throughout the cold war. A major research interest shared by the authors of this volume is: How do foreign policy bureaucracies react to a dramatic change in world affairs? In this chapter I ask: What kind of metamorphosis, if any, does a secret intelligence bureaucracy undergo when its chief foreign nemesis suddenly vanishes?

Vectors of Change

In the aftermath of the cold war, a new configuration of threats faced the United States. In some instances, the threats had actually been around for some time, but now came more sharply into focus as the disappearance of the USSR allowed policy officers in Washington to turn their attention toward the rest of the world. Understanding the intentions of the Russian republic, which still possessed a massive arsenal of strategic weaponry, remained an ongoing concern of high priority. Additional perils, immediate or potential, that required attention included the spread of weapons of mass destruction; a set of renegade states, among them Haiti, Iran, Iraq, and North Korea; flourishing drug traffickers; a spate of terrorist organizations, with the radical Islamic factions Hamas and Hezbolah high on the list; a proliferation of international criminal elements operating throughout the former Soviet republics and elsewhere; and erupting ethnic wars that threatened to engulf U.S. security and humanitarian interests, pressingly so in the Balkans (Johnson 1992–1993).

In this world setting, the CIA's managers found themselves subject to a much wider range of requests from policy officers for information and analysis than had been the case during the cold war—a condition the CIA and its twelve companion agencies viewed with ambivalence. On the one hand, the flood of new requirements threatened to overload the nation's finite intelligence capabilities; yet, on the other hand, fresh duties meant a legitimation of the secret agencies, each anxious about its funding and raison d'être now that the Soviet threat had faded into history.

Moreover, at the end of the cold war, politicians in Washington had begun to urge cutbacks in government spending, in the light of widespread concern over spiraling budget deficits and an alarming growth in the national debt—a result in large part of profligate spending during the 1980s. It was a time for government downsizing—an unpleasant prospect for the secret agencies and especially for the CIA, already under attack for failing to predict the collapse of communism.

Further, ever since conducting major investigations into the secret agencies in 1975, Congress had become deeply enmeshed in intelligence policy and was now well positioned to exercise its influence on the CIA's future in the postcommunism era. The White House was another obvious source of opinion and authority on the question of which directions the secret agencies should now take. So too were these agencies themselves, though much of the literature on bureaucracies suggests that their natural instincts would be to resist any serious change in their accustomed way of doing things (Rainey 1996; Rosati, Hagan, and Sampson 1994). In a democracy, the influence of pressure groups cannot be ignored either in any calculus of change. Nor can an influential force outside the government: the media, which would surely have opinions on how to "reinvent" the CIA.

At the level of individual policy officers, one could expect change in the CIA's activities to be shaped by the president and his top national security advisers, by the director of central intelligence (DCI), and by legislative overseers (typically few in number) with an abiding concern for intelligence policy (Johnson 1980, 1996). Occasionally, the leadership of determined, well-placed individuals can produce significant changes in policy; witness the roles of Sen. Barry Goldwater (R-Ariz.) and Rep. Bill Nichols (D-Ala.) in the well-known military reform legislation of 1986 that bears their names. Conversely, an official with little interest in a particular policy might become an obstacle to change through a lack of leadership.

Whither the CIA?

In what direction was the CIA apt to move after the cold war, when confronted with a radically changed international environment, a domestic setting where government budget cutting and downsizing were the norm, and with two chief executives in succession with startlingly different backgrounds—George Bush, the only president to have served as DCI, and Bill Clinton, who had only a peripheral interest and limited experience in foreign policy? Of the many predictions made during this time of transition, four were preeminent.

The first prediction envisioned nothing less than the abolition of the CIA. Influential journalist Seymour Hersh advocated this view with a harsh indictment of the CIA's performance during the cold war (Hersh 1994, 5). He judged it "bumbling," "perfectly irrelevant," "frequently wrong, even disastrously misleading," and, in the wake of the cold war, "probably inconsequential." His denouncement echoed an attack by Sen. Daniel P. Moynihan (D-N.Y.), who opined that the United States no longer needed "the Agency" (as the CIA is known by insiders). The senator recommended that the Department of State handle intelligence matters (Moynihan 1991).

Though less apocalyptic, the second prediction nonetheless envisioned significant reductions in funding for the CIA, comparable to the budget cuts the Pentagon was expected to endure, as policy officers searched for a "peace dividend" now that the arms race with the Soviet Union had ended. Indeed, the Clinton administration sought budget savings across the board for government agencies, a part of its promise to the electorate in the 1992 presidential contest. Vice President Al Gore's National Performance Review called for a 12 percent governmentwide personnel reduction. The clamor to ax the federal budget was even louder on Capitol Hill when the Republicans took over both chambers in 1995 (for the first time in forty years).

Less threatening from the CIA's point of view, a third prediction anticipated that intelligence spending would stay about the same as it was at the end of the cold war. The nature of the Washington budgetary process is widely described as incremental, with the bottom line for various agencies unlikely to fluctuate significantly from year to year—even if world politics change dramatically. According to this perspective, America's new status as the sole reigning superpower would entail the need for continued support of a strong intelligence capability.

More roseate still for the CIA was the fourth prediction: in something of a paradox, the intelligence agencies could actually look forward to an upward surge in responsibilities—and funding—with the end of the cold war (Combest 1995, 4). This happy outcome for intelligence bureaucrats would result from a realization among policy officers that the world remained a dangerous place, despite the end of communism.

Indeed, some reasoned further that the perils confronting the United States had grown even greater. Pent-up regional conflicts were apt to burst the boundaries once held in place by Warsaw and NATO armies in the ideological standoff that characterized the cold war. In lieu of two armed camps led by superpowers, alignments in this new world would be more ambiguous, releasing ethnic and other subnational tensions, a flood of refugees and immigrants fleeing across national lines, and a startling brio among autocrats from Iraq and North Korea to Serbia and Haiti, who would try to take advantage of the preoccupation by the large powers with their own internal economic problems and uncertainty about their international status and objectives. A post–cold war DCI, R. James Woolsey (1993–1994), took the lead in arguing for a spending increase on behalf of the intelligence community. "We live now," he repeatedly stressed, "in a jungle filled with a bewildering variety of poisonous snakes" (Woolsey 1993).

Depending on which of these points of view one accepted, spending on basic CIA activities such as collection and analysis, counterintelligence, and covert action was likely to disappear, decline, remain the same, or rise from the ashes of the cold war. Which of these predictions has proven most accurate as the postcommunist era unfolds?

The Methodology

To answer this question, we need to establish a set of baselines that capture the essential features of the CIA some years before the end of the cold war and some years after. The years selected for this analysis are 1985 through 1996. This allows us a basis for comparison to determine whether change has occurred. Among the most important features to consider are the missions emphasized by the CIA before and after the cold war, especially how it distributed resources among various types of operations; the nations and factions targeted by these operations; its budget, staffing, and organizational permutations; its responses to supervisory bodies among the three branches of government (accountability); and, finally, its relationship with outside pressure groups and the media.

Gaining access to information on intelligence policy making, most of which is held in secret, presented a challenge. I had to rely on methodologies that are more qualitative and less precise than desired; to avoid error, I did extensive interviewing and cross-checking with intelligence professionals (active and retired) and carefully sifted the limited—though expanding—corpus of documentary evidence available in the public domain. Despite the methodological vexations, the CIA is important enough as an instrument of U.S. foreign policy for us to attempt an understanding of its activities. I begin with a primer on the intelligence triad (the key missions of the CIA), then establish the baselines that permit us to appraise the agency's path of evolution over the past decade of upheaval in world affairs.

The Intelligence Triad

The bedrock purpose of the CIA is to guard against another Pearl Harbor, that is, to protect the United States from harmful threats from abroad. Toward this end, the core mission spelled out in the agency's founding statute (the National Security Act of 1947) is the collection, analysis, and coordination of information on foreign affairs. At the heart of this intelligence process is the goal of "eliminating or reducing uncertainty for government decision-makers" (Clapper 1995, 3; see also Berkowitz and Goodman 1989; Ford 1993).

Intelligence collection involves gaining access to information about foreign adversaries. For the most part, this means using open sources, but also entails using human spies (human intelligence or HUMINT; Cline 1976; Johnson 1989; Westerfield 1995) or mechanical means (technical intelligence or TECHINT; Burrows 1986; Brugioni 1993; Richelson 1990).

The CIA quickly embraced a second mission—counterintelligence (CI)—even though it was not mentioned in the founding statute. The secrets gathered by the CIA had to be guarded, and this became the responsibility of CI officers. Beyond establishing basic security measures (fences and guardhouses), CI officers are also charged with carrying out more aggressive operations—for example, penetrating a foreign intelligence service with a mole (counterespionage)—meant to thwart the efforts of adversaries engaged in espionage and harassment operations against the United States (Wise 1992; Zuehlke 1980).

The agency's third, and most controversial, mission is covert action (CA), activities undertaken "to influence events overseas that are intended not to be attributable to this country" (Deutch 1995). This "quiet option" or "special activities," as CA is sometimes called by insiders, consists of secret interference in the affairs of other nations through the use of propaganda, political manipulation, economic disruption, and paramilitary activities—which included assassination attempts in the past (Johnson 1992, 1996; Reisman and Baker 1992; Treverton 1987; Twentieth Century Fund 1992).

To what extent has each of these CIA missions undergone changes from 1985 to 1996? The analysis that follows is based on extensive interviews from 1979 to 1995 with intelligence professionals at all levels of the CIA—well over four hundred (most of whom insisted on anonymity). These interviews have been supplemented by a close search of every major scholarly and reliable journalistic work that deals with the CIA, along with all the unclassified government documents. (See, in particular, U.S. Congress, Senate Select Committee to Study Governmental Operations with Respect to Intelligence Activities 1976; Cline 1976; Colby and Forbath 1978; Darling 1990; Jeffreys-Jones 1989; Johnson 1989, 1996; Karalekas 1976; Marchetti and Marks 1974; U.S. Congress, House Select Committee to Investigate Intelligence Activities 1976; Powers 1979; Prados 1986; Ranelagh 1987; Ransom 1970; Turner 1985; Warner 1994; and, for a thorough bibliography, Lowenthal 1994). From this research, I have attempted to arrive at a judgment regarding the CIA's emphasis on various missions and responsibilities each year since its founding. In making these estimates, I took the sage advice of a historian into account: "The number and extent of the activities undertaken are far less important than the impact which those activities had on the Agency's institutional *identity*—the way people [within the CIA] perceived the Agency's primary mission, and the way policymakers regarded its contribution to the process of government" (Karalekas 1976, 45, emphasis added).

Collection and Analysis

During the last years of the cold war (1985–1991), attention to TECHINT continued to arc upward at a modest rate of progression, as it had done continually since the establishment of the CIA in 1947 (Johnson 1996). Attention to HUMINT was more erratic, descending slightly from 1986 to 1989, then beginning to rise again through the end of the cold war.

Emphasis on analysis followed a path that roughly paralleled, but always remained beneath, HUMINT. Similar to TECHINT (though at a much lower level of emphasis), coordination efforts rose steadily.

In the post–cold war years (1992–1996), attention to TECHINT continued to climb, then experienced a momentary downturn in 1994 before rising again. Following the end of the cold war, attention to HUMINT climbed steadily toward 1996, while the emphasis on analysis first rose, then dipped, then rose again. Interagency coordination efforts continued a slow upward progression.

Each of these activities displayed a modest upward surge of emphasis during the early leadership of John M. Deutch in 1995–1996. Deutch became DCI in January 1995, at a time when Washington officials were expressing ambivalent views about intelligence. On the one hand, they wanted budget cuts and intelligence reform; but on the other, they worried about ongoing and fresh threats to the United States from abroad and the need to maintain a strong intelligence shield. Skillful lobbying by Deutch, along with a growing belief among Republican leaders in Congress (especially in the House of Representatives) that intelligence warranted more support, soon shifted the debate toward enhanced funding for the CIA and the other secret agencies.

The end of the cold war failed to have a profound effect on the CIA's core missions. Some temporary zigzags did take place under Woolsey in 1994, with the dip in support for TECHINT especially noteworthy. Moreover, an upward surge was evident for all the indicators in Deutch's energetic early years. Even in the most noticeable instance of change (the TECHINT descent), the decline in emphasis proved short-lived. And during these transition years, no alteration occurred in the relative status of the four activities, compared to how they fared immediately preceding the fall of communism.

The TECHINT fluctuations that did take place in the wake of the cold war reflect the tension between two contradictory objectives advocated for the secret agencies during these years. One objective was a drawdown in spending on intelligence, associated with the search for a post–cold war peace dividend—the reason for the TECHINT decline in 1994. Yet also visible in the data was a general acceptance by 1996 of James Woolsey's "snake" hypothesis—that the world was an even more dangerous place now, and therefore, that intelligence should have its funding increased.

This inconsistency stands as the hallmark of the Woolsey era at the CIA. He paid special attention to TECHINT, a long-term personal interest of his as a Pentagon official before coming to the agency. Woolsey, however, had to contend with legislators and White House officials who favored government cutbacks, an objective clearly at odds with the DCI's affinity for expensive hardware systems.

Woolsey began his tenure in 1993 with an aggressive bid to increase funding for the intelligence agencies, not only for TECHINT but across the board—a full-fledged advocacy of a more robust intelligence service in the still hostile postcommunist world. Despite the DCI's initial urging, however, the cost-cutting ethos on Capitol Hill proved too strong to overcome; thus, the intelligence budget began to slip from its historical pinnacle of some $26–28 billion per annum in the 1989–1991 period (Weiner 1996a).

Still, Woolsey may have avoided an even more precipitous funding slide by virtue of his strenuous insistence that the United States faced an increasingly hostile world. His trial attorney style of advocacy (perceived by some members of Congress as arrogant and excessively strident) managed, however, to alienate several of the Hill's most prominent intelligence overseers—including the chair of the Senate Select Committee on Intelligence, Dennis DeConcini (D-Ariz.).

While settling initially on a vivid world-as-jungle metaphor to defend agency programs, Woolsey soon found it more prudent to rest his case less on the specter of poisonous snakes loosed upon the world than on what proved to be a more persuasive management rationale. He proceeded to a brief in favor of a short-term funding infusion for intelligence that would permit long-term savings by consolidating intelligence activities (especially TECHINT satellite programs). Congress was clearly in no mood to support increases in military or intelligence budgets in 1992–1994. Neither was the White House for that matter; during elections, politicians in both branches espoused deficit trimming as a major priority. As a consequence, Woolsey was forced to retreat from his dire warnings about "snakes" and to seek refuge in this more viable (if short-term) "better management" defense of the intelligence budget.

The funding surge would produce management efficiencies, insisted the DCI, that would soon reap savings—most notably in a reduced need for costly new satellites as older models were repositioned and assigned new duties (Woolsey 1993a). By 1997, the DCI projected a "50 percent cut in numbers of satellites and much greater than that in the number of ground stations" (ibid.). Also on the TECHINT side, the DCI foresaw a 26 percent personnel reduction in the CIA's Directorate of Science and Technology (DST), along with a reduction of seventeen hundred employees in the agency's technical support services (Woolsey 1994, 8–9).

As for HUMINT staffing, the DCI envisioned a decrease through 1997 in the actual number of case officers, the CIA's handlers of HUMINT agents ("assets") overseas. The Operations Directorate, home of the agency's espionage apparatus, would shrink by seven hundred; and the Intelligence Directorate, home of its analysts, would also experience a staffing decline of one thousand by 1997—a one-third reduction, down to 1977 personnel levels (Woolsey 1994, 7–8). Some of the savings from TECHINT program consolidation would be shifted toward new asset recruitment overseas.

These scheduled changes at the agency were quite sweeping. Emphasis on HUMINT remained relatively stable, however, because at the same time Woolsey emphasized the need to increase asset development overseas. In a roughly equal manner, this emphasis offset the reductions in staffing at headquarters and in the field stations.

Downsizing, then, was to be accompanied by the establishment of a larger number of intelligence collectors in countries the CIA often overlooked during the time of America's fixation on the USSR. The new espionage priorities would include small states that might present a future threat to the United States (near the end of the cold war, the CIA had provided policy officers with insufficient intelligence on Grenada, Panama, Libya, North Korea, and Iraq, among other trouble spots); more macroeconomic espionage (against foreign governments, not foreign business firms), a topic of increasing importance that began to absorb some 40 percent of the collection-and-analysis resources at the beginning of the post–cold war era (compared to less than 10 percent before it); and a panoply of other concerns, ranging from data on environmental threats and global health trends (AIDS, for example) to refugee and narcotics flows (Johnson 1992–1993). Of greatest concern to the CIA's managers was the fear of rampant weapons proliferation, particularly the suspected North Korean atomic bomb program.

Overall, Woolsey froze almost all hiring at the CIA and cut back on staff during his early tenure at twice the 12 percent reductions recommended by the White House (Woolsey 1993a). The agency's personnel figures projected an expected 12 percent "glide path" downward from 1994 through 1997 (Johnson 1992–1993). "We must compensate for these reductions," said the DCI, "with a structure that is flexible and responsive" (Woolsey 1994, 8).

With the arrival of John Deutch as DCI in 1995, Woolsey's blueprints underwent review and revision. A scientist from the Massachusetts Institute of Technology, Deutch was also drawn to TECHINT. In his previous assignment as second in command at the Pentagon, he had been responsible for technology planning in the Department of Defense. The revival of support for TECHINT during 1995–1996 reflected Deutch's interest in mechanical "collection platforms." He also devoted a considerable amount of time in 1995–1996 to setting up a Joint Space Management Board to coordinate expenditures for the construction of spy satellites, and crafted a new National Imaging and Mapping Agency (NIMA) to replace the faltering Central Imaging Office (CIO). (Imagery involves the conversion of TECHINT pictures obtained electronically or by optical means into viewable film, electronic displays, or other forms of media for interpretation by analysts.)

Yet Deutch hardly enjoyed the luxury of full control over planning the CIA's future. He had to take into account reform proposals from congressional committees (e.g., U.S. House Permanent Select Committee on Intelligence 1996), a presidential-legislative commission (Commission on Roles and Capabilities 1996), and various private study groups (among them, the Council on Foreign Relations; Pincus 1996) that strongly favored more HUMINT, more analysts, and greater DCI involvement in the broader "community" of secret agencies. Deutch and President Bill Clinton largely acceded to (and in some instances relished) many of the reform proposals.

Woolsey would probably have taken a similar path had he continued in office. Both men shared the "hostile jungle" perspective on intelligence needs, and an infatuation for satellites and other high-tech platforms. For Woolsey, however, the political movement toward extensive downsizing of the federal government proved an insurmountable juggernaut in 1993–1994, which plowed into the budgets of the CIA (just as it did at the Department of Defense). Forced to bow to these domestic political realities and pressed by Senator DeConcini and others, Woolsey turned to the task of planning and carrying out the intelligence community's downward slide—not happy duty for any agency head.

By the time of Deutch's appointment, however, much of the steam had gone out of the peace dividend movement. Key figures (among others, members of the Commission on Intelligence and the Speaker of the House) began to stress the priority of countering foreign threats over trimming the budget. An imbalanced budget could cause havoc; poisonous snakes could prove fatal. Although Woolsey had by then departed the CIA with low marks, his worldview and budget aspirations had at last prevailed.

The Coordination of Intelligence

The improvement of intelligence coordination was given relatively little emphasis until near the end of the cold war (Johnson 1996). The label intelligence *community* notwithstanding, America's secret agencies have been riven with internal and external divisions over the years. The dissension stems not only from differences in bureaucratic cultures (the CIA's "scholar" analysts in contrast to its covert action "cowboys," for instance), but also from ambiguous chains of command throughout the national security establishment.

The DCI is supposed to be in charge of all the secret agencies, but he soon discovers that the secretary of defense and the chairman of the Joint Chiefs of Staff can be strong rivals (not to say 800-pound gorillas). This is true on matters of tactical and strategic military intelligence—all together, some 85–90 percent of the overall intelligence budget. Sometimes prickly personalities can interfere with interagency cooperation; for a time during the 1960s, the FBI's J. Edgar Hoover refused even to speak to DCI Richard Helms.

Attempts to overcome these centrifugal forces have been frustrating for every DCI (Hastedt 1986–1987; Turner 1985, 1987). Attention to improved interagency coordination, which climbed only glacially from 1947 to 1985 (Johnson 1996), reached one of its more sustained rates of ascent in the last few years of the cold war, as Directors William Casey (1981–1987), William Webster (1987–1991), and Robert Gates (1991–1992)—responding to growing budget constraints and criticism from Capitol Hill about excessive duplication of activities in the intelligence community—began to concentrate more on melding some programs and operations.

As one important step toward overcoming the centrifugal forces in the community, DCI Casey established a Counterterrorism Center (CTC) in 1986 and a Counternarcotics Center (CNC) in 1987, both located at the CIA but composed of intelligence officers from across the community—the first of several so-called fusion centers. In 1988, DCI Webster put in place a Counterintelligence Center (CIC); and, in 1991, DCI Gates created a Nonproliferation Center (NPC), along with a parade of interagency task forces designed to improve intelligence coordination (Gates 1994).

Under Woolsey in the post–cold war era, these efforts aimed at greater communitywide coordination continued. Above all, Woolsey sought closer ties between the CIA and military intelligence, a relationship that had deteriorated over the years. A former DCI recalls that the animosity was fed by a growing "disdain" in the agency for the tendency of military intelligence analysts to propagate inflated "worst case" scenarios of U.S. intelligence requirements (Schlesinger 1994). Woolsey named an admiral as his chief deputy, established an associate deputy director for military affairs within the office of the DCI, and worked with the Department of Defense—not without tensions, and under pressure from Congress—to create and manage jointly the new Central Imagery Office for improved dissemination of imagery intelligence to the battlefield (Conner 1993, 5; Johnson 1992–1993, 64).

John Deutch continued this trend toward the "militarization of intelligence"—in spades, according to some critics. He brought with him to the CIA more uniformed military advisers than had ever been seen on the seventh floor of this proudly independent civilian agency. Deutch's "military mafia" bred resentment among many CIA officers and raised fears that nonmilitary strategic intelligence (including global political and economic matters) no longer had much importance to the DCI, and that it was being supplanted by the military's fixation on tactical intelligence (called in Pentagonese "Support to Military Operations" or SMOs). From the narrower point of view of better coordination, however, the CIA and military intelligence (the bulk of the community) had never been closer—at least at the higher reaches of their respective bureaucracies—thanks to Deutch's close ties to the Pentagon brass (including his former boss, Secretary of Defense William Perry).

During the Woolsey years, moreover, the temporary decline in resources available to the CIA—a function primarily of domestic economic constraints and a fleeting perception that the international threat level had dropped with the fall of the Soviet Union—prodded U.S. intelligence managers to search for some ways of reducing redundancies and cooperating more harmoniously with one another. One of the manifestations was the effort to pool communitywide liaison resources for contacts on Capitol Hill.

Inside the CIA, Deutch continued his predecessor's experiment in "colocating" analysts and operatives, who had once been as resistant to mixture as oil and water. On the agency's seventh floor, Deutch and his military aides waxed enthusiastic about "orchestrating the symphony" of the different parts of the CIA and the larger community, while old hands in the building smiled wryly at recollections of feckless DCI efforts in the past to mesh the secret agencies (CIA officials 1995).

Counterintelligence

Throughout two crucial decades of the cold war (1954–1974), James Angleton headed counterintelligence at the CIA. His unassailable professional and social credentials initially elevated the status of the CI staff, but his increasingly tight managerial control—not to say paranoia—over the security of "his" counterintelligence files soon led to a monastic sequestering of this mission within an isolated suite of offices at agency headquarters (Mangold 1991; Winks 1987; Angleton 1976). Angleton was eventually fired in 1974 and the CI mission entered a phase of decentralization within the CIA.

When the Reagan administration took office in 1981, the CI pendulum started to swing back toward the Angleton principle of centralization, with DCI Casey's emphasis on counterthreat fusion centers for terrorism and narcotics, followed by Webster's and Gates's centers for counterintelligence and nonproliferation. Ironically, this increased attention to a more coordinated response to foreign threats began just as the cold war was coming to an end.

After the cold war, one of the stimuli for counterintelligence change was the realization that Russia's military intelligence service (the GRU) had actually stepped up espionage in the United States since 1989 (Webster 1991; Gates 1994). This discovery reinforced Woolsey's view that the CIA would have to maintain—indeed, increase—its counterspy capabilities. Further, American corporations complained that near the end of the cold war they had become the targets of foreign espionage operations more than ever, and they requested help from the government's counterintelligence specialists (Gates 1992).

While CIA officials eschewed the more controversial assignment of industrial espionage (spying for General Motors), they were prepared to help U.S. firms block espionage operations directed against them by foreign intelligence services. Moreover, the bombing of the Manhattan World Trade Center in 1992 and of the Oklahoma City Federal Building in 1994 reminded anyone who had momentarily forgotten that counterterrorism was still an important responsibility. Moreover, America remained awash in illegal narcotics and could not afford to ignore its counternarcotics defenses.

Counterintelligence and its sister disciplines, counterterrorism and counternarcotics, thus all became growth stocks as the USSR (but not its former intelligence services) disappeared. Above all, the disclosure in 1994 of the counterspy case of Aldrich Ames—the highest-level Soviet mole known to have penetrated the CIA—ensured heightened attention to the CI mission, as executive and congressional investigators sought explanations for this disastrous failure of agency security.

Still, this mission is likely to suffer an attrition of attention; unlike TECHINT, counterintelligence lacks a strong constituency inside and outside the intelligence community. Furthermore, however important it may be, it is poorly understood beyond a small cadre of practitioners and too tedious a discipline to attract sustained focus at high levels.

Covert Action

The CA mission was also never explicitly mentioned in the CIA's founding statute. Nevertheless, it has grown in prestige and support inside the agency, from its very beginnings in 1947 through the Korean War in 1950–1953 and the Vietnam War in 1968–1970, to its apogee in the covert anticommunist crusades of the Reagan administration (Johnson 1996). As the conflict in Vietnam soured, covert action went into sharp decline, reinforced by spending cuts introduced by the Nixon administration at the insistence of the powerful House Appropriations chairman George McMahon (D-Tex.). The agency's funding fell from $5 billion in 1969 to $3 billion by 1973 (Schlesinger interview 1994). Also contributing to the decline were the tentative overtures by Nixon toward détente with the USSR and the widespread criticism of special activities—perhaps most notably with respect to CIA operations against Chile's democratically elected president Salvador Allende, disclosed in 1974 (Treverton 1987).

Interest in covert action resumed during the latter days of the Carter administration, following the Soviet invasion of Afghanistan, and especially during the Reagan administration, when the infatuation with a secret fix to America's foreign irritants soared to record levels (chiefly as a result of operations in Afghanistan and Nicaragua). After the Iran-contra scandal, however, the Reagan administration shied away from this approach; and, though President George Bush (1994) has acknowledged he found the quiet option "useful," funding for CA dropped during his presidency, eventually to less than 1 percent of the agency's total budget (Woolsey 1993a). The funding for covert action rose under President Clinton, though still to less than 2 percent of the total CIA budget (ibid.), as it gained some currency as an instrument in the CIA's struggle against its most publicly avowed bête noire—weapons proliferation. In addition, covert action was part of the administration's failed effort in 1994 to drive the Haitian junta out of power, without a U.S. military invasion.

Covert action was the change indicator that registered the greatest decline in emphasis during the years studied in this analysis. The sharply reduced reliance on CA during the Bush and Clinton administrations matched its previous low ebb, reached during 1977–1978, when a wary, reformist president Carter (suspicious of the CIA to begin with) drove this option gingerly and with the brakes on—until the Afghan invasion in 1979 shocked the president into taking a darker view of Soviet global intentions.

Regardless of the present low standing of covert action—though 1–2 percent of an estimated CIA budget of about $3.1 billion (Smith 1996) is more than pocket change—the third option has proven its resilience and may well rise again in coming years, perhaps attracting ever larger percentages of the intelligence budget in the war against weapons proliferation. "I believe that the U.S. needs to maintain, and perhaps even expand, covert action as a policy tool," DCI Deutch declared early in his tenure (1995).

Thus, waiting in the wings for presidents and DCIs with a penchant for direct secret action stand all the beguiling forms of CA, from covert propaganda to clandestine political and economic activities aimed at criminal arms merchants, and even paramilitary operations to destroy weapons production sites. In addition, future presidents may be drawn to these secret instruments for crusades against human rights abuses abroad, or against gangsterism and renewed totalitarian impulses in the former Soviet republics.

Other Vectors of Change

Additional sources of influence over the future direction of the CIA include its relationship with supervisory bodies within the government (in particular, Congress and the White House), its own internal culture, and its relationship with two important outside entities: pressure groups and the media.

Accountability

By constitutional design, the executive branch shares powers with Congress. While this can lead to frustration and inefficiency, the virtue of the arrangement lies in the accountability that sharing provides—including a prudent look over the shoulder of executive bureaucrats by congressional supervisors, a monitoring or review known by the awkward term "oversight."

In terms of oversight, the CIA has not been a part of the government throughout most of its history. It stood outside the traditional framework of checks and balances. Members of Congress deferred to the expertise of intelligence officers in the arcane realm of secret activities, and preferred in any case to avoid responsibility for errant operations such as the Bay of Pigs in 1961 (Johnson 1985). As former DCI James R. Schlesinger, recalls: "One time [in 1973] I went up to the Hill and said, 'Mr. Chairman [John Stennis, D-Miss. of the Senate Armed Services Committee's Subcommittee on Intelligence Oversight], I want to tell you about some of our programs.' To which the Senator quickly replied: 'No, no, my boy, don't tell me. Just go ahead and do it—but I don't want to know!'" (Schlesinger 1994).

With little scrutiny, the leaders of the armed services committees in both chambers quietly folded funds for the CIA into the Defense Department's annual appropriations bill. Nor did the presidency offer reliable accountability. Members of the National Security Council rarely saw the agency's budget (Johnson 1985); and many of the CIA's activities (including aggressive CA and CI operations) never received a thorough examination—or, in some cases, even approval—by the NSC (U.S. Congress, Senate Select Committee to Study Governmental Operations with Respect to Intelligence Activities 1976).

In December 1974, all this changed when the *New York Times* revealed that the CIA had spied on American citizens during the Vietnam War era (Operation CHAOS) and, further, that the agency had tried to topple the constitutionally elected president of Chile, Salvador Allende. While Congress may have dismissed the revelations about covert action in Chile as so much cold war politics as usual, spying on American citizens—voters—was an allegation difficult for legislators to shrug off. Blazing newspaper headlines demanded oversight, not overlook. Both the executive and legislative branches launched investigations during this "year of intelligence," or "intelligence wars," as some embittered CIA officers call this traumatic time (Johnson 1989; Olmsted 1996; Smist 1990).

The end result was a new era of closer supervision for the intelligence community, replete with permanent full committees on intelligence oversight in both chambers of Congress and an Intelligence Oversight Board attached to the Office of the Presidency. Some CIA officials looked upon this tightened control with dismay and anger. "Micromanagement!" became their battle cry. Many liked the idea of sharing the burden of their responsibilities with members of Congress, however. I asked each of the DCIs who served from 1966 (Richard Helms) through 1994 (R. James Woolsey) their opinions on the new oversight system. Among the eight intelligence chiefs, only Helms and William J. Casey viewed the new arrangements as an inappropriate incursion into executive prerogative. Indeed, several of the others—and especially William Colby, Adm. Stansfield Turner, and Robert Gates—expressed frustration with the unwillingness of legislative overseers to take their duties more seriously. Whatever one's view of the merits of the new oversight, one thing is clear: the CIA had become a part of the government (Treverton 1990).

In the years that followed, congressional oversight fluctuated from this high point in 1975–1976 as a function of how dedicated individual overseers were toward their supervisory responsibilities and of how often (and persuasively) the media reported incidents of wrongdoing by the CIA. Generally, however, the level of oversight remained relatively high—compared, at any rate, to its near absence in the earlier era of benign neglect. Legislative overseers slacked off during the first half of the Reagan administration; but the Iran-contra affair, revealed by a Middle East newspaper, snapped them back to the job.

In response to the Iran-contra scandal, a joint House-Senate committee investigated how administration officials had successfully bypassed the new system of oversight. Congress subsequently enacted legislation to draw the supervisory strings even tighter. Among the new laws was a provision to revamp the responsibilities of the CIA's inspector general, requiring Senate confirmation hearings for this important office and more regular reporting by the IG to Congress (Fisher 1988; Kaiser 1994). Legislators also enacted the 1991 Intelligence Oversight Act, clarifying and for the most part strengthening accountability for covert actions (Conner 1993).

Despite the ups and downs of congressional attention to intelligence review, the overall trend during the latter stages of the cold war was clear: intelligence policy had entered an era of partnership between Congress and the executive branch. As one DCI put it, the CIA now found itself poised equidistant between the two branches—and sometimes leaned toward the legislature (Gates 1992, 1994). In the 1986–1990 period, the number of CIA briefings to the congressional oversight committees, individual members, and staffers shot up from a few hundred per year to 1,040 in 1986; 1,064 in 1987; 1,044 in 1988; 947 in 1989; 1,012 in 1990; and 1,000 in 1991 (Johnson 1992–1993, 67; senior CIA official, personal communication 1991). The number of written reports sent to Congress (most of them classified) has also increased sharply since 1986. In 1991 alone, 7,000 intelligence reports went to Capitol Hill (Johnson 1992–1993, 67).

This frequency of contact has accelerated into the post–cold war era. In 1993, 1,512 meetings took place between members of Congress and the CIA's legislative liaison staff, along with 154 one-on-one or small-group meetings between legislators and the DCI, 26 congressional hearings with the DCI as a witness, 128 hearings with other CIA witnesses, 317 other contacts with legislators, and 887 meetings and contacts with legislative staff—a 29 percent increase over 1992. In 1993, the agency also provided 4,976 classified documents to legislators, along with 4,668 unclassified documents and 233 responses to constituency inquiries (CIA deputy director for congressional affairs, personal communication 1994).

Another sign of a more serious effort to monitor the CIA and keep American citizens informed of at least some of its activities was the series of congressional hearings held from 1991 to 1994, in which CIA witnesses testified in public—a rarity during the cold war (Johnson 1996). DCI Woolsey appeared in eight open hearings in 1993, whereas in previous years—even after the congressional investigations of 1975 and calls for greater openness—DCIs often never appeared in public hearings during an entire session of Congress or, if they did testify, never appeared more than once or twice. The upshot was that the agency now had two masters—the president and the Congress—and sometimes even a third (Manget 1995), as the courts increasingly adjudicated intelligence-related litigation and regularly examined requests for electronic surveillance warrants against national security targets (mandated by the Foreign Intelligence Surveillance Act of 1978).

The degree of CIA openness should not be overstated. Congress was still kept in the dark on key aspects of intelligence policy, which was startlingly underscored in 1994. Legislators learned only through a chance audit that the National Reconnaissance Office (NRO, the most secretive member of the intelligence community, responsible for the supervision of satellite manufacturing and launching) had engaged in cost overruns amounting to $159 million for its new headquarters in the Virginia countryside. Subsequent reports in 1995–1996 revealed that the NRO had also concealed from Congress a $4 billion slush fund of accumulated appropriations ("Keys to the Spy Kingdom" 1996). Moreover, in 1995 it came to light that the CIA had failed to report to Congress (as required by law) its ties with a controversial military colonel in Guatemala, Julio Roberto Alpirez, suspected of involvement in the murder of an American citizen there, and in the death of a Guatemalan man married to an American citizen (Weiner 1995a).

The CIA's degree of openness, then, has been a relative matter in the post–cold war period. Moreover, the tightening of oversight procedures came about chiefly as a result of revelations concerning the violation of U.S. domestic laws, not because of changes in the world situation.

The White House

The ties between the White House and the CIA throughout the period examined here can be summarized more briefly. During the Reagan years the agency enjoyed a particularly close relationship with the White House, primarily because DCI Casey was a personal friend of the president and had served as his national campaign manager. Casey became the first DCI ever appointed to the cabinet. Furthermore, Reagan supported Casey's enthusiasm for secretly countering the influence of the Soviet Union (which the president in the middle of his tenure labeled the "evil empire"). Unfortunately, the free rein given to the agency led to excesses such as the Iran-contra scandal.

Under Bush, the CIA had the luxury of a chief executive who understood and appreciated intelligence as well as anyone who had served in the nation's highest office (Andrew 1995). Bush was also sympathetic to most of the agency's funding requests, though he did wind down covert action.

The Clinton administration was quite a different matter, characterized by a relative inattentiveness to foreign policy (at least in its early years). Intelligence snafus in Somalia during the administration's first significant foreign policy crisis—a failure to understand the intentions, or even the whereabouts, of the Somalia tribal leader Gen. Mohamed Farah Aideed—raised doubts among NSC officials regarding the usefulness of the CIA (Aspin 1994).

In 1994, prodded by Secretary of Defense Les Aspin, Vice President Al Gore, and National Security Adviser Anthony Lake, President Clinton decided to establish a presidential commission on the roles and capabilities of the intelligence community—his first expression of interest in the direction the CIA should take during his tenure (ibid.). Sen. John Warner (R-Va.), however, had in mind quite a different commission: a legislative probe whose main purpose would be to reassure the American people that the CIA was an effective organization and needed to be preserved, not abolished or even substantially downsized. The Senate Intelligence Committee (of which Warner was a member) accepted his view and pushed for a purely congressional panel of inquiry.

The eventual compromise was a law passed in 1994 that established a joint presidential-congressional panel, called the Commission on the Roles and Capabilities of the United States Intelligence Community. The law authorized President Clinton to select nine members of the commission (all from the president's Foreign Intelligence Advisory Board, including its chair and the new commission's chair, Les Aspin), and congressional leaders from both parties selected the remaining eight members (Senator Warner among them). The commission began its work in March 1995 and, when Aspin died in May, he was replaced by another former secretary of defense, Harold Brown.

The report issued by the commission in March 1996 largely met Warner's objective. Rather than recommend sweeping reforms, the blue-ribbon panel—the first major probe into intelligence policy in twenty years—extolled the good work of the secret agencies, kept its budget intact, offered a few modest suggestions for improvement, and disappeared as a footnote to history (Commission on the Roles and Capabilities 1996).

Perhaps its most enduring legacy was the attempt to help John Deutch expand his powers over the community by recommending that the DCI have joint approval (along with the relevant department secretaries) over all intelligence agency directors. The commission further recommended that the DCI be given greater authority over communitywide budget decisions—though the individual intelligence agencies were likely to fight against these proposals, drawing upon the assistance of powerful allies in the Congress. As Deutch himself conceded in a private memorandum for the president, "Not surprisingly, the Secretary of Defense, the Secretary of State, the Attorney General and the Director of the FBI offer arguments, many cogent, against broadening the DCI's authority over appointments" (Deutch 1996a, 3).

The CIA as a Bureaucracy

The CIA's own reaction to change has appeared throughout this analysis, but a more specific word is in order on the question of internal bureaucratic resistance to change. To some observers, resistance remained evident in the agency at a deep structural level. A lawsuit brought by a woman case officer who felt she had been discriminated against on the basis of gender, for instance, argued that the CIA continued to be a bastion of "white male chauvinists" (National Public Radio 1994). The validity of this assertion aside, promotions for women and people of color in the agency rose slowly during the 1985–1994 period. "Minorities are still underrepresented in the Agency's work force," DCI Woolsey conceded, "and the advancement of women and minorities is still limited"—though he said he intended to improve the situation during his tenure (quoted in Weiner 1994a).

When Deutch took over, he made a concerted effort to place women in high office in the community. He named a woman as the agency's executive director and significantly expanded the powers of this office; and, for the first time, a woman was chosen to head a CIA directorate (for science and technology).

The cultural tensions between analysts and case officers proved a more tangled knot for Woolsey and Deutch. During the cold war, the dominant cultural ethos inside the CIA favored the clandestine side of the intelligence business: spying on the Soviets and conducting aggressive covert actions against their surrogates in other nations. In contrast, several of the

CIA's earliest leaders expressed disdain toward the brainy Ph.D. analysts while relishing the brawny officers overseas who recruited agents and (at least in the mythology) scaled walls at midnight with daggers in their teeth. Analysts and case officers traveled two separate career paths, with little interaction between the pale thought of one and the red-blooded action in the war against communism of the other.

To address this cultural bifurcation, Woolsey experimented with the concept of "co-location": placing analysts and operatives in the same suite of offices so they could work together more directly and get to know each other. Most important, the analysts could better inform the operatives about the kinds of information policy officers needed in estimates and other intelligence reports; and operatives, with rich field experience, could also critique the interpretations reached by analysts about events and conditions in the world.

Deutch continued this experiment, despite rising criticism that this "partnership" would undermine the purity of the analytic product through contamination by action-oriented operatives with field programs to defend. Deutch also named as head of the Operations Directorate the senior analyst in the Intelligence Directorate, who had never run an agent overseas—another first that did not sit well with many operatives.

Thus, changes have occurred in the internal structure of the CIA since the end of the cold war. The idea that federal agencies are so encrusted with tradition and fixed ways of doing business that they are unable to respond to new circumstances is far too glib a view of bureaucratic dynamics. Recall that in 1969, Chairman Mahon told the CIA to cut $2 billion to reduce bureaucratic bloat from the Vietnam War era—or else. And it did, quickly. Two decades later, when Congress again insisted on cutbacks, the CIA—having lost its "snakes" argument—began once again to comply with the prevailing cost-cutting sentiment in Congress. What other choice was available—particularly with a president unwilling to fight for increased intelligence spending?

As noted by former DCI Robert Gates (whose tenure bridged the two eras examined here):

> Bureaucracy is more responsive than almost anybody thinks on the outside, whether it is from self-preservation or what. There has been a *massive* [original emphasis] reallocation of resources inside CIA, because of the end of the Cold War. Take our last budget for FY 1993; in that whole budget, only 13 per cent of CIA's resources were directed against the former Soviet Union [compared to some 65 percent during the cold war—and more at times]. Huge reassignments of people have taken place. We took scores of scientists and engineers

> out of the old Office of Scientific and Weapons Research—took them off the Soviet weapons program and put them on to proliferation. And that kind of thing has happened throughout the Agency. (Gates 1994)

In tune with much of the recent scholarly literature on the subject (Rainey 1996; Rosati et al. 1994), Gates adamantly rejects the view that large government agencies—including the CIA—suffer hopelessly from inertia. "They're smarter bureaucrats than that," he observes. "You won't survive in this day and age if you do that; Congress will have your lunch. You also won't be able to respond to the questions that are being asked, as opposed to the questions that once were asked" (Gates 1994).

Gates, however, enjoyed unusual advantages, among them a close relationship with President Bush. He had worked between two and three hours a day with him for three years as deputy national security adviser, before moving back to the CIA as DCI. His close access continued and, as he recalls, the relationship had an "extraordinary" effect on his ability to gain leverage over others with whom he had to negotiate in the government, including key legislative overseers. "My ability to do deals with [David] Boren [D-Okla., chairman of the Senate Select Committee on Intelligence] on legislation—particularly in cases where [Secretary of Defense Dick] Cheney didn't like [what the intelligence community sought] was really phenomenal" (ibid.).

Gates remembers using the Hill for leverage over the intelligence community, and vice versa. "Boren and [David] McCurdy [D-Okla., chairman of the House Permanent Select Committee on Intelligence] and I conspired a fair amount [in deciding what direction to take the secret agencies into the new era]. Gates continues:

> I was able to go back to these people in the [intelligence] community and I'd say, "You've got two choices: you can do it my way, in which case you have a part in the say, or they [members of Congress] are going to tell you how to do it. They're going to go further in most of these things than I am, and they're probably not going to do it smart. We can do it smart, and we can do it radically enough that they will retreat on their legislation." (Ibid.)

In Gates's view, this is exactly what happened. "Boren rewrote his bill [the 1991 Intelligence Oversight Act], in effect to write into law what I wanted," the former DCI recalls, "and McCurdy receded altogether. So I used the Hill against the community, and that worked pretty well" (ibid.).

Two additional aspects of the CIA as a bureaucracy are worth examining: its physical growth during the period under consideration, and changes in its internal organization. Floor space provides one of the most tangible measures of growth or decline for an organization. From its barrackslike, makeshift quarters along the Mall Reflecting Pool in Washington during its early days, the CIA moved into a fabulous new building in Langley, Virginia, in 1961—one manifestation of Allen Dulles's clout in the Eisenhower administration (where his brother served as secretary of state).

Until near the end of the U.S.-Soviet standoff, the agency's headquarters at Langley changed little, not only in its physical plant but also in its basic organizational structure. The CIA's five units remained the office of the DCI and four directorates: administration, intelligence, operations, and science and technology.

The names of some organizational units changed from time to time and fluctuations have occurred in the emphasis placed on the main intelligence missions; but not until the tenures of DCIs Casey and Webster during the Reagan years did the CIA significantly expand its physical facilities and begin to experiment with major internal structural reforms. The physical expansion consisted of a second headquarters building at Langley, behind the original one—a vast, modern edifice of steel and green-tinted glass begun in 1984 and completed in 1989, with a bronze tribute to William Casey in the foyer and a transplanted graffiti-laced segment of the Berlin Wall by its side.

The primary internal reforms included a new—and, it would prove, short-lived—Directorate for Planning (1988–1992), a strengthened community management staff (CMS) established by DCI Gates to replace the intelligence community staff (which had an ineffectual record of interagency cooperation), and the series of "fusion centers" already mentioned. Like the CMS, the centers are housed at the CIA and an overwhelming majority of the professionals assigned to them are agency officers. The number of non-CIA personnel is slowly increasing in both the CMS and the centers, however, and these entities seem to represent a good faith effort by DCIs to reach out to the other intelligence agencies in search of better cooperation and coordination.

Moreover, the Ames case led to a presidential decision directive (PDD 24) that revamped counterintelligence structures in the community (Woolsey 1994, 2–3). The government now has a National Counterintelligence Policy Board set up within the framework of the NSC; and an FBI officer has been appointed director of a new interagency National Counterintelligence Center at CIA headquarters.

Adding to the confusion in this hasty effort by the Clinton administration to appear responsive to criticism over the Ames case, another FBI official became chief of the Counterespionage Group in the CIA's own Counterintelligence Center; and one or more CIA officers will assume duties at the FBI's National Security Division to work on counterintelligence at bureau headquarters in Washington. Whether this is all window dressing, an unworkable tangle of staff responsibilities, a security morass that has James Angleton spinning in his grave, or a wise restructuring that will lead to more harmonious interagency cooperation remains a matter of dispute.

Interest Groups and the Media

Just as the CIA stood aloof from government overseers for most of the cold war, its effort to keep secrets from foreign adversaries (manifested most obviously in the barbwire fences and guardhouses around its perimeter) also keeps it insulated from the other usual forces of pluralism in American society. A graph registering the presence of interest groups advocating specific intelligence policies, or one that traced CIA lobbying on its own behalf (as with the Pentagon or the FBI), would run practically flat—until 1975, when the agency found itself under siege by government and media investigators.

In that year, a senior intelligence officer resigned from the CIA to establish the Association of Retired Intelligence Officers (ARIO). The purpose, embraced by a large number of former intelligence officials who quickly swelled ARIO's ranks, was to lobby legislators and the American people on behalf of the secret agencies. Other pressure groups came into existence soon after, some for and some against the CIA. In yet another way, the CIA had become a part of the government and politics as usual. Still, compared to the extensive outreach and large war chests of most successful lobbying groups in the United States, those concerned with intelligence policy remained relatively small in number and modestly funded throughout the cold war years.

As the Pentagon's budget began to ebb after the cold war, however, industrial leaders cast an eye toward ongoing intelligence needs for espionage hardware—especially sophisticated satellites—as replacements for dwindling tank, ship, and aircraft contracts (Kohler 1994). Members of Congress in districts with weapons plants—and jobs at risk—have been solicited for assistance in procuring TECHINT deals, as they were once solicited to acquire Department of Defense contracts and to forestall base closures. The end of the cold war had ushered classic interest group politics into the once pristine domain of intelligence policy (Mintz 1995).

In the wake of the searing investigations of 1975, intelligence managers had begun to understand a lesson already well learned by the FBI and the Pentagon, namely, the importance of defending (read selling) one's programs on Capitol Hill through lobbying efforts (euphemistically known in Washington as "legislative liaison"). The number of attorneys in the agency's Office of General Counsel soared from two in 1974 to sixty-five in 1994; and the Office of Congressional Affairs expanded as well, from two staffers in 1974 to over a dozen in 1994. Forced (somewhat) out into the open by the *Times* allegations of illegalities in 1974, the CIA began to devote additional resources to its public defense, in the manner of most other government agencies.

As for the media, journalists continue to provide the public with the most telling information on the abuse of power by the CIA, whether based on leaks or skillful investigative probing—usually a combination of both. Yet, even though the media have served as an indispensable safeguard for democracy over the years, reporters have hardly been an infallible check on improprieties (Johnson 1989). The agency's fortress has proven largely inviolable to outsiders, including the media corps. This has changed little since the end of the cold war, though CIA officials have been slightly more forthcoming in their public release of selected documents from the organization's early history, including analytic papers on the USSR in the 1950s and documents on the Cuban missile crisis (see Deutch 1996b; Hedley 1994; "U.S. Spy Satellite Photos Go Public" 1995, 8).

With its subpoena powers, budget review, control of the CIA's purse strings, and the capacity to focus public attention with public hearings, the Congress remains the strongest *potential* intelligence overseer in the post–cold war era. This potential rests, however, on whether its members have the will to perform these vital duties—and the record is mixed so far (Johnson 1996).

Conclusion

One might expect the collapse of an imposing empire such as the USSR to bring in its wake dramatic changes in other parts of the world as well, even within the government of its arch rival, the United States. This surprising event did indeed set off several vectors of change for the CIA.

Responding to the new era, the agency instituted a number of fresh policies, reducing its concentration somewhat on technical intelligence while shifting resources incrementally toward the further development of human spy networks in regions beyond the old Soviet Union. A large portion of both types of collection systems—TECHINT and HUMINT—are now being reoriented toward formerly slighted targets in the developing world (in particular, unfriendly microstates harboring military ambitions) and away from saturation coverage of the former Soviet republics, whose current openness makes clandestine coverage less necessary.

Further, the agency has begun to be more concerned with analysis than with covert action—a victory for the thinkers over the "snake eaters" (slang from the Vietnam War days for paramilitary officers who crawled through the jungles on village raids). The CIA also began to focus more attention on improving the coordination of its activities with its companion agencies. This initiative was in part a cost-saving move in times of fiscal stress; but, more important, it reflected John Deutch's skill in elevating the authority of the DCI and the widely felt sense (stemming from intelligence malfunctions in the Persian Gulf War and Somalia) that the community lacked sufficient interagency synergism.

Paradoxically, the CIA increased its attention to counterintelligence after the cold war. This belated response was a result of ongoing—indeed stepped-up—foreign espionage in the United States (despite the cold war's end), a resurgence of terrorist incidents and ongoing narco-terrorist trafficking, and above all, the revelation of serious security lapses at the CIA, which were exposed by the Ames case. Facing a diminishing need to combat Soviet intelligence agencies in wars of liberation throughout the developing world, the CIA began (at the direction of a Reagan-Bush White House, recoiling from the Iran-contra blowup) to wind down its covert actions well before the fall of the Soviet Union. This minimal emphasis on "special activities" has continued, with covert action accounting for only a small portion of the CIA's annual budget by 1992 and rising only slightly under President Clinton.

Under DCI Woolsey, the overall intelligence budget underwent a momentary upward surge to consolidate collection platforms, then began a decline, accompanied by a 12 percent drop in agency personnel. As political sentiment shifted from cutting the intelligence budget toward preserving America's intelligence capacity to warn against foreign dangers, Woolsey's successor, John Deutch, reaped support for a renewed emphasis on TECHINT, HUMINT, analysis, and augmented DCI authority over the community. It was not the feast of the Reagan era, but Deutch also did not face the belt-tightening that Woolsey had to endure following his program to consolidate collection platforms.

Spurred by lingering resentment over the Iran-contra abuses, then the Ames shock, and a general feeling that the intelligence community needed housecleaning (suggested by NRO fiscal irresponsibility and intelligence failures in Iraq and Somalia), executive and legislative overseers sought a tighter rein over intelligence policy. In 1991, Congress passed significant oversight provisions, and, from 1990 to 1994 held a series of public hearings on intelligence. In 1994, President Clinton and the Congress created a special commission to recommend new directions for U.S. intelligence policy. At the same time, in the ongoing Washington tug-of-war between saving and spending, some legislators joined with defense contractors to lobby on behalf of expensive TECHINT acquisitions; the end of the cold war witnessed the beginning of interest group politics for the secret agencies.

Thus, the demise of the Soviet Union was hardly the only influence bringing about changes at the CIA. Several of the agency's most significant policy departures came in the very midst of the cold war. Covert action began a sharp decline during 1970, shot up to its highest levels of emphasis during the Reagan defense buildup, began to plummet after Iran-contra (two years before the Berlin Wall fell), and continued downward during the Bush administration, matching its lowest levels since the early Carter years. The end of the cold war simply accelerated covert action's downward slide.

Despite the useful reminder from DCI Gates that bureaucracies can react to a changing environment, the forces of bureaucratic inertia—Newton's first law applied to politics—cannot be dismissed altogether. In 1992, DCI Woolsey initially advocated budget increases at a time of economic retrenchment, in part because that is the expected role of agency heads; to have done otherwise would have invited sagging morale at the CIA—or outright rebellion, as a besieged DCI Stansfield Turner discovered when he cut back the agency's clandestine personnel slots during the Carter administration.

Moreover, scandal can play a significant role in organizational change. The CIA's chilling involvement in domestic spying (disclosed in 1974 in the midst of the cold war) and in the Iran-contra affair (1987) did more to bring about serious changes in intelligence accountability than anything associated with the end of the superpower rivalry (though the events that led to the scandals were themselves offshoots of an overzealous pursuit of cold war objectives).

Finally, changes at the CIA during the early stages of the postcommunist world were affected as much by the state of the U.S. domestic economy as by anything else. This condition was influenced, to be sure, by the perception of a declining external threat. And in turn, this persuaded government officials in 1992–1994 that they could safely direct their attentions toward roping in runaway deficits—a fleeting sentiment.

The original research question was: Has the end of the cold war brought changes to the CIA? The answer is an unequivocal yes: in the agency's metamorphosis, world events—including the end of the cold war—have exercised an influence on intelligence policy at home. So, however, have domestic economic distress and a complicated interplay of institutional and group demands, scandals, bureaucratic mores, and the personal predilections of a range of individual policy officials from DCIs to presidents and legislative overseers—the rich mix of variables that makes the study of politics both frustrating and fascinating.

Kimberly Marten Zisk

7. The Threat of the Soviet Decline

The CIA, The Joint Chiefs of Staff, and the End of the Cold War

Why do some organizations adapt quickly and easily to radical change in the environment, while others struggle against change and thus respond sluggishly? I attempt a partial answer to that question by examining the differing responses of two American security organizations—the Joint Chiefs of Staff (JCS) and the Directorate of Intelligence (DI) at the Central Intelligence Agency—to the changes in their operating environments caused by the collapse of the USSR and the emergence of an independent Russia. Three questions will orient this discussion. First, to what extent was flexibility in a changing environment either limited or enhanced by structural organizational characteristics? Second, how important were particular individuals in creating or blocking the conditions for effective reaction to change? Third, did change in the international environment either cause organizational change or act as a further catalyst to organizational change that was already under way? As we examine these three questions across two cases, we should gain a greater understanding of how domestic and international factors interact to cause change in U.S. government organizations.

The JCS, under the leadership of chairmen Adm. William Crowe and Gen. Colin Powell, orchestrated the transformation of the basic mission of U.S. military forces. In remarkably quick order, strategic military planning was reoriented from its forty-year focus on the Soviet superpower threat to contingency planning for various threats in formerly peripheral areas.

Crowe actively contributed to the decline in the U.S. perception of a Soviet threat through his support of military-to-military contacts between the United States and Russia. These contacts are continuing now at the bilateral level as American and Russian military troops plan joint military exercises. They are ensconced even more firmly as a vital component of the U.S. relationship with other former Soviet states and former members of the Warsaw Pact. Later, Powell spearheaded the effort to reshape U.S. force structures away from the old Soviet threat to a new regionalism, and he is credited with working with field commanders to overcome the inertia of existing service interests. The JCS worked to point the reluctant U.S. security bureaucracy in a new direction.

The analytic arm of the CIA, in contrast, gained a reputation in the late 1980s for inflexibility and an unwillingness to let the Soviet threat go. Former secretary of state George Shultz (1993, 864) remembers the CIA as follows:

> When Gorbachev first appeared at the helm, the CIA said he was "just talk," just another Soviet attempt to deceive us. As that line became increasingly untenable, the CIA changed its tune: Gorbachev was serious about change, but the Soviet Union had a powerfully entrenched and largely successful system that was incapable of being changed, so Gorbachev would fail in his attempt to change it. When it became evident that the Soviet Union was, in fact, changing, the CIA line was that the changes wouldn't really make a difference.

In Senate hearings in fall 1991 on the nomination of Robert Gates to be director of central intelligence, the CIA was publicly chastised for its failure to predict Soviet upheaval. Gates in particular was accused by some of fitting the intelligence product to meet the preexisting beliefs of hard-line CIA managers (U.S. Congress, Senate Select Committee on Intelligence 1991; hereafter SSCI). An in-depth review of DI output during the Gorbachev years, written by Kirsten Lundberg (1994) with CIA support, demonstrates that at least some DI analysts did in fact unearth trends, beginning in the early 1980s, indicating that radical change in the Soviet Union and in Soviet foreign policy was a possibility. Yet much of this analysis was not forcefully communicated to policy makers. For example, an important 1988 paper, predicting that the Soviet Union might undertake unilateral defense spending cuts to ease its economic burdens, reportedly spent almost nine months languishing in the internal CIA publication process and was virtually ignored when finally released to policy makers because it did not accord with their predominant views. Lundberg (1994, 28) quotes Douglas MacEachin, then chief of SOVA (the Office of Soviet Analysis, the DI division responsible for analyzing the Soviet Union) as saying: "Nobody was standing up to the Reagan administration." DI analysts were doing their jobs well, but the directorate as a whole seems to have been ineffective in the face of a changing strategic environment. While leaders of the organization reacted to change in Russia, they did so only after the organization faced domestic political pressure to change.

Why were the responses to change in the international system so different from each other in the two organizations? There are a great many differences between the JCS and the CIA as organizations (see U.S. Congress, Senate Committee on Armed Services 1985, hereafter SCAS; Breckinridge 1986, 7–53; Gentry 1993, 5–17). The JCS was created during World War II to direct the U.S. war effort; since it predated the cold war, the JCS had a history of adapting to new missions (Huntington 1994). The CIA, on the other hand, was created through the National Security Act of 1947. At its very first meeting, the National Security Council instructed the CIA to "undertake covert psychological operations against Soviet programs" (Breckinridge 1986, 31), thereby establishing the CIA's cold war mission. As one senior official recently said, "If there hadn't been a Soviet Union, there wouldn't have been a CIA, at least not of the type it was." The need to obtain information about an adversary whose borders and society were closed determined the development of the CIA's secretive, compartmentalized, and Soviet-oriented structure and procedures.

Beyond this difference in historical experiences, the policy missions of the two organizations differ. The JCS is responsible for strategic planning and for the establishment and oversight of joint military command structures; it also serves as the principal military adviser to the president. The DI's primary responsibility, in contrast, is to provide intelligence judgments to the president and other senior policy makers; it is explicitly not designed as a policy-making organ. In the past, the DI and the Directorate of Operations (DO)—the arm of the CIA responsible both for the covert collection of information and for other covert activities that might be considered policy making—were almost completely disconnected. The analytic arm of the CIA thus played little if any direct operational role. The focus of the JCS is thus much more operational than that of the DI, even though its advisory role to some extent parallels the DI's mission.

Yet despite these obvious differences, there were clear similarities between the two organizations as they entered the mid-1980s, similarities that should have made both organizations conservative in their outlook and therefore capable of adapting only with difficulty to radical change in the international environment. Both spent the forty-odd years of the cold war focused primarily on the Soviet threat, and thus should have found the prospect of that threat's disappearance disquieting to their organizational purposes. Both had little if any direct contact with actual Soviets or with life in the USSR before the glasnost of the Gorbachev era. In the case of the CIA, this again reflected the disconnection between the DI and the DO; for the JCS, this was because the military-to-military contacts program began only in 1987. Thus both were equally apt to suffer from too heavy a reliance on secondhand information in forming their analyses. Both were characterized by strict hierarchical personnel structures, which tend to inhibit the expression of unconventional ideas. Both were dominated by a community of inside professionals, whose shared background training should have fostered a more homogeneous outlook than is found in open organizations with varied memberships. Further, neither organization appeared to have entered this period with a sense that it was under threat from competitors for either missions or resources; the Reagan-era focus on "peace through strength" should have made members of both organizations feel secure in their traditional, hard-line views of the Soviet threat.

In fact, it is widely accepted among organization theorists that most organizations tend to follow in the grooves set by past behavior (Cyert and March 1963; March and Olsen 1989). Organizations that are accustomed to facing constant radical change in the environment will develop procedures for reacting effectively to such change (March 1981; Rosenau 1986), but there is no reason to expect less challenged organizations to adopt such procedures. Given the unchanging nature of the forty-year perceived Soviet threat, and given their comfortable resource bases, there is no reason to expect that either the JCS or the CIA would have had built-in procedures for reacting quickly to radically changed environments.

Presumably, when previously unchallenged organizations face a radically new environment, those with a pattern of promoting innovative thinking are likely to adapt best. Ingrained structures that foster conservatism are not usually associated with adaptability in the face of radical change. The structural factors we might associate with organizational innovation (Walker 1981, 86) appear in fact to have been absent from both the JCS and the CIA in the mid-1980s. Innovative organizations tend to give their members autonomy from retribution for the expression of unconventional ideas, a characteristic usually lacking in very hierarchical organizations such as the JCS and the CIA; they tend to promote the wide circulation of ideas among both insiders and outsiders, a process difficult to achieve in a closed professional environment such as that characterizing the JCS and the CIA; and innovation tends to occur most in organizations that need to compete to survive, a prospect that neither the JCS nor the CIA had to face during the Reagan years.

Given the set of characteristics outlined above, it is therefore not surprising that the DI was so slow to react to change in the Soviet Union. It simply was not structured to be an innovative organization. What is surprising is that the JCS overcame similar structural circumstances to be on the leading edge of recent change in U.S. security policy.

Given these crucial organizational similarities between the JCS and the CIA at the beginning of the Gorbachev era, it is probable that one of the key explanations for the different performances of the two organizations in succeeding years was the fact that the organizational structure of the JCS was undergoing drastic change at the same time that the Soviet Union was undergoing its own revolution. A critical factor explaining JCS adaptability in reacting to change in the Soviet Union seems to have been the Goldwater-Nichols Defense Reorganization Act of 1986, which was designed to overcome years of criticism about JCS performance. The CIA, and the DI in particular, did not undergo any major structural changes at this time that would have overcome its innate conservatism. Since 1991, however, major changes have occurred in DI.

The CIA Directorate of Intelligence

Any discussion of the DI in the middle to late 1980s must recognize the newly revealed fact that Soviet mole Aldrich Ames introduced "illusory threats" into the material received and disseminated by DI analysts beginning around 1986 (Weiner 1995b). Undoubtedly, Ames's actions complicated the CIA's efforts to respond to the decline of the Soviet threat, and it would be unfair to single out the DI for blame (even if we believe that counterintelligence should have prevented Ames's success). But many of the apparent shortcomings in the output of the DI began before Ames's work for Moscow.

Those shortcomings were first made apparent with the accusations aired in the 1991 Senate hearings on Robert Gates's appointment as director of central intelligence. Several DI employees and senators accused Gates, as well as the late Bill Casey (the DCI under whom Gates had worked as deputy director for intelligence, or DDI, the chief of CIA analysis), of politicizing the intelligence product to make it fit President Reagan's conservative foreign and military policy agenda. On one side of the debate were half a dozen detractors of Gates from inside the agency, who claimed that he hurt DI morale by quashing analyses that did not match Casey's views. On the other side were half a dozen Gates supporters, also from inside the agency, who claimed that the detractors were malcontents with personal axes to grind, and who cited numerous examples of Gates's willingness to stand up to Casey and to take independent analytic positions (SSCI 1991).

There is no way for an outsider to determine which side's arguments have the most truth behind them. There were clearly personal antagonisms influencing the testimony on both sides. While the Senate did vote to confirm Gates as DCI, some prominent senators objected that the evidence of politicization was too strong for them to support Gates's promotion (see statement of Ernest Hollings, SSCI 1991, 218), indicating that even those who had access to classified testimony were unable to reach agreement on the issue.

Regardless of whether Gates as an individual played a positive or negative role at the DI, the hearings did clearly lead to one incontrovertible conclusion: morale inside the DI was poor throughout the 1980s, particularly in SOVA (renamed the Office of Slavic and Eurasian Analysis, or OSE, in 1992). Perhaps the best evidence of a morale problem within the DI was the high level of personnel turnover at midlevel positions, which one reporter outside the agency has called a "hemorrhage of the CIA's brightest minds" (Perry 1992, 404). Perry estimates that 20 percent of all SOVA analysts left between 1984 and 1987, arguably a key period for analyzing change in the USSR. According to John Gentry (1993, 59–60), a DI analyst who resigned in anger over the agency's personnel oversight and review policies, a 1991 survey within SOVA about employees' feelings revealed that "18 of 22 respondents sa[id] they would move to another division if they could." Gentry is a former army officer with a reputation for conservatism, and his own letter of resignation, widely circulated within DI, is said to have caused an uproar (Perry 1992, 402–03), though senior officials point out he never worked in SOVA himself.

According to Jennifer Glaudemans, a former SOVA analyst who testified at the Gates hearings (SSCI 1991, 161–62), SOVA went through disruptive reorganizations at least five times during the 1980s; the resulting personnel dislocations, in her words, created "a break [*sic*] on the flow of papers getting out of SOVA Third World Division." As the Gates hearings revealed, the Third World Division was a particularly important source of information about change in the Soviet Union. It was here that reports began surfacing (and some say, were quashed) in the early 1980s, saying that the Soviet Union could no longer afford to maintain its current level of military influence abroad, and that therefore significant change in the direction of Soviet foreign policy might be forthcoming.

A major part of the SOVA morale problem seems to have been infighting between the SOVA office and "the Seventh Floor," agency lingo for the top CIA managers. The Seventh Floor apparently believed that the SOVA analysts "had too benign a view of the USSR," (SSCI 1991, 102) while many SOVA analysts believed that the Seventh Floor had been blinded to change in the direction of Soviet foreign policy by Reagan's cold war agenda. According to Melvin Goodman, the former SOVA analyst who made the strongest attack against Gates at his nomination hearings (and in fact, the leader of an anti-Gates faction within DI), top DI managers believed that SOVA had a "counterculture" that was hostile to the Seventh Floor, leading to continual conflicts (SSCI 1991, 103). Graham Fuller, former National Intelligence Officer (NIO) for the Near East and South Asia, may have summed up the views of many of the more conservative Seventh Floor managers when he said: "Many SOVA analysts may perhaps have been expert on Soviet writings on Third World issues, but few of them had gotten their feet dirty . . . in the dust of the Third World, had not watched Soviet embassies work abroad" (SSCI 1991, 103). In other words, to the Seventh Floor, SOVA analysts seemed naive. Wayne Limberg, a SOVA branch chief, testified that Gates "let it be known that he suspected SOVA and that its work was subject to special scrutiny. The result was that morale fell, production declined, and analysts, rightly or wrongly, began to censor themselves," leading to less creative analysis (SSCI 1991, 103). The negative energy moved in both directions. Former SOVA chief Douglas MacEachin (who later became DDI himself) testified that SOVA failed to predict the Soviet invasions of both Czechoslovakia in 1968 and Afghanistan in 1979, partly because of "our hang up in internal debates. . . . We routinely got bogged down in an internal contest as to whose views would win the institutional place" (SSCI 1991, 205). John Hibbits, a SOVA analyst, added that relations between SOVA and the National Intelligence Council (NIC, the team responsible for drafting the National Intelligence Estimate) were "adversarial rather than collegial," with the Seventh Floor frequently sending back SOVA analysis for significant substantive changes (SSCI 1991, 107).

This situation brings us to the first structural lesson to be learned from the morale problem within the DI: ingrained rivalries over the content of output within an organization lead to loss of productivity and creativity. When factions become institutionalized, people focus too much attention on proving their own views correct and on defending themselves from perceived internal enemies. Objectivity and innovation are lost as subgroups within the organization become hostile to each other, and the potential for cross-fertilization of ideas and perspectives declines precipitously. Regardless of who is at fault in the beginning, factionalism can expand to destroy an organization from within.

A particular feature of the DI exacerbated this factional antagonism: its stringent hierarchical structure. According to a former CIA analyst (Ott 1993–1994, 140), each piece of analysis had to go through eight layers of review before it landed outside the DI. Gentry (1993, 21–29) describes a typical example of such review in excruciating detail. At each of the review points, the analysis could be bounced back all the way to the original analyst with demands ranging from minor editorial restructuring to a major substantive rewrite, and sometimes with the demand that the analyst reach the opposite conclusion of the one originally put forward.

Some employees of the agency, such as thirty-two-year veteran Arthur Hulnick (1991, 91), defended this process as an absolute necessity, which "tends to eliminate personal biases, prejudice and policy advocacy." Gentry notes, however, that the hierarchy of analytic review within the agency was identical to the hierarchy of promotion decisions, with the same set of supervisors responsible for both decisions. The fact that the reviewers were the same people who would determine the analyst's career advancement path tempted employees to "craft analysis heavily to serve senior Agency officials" (Gentry 1993, 29), especially in an atmosphere where analysts believed that complaints against their supervisors would merely result in their being labeled "malcontents" (ibid., 35).

In the Gates hearings, the accusation against the Seventh Floor that seemed to carry the most weight was not that intelligence output was politicized by the desire to please the president or other outside officials, but that output was largely shaped by the preexisting beliefs of the senior DI managers. Repeatedly, analysts spoke of their need to censor themselves to avoid the wrath of the Seventh Floor. Analysts claimed that their views on a wide variety of subjects—including whether the Soviets were responsible for the 1981 assassination attempt against Pope John Paul II (SOVA thought they were not), and whether or not terrorists financed by Syria, Libya, and Iran were actually supported by Moscow (again, SOVA thought no)—were first requested and then ignored or overturned further up the hierarchical chain. Outsiders who were known in advance to support the Seventh Floor's more hard-line views were brought in to duplicate SOVA efforts (SSCI 1991, 107, 126); internal DI criticisms of papers in circulation among policy makers were not publicized (ibid., 114–15); and SOVA analysts were reportedly not allowed to put "footnotes," or statements of counterfindings and criticisms, on reports (ibid., 126, 131).

SOVA analysts began to feel their work was wasted. The feeling was so strong and so well known within the agency that in 1988, an internal inspector general's report was commissioned to determine whether politicization of intelligence in fact existed within DI. The report concluded that while no direct evidence of politicization could be found, the perception that such politicization existed was rampant (SSCI 1991, 104 and 161). Thus, while no evidence indicated that any manager had knowingly impeded the intelligence process, the intelligence process was probably being impeded. People who were closest to the evidence, particularly those with unorthodox views, were either afraid to stick to their guns against their supervisors, or were shot down by midlevel supervisors afraid to let controversial analysis reach the Seventh Floor.

George Shultz (1993, 710–11) mentions in his memoirs that he noticed this. As secretary of state, he held informal Saturday policy discussions that included junior analysts, and he writes that he learned more from those informal discussions than he did from the formal reports that crossed his desk every morning. According to Shultz, "I saw [at these sessions] that there was at least healthy ferment in the agency." Continuing the enzyme metaphor, Marvin Ott, the former senior analyst, seconds the claim that the review process led to bland formal analysis: "It is Cheez Whiz rather than sharp Cheddar" (1993–1994, 141).

The negative consequences of this atmosphere bring us to the second structural lesson for those wishing to create organizations that can react quickly to changing environments: there needs to be an institutionalized mechanism allowing disagreement on important points to be incorporated into the product that reaches decision makers, without punishment for the dissenters. Presenting a false appearance of unanimity can degrade both the quality of the immediate product and the morale within the organization, leading to a spiral of counterproductive self-censorship. Analysts are certainly subject to personal biases and prejudices, but then again, so are senior managers. Letting debate show is probably the best way to keep everyone honest.

A final condition within the DI that limited its ability to respond to change was the set of constraints placed on analysts' contact with outsiders. The CIA itself was extremely compartmentalized, according to most reports; in particular, the DI and DO were separated from each other and viewed each other as competitors. Former operations officer Charles G. Cogan (1993a) argues that the DI and DO have opposing organizational cultures. There was almost no career mobility across the two directorates; someone with experience on the ground in the USSR was unlikely to become an analyst of Soviet politics. According to Ott (1993–

1994, 144), "in the early 1980s it was not atypical to have a DI branch chief for a major East European country who had never set foot in that country and spoke none of the local languages."

It is widely rumored that previous contact with actual Soviets or other citizens of potentially hostile countries (for example, during area studies field research at graduate school) severely hampered the clearance procedure for analysts. If these rumors are correct, it would indicate that the less experience one had with a country under study, the better the chance of passing the screening test and being hired. In addition to the initial screening procedure, analysts are supposed to undergo a full polygraph examination once every five years; according to the popular press reports on the Aldrich Ames case, every CIA employee who travels abroad is also supposed to undergo interrogation upon return. (In reality, it is doubtful there are sufficient personnel resources to perform these exams.) According to Ott, "The more professional (or even social) contacts one has outside the agency, the more likely one will have trouble with the polygraph—further reinforcing the insularity at Langley" (1993, 94, 144). The polygraph test has a reputation for arbitrariness. It thus might seem rational to analysts to avoid any behavior, however innocent, that could be subject to polygraph questioning.

Ott (1993–1994, 145) also claims there has been little effort to welcome midcareer outsiders such as academics into the agency in positions of responsibility. While the CIA has always turned to scholars for consultation on particular issues, it is unclear whether these outside views had a significant impact on classified analysis in the 1980s, especially if they disagreed with the position of the Seventh Floor. Overall, the DI appears to have been fairly isolated.

Clearly, an organization that is by its very nature secretive faces a dilemma on these points. It is unlikely that someone could live for months at a time in a foreign country, as many area studies graduate students and academics do, without developing friendships there in addition to a wide circle of acquaintances. Such relationships must make background checks a nightmare to complete, especially since in the Soviet era it was safe to assume that every foreigner would encounter a KGB agent or two during a visit, even if the foreigner was never aware of it. At the same time, a good argument can be made that until one has spent time in a country such as the Soviet Union and gotten to know individual citizens, a thorough understanding of the society is impossible. Similarly, the more contact one has with area specialists in various nongovernment positions—including international businessmen and journalists as well as academics—the better informed one's judgments about that area is likely to be, even if one does encounter a foreign agent or two among the lot.

It appears that Gates expended a good deal of effort and political capital on this particular problem. Gates was responsible for at least two programs that may have overcome the isolation of DI to some degree. First, he approved an unusual unclassified cooperative research project with Harvard University's Kennedy School of Government in 1987, designed to encourage outside researchers and agency insiders to work together to improve CIA communication with policy makers, and to understand why communication problems had occurred in the past (Gelbspan and Ackerman 1987). Outside academic specialists are also regularly brought in on issue-specific panels, for day-long brainstorming sessions with CIA analysts. (One senior official noted that it is currently difficult for DI to go beyond this point and bring in academics as long-term visiting scholars, since that entails payment of a salary that would eat up the agency's already stretched personnel budget.) Second, Gates worked to create so-called fusion centers, where members of the operations, intelligence, and technical directorates would work together on substantive issues, including counterproliferation and the drug trade (Cogan 1993b). Presumably, this will not only overcome the past compartmentalization of much of the agency's work, but will also provide analysts with more direct contact with those who have worked on the ground in foreign countries.

Furthermore, according to senior officials, throughout the 1980s increasing emphasis was put on placing DI analysts in overseas embassy stations, especially in eastern Europe. What started out as a program to replace the State Department's foreign service officers on summer leave has since become an institutionalized opportunity for analysts to obtain operational experience. In addition, senior officials are pleased that about half of all OSE analysts now have a working knowledge of Russian, a situation encouraged by the priority placed on language instruction within DI during Gates's tenure as director of central intelligence.

Senior officials nonetheless believe that the most important changes in the DI came in spring 1993, after Gates's departure as director of central intelligence. In particular, one senior official confirms that despite the positive changes Gates introduced, the review process he kept in place over analytic output was "suffocating." Political correctness, this official claims, was "communicated through body language, if not direct orders." The DI head office had final say regarding whether any paper longer than three pages went out from the agency. Publication of such papers was a prerequisite for promotion, and thus if an analyst misjudged what the Seventh Floor wanted, it could "muck up [the analyst's] life."

Under new rules implemented in March 1993, mandatory Seventh Floor review of finished products was eliminated. Now such review occurs only if the DI or assistant director directly ordered the product, or if the production component itself requests such review on a particularly sensitive topic. In the year following the rule change, according to then-DDI Douglas J. MacEachin, only about a dozen products underwent such review (MacEachin 1994, 6–7).

Furthermore, rules for promotion inside DI have been undergoing change. MacEachin (1994, 4–5) describes how under the old system, promotion value was placed on long, analytic, academic papers that passed the Seventh Floor review process. Now, in contrast, the DI has consciously adopted the precepts of the "total quality management" business style, and wants to base promotion on responsiveness to the needs of the intelligence customer—the policy maker. This customer is likely to already know a fair amount about many subjects under study, and is very likely over the course of a career to have developed ingrained, independent views on most issues (Heymann 1985; Johnson 1989, 63–64; Lowenthal 1992a). Thus, the DI analyst must provide "value added." Senior officials say that outside academic area specialists and on-site news reporters are already providing high-quality, long-term, contingency-based analysis of issues; DI analysts should be rewarded for filling in the blanks with secret information and passing on the crucial missing links to the customer in a way that responds to the customer's immediate needs. These officials are proud that in 1994, OSE did 83 percent of its intelligence in response to a policy maker's request for information on a specific issue. They cite this as evidence that performance standards are no longer set by arbitrary, internal criteria.

Senior officials hoped these changes would eventually lead to improved morale. Morale certainly plummeted in the early to middle 1990s. In response to budget cuts, and in anticipation of further cuts, DI personnel levels as a whole were to be downsized by 17.5 percent, and the offices most responsible for post-Soviet analysis were taking the hardest hits. OSE was slated to be reduced by 42 percent between 1992 and 1997. While it was hoped that these decreases would occur through buyouts, retirement, and attrition, there was a new climate of fear about job security throughout DI. Senior officials note that it is psychologically difficult for Soviet analysts to go from being the center of attention (SOVA was the largest office in DI, even though it was the only office to cover only one country) to being the office hardest hit by budget cuts.

The content of OSE analysis has simultaneously undergone drastic change. More than 70 percent of SOVA effort was directed at military analysis, often based on hard signals and photographic data. Now, according to senior officials, the effort is equally divided among military, political, and economic analysis, and the kind of softer data required is far different from what most analysts were used to handling in the past. Increased responsiveness to the immediate demands of particular customers has also meant that analysts skilled in so-called academic writing—longer papers written on highly specialized themes and involving weeks or months of background research—have had to adjust to new economic realities. Senior officials note that increased responsiveness to customers, changed analytic requirements, and decreased personnel resources have all hit at once. They nonetheless hope that the heavy workload and uncertain future are balanced by the new opportunity analysts have to express their findings honestly and to engage in meaningful debate.

The reform process within the CIA can provide one additional lesson about making organizations more responsive to changing environments: there must be a push for such reforms from within the organization, not merely from outside policy makers, and reformist ideas must particularly take root among those who have responsibility for personnel advancement. This is a concept familiar to those who have studied reform in military organizations, for example (Davis 1966–1967; Snyder 1984; Rosen 1991; Zisk 1993). It seems to be borne out by the recent history of CIA reform attempts. Director of Central Intelligence William Webster is said to have ordered six studies of the morale problem at the CIA during his tenure in the Bush administration (Perry 1992, 404). But because he lacked experience in intelligence work—he was widely thought among analysts not to be interested in foreign policy—he failed to gain much support for reform even among those within the agency who were themselves reformers (Perry 1992, 323–24 and 407; Gentry 1993, 50 and 121 n. 82). It was an insider, Robert Gates, who despite his controversial history within the agency seemed most able to achieve the internal consensus necessary to begin the pursuit of reform efforts. Later Douglas MacEachin, head of SOVA during one of its most difficult years, was the insider who spearheaded the overhaul of procedures within DI.

What is perhaps the most interesting finding from conversations with senior officials is that change in the Soviet Union and Russia is not seen as the primary source of change within DI. According to one official, it was the Gates hearings themselves that galvanized the internal reform effort. Everyone knew that changes were necessary, he argues, but it was the Gates hearings that brought them to the "jumping-off point." This senior official calls the hearings, arguably one of the toughest challenges the agency ever faced until that point, a "catharsis." Obviously, the scrutiny that was turned on the agency because of the Aldrich Ames case is now acting as an even stronger impetus to major structural transformation. Change in the Soviet Union and Russia allowed the spring 1993 reorganization to take place, but it is seen as more of a catalyst than a cause of reform. The same argument is also heard among Pentagon officials about change in the Joint Chiefs of Staff.

The Joint Chiefs of Staff and the Goldwater-Nichols Reform

While the list of problems faced by the Joint Chiefs of Staff in the early 1980s does not exactly match that of the DI, there are remarkable similarities in the criticisms that were leveled against each organization. For decades, various blue-ribbon panels had recommended reform of the JCS system, and all the panels cited very similar shortcomings within the existing system. The major problem cited was that rivalries among the various military services dominated JCS decision making.

The JCS is made up of the chiefs of staff of each of the individual services—army, air force, navy, and marines—plus a chairman appointed by the president (Goldwater-Nichols added a vice chairman). Supporting these members is the Joint Staff, a large organization of military personnel divided into functional directorates.

There is almost universal agreement that, before Goldwater-Nichols was implemented, the interests of the individual services dominated the JCS. The chairman set the agenda for JCS meetings and presided over those meetings, but he had no statutory authority to communicate to the president anything other than the corporate views of the JCS (SCAS 1985, 151). Given that the JCS found it difficult to reach agreement on many important policy issues, this often meant that the advice communicated to the president was very limited. Furthermore, since interests were communicated and benefits bestowed at the service level, the most talented officers tended to be promoted within their individual services, and were usually not rotated into the Joint Staff. The Joint Staff, according to one official, was a "backwater."

While there is no indication that the JCS was riddled with the kind of personal animosities or low morale that permeated the DI, the effects of interservice rivalry on the JCS do parallel many of the criticisms made about the effectiveness of the DI (SCAS 1985, 157–79). The JCS was perceived to have focused its efforts on competition between the services rather than on joint military planning. Many observers, including both JCS insiders and outsiders, noted a resulting inability in the JCS to achieve either fiscal restraint in arms acquisition or rational unified planning in military theaters. Thus, as in the DI, institutionalized factionalism led to ingrained patterns of competitive behavior, making it harder for the organization as a whole to adapt to changing circumstances.

Furthermore, as in the case of Shultz's complaints about the quality of information received from DI, many observers lamented that the perceived need to present a unified front among conflicting service interests made JCS advice to the executive branch bland and muddy (see Trainor 1986). In the words of former JCS chairman Gen. David Jones, "The corporate advice provided by the Joint Chiefs of Staff is not crisp, timely, very useful, or very influential. And that advice is often watered down and issues are papered over in the interest of achieving unanimity" (quoted in SCAS 1985, 158). The JCS, like the DI, appeared to be producing Cheez Whiz.

As mentioned above, multiple expert panels, meeting as early as 1949 and continuing through the early 1980s, found the same problems cropping up in the JCS over and over again. While there was much talk about the need to reform the system, nothing of much substance had ever been accomplished. According to Rep. Richard White (D-Tex.), chair of the Subcommittee on Investigations of the House Armed Services Committee (U.S. Congress, House Committee on Armed Services 1982, 2; hereafter HCAS), a major factor impeding the adoption of reform proposals was that they tended to come from civilian outsiders. As in the case of the DI, reformers needed to be insiders to obtain organizational support for their programs.

This appears to be one of the primary reasons for the success of the Goldwater-Nichols Act. The act followed on the heels of recommendations made by JCS Chairman Jones. Both Jones, while serving as JCS chairman, and Gen. Edward Meyer, while serving as army chief of staff on the JCS, published articles in 1982 calling for a major restructuring of the JCS system. Both wanted to strengthen considerably the power and authority of the chairman over the chiefs, and both wanted to encourage officers to obtain more joint service experience before moving up their individual service hierarchies. This is precisely what Goldwater-Nichols did (see Davis 1991).

Under Goldwater-Nichols, the JCS chairman became, as an individual, the top uniformed military adviser to the president. Consensus among the service chiefs was no longer required for that advice to be given, and the

JCS officially became merely a "committee of advisers" to the chairman. The chairman was also given new responsibility as an individual for oversight of the eleven joint unified and specified theater commands. Ironically, then, the institution of more hierarchy can actually improve organizational innovation, as long as the person sitting at the top of the hierarchy is an innovator.

It might be argued that to promote innovative thinking, competition between organizations is necessary, and therefore that competition among the services keeps them on their toes. Since JCS reform lessened that competition, the argument would go, it may have actually detracted from the innovative capacity of American military forces. However, under Goldwater-Nichols, any service chief who disagrees with the chairman's advice can still gain separate access to the executive branch (or, in terms familiar to the DI, can take a footnote). This serves as a necessary balance to the strengthening of the top of the pyramid. If, at some future point, a mistake is made and a closed-minded bureaucrat somehow receives the chairman's post, innovative service chiefs have a means to circumvent him.

Under Goldwater-Nichols, a record of outstanding joint service work (in military terms, "purple-suiting") became for the first time a prerequisite for promotion to the senior officer corps. Practically overnight, joint service went from being a backwater assignment to being the center stage, as the brightest young people in the military were funneled in that direction. It was suddenly in the interests of the individual services to encourage their best officers to think jointly, since only jointly oriented officers would be allowed top service positions. Pentagon officials agree that the quality of Joint Staff personnel improved dramatically as a result of Goldwater-Nichols, and they refer to the Joint Staff proudly as "a superb instrument" and the "best staff in Washington." There are persistent rumors that at least one service, the air force, puts personnel returning from the Joint Staff through "re-bluing sessions" to wash off the purple hue. Nonetheless, the ability of the services to work jointly at an operational level has vastly improved in recent years; the successful pursuit of the 1991 Persian Gulf War is clear evidence of that fact.

Jones was careful to build support for his ideas internally within the military before he made his proposals public (Hadley 1988, 22). He commissioned a study on JCS effectiveness and reform by a panel of retired JCS officers, believing they would provide an objective view of JCS problems while being shielded by their retirement from institutional pressures (HCAS 1982, 47). Certainly there was far from universal support for his proposals within the military. Both Adm. Thomas Hayward, chief of naval operations, and Gen. Robert Barrow, marine commandant, testified against the reform proposals, claiming they would create a U.S. General Staff system with loss of civilian control over the uniformed military (HCAS 1982, 103, 196). Yet Air Force Chief of Staff Gen. Lew Allen Jr. joined Meyer in supporting Jones's plan (HCAS 1982, 178). Four years later, when personnel had changed and the Goldwater-Nichols bill was under discussion in Congress, service objections heated up, and each JCS member and armed service secretary actually wrote letters of protest to Sen. Barry Goldwater (R-Ariz.), complaining about the loss of power for the individual services ("Changes Draw Protests" 1986). The new chairman, Adm. William Crowe, nonetheless made it known that he was, in the words of one observer, a "discreet" ally of reform proponents ("Changes Draw Protests" 1986). Thus, while approval within the military was far from overwhelming, a sufficient number of powerful and respected current and former JCS officers gave their support to ensure that the reforms would be implemented after they were adopted. Maj.-Gen. Howard D. Graves, the deputy director of the Joint Staff, reported a "new attitude" within the JCS after the Goldwater-Nichols reform (quoted in Halloran 1986): "Before we were struggling for consensus. Now the word is to solve problems and get things done."

While there was initially some criticism of the slow pace of implementation of Goldwater-Nichols reforms (see Blackwell and Blechman 1990a; Hammond 1990; Trainor 1989), on the key issues that interest us here—the quality of advice given to the president by the chairman, and especially, the action taken by the JCS in regard to change in the Soviet Union—there seems to be fairly universal agreement that Goldwater-Nichols was a smashing success (Davis 1991; Hilton 1990). Freed from the burden of having to pass recommendations through the service chiefs, Crowe first, and Powell even more strongly, moved forward quickly with innovative ideas.

Before the implementation of Goldwater-Nichols, the JCS kept a low profile on sensitive political issues. For example, while the JCS had believed that the United States should respect the arms limitations of the unratified SALT II treaty in the early 1980s, disputing President Reagan's position on the issue, they chose to remove themselves from the debate rather than press the matter (Gordon 1986). Yet by March 1987, within six months of the signing of the act, Crowe was actively advising Secretary of State Shultz in Shultz's capacity as a National Security Council member, angering Defense Secretary Caspar Weinberger in the process, who wanted control over who received Crowe's advice. Crowe was quoted as saying that now he had "more opportunity and authority to cut through some of the bureaucratic problems" (quoted in Halloran 1987b).

Within a year, Crowe had made history by reaching out to Soviet Chief of the General Staff Marshal Sergei Akhromeev, inviting him to breakfast in at his office at the Pentagon, with only interpreters present, at the time of the INF treaty signing (Halloran 1987a). In December 1987, Crowe characterized Akhromeev, who at the time was still one of his chief cold war enemies (the Soviets had showed no public signs of dismantling the Warsaw Pact, there had as yet been no free elections in the USSR, and Soviet troops were still fighting in Afghanistan), as "straight-forward, candid, [and] nonpolemical." The two discussed the possibility of establishing regular military-to-military meetings and programs between the two sides, and of signing a protocol on avoiding dangerous military incidents. By July 1988, these plans had been formalized in a two-year program of military exchanges, and in the establishment of a working group on avoiding unintended military confrontations during routine patrols and exercises (Gordon 1988).

Crowe did not act alone. Maj. Gen. George Lee Butler, first as vice director and then as director of J-5 (the Strategic Plans and Policy Directorate of the Joint Staff), acted forcefully to articulate his vision of a declining Soviet threat and a new need for regionalism in U.S. military planning. Butler also headed the negotiation team for the agreement on the prevention of dangerous military activities (Jaffe 1993, 6–9). Furthermore, military-to-military activities had to be negotiated within the U.S. foreign policy bureaucracy, and according to Pentagon officials, this involved sometimes acrimonious discussions with representatives from the State Department who disliked the notion of a separate military channel of diplomacy. Yet Crowe was by all accounts a pioneer and was willing to fight hard against civilians in the Reagan administration who thought that such overtures to the Soviets were dangerous (Campbell 1991, 54–56). Under his post–Goldwater-Nichols leadership, the JCS also argued against the pursuit of Star Wars technology, for the preservation of the ABM treaty, and for U.S.-Soviet negotiations to curb short-range missile development in Europe—in each case, against administration civilian hawks (Cushman 1988; Gordon 1989). It is clear that Goldwater-Nichols gave the chairman a stronger voice on issues relating to change in the U.S.-Soviet security relationship.

Many government officials, including both those currently in the Pentagon and those who have since retired, agree that despite Crowe's achievements, it was Powell who, working with Butler, truly used the power of Goldwater-Nichols to lead and implement the strategic changes designed to retain U.S. military effectiveness in a new international environment. During Crowe's tenure, the traditional concept of forward defense against the Soviet Union in Europe began to be modified to allow for greater regional flexibility and to deal with expected budget cuts (Jaffe 1993, 2–10). However, Crowe is widely seen among knowledgeable officials as a transitional figure in JCS change, a chairman who did not "push the envelope" on what Goldwater-Nichols could accomplish. Some explain this by pointing to his personality, which tended toward consensus building; others note that he had to try to implement Goldwater-Nichols with the Joint Chiefs of Staff and the staff personnel that had served with him before the reform, most of whom were opposed to it. Still others suspect that because Crowe put so much effort into the Soviet military-to-military relationship he did not have sufficient time or energy to concentrate on other Goldwater-Nichols opportunities.

Powell, his successor, continued to work on improving military relations with the Soviet Union. Powell had earlier received an award from Secretary of State Shultz for his "consummate skill" in shaping the INF treaty negotiations as President Ronald Reagan's assistant for national security affairs (Engleberg and Rasky 1988). Perhaps this negotiation experience exposed him to the kind of new ideas that were necessary to overcome cold war ways of thinking. An "anonymous Pentagon planner" is quoted as saying of Powell: "A few of us were running here saying, 'The Russians aren't coming! The Russians aren't coming!' There were people all around Washington who wouldn't deal with it—it was just suicide to do so. But Powell was dealing with it in secret" (quoted in Means 1992, 279; corroboration of this reputation is found in Rosenthal 1989). At that time, Powell met with a variety of Soviet leaders and became convinced that the changes the USSR was undergoing were significant and real (Jaffe 1993, 11). When Powell became JCS chairman, he demonstrated these beliefs by, for example, participating in the first annual short-course on democracy for Soviet military officers at Harvard's Kennedy School of Government in 1991 (Black 1991).

From the perspective of military officers, however, Powell's key contribution as chairman was his willingness to fight both ingrained service interests and skepticism among civilian Defense Department leaders (especially Secretary of Defense Dick Cheney and Undersecretary of Defense for Policy Paul Wolfowitz), to insist that fundamental change in the basing scheme for U.S. forces was necessary to preserve American superpower status in an uncertain future (for a detailed description of Powell's activities, see Jaffe 1993, esp. 18, 20, 23–24, 27, 29–30). Realizing that the service chiefs, who were primarily interested in maintaining their current program objective memorandums (POMs) to whatever degree possible, could not be won over to his viewpoint, Powell did not seek to build consensus among them. Instead, he directly lobbied both top DOD policy makers, and (when the DOD proved unyielding) the wider foreign policy establishment, using the resources of a staff newly trained and selected for their ability to work jointly.

While the base force concept that was eventually accepted by the DOD, approved by Congress, and implemented in operational planning was the result of compromise among each of the actors involved, Powell was the undisputed policy entrepreneur. He focused attention on the need for a basic rethinking of U.S. military strategy, at a time when many of those who were responsible for U.S. international security policy were reluctant to consider drastic change.

Obviously, individual personalities mattered here. Nothing predetermined that the JCS would be led for eight years by men who had the foresight to understand that the Soviet Union was changing. If either Crowe or Powell had turned out to be a stagnant thinker, it is likely that none of the changes in U.S. military policy toward the Soviet Union or Russia would have happened, or at least, they would not have happened so quickly. Nonetheless, it is doubtful that either Crowe or Powell would have been able to express his views forcefully, much less implement the kinds of military-to-military programs and force planning changes that each did, if Goldwater-Nichols had not overcome the previous JCS logjam. Good organizational structure cannot create insight among its members. It can, however, encourage members to act on their insights, bringing innovative policy ideas to bear on a changing environment.

Conclusion

Russia now seems to be sliding back into the role of rival to the United States. This fact casts doubt on the optimism of those who believed that outreach alone could ensure Russia's entry into the Western community. Nonetheless, it is clear that the relationship between Russia and the United States has fundamentally changed. The perception of hair-trigger threat between the military forces on both sides appears to be a relic of the past, regardless of the level of political conflict that arises in the future. The major conflictual strategic issues facing the relationship today—whether NATO should admit its former enemies as regular members; whether joint U.S.-Russian military exercises should be held on Russian soil; whether U.S. Defense Department funds should be allocated to Russian nuclear warhead destruction and nuclear facilities security; whether joint U.S.-Russian commercial cooperation in space should face sanctions because of Russian sales of dual-use technology abroad—would have been denigrated as pipe dreams in 1985.

The need for fundamental change in both U.S. analytic intelligence techniques and strategic operational planning from cold war days is now obvious. From the cases reviewed above, it seems that key personnel in both the CIA and the Joint Chiefs of Staff recognized the need for change when it arose. Yet organizational structures and procedures in the DI served to stymie creative reaction to that change, even though insiders recognized the disabilities of the organization. Domestic political pressure seemed to be the main factor leading the CIA to finally react to a changed environment. In the Joint Chiefs of Staff, in contrast, exceptional individuals used the opportunity of organizational transformation to become leaders in the battle to reorient the U.S. security bureaucracy toward a new set of challenges. That organizational transformation was not a response to international change, however; it was instead a response to decades of criticism by domestic political actors.

The international environment, and especially the aftershocks of the Soviet breakup, will continue to present U.S. policy makers with surprises in the coming years; few, if any, will be able to predict what those surprises will be. As policy makers face a world where their preexisting notions are likely to be challenged repeatedly and frequently, the best we can hope for is that the foreign policy bureaucracies that are charged with providing them with information and advice will be able to adapt rapidly and creatively to this maelstrom. Planning based on past trends is unlikely to bring success; experimentation, even when it is risky, will be necessary.

What this review suggests is that organizations beset by factionalism, infighting, isolation, and morale problems are unlikely to be effective at a new set of tasks. Instead, they will be mired in old struggles over issues that are fast becoming obsolete. Organizations that provide their members with incentives to overcome factionalism and with opportunities for open expression of competing ideas are more likely to be innovative in adapting to an uncertain environment. Whether one agrees with the policy prescriptions of the DI or the JCS in the middle to late 1980s, it is clear that Goldwater-Nichols gave the JCS an opportunity that was denied the CIA: the freedom to break out of old patterns of thinking and to take risks in search of new effectiveness. In an interesting twist, the new DCI appointed in 1995, John Deutch, brought in to the CIA a number of outsiders who, in the words of one observer, were "steeped in the modern military culture," and "hoping to transfer to the CIA some concepts from the military services" (quoted in Risen 1995). Perhaps, then, the changes currently under way in the DI and throughout the CIA will prove to be as effective in their own way as Goldwater-Nichols was for the JCS.

Many organizations have grown up in a relatively unchanging atmosphere; many have undoubtedly institutionalized policy rivalries of one sort or another; and many are staffed predominantly by professional insiders who lack adequate access to outside ideas and perspectives. Whether the specific choices of the Goldwater-Nichols Act have any bearing on these organizations, their reformist members may find it useful to judge their own options based on the degree to which they overcome this common set of problems. Once the roots of innovative organizational behavior are traced, it should become easier for organizations to structure themselves to weather uncertain times.

PART III

POLICIES

Peter L. Hahn

8. Grand Strategy

In this chapter, I explore changes in U.S. grand strategy since the end of the cold war. I examine two historical case studies of change in American grand strategy in the aftermath of war, focusing on debates within the Truman administration in 1947–1948 and the Eisenhower administration in 1953. The primary purpose of this chapter is to shed light on the degree of change in grand strategy following the cold war. Charles Levine (1980) suggests that institutional decline can be attributed to external variables such as "problem depletion" or "environmental entropy." I will suggest that these external variables both stimulate and limit the changes that occur in American grand strategy.

Grand Strategy

The concept of grand strategy emerged from the work of military analyst Basil H. Liddell Hart. Reflecting upon the thinking of Carl von Clausewitz, Liddell Hart conceived of "grand strategy" as a nation's all-encompassing approach to war. Grand strategy has "the sense of 'policy in execution,'" he explains. "For the role of grand strategy—higher strategy—is to co-ordinate and direct all the resources of a nation, or a band of nations, towards the attainment of the political object of the war—the goal defined by fundamental policy" (Liddell Hart 1967). A viable grand strategy involves coordinated mobilization of a nation's economic, moral, political, and military resources. Liddell Hart also elaborates the importance of postwar peace planning in formulating grand strategy.

Liddell Hart's conception of grand strategy revolutionized the way experts viewed strategy. His observations centered the attention of analysts on nonmilitary dimensions of strategy such as economic-industrial mobilization, diplomacy, and domestic political culture. These observations underscored that peace and war are equally significant. They stressed the importance of balancing ends and means. As Paul Kennedy notes (1991, 4–5), Liddell Hart showed grand strategy to be "a complex and multilayered thing." Under Liddell Hart's influence, Rosecrance and Stein add (1993, 4), "Grand strategy came to mean the adaptation of domestic and international resources to achieve security for a state. Thus, grand strategy considers *all* the resources at the disposal of the nation (not just the military ones), and it attempts to array them effectively to achieve security in both peace and war."

U.S. grand strategy, then, involves the country's ability to mobilize all its resources—military, economic, political, cultural—in aspiring toward a given aim. Studying grand strategy means considering how officials balance means and aims, how they manage the transition between war and peace, and how they arrange their resources for the tasks deemed essential to the national interest.

Certain difficulties arise in a study of U.S. grand strategy. On a fundamental level, one difficulty is the absence of a bureaucracy with clear responsibility for formulating and implementing a centrally designed grand strategy. In other words, the U.S. government has never had a Department of Grand Strategy. Rather, grand strategy is formed by the decisions of officials in a variety of government posts. Debates over it usually involve the president, the State Department, the Pentagon, and occasionally members of Congress and the public.

A second and related difficulty is that the officials who make grand strategy rarely if ever use that term. This curious pattern of omission suggests that these officials lack a clear understanding of what they are formulating. Grand strategy, in other words, is often formed without the cognizance of the decision makers. In fact, experts have only recently conceived and refined the term and endowed it with a particular meaning. Most writers, moreover, treat grand strategy as a wartime concern only, overlooking its evolution in periods of peace.

Further complicating a study of grand strategy is theoretical research suggesting that national security decisions do not necessarily result from rational thought by government officials about clearly understood problems. In other words, grand strategy might best be considered a retrospective construct devised to explain policy decisions reached under conceptual, cognitive, and informational handicaps (Simon 1964). To borrow the words of Cohen, March, and Olsen (1972, 1), the national security bureaucracy could be cited as an "organized anarchy" that "operates on the basis of a variety of inconsistent and ill-defined preferences" and involves a constantly changing roster of officials.

Despite these difficulties, I intend to shed light on the formulation of U.S. grand strategy. I examine debates about grand strategy among officials of the federal government at the dawn of three postwar periods: 1947–1948, 1953, and 1990–1994. In each era, the end of a war or cold war—what Levine (1980) calls "problem depletion"—compelled policy makers to reformulate grand strategy. In all three eras, government officials debated how to mobilize the country's resources to achieve certain foreign policy objectives; in other words, they repeatedly discussed policy issues and problems that shaped what could later be identified as their grand strategies. Among these issues were economic mobilization, domestic political support for foreign policies, propaganda against foreign adversaries, and cooperation with allies.

Given that there is no single bureaucracy responsible for grand strategy, I will concentrate on two central elements of the debate: the appropriate level of defense spending and the proper role of the military services. I will also briefly address other issues, such as the proper degree of U.S. involvement in multinational security institutions and initiatives. This approach is justified for two reasons. First, the available historical record reveals that key strategy debates among elite policy makers in each era usually devolved into arguments over the amount of funding the Pentagon needed to safeguard the vital interests of the country, the level of spending the government could afford without undermining traditional principles of governance or exhausting the tolerance of taxpayers, and the correct roles and missions for the military services. To a lesser degree, discussion also focused on American interaction with multinational security apparatuses. Second, debates over how to balance means and ends were at the core of the formulation of grand strategy. By studying these salient issues, we can open a window through which fundamental aspects of American grand strategy can be viewed.

The Truman Administration

The first of the historical case studies centers on crucial debates within the Truman administration over the proper level of defense spending and the appropriate mission for the armed services in the post–World War II era. These debates peaked in 1947–1948, a point at which demobilization from the world war had been completed, the Truman administration had launched its policy of containment of the Soviet Union, and the armed services had been unified into the National Military Establishment (later the Department of Defense).

With the global war won, the Truman administration sought to balance the nation's foreign and domestic interests. As Melvyn Leffler (1992) suggests, Truman first and foremost sought to create a stable, liberal, and capitalist international order that would ensure U.S. security and economic interests. Convinced that isolationism had contributed to the Great Depression, the rise of fascism, and World War II, the president decided that the country had to remain involved and powerful in the postwar world. He implemented the policy of containment of the Soviet Union, deemed the only probable challenger of the new world order as America envisioned it. At the same time, Truman gave high priority to certain domestic objectives, such as liberal social welfare reforms and balanced federal budgets, and therefore inclined toward reductions in defense spending. As Leffler (1992) argues, such a policy created a perpetual discrepancy between foreign commitments and the ability to honor those commitments. Yet it also showed that Truman understood the essence of a grand strategy; he remained concerned with domestic stability as well as military success and he looked to preserve vital U.S. interests in the period of peace that immediately followed the upheaval of the international order.

One element of Truman's grand strategy was his concern for economy, and in 1946 and 1947, administration officials followed a policy of limiting defense spending to promote domestic fiscal stability. As Secretary of Defense James V. Forrestal explained in December 1947 to Sen. Chan Gurney, chair of the Senate Armed Services Committee, the United States would take a "calculated risk" in Europe. It would neither abandon Europe to Soviet control, which would raise the specter of Old World aggression against the New World, nor deploy vast numbers of troops to defend the continent against Soviet ground threat, which would break the budget of the government. Instead, the United States would base its commitment to European defense on its nuclear monopoly, dominant airpower, and superior industrial base, and would use the period of its nuclear monopoly to "restore world trade, to restore the balance of power, . . . and to eliminate some of the conditions which breed war" (Schilling 1962, 33). Accordingly, in early 1948 the administration proposed fiscal year 1949 defense spending of $10.0 billion, a reduction of $.5 billion from fiscal year 1948 and $1.8 billion from fiscal year 1947 (Schilling 1962).

During the escalation of the cold war in early 1948, however, Truman administration officials vigorously debated the wisdom of continuing to limit defense spending. On the one hand, Pentagon officials questioned the sagacity of defense cuts in light of mounting tensions in Europe, the Middle East, and Asia. With the armed services reduced to 1.3 million personnel, Gen. Alfred Gruenther warned at a White House meeting on February 18, 1948, that the Pentagon lacked the manpower to intervene promptly in "possible explosive points" such as Korea, Palestine, Greece, and Italy (quoted in Condit 1979, 192). "We are playing with fire while we have nothing with which to put it out" (quoted in Schilling 1962, 41), Marshall told the National Security Council (NSC), and on March 24, the Joint Chiefs of Staff urged Truman to ask Congress to approve a $9 billion supplemental appropriation, nearly equal to the amount originally requested. Distancing himself from his message to Gurney of December 1947, Forrestal testified to the Senate Armed Services Committee on March 25 that the United States needed "a balanced strength in manpower—on the ground, on the sea, in the air" (quoted in Condit 1979, 192, 195). While it seemed unlikely that the Soviets would deliberately provoke a war, the Joint Intelligence Committee at the U.S. embassy in Moscow concluded on April 1 that "there is real danger of war within one or two years. The only deterrent" would be certainty in the Kremlin "that in fact the United States was preponderant in military strength and potential and that war would eventually result in peril to the Communist regime" (*FRUS, 1948* 1973, 1:550–57).

On the other side of the debate, economizers within the administration opposed significant increases in defense spending. Officials such as Bureau of the Budget Director James Webb, Secretary of Treasury John Snyder, and presidential assistant John Steelman wanted to reduce taxes and thereby enable the free market to flourish. White House Counsel Clark Clifford and Council of Economic Advisers member Leon Keyserling welcomed new taxes but only to finance welfare measures. All these officials united in opposing additional spending on defense. With regard to spending in FY 1950, Edwin Nourse, chairman of the Council of Economic Advisers, warned Truman on March 24: "The additional pressures coming from the expenditure, the appropriation, or even the consideration of some additional billions of government money [for defense] must inevitably aggravate this danger" of inflation. Increasing defense spending would force the president to suspend "free market practices" and impose "a rather comprehensive set of controls of materials, plant operations, prices, wages, and business credit" (quoted in Schilling 1962, 47–48, 136–37).

Torn by the debate, Truman made concessions to the Pentagon but ultimately sided with the economizers. For example, the president asked Congress to resume the draft, approve universal military training, and authorize supplemental defense spending of $3 billion, twice the amount he originally thought the Pentagon needed. On the other hand, Truman remained convinced of the necessity of economy in defense, in part because of Republican proclivity to reduce taxes and spending, evident in a tax reduction passed by Congress on March 24, 1948. "We must be very careful," Truman wrote to Nourse, "that the military does not overstep the bounds from an economic standpoint domestically. Most of them would like to go back to a war footing—that is not what we want" (quoted in Schilling 1962, 137). Congress approved the requested supplement, eventually authorizing FY 1949 defense spending of $13.8 billion (including $800 million for aircraft procurement) (Condit 1979).

Truman reached this decision in part becase he believed that Pentagon demands for higher budgets stemmed from interservice rivalries, which peaked in 1948. For example, armed service leaders had agreed that in the event of another world war the United States would seek to defeat its enemy (likely the Soviet Union) by means of a punishing strategic air offensive. But they vigorously debated which service would deliver the blast. The army and air force wished to rely on land-based bombers; the navy argued that carrier-borne aircraft were more reliable and defensible than designated air bases in Europe and the Middle East. In March 1948, Forrestal assembled the JCS in Key West, Florida, to reach an agreement on "roles and missions," an agreement that allowed for redundant capabilities among the services. Because the Pentagon's request for $9 billion in additional funding followed the Key West accord, many economizers concluded that the extra money was not really needed to defend national security (Leffler 1992).

The debate over grand strategy continued in early May 1948 as defense spenders and economizers sparred over proposals for defense funding in FY 1950. Budget director Webb favored a ceiling of $15 billion, if not a small decrease to keep expenditures frozen despite inflation. To allow growth in military expenditures would result in mounting defense budgets in the early 1950s, a tendency that would demand new taxes, government controls of market activities, or deficit financing, all of which Webb abhorred. "Is the world situation such," Forrestal countered, "as to warrant appropriations of this order at the present time?" (quoted in Schilling 1962, 139). The crises of early 1948, he explained, compelled him to suspend his own fiscal conservatism and urge that a gamble be taken with domestic problems rather than military capabilities. In the Pentagon's view, the grave world situation sufficiently justified a defense buildup despite the risks of taxes, controls, and deficits. Especially after George Marshall endorsed Webb's argument, Truman sided fully with the economizers on the matter of the FY 1950 budget. Suspicious that Defense Department requests were fueled by interservice rivalry more than real defense needs, the president decided on May 7 to deny Forrestal's request for additional resources (Schilling 1962).

Nursing the wounds of defeat in the budget battles, Forrestal provoked a second round of debate on grand strategy in mid-1948. In early July, he circulated a memorandum stressing that the NSC had to assess the dangers facing the United States to ensure that the Pentagon received adequate funds to preserve national security. "If the dangers are great, immediate and of a military character," he asserted, "this fact should be clearly reflected in our military budget and our military strength adapted accordingly" (*FRUS, 1948* 1973, 1:589–92). In Forrestal's view, of course, the dangers facing the United States were severe. Even though the Soviets were unlikely to start a war by design, he reasoned, "It does not follow . . . that some country, or combination of countries, will not miscalculate the risks and, by taking some aggressive action or precipitating some local conflict, create a situation in which the United States might be required to use military force to protect its own security or to prevent a breakdown in world order" (ibid.).

To justify a larger (and more expensive) mission for the Pentagon, Forrestal suggested that the NSC examine the prospects of several types of wars: "An aggressive war by Russia; a conflict precipitated by some miscalculation on the part of Russia or one of her satellites; Communist expansion through power diplomacy, through the creation of internal dissension and civil strife, or through political terrorism and propaganda; the outbreak of a major war as a result of some eruption in one of the 'tinderbox' areas of the world" (ibid.). Until U.S. officials appraised the threats of each scenario and determined how best to counter them, Forrestal continued, "No logical decisions can be reached as to the proportion of our resources which should be devoted to military purposes." Perhaps exploiting Truman's avowed globalism, Forrestal urged the president to order the NSC evaluation before deciding the FY 1950 budget (ibid., 1:589–93; Leffler 1992).

Economizers in the State Department contested Forrestal's extreme view of the Soviet danger and advocated spending restraints. George F. Kennan and others on the policy planning staff (PPS) warned that no amount of spending would buy complete security since the Soviets would adapt to whatever precautions the United States took. In late August, officials at Foggy Bottom also circulated NSC 20/2, a policy proposal drafted by the PPS in June. The PPS advocated that the United States prepare for an enduring contest with Moscow rather than try to maximize defense capabilities for a certain future point of peak danger, such as the moment when the Soviets acquired atomic capability. Given the unlikelihood that the Soviets sought war or that they would provoke it once they broke the American atomic monopoly, the United States should maintain "a permanent state of adequate military preparation" rather than "a defense effort pointed toward a given estimate peak of war danger" (*FRUS, 1948* 1973, 1:615–24). Facing uncertain reelection prospects, Truman sided with the economizers and rejected the study proposed by Forrestal (ibid., 1:599–601; Leffler 1992).

In late 1948, Forrestal doggedly tried to enlist State Department officials as allies in his campaign for more defense spending. In the absence of spending increases beyond Truman's ceiling of $14.4 billion, he wrote to Marshall on October 31, the Pentagon would have to cut personnel strength and thus surrender its ability to fight. Before Marshall, who was in Paris, could possibly respond, Forrestal convinced Kennan and acting secretary Robert Lovett to agree informally that international tensions had not abated sufficiently to justify personnel reductions. Yet others in the department, such as Counselor Charles E. Bohlen, resisted Forrestal's pressuring. Bohlen thought the threat of retaliatory air strikes would deter Soviet expansion and that excessive spending on defense would "impair the potential productivity of our national economy," which served as "the general restraining factor in the world today" (*FRUS, 1948* 1973, 1:652–54). Marshall endorsed the economizers' view and repudiated Lovett's concession to Forrestal. The previous spring, Marshall asserted, "I told Forrestal that he should plan on building his forces within a balanced national economy, and that the country could not, and would not, support a budget based on the preparation for war. This view still holds. It has nothing to do with the international situation as such—it is designed to get the most security without putting the nation on a war-time footing" (ibid., 1:644–50, 654).

The economizers' arguments rang out loud and clear when the NSC debated NSC 20/4 on November 23 and Truman approved it the next day. The Soviet Union seemed unlikely to provoke war, the final policy paper posited, yet "the risk of war with the USSR is sufficient to warrant, in common prudence, timely and adequate preparation by the United States" (ibid., 1:662–69). On the other hand, the NSC also decided that

U.S. security could be undermined by either "inadequate or excessive armament" or "an excessive or wasteful usage of our resources in time of peace" (ibid.). Washington should seek "to reduce the power and influence of the USSR to limits which no longer constitute a threat to the peace" and to convince Moscow to conduct foreign policy according to UN principles. "In pursuing these objectives," the NSC added, "due care must be taken to avoid permanently impairing our economy and the fundamental values and institutions inherent in our way of life" (ibid.).

Forrestal and others in the Pentagon tried one more time in late 1948 to secure greater defense appropriations. In early December, Forrestal warned Truman that the JCS "do not believe that our national security can be adequately safeguarded with the forces which can be maintained under this 14.4 billion dollar budget" (ibid., 1:669–72). Although the chiefs wanted $23 billion, Forrestal requested $16.9 billion. Although he claimed to have Lovett's endorsement, however, he could not persuade Marshall to back him. The secretary of state refused to endorse higher ceilings because he favored European recovery over U.S. rearmament, because he deemed the situation in Europe less grave than Forrestal considered it, and because he deplored the Pentagon's campaigning to reverse a presidential decision. On December 9, Truman invited Forrestal to the White House to make his bid for the $2.5 billion increase. After listening for an hour, the president denied the request because he found no reason to reverse the policy he had followed since spring (Schilling 1962).

Thus in 1948 Truman maintained his balance between foreign threats and domestic restraints. Indeed, prior to the eruption of the Korean War, Truman continued stringently to limit defense spending. In January 1949 he requested $14.7 billion for fiscal year 1950 (excluding $800,000 earmarked for universal military training), and in early 1950 he asked for $13.5 billion for fiscal year 1951 (Condit 1979; Schilling 1962). Leffler (1992) stresses that NSC 20/4, by reaffirming global commitments while limiting expenditures, fostered a perpetual dilemma between goals and means. This may be true, but seen in a different light, NSC 20/4 could be considered a reflection of Truman's grand strategy that sought to preserve the domestic resources of the nation in peacetime, in case war should recur.

Interestingly, Warner R. Schilling (1962) argues that Forrestal might have changed the outcome of the debate by arguing that economic as well as military concerns demanded larger defense budgets, namely, that increased defense spending might spur economic growth. In other words, Forrestal and other Pentagon officials failed to realize the importance of peacetime domestic priorities in Truman's calculations. Forrestal argued on the basis of strategy, and not grand strategy, and that approach brought about the defeat of his objectives.

In addition to defense spending and military missions, other concerns occupied Truman administration officials who shaped grand strategy after 1945. Convinced that isolationism and autarky had exacerbated the financial depression of the 1930s and widened the scope of World War II, officials in Washington sought to project American influence throughout the world. In 1948, for example, despite perceived risks to economic stability at home, Truman implemented the Marshall Plan, a major initiative to remold European institutions on American models. Based on the calculation that promoting free enterprise in western Europe would perpetuate liberal democracy there, to America's benefit, the Marshall Plan promoted deep U.S. involvement in the political, economic, and social affairs of Europe. Based on similar reasoning, U.S. officials also committed themselves to political entities such as the United Nations, to financial institutions such as the World Bank and the International Monetary Fund, and to trade pacts such as the General Agreement on Tariffs and Trade (Hogan 1987; Leffler 1992).

Security concerns also encouraged American internationalism. Pentagon officials sought to establish access to military facilities worldwide in order to set up defensive barriers that would deter future attacks on the homeland. The Truman administration also signed the Rio Pact and several bilateral defense agreements and disseminated propaganda to discourage foreign states from becoming dependent on Moscow. The NATO alliance and the European military assistance program served in 1949 as capstones of a concerted diplomatic effort to enlist the states of western Europe as backers of Washington's anti-Soviet and anticommunist objectives (Condit 1979; Kaplan 1988; Leffler 1992). In short, American diplomatic initiatives of the late 1940s showed that American grand strategy included a clear departure from isolationism and an assumption of great power status.

The Eisenhower Administration

A second postwar debate over grand strategy occurred in the early months of the Eisenhower administration, following the end of the Korean War. The debate centered primarily on the level of defense spending inherited from the Truman administration. During the Korean War, Truman abandoned his policy of limiting defense spending and launched a massive armaments buildup. Days before leaving office, Truman proposed a fiscal year 1954 budget of $78.6 billion, including $45.4 billion for the Pentagon and a projected deficit of $9.9 billion. On January 19, 1953, hours before his term expired, Truman approved NSC 141, a policy paper that endorsed continuation of the military buildup and the disbursement of economic and military aid to allies. NSC 141 acknowledged that "a healthy society is the essential basis of a strong defense, and economic capabilities set a limit to the size of the defense program a society can . . . safely undertake" (*FRUS, 1952–1954* 1984, 2:142, 209–22). It applied this maxim, however, only to other political states, as a rationale for shifting spending from military to economic aid (Leffler 1992; Snyder 1962).

Dwight D. Eisenhower brought to the presidency principles on defense and economy that differed from those Truman displayed during the Korean War. "The clash with the Russians," writes revisionist historian Robert Divine (1981, 11), was for Eisenhower "a problem to be managed, not an all-consuming crusade against the forces of evil." A fiscal conservative with a realistic grasp of defense needs, Eisenhower also possessed an impulse to limit military spending in order to devote national resources to human and social needs. In the Truman administration debates of 1949, he had endorsed the White House conviction that the Pentagon could function on $15 billion per year. On April 16, 1953, the new president said in a public address: "Every gun that is made, every warship launched, every rocket fired signifies, in the final sense, a theft from those who hunger and are not fed, those who are cold and are not clothed. This world in arms is not spending money alone. It is spending the sweat of its laborers, the genius of its scientists, the hopes of its children" (Eisenhower 1953, 182; Leffler 1992).

To honor these principles, Eisenhower aimed to formulate a new grand strategy. "The first thing that any nation . . . must do, before they can really defend themselves," he explained publicly in April 1953, "is to be able to make a living. That is the thing you are constantly trying to correlate in this job of security. . . . How do you make a living and bear this expense?" If economic and military affairs "are allowed to proceed in disregard one for the other," he added a week later, "you then create a situation either of doubtful military strength, or of such precarious economic strength that your military position is in constant jeopardy." Although he did not call it such, Eisenhower strove for a grand strategy that took into consideration the nation's foreign *and* domestic needs and its wartime *and* peacetime interests. He would "bring American military logic and American economic logic into joint strong harness" (Eisenhower 1953, 209, 239–40).

During his first month in office Eisenhower directed his top advisers to examine the policy of military buildup inherited from Truman in terms of its costs to U.S. fiscal stability. He wished to find a way to maintain national security while balancing the federal budget. The "great problem," the president told the NSC on February 11, 1953, "was to discover a reasonable and respectable posture of defense. . . . It may be possible to figure out a preparedness program that will give us a respectable position without bankrupting the nation" (*FRUS, 1952–1954* 1984, 2:236–37).

This charge from the president touched off a heated debate within the top echelons of the administration over the correct balance between financial and national security objectives. Specifically, top officials argued over whether to approve an annual defense budget of $45 billion, as Truman had proposed, or to cut such expenditures to $33 billion in order to balance the budget. Pentagon officials vociferously opposed substantial reductions in defense spending on grounds of national security. At the NSC meeting of March 25, 1953, Army Chief of Staff Gen. J. Lawton Collins warned that "the proposed cut would have not only grave military implications for national security, but would give rise to equally serious political and diplomatic difficulties." Chief of Naval Operations William Fechteler added that the effects on the navy would be "hardly less serious than for the Army." Marine Corps Commandant Gen. Lemuel Shepherd Jr. warned that "the effect of the proposed reductions on the contribution of the Marine Corps to the national security, was such as to deprive the proposed reductions of any justification." Air Force Chief of Staff Gen. Hoyt Vandenberg stressed that the cuts would "inflict on the Air Force" similar difficulties. Chairman of the Joint Chiefs of Staff Gen. Omar Bradley, Assistant Secretary of Defense Frank Nash, and Secretary of Defense Charles Wilson also added bleak prognoses (ibid., 2:258–64).

When the NSC reconvened on March 31, Wilson reported that the Pentagon would prefer a budget of $41 billion, that it could accept an allocation of $36 billion by retracting commitments and demobilizing in Korea, and that it would aim for a budget of $33 billion by FY 1958. For the short term, he stressed, the $36 billion budget, though necessary on grounds of economy, was "the maximum that could be cut from a political and psychological point of view." Seven civilian consultants recruited by Eisenhower to assess the defense budget agreed with Wilson's report (ibid., 2:264–81).

On the other side of the debate were economizers such as Secretary of Treasury George M. Humphrey and director of the Bureau of the Budget Joseph M. Dodge. Humphrey "stated very emphatically" to the NSC on February 11 "that from now on out this Government must pay its way."

Deficit financing would spawn inflation and "end with a resort to controls and a planned economy along New Deal lines," he added later. "The money and resources required by the great security programs which had been developed since Korea to the present time, simply could not be borne by the United States unless we adopted essentially totalitarian methods." On March 31, 1953, he warned the NSC of "the vital need for a reversal of the previous Administration's spending policy. Continuation of this policy would bankrupt the free world and force the United States itself to abandon its way of life" (ibid., 2:236–37, 258–64, 264–81). "Vigorously and bluntly," Emmet John Hughes (1963, 72) later wrote, Humphrey "enlivened almost every Cabinet session with little polemics on checking deficits, spoken as ardently as [John Foster] Dulles' exhortations on checking Communists."

To Eisenhower fell the task of reconciling the positions argued by Wilson and Humphrey. Exasperated by the debate at a late March NSC meeting, he wondered aloud "whether national bankruptcy or national destruction would get us first." He also expressed genuine sympathy for both sides, recognizing the value of defense capabilities but also commenting that "if we must live in a permanent state of mobilization our whole democratic way of life would be destroyed in the process." On March 31, the president negotiated a compromise among NSC members. They came to a consensus that balanced budgets were essential because "the survival of the free world depends on the maintenance by the United States of a sound, strong economy." Because security commitments could not be retracted at once, however, the United States would pursue this goal of balanced budgets over several years (*FRUS, 1952–1954* 1984, 2:258–64, 281–87).

Upon reaching this decision, Eisenhower worked to sell it to Congress, the public, and members of his administration. The United States faced a "dual threat," he told members of Congress in late April, "the external threat of Communism and the internal threat of a weakened economy." His policy would give precedence to the external threat but "would no longer ignore the internal threat" (ibid., 2:36–17). In early May, Dulles testified before the Senate Foreign Relations Committee and the House Foreign Affairs Committee, "We and our allies alike must maintain an essential balance between our economic health and our military effort. . . . If economic stability goes down the drain, everything goes down the drain" (U.S. Department of State 1953, 737). At a press conference days later, Eisenhower observed that the United States would become "a garrison state" if it continued its prolonged military mobilization. "We don't want to become a garrison state," he added. "We want to remain free. Our plans, our programs, therefore, must conform to the practices of a free people, which means essentially a free economy" (*FRUS, 1952–1954* 1984, 2:326–27). "If you demand of a free people over a long period of time more than they want to give," the president informed his top aides in the summer of 1953, "you can obtain what you want only by using more and more controls; and the more you do this, the more you lose the individual liberty which you are trying to save and become a garrison state (American model)" (ibid., 2:394–98).

The consensus that Eisenhower promoted in the NSC and sold to the public informed his subsequent policy decisions. In NSC 153/1, approved on June 10, 1953, the administration identified "two principal threats to the survival of fundamental values and institutions of the United States: a. The formidable power and aggressive policy of the communist world led by the USSR. b. The serious weakening of the economy of the United States that may result from the cost of opposing the Soviet threat over a sustained period." Officials in Washington realized that "the basic problem facing the United States is to strike a proper balance between the risks arising from these two threats" (ibid., 2:378–86).

In autumn 1953, a second round of debate opened on the question of defense versus economy. NSC 162, circulated for discussion in late September 1953, affirmed the basic consensus reached in March. Pentagon advocates of spending increases, however, launched a frontal assault on the consensus. Alarmed by the successful Soviet test of a hydrogen bomb on August 12, by persistent tensions in Asia despite the end of the Korean War, by growing political commitments incurred by the United States, and by perceived weaknesses in U.S. conventional forces, the JCS argued that the government should bear all costs necessary to assure national defense and demanded a fiscal year 1954 defense budget of $42 billion (ibid., 2:489–503; Snyder 1962).

The economizers quickly countered these calls by insisting that spending more than $35 billion on defense would imperil the U.S. economy. While recognizing the seriousness of Soviet nuclear capability, Dodge argued that economic warfare "was a very successful element of the Soviet strategy. . . . The threat to the economy was part and parcel of the Soviet threat." Humphrey added that "the essence of the issue" was that "over the long haul we could easily be destroyed by either of the two threats, external or internal" (*FRUS, 1952–1954*, 2:514–34). The debate grew quarrelsome. When Humphrey admitted under pressure that "no one wanted to balance the budget at the sacrifice of the national security," Wilson mockingly dared him to repeat the point in public. Humphrey retorted instead that "the military ought to be so damned dollar conscious that it hurts" (ibid., 2:514–49; Snyder 1962).

Both sides to the dispute carried their arguments to the public arena. Pentagon officials criticized the idea of diminishing conventional force strength and relying on nuclear capability on grounds of economy. "Our plans must be flexible and must prepare us to meet any type of emergency," Secretary of the Army Robert Stevens said in an armed forces journal, "for we can hardly count on the cooperation of the aggressor. As long as the initiative remains with him, he is likely to attempt to avoid our strength and exploit our weaknesses" (quoted in Snyder 1962, 434). Humphrey conveyed his views to the public as well. "There would be no defense but disaster in a military program that scorned the resources and problems of our economy—erecting majestic defenses and battlements for the protection of a country that was bankrupt and a people who were impoverished. We know that a sick American economy would fulfill the Communist dream of conquest just as surely as disaster on the battlefield." The country's greatest defense was "the power and potential of American mass production" (quoted in Davies 1953).

To the relief of the economizers, Eisenhower decided to deny the Pentagon's request and reaffirm the decision he had made in March. He criticized the JCS for suggesting "that we should do what was necessary even if the result was to change the American way of life. We could lick the whole world if we were willing to adopt the system of Adolf Hitler." The NSC policy paper should clarify that "after all we were engaged in defending a way of life as well as a territory, a population, or a dollar." Indeed, the final draft of the paper, approved by Eisenhower as NSC 162/2 on October 30, 1953, declared that the basic problem confronting the United States was "to meet the Soviet threat to U.S. security" and "in doing so, to avoid seriously weakening the U.S. economy or undermining our fundamental values and institutions" (*FRUS, 1952–1954* 1984, 2:514–34, 567–76, 577–97).

Like the Truman administration, Eisenhower and his policy advisers decided many other matters relating to grand strategy by balancing security, political, and economic concerns. Eisenhower tried to reinvigorate U.S. containment policy through the "New Look" policy, which included nuclear deterrence, military alliances, psychological warfare, covert operations, and a willingness to negotiate as a means to promote American vital interests in an economical manner (Gaddis 1982). Shortly after taking office, Eisenhower affirmed the wisdom of the Marshall Plan and declared his determination to support similar plans "to help build a world in which all peoples can be productive and prosperous" (Eisenhower 1953, 186).

In addition, Secretary of State John Foster Dulles informed a congressional committee in May 1953 that the United States would pursue "mutual security . . . on a global basis," on the reasoning that all "free nations" must "continue to make a vital positive contribution to peace and security" (U.S. Department of State 1953, 736–38). Accordingly, Eisenhower readily shored up the U.S. relationship with NATO and extended the premise of collective defense by establishing the Southeast Asia Treaty Organization and the Central Treaty Organization (Kaplan 1988). Finally, NSC officials determined that the government needed actively to "assure the vitality and soundness of our free, democratic institutions," to mobilize public opinion to support cold war policies, and to counter subversion "through methods consistent with the maintenance of a vital and democratic society" (*FRUS, 1952–1954* 1984, 2:378–86).

The grand strategy formulated by the Eisenhower administration in the wake of the Korean War, then, struck a balance between the imperatives of the cold war and the demands of the domestic political economy. As in the Truman years, extensive arguments between defense advocates and economizers preceded the formulation of this grand strategy. Extremely cautious about perceived threats from foreign rivals, the defense advocates urged the allocation of maximum resources to military readiness programs. Worried that excessive spending would bankrupt the national treasury and imperil the domestic economy, economizers favored reductions in defense spending. Eisenhower sought a middle position between these two, but leaned toward economy when forced to choose sides. Consistent with NSC 162/2, he proposed in January 1954 a fiscal year 1954 defense budget of $37.6 billion, a sum requiring reductions in personnel from 3.3 million to 3.0 million troops by June 1955. In the aftermath of war, Eisenhower found sufficient comfort to favor economy over readiness in his grand strategy (Snyder 1962).

Grand Strategy After the Cold War

A third postwar debate over grand strategy began as the Soviet empire in eastern Europe collapsed in 1989 and the Soviet Union dissolved two years later. These momentous developments ended the cold war and created a global situation resembling the conditions that confronted Truman in 1947–1948 and Eisenhower in 1953. The fluidity and uncertainty of the post–cold war world compelled American officials to address anew the grand strategy of the country. The public record of the debate over grand strategy since 1989 reveals that the discussion, like the debates of 1947–

1948 and 1953, centered on the appropriate balance between defense spending and domestic priorities. Moreover, Presidents George Bush and Bill Clinton affirmed the country's internationalism, even as they wrestled with questions about the range of countries with which they wished to associate. Unlike the debates of the Truman and Eisenhower eras, on the other hand, in the recent discussions on defense spending and missions both presidents sided with Pentagon advocates against economizers in the executive branch and Congress.

The recent round of debate over grand strategy originated in a context of shrinking defense budgets. As American-Soviet relations improved dramatically after 1985, Congress reduced annual defense budgets by 2 percent per year (adjusted for inflation). The collapse of the Soviet empire in 1989 triggered a debate among U.S. policy makers over whether to accelerate the pace of reduction. Backed by Bush, Pentagon officers opposed additional cuts on the grounds that they needed the means to fulfill new responsibilities, for instance, pacifying hot spots such as Panama—which U.S. forces invaded and occupied in December 1989—and interdicting narcotics trafficking. "In this world of change," Bush explained in January 1990, "one thing is certain: America must be ready. . . . This is not a time when we should naively cut the muscle out of our defense posture" (quoted in Rosenthal 1990).

Other voices, however, argued that the Pentagon's operations in Panama offered no reason to delay reductions in defense spending that were justified by the diminution of the Soviet threat. Les Aspin (D-Wis.), chairman of the House Armed Services Committee, disputed what he called the Pentagon's demands for a "robust defense budget" in the aftermath of the action in Panama. Lawrence Korb, a fellow at the Brookings Institution and an expert on defense administration, observed that the military deployed none of its aircraft carriers, B-1 bombers, or M-1 tanks, and only 25,000 of its 2.1 million troops during the invasion. Operations in Panama, Korb suggested, showed that the Pentagon could endure substantial additional reductions (Engelberg 1990).

To head off pressures to reduce defense spending dramatically, the Pentagon, with Bush's approval, imposed a restructuring plan on itself in summer 1990, including limited personnel reductions and organizational reforms. The so-called base force plan was leaked to the press, which suggests that the services sought to address congressional and public demands for drastic reductions in defense spending. Kohn (1994) argues that Gen. Colin Powell, chairman of the Joint Chiefs of Staff, conceived the plan to deflect congressional criticisms that mounted as the Bush administration talked vaguely of a "new world order." The plan also reflected changes in the services' thinking about European military security in the aftermath of the Soviet withdrawals from eastern Europe. Pentagon war plans had traditionally assumed that the Soviet Union would need two weeks to mobilize before attacking western Europe. After the withdrawals, military officers calculated that the Soviet army would need two full years to gear up for an assault. On this supposition, the Pentagon proposed reducing service personnel by 25 percent (from 2.1 million to 1.6 million soldiers), restructuring command lines, and relying on reserves to defend western Europe. The army would shrink from eighteen to twelve active divisions, the navy from fourteen to twelve carrier groups, and the air force from thirty-six to twenty-six wings. Most troops would be stationed stateside and mobilized rapidly during crises to forward staging areas and weapons stockpiles (Gordon 1990).

Bush publicly outlined the rationale behind the base force plan on August 2, 1990. "The United States would be ill-served by forces that represent nothing more than a scaled-back or shrunken-down version of the ones we possess at the present," he declared, to counter those advocating blanket reductions in the defense budget. "If we simply . . . cut equally across the board, we could easily end up with more than we need for contingencies that are no longer likely and less than we must have to meet emergency challenges" (quoted in Dowd 1990). To reassure allies and deter rivals, Bush also vowed to preserve America's ability "to respond to threats in whatever corner of the globe they may occur. . . . Threats remain. Terrorism. Hostage-taking. Renegade regimes and unpredictable rulers—new sources of instability—all require a strong and engaged America" (ibid.). The base force plan took effect in late 1990, and not even the mobilization for Operation Desert Shield and Operation Desert Storm slowed its pace. In fact, the base force plan's proposal to phase out battleships was announced in February 1991, on the very day the *USS Missouri* shelled Iraqi forces in Kuwait (Gordon 1991a, 1991b).

The 25 percent reduction proposed in the base force plan failed to satisfy advocates of defense reductions once the Soviet Union collapsed in 1991. On Capitol Hill, pressure mounted in favor of cutting military spending by as much as 50 percent. Citing the mounting federal deficit and the economic recession of 1991–1992, Representative Aspin accused General Powell of showing insensitivity to the fiscal crisis facing the country and of exaggerating the threats facing the nation in the post-Soviet world. In August 1992, Aspin demanded cuts substantially deeper than the base force plan targets. The base force plan aimed for 1.6 million personnel, 15 tactical air wings, 450 navy ships, and 12 army divisions. Aspin proposed 1.4 million personnel, 10 tactical wings, 340 navy ships, and 9 army divisions. Senate Armed Services Committee Chairman Sam Nunn (D-Ga.) and Senate Majority Leader George Mitchell (D-Maine) endorsed Aspin's demands. Nunn and Mitchell proposed reductions in the defense budget of $100 billion to $150 billion over five years, sums that were two and three times the amount the White House agreed to cut. Once the Soviet Union dissolved, Sen. Edward Kennedy (D-Mass.) asserted, "We need to go deeper, and we can afford to do so" (quoted in Schmitt 1992a, 1992b, 1992c, 1992d). The Bush administration and Pentagon officers resisted this congressional pressure. General Powell defended the base force plan as entirely reasonable, noting in January 1992: "We'll be fighting a legislative war this year instead of one with people getting killed and injured" (quoted in Schmitt 1992b). President Bush proposed a fiscal year 1993 defense budget of $281 billion, a $10 billion reduction from fiscal year 1992. "This deep, and no deeper," the president said in his State of the Union Address. Because they would weaken military capabilities and morale, Secretary of Defense Cheney added bluntly, deeper cuts would be "stupid." In testimony to the Senate Armed Services Committee on the FY 1993 budget request, a more composed Cheney admitted that "the threats [to U.S. security] have become remote, so remote that they are difficult to discern" (quoted in Schmitt 1992d). Issues such as nuclear proliferation and enduring regimes such as Saddam Hussein's dictatorship in Iraq, however, justified adherence to the base force plan. General Powell further defended the plan as "a reshaping, not a demobilization" (quoted in Schmitt 1992d).

As the debate ensued over the base force plan, the Pentagon conceived a second blueprint for the post–cold war era that demanded additional defense spending. Although the final report, eventually entitled "Roles, Missions, and Functions of the Armed Forces of the United States," remained secret until February 1993, large sections were leaked to the press in early 1992, apparently to cultivate public support for the services' demands. Reminiscent of James Forrestal's plan in NSC 20 of July 1948, the roles and missions plan envisioned seven scenarios in which the United States might be forced to deploy military forces during the post–cold war era: Iraqi aggression against Saudi Arabia and Kuwait, a North Korean invasion of South Korea, simultaneous Iraqi and North Korean assaults, a Russian attack on Lithuania, a coup d'état in the Philippines that threatened U.S. citizens, Panamanian internal unrest that endangered U.S. access to the Panama Canal, or expansionism or global military competition by "a single nation or coalition of nations" designated the "resurgent/emergent global threat" (REGT). The report claimed to reflect "a shift in planning focus from a single monolithic global scenario to an array of regional scenarios" and emphasized that the seven scenarios were "illustrative" and "not predictive." General Powell refused to identify potential enemies but added: "I know the neighborhoods they live in" (quoted in Tyler 1992a).

The leaked draft of the report on military roles and missions found few converts among the congressional skeptics of Pentagon spending. Voices on Capitol Hill questioned whether the scenarios were realistic, whether the threats were as severe as the report described them, and whether the scenarios justified budget hikes after mid-decade. "If during the cold war we did not have to worry about fighting Iraq and North Korea simultaneously," one congressional staff member queried, "why do we have to worry about it now when the major adversary has disappeared?" (quoted in Tyler 1992b). On July 2, 1992, Senator Nunn demanded that the Defense Department "thoroughly overhaul the services' roles and missions" and eliminate duplicate roles and missions in order to achieve economy (quoted in Gordon 1992b).

In his campaign for the presidency in 1992, Democratic nominee Bill Clinton endorsed the call for major restructuring of the Pentagon's roles and missions to reduce duplicate responsibilities among the services. "I agree with Senator Sam Nunn that it is time to take a fresh look at the basic organization of our armed services," Clinton asserted in a campaign speech on August 13, 1992. "While respecting each service's unique capabilities, we can reduce redundancies, save billions of dollars, and get better teamwork" (ibid.). With Clinton favored to win the general election, in late summer Pentagon officers anticipated substantial spending reductions. "Today's fiscal environment shows no sign of being cyclical in nature," a secret navy memorandum, leaked to the press, observed. "Reversal of current projected resource reductions is not foreseen" (quoted in Schmitt 1992a).

After Clinton won the presidential election, General Powell tried to stem the momentum toward greater cuts by offering an alternative package of limited reforms, including establishment of a central command to unify joint training and to oversee operations such as peacekeeping and disaster relief. "There are a number of advantage[s] in having similar, complementary capabilities among the services," Powell stressed in an official report to the president dated December 31, 1992. "The similar but specialized capabilities of the Armed Forces are not unlike the safety features of modern automobiles, which come equipped with automatic shoulder restraints, lap safety belts, and air bags" (quoted in Gordon 1992b). Whereas critics such as Nunn and Clinton emphasized that the United States had four air forces, Powell responded that "each is different, playing a unique and complementary role" (ibid.). Powell (1993b, 41) also argued publicly that lurking dangers in the post–cold war world necessitated the vigilance and preparedness proposed in the base force plan. Since the Soviet Union had collapsed, "tectonic plates shift beneath us, causing instability in a dozen different places."

When Clinton assumed office in January 1993, a major struggle loomed between the White House and the Pentagon over the proper level of defense spending. Clinton named economy-minded Representative Aspin as secretary of defense and in February announced plans to reduce the defense budget over five years by $60 billion more than Bush had planned to reduce it. When the Pentagon, on the other hand, released the official version of its "Roles, Missions, and Functions" report on February 12, it had removed even the modest changes General Powell had suggested in December. The service chiefs subsequently protested that additional cuts would imperil national security. "In the case of the Army," Chief of Staff Gen. Gordon Sullivan said, "We are on razor's edge" (quoted in Gordon 1993b). Marine Corps Commandant Gen. Carl Mundy added, "Our operations and maintenance account is strapped," and Chief of Naval Operations Adm. Frank Kelso warned: "We're on the ragged edge in readiness" (ibid.). Even director-designate of central intelligence James Woolsey, a Clinton nominee, testified to the Senate Intelligence Committee, in defense of CIA's budget, that although the United States had "slain a large dragon . . . we live now in a jungle filled with a bewildering variety of poisonous snakes. And in many ways, the dragon was easier to keep track of. . . . Today's threats are harder to observe and understand than the one that was once presented by the U.S.S.R." (quoted in Gordon 1993b; Gordon 1993c; Jehl 1993).

Despite his early stance as an economizer, Clinton buckled under the strong pressure from defense advocates. In September 1993, after months of intragovernment debate, the president approved a Pentagon strategic plan in line with the Pentagon's wishes on defense missions and budgets. With the White House's full approval, Secretary of Defense Aspin, shifting toward the defense advocates' position, publicized the so-called win-win plan, under which U.S. armed services would maintain the capability to prevail in two simultaneous regional wars. In approving "win-win," the administration rejected an alternative plan, called "win-hold-win," under which the military would have sought consecutive rather than simultaneous victories in two regional wars. Without "win-win" capabilities, Aspin explained, potential aggressors would be tempted to strike should the United States become embroiled in one war (Gordon 1993f).

The "win-win" plan strongly resembled the blueprint hatched during the Bush presidency. It would reduce the armed services from 1.7 million to 1.4 million personnel. The plan proposed reducing the number of navy carriers from fourteen to twelve, air wings from twenty-four to twenty, and army divisions from twelve to ten. The marine corps would actually regain scheduled losses and remain at 174,000 marines, compared to 159,000 proposed by Bush. The "win-win" plan "ought to be quite similar" to Bush's blueprint, General Powell explained, "because the world looks the same to us." The plan also discounted the prospect of allied assistance in war. "Our forces must be sized and structured to preserve the flexibility and the capability to act unilaterally," Aspin asserted, "should we choose to do so." The estimated cost of "win-win" also approximated the Bush administration's spending projections: $1.2 trillion over five years (quoted in Gordon 1993f; Gordon 1993e; Schmitt 1993).

Clinton again sounded a retreat from economizing by siding with the Pentagon and against the Office of Management and Budget in a financial quarrel in December 1993. The Pentagon and the Council of Economic Advisers calculated that inflation and a congressionally mandated pay raise valued at $14.5 billion would produce a $31 billion shortfall in the Pentagon budget between 1995 and 1999. "Something will have to give if we don't get the funds," one officer said. "We will either have to cut the forces and throw the strategy overboard, give up some weapons modernization, or get the funds we need from domestic programs." Another officer added, "This is a real war. It is a war with OMB and a war among ourselves" (quoted in Gordon 1993e). Aspin called on Clinton to commit additional funds to preserve the "win-win" strategy. OMB Director Leon Panetta, by contrast, encouraged the president to refuse extra funding because it would imperil domestic reform programs (Gordon 1993g).

After meeting with Aspin and Panetta in mid-December, Clinton decided to guarantee funding for the "win-win" strategy despite the risks such a step incurred for his domestic programs. "The President said he is committed to funding the strategy. That will be the assumption," National Security Adviser Anthony Lake reported (quoted in Gordon 1993g). Within days, Clinton approved an additional $10 billion in the defense budget to offset the costs of the mandatory pay raise. To help fund this hike, the president siphoned $2.5 billion from a package of domestic programs—

including scientific research, education, job training, and transportation—whose budget had already been reduced from $30 billion to $16 billion (Gordon 1993d).

Defense budgets also signaled Clinton's retreat from his economizing agenda. Congress approved defense budgets of $261 billion in fiscal year 1994 and $263 billion in fiscal year 1995. The latter figure was five times greater than Russia's defense budget, equal to defense spending by the rest of the world combined, and 85 percent as large as the average defense budget during the cold war (in constant dollars). "This year, many people urged us to cut our defense spending further to pay for other government programs," Clinton declared in his January 1994 State of the Union message. "I said no. . . . We must not cut defense further" (quoted in Schmitt 1994a). Although Secretary of Defense William Perry asserted that "there are no cold war relics in the budget," in early 1994 the military remained as large as it was in 1990 ("More Is the Pity at the Pentagon" 1994). It included nineteen divisions of ground troops (thirteen of them active), thirty-five air wings (twenty-six active), and twelve carrier groups (Schmitt 1994d, 1994b).

The Republican-controlled Congress that convened in January 1995 created a climate in Washington that made it politically difficult for Clinton to return to his original commitment to economy. Republican lawmakers criticized the White House for permitting a so-called readiness gap, charging that the Clinton administration had allowed both soldiers and equipment to reach such a state of unpreparedness that vital national security interests were in danger. Rep. Floyd Spence (R-S.C.), who chaired the House National Security Committee, argued that "the military is suffering through the early stages of a long-term readiness problem" (quoted in Spence 1995). To close the readiness gap, congressional Republicans eventually passed a fiscal year 1996 defense budget of $265 billion, some $7 billion more than the Clinton administration requested. "This is not an increase," Rep. Curt Weldon (R-Pa.) declared, "It's just stopping the hemorrhaging" (quoted in Lewis 1996; Schmitt 1995a).

Pentagon officials and other defense advocates exploited the position of the Republican legislators. Allen Harris, national vice president of the Air Force Association, warned that spending reductions imperiled readiness to prevail over "rogue regimes unfettered by public debates about military spending" (quoted in Harris 1995). Gen. John Shalikashvili, chairman of the Joint Chiefs of Staff, said in early 1995 that "the dangers are very, very real and very great" in delaying purchases of new equipment (quoted in Schmitt 1995c). Maj. Gen. Richard L. Phillips, inspector general of the air force, added: "At some point in the near future, the current funding strategy will ultimately undermine the Corps' ability to meet war-fighting and peacetime presence requirements" (ibid.).

Economizers disputed the "readiness gap" charge. The *New York Times* pointed out in late 1994 that the current Pentagon budget for "operations and maintenance," which accounted for readiness, was double that in 1980 and a third more than 1985, even though personnel in uniform had declined by 25 percent since then ("Are U.S. Forces Ready to Fight?" 1994). Lawrence Korb (1995a) decried the "readiness gap" allegation as "a hot-button issue subject to easy manipulation by Congress and a Pentagon set on preserving its share of the federal budget." Sen. Carl Levin (D-Mich.), argued, "There is no sudden increased threat to justify the hefty boost" in defense spending (quoted in Schmitt 1995a). Other critics pointed out that much of the additional funds allocated was designated for the purchase of military equipment built in the congressional districts of those voting for the funds. The fiscal year 1996 budget, in the view of the *New York Times,* was "an irresponsible indulgence that the country cannot afford" ("The Pentagon Jackpot" 1995; Lewis 1996; Schmitt 1995b).

Without access to the secret records of these debates, we can only speculate on why Clinton retreated from his promises of economizing. Part of the reason might be the natural inclination of leaders, upon assuming office, to defend what they criticized as extravagances while outside of power. Second, perhaps Clinton appeased the military establishment to repair his strained relationship with it. In honoring Pentagon wishes, he might have wished to end the tensions stemming from his youthful avoidance of military service, his unpopular policy initiatives regarding women in combat and homosexuals in the services, and his restrictions on military deployments in Somalia. Third, Clinton might have been motivated in part by arguments regarding domestic politics and economics. The win-win plan, for example, specified that the Pentagon would purchase a third Seawolf attack submarine and an additional aircraft carrier, not on grounds of military necessity, but to preserve the industrial base that produced them.

Fourth, Clinton administration officials shared the Bush view that the perils of the post–cold war era resembled those of the cold war and even of World War II. "The same idea attacked by Fascism and Communism remains under attack today," National Security Adviser Anthony Lake observed in September 1994. "We are at the start of a new phase in this old struggle. . . . The enemies . . . are extreme nationalists and tribalists, terrorists, organized criminals, coup plotters, rogue states and all those who would return newly free societies to the intolerant ways of the past" (Lake 1994). Finally, once the Republican Party captured control of Congress in 1995, Clinton faced extraordinary political pressures not to economize on defense spending.

In any case, by 1994 it appeared to critics that the Pentagon had won the battle of the budget during the early Clinton presidency. "Instead of [Clinton] reinventing the Pentagon," Lawrence Korb (1994) observes, "the Pentagon reinvented the threat" facing the country. Korb deemed it unwise for the United States to prepare for simultaneous wars against regional threats such as North Korea and Iraq, whose combined defense spending totaled $40 billion, with a force structure similar to that maintained to deal with the Soviet Union, whose last defense budget exceeded $300 billion. The Pentagon inflated the threat facing the country, Korb observed, by completely discounting the contributions of allies and by avoiding reconsideration of duplicate roles and missions between the branches. Korb estimated that a budget of $200 billion would enable the Pentagon to defend the vital interests of the country (Korb 1995c).

In addition to debating military roles and missions, the Bush and Clinton administrations also debated the appropriate role of the United States in international organizations. Eschewing any return to pre-1941 isolationism, they affirmed America's centrality in the international community. U.S. participation in such international trade and financial institutions as GATT, the World Bank, and the IMF continued to encourage global-based trade, a trend advanced in the ratification of the North American Free Trade Agreement (NAFTA) in 1993. U.S. membership in political bodies such as the United Nations seemed to be taken for granted. American officials also affirmed the country's central role in military and security organizations, including NATO and the Conference on Security and Cooperation in Europe (CSCE). The premise of the "win-win" plan, that the United States must remain capable of independent military action, should be viewed more as a Pentagon ploy to secure resources than an indication of flagging confidence in NATO (Gaddis 1992; Wells 1992).

The triumph of U.S. internationalism was not devoid of complicated policy issues. For example, U.S. officials in the immediate post–cold war years wrestled with the issue of the proper scope and role of the NATO alliance. The end of the cold war raised the prospect of friendship between European states formerly divided into rival blocs. As early as July 1990, NATO members signaled to the Soviet Union and eastern European governments that they would welcome military consultations aimed at resolving conflicts and reducing the likelihood of war (Garthoff 1994). Determined to stem political instability in eastern Europe, manifest in crises such as ethnic warfare in the Nagorno-Karabakh region of Azerbaijan, the Bush administration conducted a series of conferences that led to the creation of the North Atlantic Cooperation Council (NACC) in November 1991. Heralded by NATO ministers as a "new security architecture," NACC was designed to foster communication about security issues among NATO and former Warsaw Pact states. By the time of its first ministerial summit in June 1992, NACC boasted thirty-seven member countries, including Russia and all the other successor states to the Soviet Union (Crossette 1992; Kempe 1991).

Despite Bush's apparent ease in enlisting Russia in NACC, President Clinton confronted more perplexing dilemmas regarding the long-term relationship between NATO and Russia. In mid-1993, Clinton considered honoring requests from Poland, Hungary, and the Czech Republic to join NATO. Besieged by mounting nationalism among Russian citizens, however, President Boris Yeltsin retracted earlier assurances that Russia would not object to such an expansion of NATO. Because it "would bring the biggest military grouping in the world, with its colossal offensive potential, directly to the borders of Russia," Yevgeny M. Primakov, director of Russia's intelligence service, declared, such an expansion would necessitate "a fundamental reappraisal of all defense concepts on our side" (quoted in Erlanger 1993).

Leery of the rising tide of Russian nationalism, Clinton delayed his decision regarding expansion of NATO. Then, after the ultranationalist party of Vladimir Zhirinovsky finished surprisingly well in Russian parliamentary elections on December 12, 1993, the U.S. president indefinitely suspended the initiative. Rather than NATO membership for eastern European states, he proposed a "partnership for peace" (PFP). This initiative denied eastern European states the security guarantees provided to NATO members, but invited them to participate in NATO training exercises, conduct joint military actions for peacekeeping and humanitarian relief purposes, consult NATO if a foreign threat materialized, and negotiate eventual entry into the alliance. Senator Nunn heralded the partnership as a balance between ensuring the security interests of Russia and those of eastern European states, and between mollifying Russian nationalism and admonishing Moscow to contribute to international stability (Nunn 1993b). "The 'partnership for peace' proposal was a very skillful compromise between people who said we should do nothing to offend the Russians, and people who said we should let the Europeans in now," an American diplomat noted in January 1994. "The beauty of the proposal is that it's a framework on whose canvas we can paint what we want" (quoted in Whitney 1994b).

The PFP proposal triggered widespread public debate. Some critics assailed it as an unwise appeasement of Russian nationalism. As Craig Whitney wrote in the *New York Times,* "The underlying assumption is a huge strategic gamble, a bet that the success of democracy in Russia is what counts most, and that concessions to wounded national pride there will keep the wounds from becoming malignant. . . . The result could be exactly the opposite" (Whitney 1994c). In an endorsement of the PFP, on the other hand, Raymond Garthoff of the Brookings Institution argued that the United States would needlessly provoke Russia by enlisting eastern European states in NATO without soothing its nationalistic pride (Garthoff 1994, 792).

Clinton weathered the criticisms and eventually coaxed Russia to join the PFP, but not without effort. Russian foreign minister Andrei Kozyrev hinted in April 1994 that Yeltsin would enroll in the partnership, but Clinton's decision days later to launch an air strike against Bosnian Serbs without first consulting Yeltsin infuriated Russian leaders and soured them on the partnership. To mollify the Russians, the United States and other NATO states conceded during the following month that Russia deserved more respectful treatment than the smaller, less powerful, and non-nuclear states of eastern Europe. But they rejected Russia's call for a "full-blooded strategic relationship" and denied Russia's demand for special veto powers in NATO decisions (Sciolino 1994b). Instead, as Secretary of State Warren Christopher explained, the United States envisioned Russia's membership in the PFP and supplementary agreements on matters in which Russia and the United States shared mutual concerns, such as nuclear weapons dismantlement and nuclear nonproliferation. Although denied the special status it sought, Russia joined the PFP on June 22, 1994 (Erlanger 1994a; Greenhouse 1994b; Schmidt 1994; Sciolino 1994c; Whitney 1994a).

Russia's membership did not permanently solve the issue. Although American-Russian cooperation ensued in late 1994 on issues such as trade, nuclear nonproliferation, and mutual disarmament, Russian officials grumbled about the appearance of inequality between Moscow and Washington in the PFP. In response to talks in the West about accelerating the timetable for eastern European states to join NATO formally, Moscow laid plans to reunite the states of the former Soviet Union in a common defense alliance against Western encroachments (Karatnycky 1994; Migranyan 1994; Sestanovich 1994a, 1994b).

Russian opposition continued to delay the expansion of NATO in 1995 and 1996. At the December 1994 CSCE meeting in Budapest, Yeltsin delivered a caustic warning against expanding NATO to eastern Europe, a message that one American official called "a shot across the bow" (quoted in Erlanger 1994b). To soothe Russia, in March 1995 Clinton sent Yeltsin written assurances that he would consult Russia carefully on NATO expansion. "It is important to develop a new relationship between Russia and NATO that is parallel to the process of NATO expansion," a U.S. official remarked (quoted in Greenhouse 1995b). "Whatever one may think of NATO," an unreassured Foreign Minister Andrei Kozyrev stated, "it's still a military alliance that was created when Europe was divided. It should be replaced by a new model based on comprehensive security" (quoted in Whitney 1995b). This gap in the American and Russian positions remained, despite Clinton's call during a summit meeting with Yeltsin in Moscow in May 1995 for "a special relationship between NATO and Russia" (quoted in Apple 1995; Greenhouse 1994c; Jehl 1995; Sciolino 1994g).

Russian leaders agreed to conduct secret discussions with U.S. officials on the issue, but warned that Russia would resign from PFP if NATO expansion ensued. Mikhail Gorbachev warned in February 1996 that Russians viewed NATO "as a war machine that is trying to take advantage of our troubled political and economic situation" (Gorbachev 1996). Yevgeny Primakov, recently promoted to foreign minister, stressed to Secretary of State Christopher that NATO expansion threatened Russia's equality and was therefore intolerable (Erlanger 1995, 1996c; Gorbachev 1996; Greenhouse 1995e).

Clinton administration officials did not completely abandon their plans to enlarge NATO to include eastern European states. In September 1995, NATO members approved documents to facilitate the process of joining. "NATO has made a commitment to take in new members, and it must not and will not keep the democracies in the waiting room forever," Christopher declared. "NATO enlargement is on track and it will happen" (quoted in Erlanger 1996a). In light of Russian sensitivities, on the other hand, the effort to expand NATO would take years to complete (Erlanger 1996a; Whitney 1995a).

Conclusion

In certain ways, the debate over grand strategy in 1990–1996 resembled the debates of 1947–1948 and 1953. In all three eras, "problem depletion"—the end of a major foreign conflict—triggered debates. In all three periods, government officials who formulated grand strategy debated the appropriate level of military spending and the appropriate roles for the armed services in defending the country's national security. All the debates involved defense advocates, usually uniformed officers who insisted that the Pentagon needed additional resources to defend the country against foreign foes. In fact, Pentagon officials who wrote the seven scenarios assessment of 1992–1993 borrowed from the tactics of James Forrestal, who in 1948 underscored in NSC 20 the severity of potential foreign threats facing the nation as a justification for raising defense spending at the expense of domestic programs. The debate pitted such defense advocates against economizers, generally executive branch officials and members of Congress who wished to reserve scarce financial resources for domestic programs, to avoid higher taxes and government controls, and otherwise to preserve what they viewed as essential principles of governance. In all three eras, the debates ultimately involved presidential decision making.

Despite these similarities, the debates over grand strategy differed in significant ways. In the first two periods, for example, presidents resisted Pentagon pressures and sided with the economizers. Wary of duplicate responsibilities among the armed services, Harry Truman refused to sacrifice his domestic aims for increased defense spending in peacetime. In the aftermath of the Korean War, Dwight Eisenhower ordered deep reductions in defense spending over Pentagon protests, to safeguard the economic stability of the republic. After the cold war, by contrast, George Bush and Bill Clinton broke these precedents. They endorsed Pentagon assessments of enduring threats to national security, approved defense funding close to levels provided during the late cold war, and left intact a force structure similar to the one that had been arrayed against the Soviet Union at its height. Truman's and Eisenhower's grand strategies balanced foreign and domestic imperatives. Despite a mounting national debt, Bush and Clinton showed less regard for domestic stability in the formulation of their grand strategies. To borrow Levine's terminology (1980), differences in the degree of environmental entropy account for such policy differences. As advocates of balanced federal budgets, Truman and Eisenhower imposed strict limits on defense spending, while Bush and Clinton, accustomed to deficit spending, withheld restraints. Despite suggestions to the contrary, the two recent presidents declined opportunities substantially to alter grand strategy in the post–cold war period.

Several conclusions about grand strategy after the cold war can be drawn from this comparative analysis. First, we might accept the suggestion, made in chapter 1, that political factors such as antitax sentiment determined post–cold war restructuring. Both Truman and Eisenhower clearly formulated grand strategies with an eye to the limited public tolerance for taxes and big government. Bush and Clinton showed less regard for antitax sentiment, but both men demonstrated sensitivity to other public demands, such as job security for defense industry workers.

Second, Morton Halperin (1974) is correct in observing that bureaucracies resist proposed changes that would require them to forfeit their missions. In 1948, 1953, and 1990–1994, Pentagon bureaucracies interpreted pressures to demobilize as threats to their very livelihoods. They resisted such demands by stressing that new and more perilous dangers were replacing the threats the country had survived. Third, my analysis confirms the observation that the Pentagon often mixes stonewalling and co-optation in pursuit of its aims. Facing strong pressures to demobilize in 1990, for example, the Pentagon, in the base force plan, voluntarily accepted a 25 percent cutback, and then adamantly refused additional reductions in its resources.

After the cold war ended, U.S. grand strategy changed in only minor ways. Even after Soviet power evaporated, the Pentagon's annual budget, force structure, and roles and missions remained similar to those of the cold war era. George Bush, in his endorsement of the base force plan, and Bill Clinton, in his decision to sustain defense spending, remained committed to cold war policies, despite the cost to domestic policy initiatives. While U.S. officials identified new types of adversaries and different conditions under which they would deploy military force, they left intact the overall grand strategy followed during the last phase of the cold war.

The evidence presented in this chapter suggests several reasons for the absence of change. First, one important bureaucracy, the Pentagon, resisted substantial and pervasive change in its budgets and missions. Second, time has not permitted significant reform of that bureaucracy, a development that might facilitate policy change. The evidence also suggests a third reason, namely, that both Bush and Clinton, claiming to be prudent about lurking dangers to American security, rejected suggestions from economizers that defense spending could be reduced safely. Slow to clarify changes in national security interests in the post–cold war era, Bush and Clinton continued to operate on the same strategic assumptions that determined policy for the last decade of the cold war. The reluctance of a large, powerful bureaucracy to change its missions and size and the reluctance of elite policy makers to change security policy combined to perpetuate the grand strategy of the late cold war period.

Duncan L. Clarke and Daniel O'Connor

9. Security Assistance Policy After the Cold War

Security assistance (SA), which includes military aid and other security-related categories of foreign assistance, has been a prominent feature of U.S. foreign policy since 1946. Every cold war president considered SA vital to national security, especially for containing the Soviet Union and its allies. The program faced fundamental questions about its future direction by 1989 and certainly after 1991. However, both George Bush and Bill Clinton assigned SA major roles in implementing several national objectives, from building democracy in eastern Europe to advancing peace in the Middle East. Much of the traditional SA budget, such as aid to Israel and Egypt, was largely unaffected by the end of the cold war, but other program elements changed significantly. Future programmatic change will be affected by evolving international events, fiscal constraints, interest groups, and especially, the disposition of the U.S. Congress.

Foreign aid is influenced, often decisively, by Congress. Indeed, the foreign assistance bill is Congress's most visible and important mechanism for affecting foreign policy. Even those who dispute the view that Congress has been notably assertive in foreign policy since the early 1970s acknowledge that presidents regularly "bargain for whatever foreign assistance they get" and that, at least in this area, "Congress has *not* acquiesced to the executive branch" (Hinckley 1994, 106). Therefore, in addressing one of the central issues of this book—the relationship between the substance of post–cold war U.S. foreign policy and changes in the policy process and structure—we will focus particular attention on Congress.

Major Elements of Security Assistance

For most of the cold war, SA constituted more than 50 percent of all U.S. foreign aid. Only in fiscal year 1992, for the first time in many years, did SA dip slightly below 50 percent. The figure stood at 45 percent in fiscal year 1996 (U.S. Agency for International Development [hereafter USAID] 1995, 4; U.S. Department of State 1995).

Together, the Foreign Military Financing (FMF) program and the Economic Support Fund (ESF) constituted about 95 percent of U.S. SA in the Bush and Clinton administrations. FMF aid for the purchase of U.S. military equipment was the largest component. The FMF program, which before 1989 was called the Foreign Military Sales (FMS) credit program, provided recipient countries with $43 billion in loans and $50 billion in grants from 1946 through 1995. Prior to 1989, when it was abolished, the Military Assistance Program (MAP) distributed another $59.2 billion in grants for the purchase of U.S. defense equipment and services (USAID 1995, 4; U.S. Department of State 1995, 520, 523).

The International Military Education and Training (IMET) program is a distinct military aid program established in 1976. Grants from IMET and its predecessor programs have provided professional military education and technical training to about 550,000 persons from allied and friendly armed forces. Since 1991, IMET has also funded the education and training of civilian as well as military officials in new democratic nations, including former Warsaw Pact countries and the newly independent states (NIS) of the former Soviet Union, in areas such as managing defense budgets, creating military codes of conduct, and instituting military judicial systems. From 1950 through 1995 IMET and its predecessors spent $2.6 billion (USAID 1995, 4; U.S. Department of State 1995, 524).

The Economic Support Fund was created in 1978, but it had several predecessors dating from 1951. During the 1950s the program provided budget support to western European nations, South Korea, Taiwan, and others, to enable them to channel more resources into defense infrastructures. In the 1960s and early 1970s, in addition to sustaining defense capabilities of friendly nations, its scope was expanded to promote political and economic "stability," especially in Southeast Asia. After 1978, ESF increasingly moved away from direct support of U.S. overseas military interests and toward more "political" objectives. This was most evident in the Middle East, where the justification for ESF was that it promoted peace between Israel and Egypt. A congressional report that accompanied the 1978 amendment to the Foreign Assistance Act of 1961 establishing the ESF says it is to assist "countries of political importance to the United States" (U.S. Congress, House Committee on Foreign Affairs [hereafter HFAC] 1978, 44; Nowels 1987, 6, 50–52). Although components of the program include development projects and commodity import credit, most ESF aid in recent years has taken the form of direct cash transfers. ESF has been the largest U.S. economic aid program since 1978, with Egypt and Israel receiving the lion's share. Between 1951 and 1995 the United States provided $78 billion in aid through ESF and its predecessors (USAID 1995, 4; U.S. Department of State 1995, 526).

Smaller SA programs include antiterrorism aid, international narcotics control, and voluntary peacekeeping operations (PKOs). Only two PKOs were funded through the voluntary account before fiscal year 1994: the Multilateral Force and Observers in the Sinai Peninsula, and the United Nations force in Cyprus. Annual costs averaged about $30 million. The Clinton administration raised this voluntary PKO fund to about $75 million per annum to cover a variety of missions (U.S. Department of State 1995, 206).[1]

All aid to Russia and other NIS is intended to further U.S. security interests. Congress stated expressly that "the purpose of providing aid to Russia is to increase the likelihood that . . . democracy and free market reforms will take hold, and that our defense budgets will not return to astronomical levels" (U.S. Congress, House Committee on Appropriations 1994a, 10). The effort that most directly addresses security concerns is the Nunn-Lugar Cooperative Threat Reduction (CTR) program which, among other things, seeks to safeguard or destroy various classes of nuclear weapons ("loose nukes") and other weapons of mass destruction in Russia, Ukraine, Belarus, and Kazakhstan. While Nunn-Lugar is funded through the Department of Defense budget and is not a *formal* SA program, it is certainly in the nature of security assistance. Through FY 1996, $1.8 billion had been appropriated for the CTR program (Tarnoff 1995, 16).

Security Assistance Budget Process: Executive Branch

The three major stages of executive participation in SA budgetary matters are formulating a budget request to Congress, supporting the request before Congress, and implementing foreign assistance legislation.

Much of the SA budget is substantially shielded from the budgetary process sketched here (see "Security Assistance" 1991, 1–7; Burke 1990, 119–25).[2] That is, Israel is accorded favored treatment, as is Egypt, because of Israel. This preferred standing was institutionalized in the Reagan administration following the formal commencement of "strategic cooperation" between Israel and the United States. A joint planning group composed of American and Israeli officials has met annually since 1984 to negotiate Israel's grant from Washington. Only after the group meets does Israel's budget package go to a receptive Congress. No other country is treated that way (Puschel 1992, 94–95).[3]

Every administration provides overall policy guidance for SA and commercial arms transfers. (Commercial arms sales are formally classified as security assistance. Because they are not foreign aid, they are outside the scope of the chapter.) The process usually begins with a determination of whether to increase or decrease the prior fiscal year's SA budget, or, in the case of an incoming administration, whether to establish a new baseline. Several factors may affect this initial decision, including: Office of Management and Budget (OMB) guidance; anticipated congressional reaction; the national political and economic climate; U.S. strategic and foreign policy priorities; and the needs of recipient countries. Unanticipated events may also prompt the administration to request a one-time supplemental appropriation.

The Department of State has the policy lead in SA and foreign aid generally. State's bureau of political-military affairs (PM) provides the undersecretary of state for arms control and international security affairs with support in this area. PM coordinates policy papers and early budget projections internally within the department and through State-DOD interagency groups. (The interagency committees during the Reagan-Bush era were called security assistance program review working groups [SAPRWGs]. The Clinton administration discontinued the SAPRWGs in late 1993.) PM works closely with DOD's Defense Security Assistance Agency (DSAA). Neither DSAA nor PM has an institutional identity with a particular region or country.

Regional and country interests are well represented, however. All U.S. embassies in countries with SA programs prepare an annual integrated assessment of security assistance (AIASA). The AIASA is the principal vehicle for stating SA requirements in preparing budgets for those countries that do not have periodic formal planning sessions with the United States. That is, the AIASA is less important for countries such as Greece, Turkey, Egypt, and Israel. In preparing AIASAs, embassies consult their own SA offices and the host governments. The regional U.S. commanders in chief (CINCs) also comment on AIASA submissions of U.S. missions. Regional interests are also well represented throughout the larger process. In both informal consultations and interagency meetings, State's regional bureaus and officials from the Office of International Security Affairs (ISA) in the Office of the Secretary of Defense (OSD) usually share common interests. For them, SA is a currency of diplomacy, and, predictably, they generally seek funds for "their" regions or countries.

The major actors in DOD are DSAA, the assistant secretary of defense for ISA (ASD/ISA) and ISA's regional divisions, the Joint Staff (J-5, plans and policy) of the Joint Chiefs of Staff, and the undersecretary of defense for policy. Certain SA issues are cleared through offices dealing with, for example, counterproliferation and human rights. The DOD units work closely with their counterparts at State, but only DSAA works full-time on SA and arms transfers. The ASD/ISA or, if necessary, the undersecretary of defense ultimately resolves internal DOD disputes.

White House involvement is usually through OMB, or, far less commonly, the National Security Council. OMB's influence depends on such factors as the style, character, and preferences of the president, and the president's relationship with the OMB director and the secretary of state. OMB has had a prominent role in the Clinton administration, but its traditional mission of limiting program increases was weakened during the Reagan years by the president's strong support for defense and SA expenditures and by OMB Director David Stockman's early, losing ("I got rolled") confrontation with Secretary of State Alexander Haig (Stockman 1986, 116–17). Foreign assistance was effectively capped during the Bush administration in FY 1991–1993, not by OMB, but by the Budget Enforcement Act of 1990 (P.L.101-508).

Following interagency meetings, the undersecretary of state attempts to form an integrated budget and resolve outstanding issues. The deputy secretary of state then provides final program and funding recommendations to the secretary of state for a decision. After making revisions, the secretary forwards the package to OMB in the fall. State and OMB often wrestle over the appropriate figure. Once a final total is established, it is forwarded to Congress in January in the federal budget for the next fiscal year. Detailed supporting information is contained in what in 1996 was titled the *Congressional Presentation for Foreign Operations*.

State Department officials and executive branch congressional liaison offices often consult with key members of Congress and their staffs before budget submission. They also testify at authorization and appropriation hearings; meet privately with legislators, especially when the House and Senate appropriations committees begin to mark up the FA act; and provide material for presentation to the budget committees. With SA budgets effectively frozen or declining since fiscal year 1985, the executive branch has focused much of its attention on the proportion of security to development aid, reducing congressional earmarks and conditionality,[4] seeking additional funds for unforeseen crises, and challenging extraneous amendments to the foreign aid bill.

Once that bill is signed into law, DSAA implements the military aid portion and the Agency for International Development (AID) manages the ESF portion. However, neither DSAA nor AID has monitored SA expenditures effectively (see U.S. General Accounting Office [hereafter GAO] 1993a, 1993b). For instance, despite scandals involving illegal diversions of about $100 million in U.S. military aid by Israeli officials, Israel's large-scale use of FMF for direct commercial contracts with U.S. firms has never been systematically audited. When DSAA tried to improve oversight in 1993 by requiring Israel and other countries to make FMF purchases of American goods only through government-to-government channels, Israel complained and the Senate then blocked DSAA's action (U.S. Congress, House Subcommittee on Oversight and Investigations 1993, 1–4; U.S. Congress, House Subcommittee on Oversight and Investigations 1992, 69–77).

Except for an incoming administration's usual changes in personnel, titles, and some organizational arrangements, the overall SA budget process remained substantially intact in 1993–1995. Clinton did attempt to move away from a country-specific approach in 1994, but Congress, and de facto the executive branch, continued to allocate most SA on a country basis. Deputy Secretary of State Strobe Talbott was a major player in aid to the NIS.

Security Assistance Allocations: 1949–1989

The United States provided only economic assistance to postwar Europe before 1949. That year, the establishment of NATO and the passage of the Mutual Defense Assistance Act (P.L. 81–329), which created the MAP, made mutual security pacts and SA integral, intertwined elements of the doctrine of containment. The lion's share of military and economic SA grants went initially to western Europe. However, except for the base rights countries of Spain, Greece, and Turkey, SA aid to Europe was largely phased out by the mid-1950s.

SA was thought to fit well with President Eisenhower's cost-conscious New Look defense policy. Administration officials asserted it was cheaper to maintain a foreign soldier than an American soldier. The focus of aid shifted gradually to the Third World, especially Asia. One-half of all U.S.

foreign assistance went to East and Southeast Asia by fiscal year 1955. Two-thirds of the Asian aid from fiscal year 1954 through fiscal year 1961 went to South Korea ($4.2 billion), Taiwan ($2.7 billion), and South Vietnam ($2.2 billion).

Military and economic SA constituted 83 percent of all U.S. aid to this region (USAID 1991). Its overriding purpose was to maintain anticommunist regimes friendly to the United States and to secure military bases or facilities in Japan and the Philippines that could be used in a conflict with China or the Soviet Union.

It was assumed that alleviation of poverty in the Third World would inhibit the spread of communism. Hence, development assistance, like SA, was viewed largely in a security context. Moreover, congressional support for economic development aid was much more likely if this aid could be portrayed as an important element of U.S. security policy. By 1960, development aid had risen to 41 percent of all foreign aid. An annual average of 55 percent of the foreign aid budget was development assistance during the Kennedy-Johnson years, and Latin America was a major recipient (Heginbotham and Nowels 1988, 19).

The 1960s also saw a sharp, absolute increase in SA. From fiscal year 1963 through fiscal year 1973, the East and Southeast Asian regions continued to dominate the program. South Korea received $4.1 billion in military aid during this period, but the Vietnam War drove the program. In addition to the usual aid, a special fund was created for Vietnam: the Military Assistance Service Fund (MASF). Despite its location in DOD's budget, MASF was clearly an SA program, and it distributed more than $15 billion between fiscal year 1966 and fiscal year 1975 (USAID 1991; Grimmett 1985, 23–24).

In 1969 Richard Nixon declared that, while the United States would honor its commitments, America's allies and friends would have to bear the primary burden of their own defense. "Central" to the Nixon Doctrine, said the president, was a pledge of substantial foreign aid to allied and friendly nations (Nixon 1970, 294). Central as well were commercial arms sales, particularly to regional surrogates such as Iran and Saudi Arabia.

Aid to Israel escalated more than 600 percent, to $634 million in fiscal year 1971, as Congress passed the first in what became an unbroken series of large, earmarked aid packages to the Jewish state. The Middle East was absorbing 70 percent of U.S. SA by the mid-1970s, eclipsing Asia as the leading regional aid recipient. Most of this aid went to Israel and Egypt under the rubric of furthering peace and stability (Mark 1995, 14).

Congress became increasingly critical of conventional arms transfers and U.S. military aid during the 1970s. Restrictive legislation was enacted every year from 1973 to 1976. The most notable was the Arms Export Control Act of 1976 (AECA) (P.L. 94–329). The AECA imposed specific constraints on the president in this area and stated for the first time in legislation that arms transfers contributed to regional conflict.

The SA allocation pattern of 1974–1976 continued throughout the Carter administration. Carter's attempt to steer U.S. foreign policy away from its fixation on the Soviet Union had failed by 1979 and his successor, Ronald Reagan, possessed what Robert McFarlane called a visceral "disdain for Commies" (quoted in Cannon 1991, 316–17). Foreign aid levels soared in the first Reagan administration. Between fiscal year 1981 and fiscal year 1985 overall aid rose from $11 billion to $19 billion per annum. ESF doubled from $3 billion to $6 billion and FMF increased from $4.6 billion to $6.6 billion (Heginbotham and Nowels 1988, 17).

SA (including commercial arms sales) was a major foreign policy tool and a factor in defense planning for a global "full-court press" against Moscow and its supposed proxies. The number of ESF recipients went from twenty in 1981 to almost sixty in 1985. Congress permitted the Reagan administration to extend the MAP, which otherwise would have lapsed. Finally, to provide recipient countries with better-quality aid (less debt burden), the administration shifted SA away from loans. More than 90 percent of SA was in grant form by 1989 (U.S. Congress HFAC 1989b, 10–11; Nowels 1989, 8).

There were distinct categories of SA recipients. Israel and Egypt were the most privileged. They accounted for 57 percent of worldwide SA during the Reagan era. The base rights nations of Greece, Turkey, Spain, Portugal, and the Philippines were a second group. They received annually 15–20 percent of all SA. A third category, labeled "frontline states," bordered countries whose governments were backed by the Soviet Union: Pakistan, Thailand, the Sudan, and others. Overlapping the frontline states was a Central American-Caribbean grouping, including especially El Salvador and Honduras (USAID 1995). SA continued to dominate aid budgets in the second Reagan administration, but it came under increasing attack. Congress reacted to the 1985 Gramm-Rudman-Hollings deficit reduction plan, the shift away from development aid, human rights abuses, and a thawing of the cold war, by reducing the program. Indeed, while sometimes restored in supplemental funding, SA was cut by Congress every year from 1985 through 1994 in the regular appropriation. Congress also began earmarking almost everything. For instance, the Reagan administration distributed 44 percent of appropriated ESF funds as it wished in fiscal year 1985. By fiscal year 1989, 98 percent of ESF was earmarked (U.S. Congress HFAC 1989a, 194).

Post–Cold War Security Assistance

Bush Administration

The dramatic events in eastern Europe in 1989, followed by the collapse of the Soviet Union in 1991, eliminated a cold war rationale for SA. Changes in the program came slowly, however. Sometimes change was prompted by international events, sometimes it was driven (or impeded) by Congress.

The end of the cold war, criticism of military aid by some members of Congress, and public antipathy toward foreign aid merged with new federal budget constraints to further reduce SA. Indeed, most SA recipients during the Reagan era were cut off completely by fiscal year 1993.

The Budget Enforcement Act of 1990 set strict caps on fiscal year 1991–1993 budget authority and outlays for, among other things, the international affairs function of the federal budget (of which foreign assistance is a central component). This meant in effect that any additional funding for SA would either have to come from supplementals, as with the Gulf War in 1990–1991, or from direct trade-offs among accounts within the international affairs budget (Nowels and Collier 1991, 3). The budgetary walls separating international affairs, defense, and domestic spending that were enforced by the 1990 legislation came down in fiscal year 1994. This allowed the international affairs budget to "raid" DOD's budget for aid to Russia, but also exposed foreign aid to even greater reductions than during the Bush years.

In addition to furthering several foreign policy objectives, the Bush 1991 national security strategy statement envisioned SA supporting three of the four "fundamental elements" of U.S. defense strategy: crisis response, reconstitution, and (especially) the forward presence of U.S. armed forces. The statement asserted that SA "must enhance the ability of other nations to enhance our deployments" (Bush 1991b, 9). The 1993 national strategy document, issued just days before George Bush left office, reiterated these themes, but also said it was time to "refashion" security assistance and ease the "transition of foreign militaries to democratic systems" (Bush 1993, 14–15, 20).

The IMET program held its own despite criticism from some liberal members of Congress. Since antiterrorism and international narcotics control related to domestic concerns, they actually increased in size. Similarly, two countries with influential domestic constituencies maintained their levels of aid—Israel and, to a lesser degree, Greece. Indeed, Israel (and Egypt) did quite nicely. A pattern set in fiscal year 1985 held throughout the Bush and Clinton period. Annually, Israel received $1.8 billion in FMF and $1.2 billion in ESF, while Egypt received $1.3 billion in FMF and $815 million in ESF. From fiscal year 1981 through fiscal year 1993, Israel received a total of $21.9 billion in FMF and $16.4 billion in ESF. During the same period, Egypt received $15.7 billion in FMF and $11 billion in ESF. Egypt also had $6.7 billion of its military assistance loans from the United States forgiven in 1990, in recognition of its dire fiscal situation and role in the Gulf crisis (P.L. 101–513). Israel fared even better. Among other things, in 1989 it was allowed to refinance outstanding military assistance loans at very favorable rates; during the buildup to the Gulf War $700 million in surplus U.S. military equipment was authorized for Israel; and it received supplemental ESF aid of $650 million in 1991. Beyond this, Israel received, and still receives, numerous unique benefits, including: the right to annually spend $475 million of its FMF aid in Israel (offshore procurement), rather than in the United States; receipt of all SA early in the fiscal year, enabling Israel to earn about $70–100 million dollars interest annually on U.S. Treasury notes; substantial indirect aid through DOD's politically less visible budget (such as the largely U.S.-funded Arrow antitactical ballistic missile); and several categories of nonsecurity assistance ranging from aid (since fiscal year 1973) to settle Jewish refugees to housing loan guarantees (beginning in fiscal year 1972 and culminating with a $10 billion loan in fiscal year 1993) to the United States, paying for some of *Israel's* foreign aid program (Clarke 1994; Mark 1995; Nowels and Mark 1994; U.S. Department of State 1993a).

Development aid under the Support of East European Democracy (SEED) Act of 1989 (P.L. 101–79) and some IMET funds had begun flowing into eastern Europe by fiscal year 1990. SEED aid reached an annual level of $400 million by fiscal year 1993. However, aid to the former Soviet Union, beginning in fiscal year 1992, was the most stunning occurrence. The key legislation was the Freedom Support Act of 1992 (P.L. 102–511). Aid eventually assumed several forms, including DOD funds for dismantling nuclear weapons and military facilities, ESF, development aid, and special aid. Virtually all the aid was motivated by security considerations; that is, it was designed to ease Russia and other NIS toward democracy and greater stability, free market economies, and less threatening military postures (Nowels 1993, 7, 16; Tarnoff 1995, 1–14, 16).

Following the December 1989 U.S. invasion of Panama and the February 1990 election in Nicaragua that ousted the Sandinista government, Congress appropriated $420 million for Panama and $300 million for Nicaragua, primarily in ESF. By fiscal year 1993, virtually no SA went to either country. No Latin American nation received more U.S. aid during the Reagan era than El Salvador. But human rights violations contributed to aid reductions and, following the January 1992 peace agreement between government and rebel forces, SA to El Salvador all but vanished. Honduras, another large aid recipient in the Reagan period, also saw its SA disappear (USAID 1994, 97, 102; U.S. Department of State 1993).

Aid to Pakistan was a casualty of the Soviet withdrawal from Afghanistan and nuclear proliferation concerns. The president no longer certified Pakistan as not having a nuclear device, a prerequisite for SA under the 1985 Pressler Amendment. Pakistan had been the fifth largest SA recipient during the 1980s, but it has received no military aid since 1991 (USAID 1995, 137).

Base rights countries also suffered. The United States withdrew from military installations in the Philippines in 1992. Greece, Turkey, and Portugal continued to get SA, but the level and quality of aid declined. Only $980 million, primarily in concessional loans, went to these nations by fiscal year 1993. The executive branch had long opposed the congressionally mandated 7:10 aid ratio between Greece and Turkey ($7 of aid to Greece for every $10 to Turkey). Since before 1989, Greece had been considered of much less strategic value to the United States than Turkey. However, Congress again came to Athens's defense (Clarke and O'Connor 1993).

The Clinton Administration

The central objectives of the Clinton administration included the promotion of democracy, stability, free market economies, and denuclearization in Russia, the other former Soviet republics, and elsewhere. In 1993, Congress granted the administration's request for a $2.5 billion aid package (of which SA was only one element) for the former Soviet republics. However, this was politically feasible only because Congress insisted upon a trade-off under which it simultaneously and severely cut aid to most other regions and countries (except, of course, Israel and Egypt) (Rosner 1995, 45–64). For example, Congress approved only 43 percent of the administration's foreign aid request for Latin America. For Russia and the other NIS, however, total U.S. foreign aid (excluding the DOD-budgeted Nunn-Lugar aid) amounted to $2 billion in fiscal year 1993, $904 million in fiscal year 1994, and $842 million in fiscal year 1995. The administration reduced its fiscal year 1996 aid request for the former Soviet region in the face of congressional concerns about the ineffective use of some aid, and allegations of arms control treaty noncompliance and human rights violations (Tarnoff 1995).

Relative to development aid and most other forms of assistance, SA actually increased as a percentage of the budget. SA went from 38 percent of a $16.3 billion foreign assistance budget in fiscal year 1993 to 45 percent of a $12.1 billion budget in fiscal year 1996 under the Republican-controlled 104th Congress. There were several reasons for this. First, as the foreign aid budget fell, the bulk of SA—aid to Egypt and Israel—remained frozen at customarily high levels. Also, the conservative 104th Congress was less critical of security aid than were its more liberal predecessors. Finally, President Clinton, like other presidents before him, discovered that foreign aid, and SA in particular, was a useful tool of foreign policy. Indeed, in 1995 Clinton's national security adviser, Anthony Lake, denounced "backdoor isolationists" in Congress who slashed foreign aid, thereby damaging "tools America has used for fifty years to maintain our leadership in the world" (Lake 1995a).

It was in the Clinton administration that the United States truly began to pursue a postcontainment foreign policy, and with it, a post–cold war SA program. However, that program retained a decided continuity with the past in many respects. This was nowhere more evident than in President Clinton's conventional arms transfer policy, which was announced in February 1995 in Presidential Decision Directive 34. The Clinton policy was squarely in line with the largely open-ended Reagan-Bush approach. That is, arms transfers were justified and encouraged on a wide variety of often vague or even contradictory grounds (Grimmet 1995; Lumpe 1995, 9–14).

Clinton's national security statements linked SA to four of the five principal elements of this foreign policy: enlarging the community of free market democracies, maintaining strong military forces with peacetime forward presence commitments, responding to global threats such as those posed by terrorists and narcotics traffickers, and meeting other security needs such as supporting multilateral peace operations. These declaratory policy statements gave SA a prominent role "through training programs, . . . military contacts, and security assistance programs that include judicious foreign military sales," by which the United States "can strengthen . . . our friends and allies" (Clinton 1995, 1–17). This was as vigorous a rationale for SA as was set forth by the Bush administration.

Only $13.7 billion was appropriated for foreign aid in fiscal year 1994 and again in fiscal year 1995, and several accounts were reduced. Greece and Turkey received just $770 million in Treasury rate (i.e., not concessional) loans in fiscal year 1994 and $620 million in fiscal year 1995. Despite the Clinton administration's assessment that more military aid was required to help dismantle drug trafficking operations in South America, the State Department's international narcotics control budget was reduced by Congress, until the 104th Congress increased it in fiscal year 1996. The process of decapitalizing the Special Defense Acquisition Fund (SDAF) also began at this time. The SDAF was established in 1982 to ensure that U.S. defense stocks would not be seriously depleted if an ally needed rapid delivery of military equipment (Nowels 1995, 11).

Responding to congressional directives, the IMET program—which retained most of its funding—expanded its mission in 1991 and 1992 to include instruction in civilian control over the military, improvement of military justice systems, and training of national legislators for overseeing their national militaries (P.L. 101–513; P.L. 102–391). IMET and a parallel Pentagon program focused heavily on eastern Europe and the former Soviet region.

Some other accounts actually increased. Voluntary U.S. funding of the United Nations' peacekeeping operations rose from $27 million in fiscal year 1993 to $68 million in fiscal year 1996. A new account, the Nonproliferation and Disarmament Fund (NDF), was established with $10 million in fiscal year 1994 to help create viable export control systems in the former Soviet republics. The NDF was under the rubric of Nunn-Lugar, but funded out of International Affairs, rather than the DOD budget. The allocation for the NDF rose to $25 million in fiscal year 1996 to support science centers in Kiev and Moscow as well as export controls (U.S. Department of State 1995, 190).

Regionally, SA continued to be virtually synonymous with the Middle East. In addition to Israel-Egypt, Jordan began to receive some SA by fiscal year 1993 and obtained $275 million in debt forgiveness that year. Another "peace process recipient," the West Bank/Gaza Strip, received $75 million in fiscal year 1995 and again in fiscal year 1996. In Europe, loans continued to Greece and Turkey, but Portugal was "graduated" as an aid recipient. Very little SA went to either Asia or Africa, and Latin America experienced a continued reduction in both ESF and FMF aid. While much of the small counternarcotics and IMET programs went to Latin America, only Haiti—in the wake of the U.S. intervention—received a notable level of security assistance (USAID 1995; U.S. Department of State 1995).

By April 1993, the Clinton administration had begun to broaden and deepen its relations with the non-Russian former Soviet republics. Whereas President Bush had used Nunn-Lugar aid as an incentive to persuade the former Soviet republics to denuclearize as a precondition to a more broad-based relationship with the United States, Clinton's approach was across-the-board constructive engagement.

The Clinton administration became an ardent advocate of a CTR program that it viewed as opening valuable channels of communication, affording the United States a "seat at the table" for regional security affairs, and ultimately, achieving the denuclearization of Ukraine, Kazakhstan, and Belarus. There was enthusiastic support for CTR within the national security bureaucracy, largely because of a shared perception that it made sense to help eliminate a former enemy's nuclear weapons and convert much of its defense industry to peaceful purposes. The 103d Congress agreed; it fully supported Nunn-Lugar.

This situation changed in 1995, especially in the House of Representatives. Some House members, particularly conservative Republicans, charged that Russia had not complied with its arms control obligations concerning chemical and biological weapons, that Russia was using CTR funds to modernize its weapons of mass destruction, and that the General Accounting Office was critical of the program (USGAO 1995). The House then slashed the administration's $371 million CTR budget request for fiscal year 1996 to a mere $200 million. However, the Senate was more supportive and $365 million was ultimately appropriated.

Nunn-Lugar, while certainly not problem-free, was considered vital by most U.S. security specialists, whether inside or outside government. Moreover, the cumulative cost of the CTR program through fiscal year 1996 was relatively modest—one-third less than the *annual* U.S. SA subsidy to Israel.

Congress and Security Assistance

Congress takes a keen interest in foreign aid. The foreign aid bill is the only regularly scheduled foreign policy debate in Congress. It is with foreign assistance, perhaps more than any other area, that Congress can affect foreign policy most directly (Warburg 1989, 231–73; Hinckley 1994, 101–24). Since foreign assistance involves the transfer of American tax dollars to nonvoting foreigners, Congress also has an incentive—albeit a highly selective one—to oversee the executive's expenditure of these funds. Moreover, legislators know that foreign aid, while often supported by elite opinion, does not enjoy sustained, broad-based support from the American public. This is especially the case for military aid (see Rielly

1991, 93; Wittkopf 1990, 151–53). There are few political costs for voting to cut foreign aid, except from highly specific constituencies such as wheat farmers, Jewish Americans, and defense firms that profit from arms transfers.

Members of Congress have expressed several policy concerns over the years about SA. Many members want more development aid and less military aid. Concerns are regularly voiced that aid (of any kind) "just doesn't work," that it diverts resources from domestic priorities and worsens the U.S. balance of payments. Congress has worried that SA might entangle the United States in ill-considered commitments. Legislators, especially liberal and moderate ones, fault SA for sometimes maintaining repressive regimes. This same group also tends to view military aid as a force for regional instability in that it contributes to conventional arms races and military coups. Still others oppose aiding countries—such as Pakistan—that have acquired or are acquiring nuclear weapons (even though they support aid to a nuclearized Israel). Because of such misgivings and the political volatility of foreign aid, Congress moved to restrict the president's flexibility to dispense SA. The original Greek-Turkish Aid Act of 1947 contained comparatively few restrictions on the president. But successive laws governing SA embodied more stringent requirements for the allocation and receipt of such aid. Congress has not hesitated to exercise its budgetary prerogatives. Long before the end of the cold war the president's SA request was often reduced by 10 percent or more and, beginning in the 1970s, Congress earmarked ever larger portions of the SA budget for favored nations and programs.

American SA policy is ultimately the product of bargaining and compromise between the president and Congress. The president usually proposes and presents a program he believes meets national security requirements and at least some major congressional concerns. However, especially since the mid-1970s, Congress has often determined significant SA policies, even over executive branch opposition.

From 1981 through 1995 Congress succeeded in passing foreign assistance authorization legislation only twice: in 1981 (for fiscal year 1982–1983) and 1985 (for fiscal year 1986–1987). The House usually considers authorization measures before the Senate. During the 1981–1994 period the authorization process typically began to break down when the House bill became overladen with amendments and provisos. The administration then indicated its opposition to the House measure and started working with the appropriations committees to fashion a more acceptable bill. At this point the Senate had little incentive to consider an authorization bill

(Warburg 1989, 233–35). If the House did pass one—as in 1984, 1987, and 1993—the Senate allotted insufficient time to produce a bill of its own, even when the Senate Foreign Relations Committee reported one. A foreign aid authorization bill reached the president's desk in 1981 only because of strong backing from an incoming Reagan administration. This happened again in 1985 when the chairmen of the authorizing committees actively pushed the bills by limiting amendments.

When there is no foreign aid authorization legislation, authorization is folded into the appropriations legislation. Hence, the primary tool for Congress to decide annual funding and policy matters since 1985 has been the annual foreign operations appropriation. Foreign aid appropriations bills are generally freestanding. However, during much of the Reagan period foreign aid appropriations were often submerged as just one component of huge, omnibus continuing resolutions that lumped foreign aid with other federal programs.

Such continuing resolutions had a certain appeal to the administration and Congress. For supporters of foreign aid they offered protection from legislators who might otherwise gut the bill with amendments. For the administration they meant fewer earmarks and conditions on aid. The executive branch also negotiated with fewer legislators: the two foreign operations subcommittees of the appropriations committees and the leadership. The authorizing committees could be bypassed (Obey and Lancaster 1988, 147–48). For Congress, omnibus continuing resolutions provided protective political cover for members who did want to go on record by voting for a separate, visible foreign aid bill. Yet continuing resolutions reflect weakness in the democratic process because they promote avoidance of accountability, effectively require a "yes" vote lest government close down, and are "strong indicators of dissensus [which] testify to a breakdown . . . in ordinary modes of accommodation" (Wildavsky 1992, 234–36).

Overhauling Foreign Aid

Proposals to reform foreign assistance are nearly as old as the program itself. Successive presidential commissions during the cold war, from the Fairless Commission in 1957 to the Gorman Report in 1988, assessed SA programs, generally with an eye toward gaining more resources from a frequently skeptical Congress (Clarke and Woehrel 1991, 231–33).

As the cold war wound down in 1989, a House Foreign Affairs Committee Task Force headed by Reps. Lee Hamilton (D-Ind.) and Benjamin

Gilman (R-N.Y.) issued an important report. The task force found that the foreign aid program had contradictory goals, outdated and ambiguous provisions, and severe management and accountability deficiencies. The task force also concluded that congressional earmarks, onerous reporting requirements, and restrictions subverted effective program implementation. The report recommended repealing the governing legislation: the Foreign Assistance Act of 1961 (P.L. 95–384), as amended. In its stead, the task force urged enactment of new legislation to, among other things: give the president greater flexibility by lifting most restrictions imposed by Congress; establish a new core of program goals emphasizing development, humanitarian, and environmental concerns; end military aid to base rights nations; create a single military assistance account; and move ESF project aid to the development assistance account (Clarke and Woehrel 1991, 233–41; Nowels 1990; U.S. Congress HFAC 1989b).

The House accepted most of the recommendations, except for reducing earmarks and phasing out base rights aid. A foreign aid reform bill was passed by the House in 1989, but it died because of Senate inaction and lack of support from the Bush administration. Still, some task force prescriptions were realized. The termination of MAP that year essentially created a single military assistance account and, by fiscal year 1993, grant aid to base rights countries had virtually ended. House and Senate conferees in 1991 made headway toward restructuring foreign aid (H.R. 2508), but the bill was not a comprehensive overhaul like the Hamilton-Gilman initiative, and the House rejected the conference report (Nowels 1992, 39).

Under pressure from a Congress still controlled by Democrats, the Clinton administration in 1994 attempted to overhaul the entire foreign assistance program and, in so doing, offer its vision of the future of SA. The proposed Peace, Prosperity, and Democracy Act (H.R. 3765), which was transmitted to Congress in early 1994, abandoned the practice of budgeting foreign aid resources around functional accounts such as FMF, ESF, development aid, and so forth. Rather, it sought to reorganize foreign aid policy and budget allocations around five thematic foreign policy objectives: encouraging sustainable development, building democracy, promoting peace, providing humanitarian and crisis aid, and spurring economic growth through trade and investment (Nowels 1994).

The administration asserted that this new framework would strengthen public and congressional support for foreign aid by restoring coherence and direction to the program through a focus on the goal of "enlarging" the sphere of democracy. All foreign aid was intended to support one or more thematic objectives, and was not to be country oriented; instead, it was designed to advance broad U.S. goals (democracy, free market economies, etc.) and to meet shared global concerns, such as weapons proliferation, refugees, and so forth. Most SA in the draft bill fell under Title II (Building Democracy) and especially, Title III (Promoting Peace). Title II would direct economic and military aid to countries making the transition to democracy, though authorization of aid to the NIS and eastern Europe would remain, respectively, under the Freedom Support and SEED Acts. Title III stated that regional conflicts posed continuing threats to the United States; it noted the U.S. interest in Middle East peace; and, most sweepingly, it allowed the use of aid for any of three purposes: to resolve conflict, counter security threats, or promote collective security.

H.R. 3765 was somewhat elusive about how funds would be programmed but the president was granted broad authority to offer aid for political, economic, and security reasons. There was a provision, however, for Congress to separately authorize and appropriate military aid programs administered by DOD, thereby allowing Congress to set the respective levels of military and economic aid. Sensitive to congressional concerns about global arms transfers, the bill stipulated—but did not require—that the president lean toward development assistance once regional threats subside. Much to the chagrin of many members of Congress, the bill was also framed to pursue one of the principal recommendations of the 1989 Hamilton Task Force: the virtual elimination of earmarks. However, *none* of the traditional functions performed by SA programs would have disappeared under the proposed legislation; only their packaging, organization, and (perhaps) funding levels would have changed.

But Congress failed to act in 1994 and H.R. 3765 was a short-lived attempt to reform the cumbersome foreign aid program. Many members of Congress objected that the proposed Peace, Prosperity, and Democracy Act would shift excessive power to the president. Moreover, there was no political constituency for reform. In fact, the powerful pro-Israel lobby opposed changing a system under which it was the primary beneficiary. With the onset of a Republican Congress in January 1995, other priorities took precedence. Indeed, Sen. Jesse Helms (R-N.C.), the new chairman of the Senate Foreign Relations Committee, denounced foreign aid as this "stupid business of giving away taxpayers' money" (quoted in Goshko 1994a). Senator Helms then launched a campaign to abolish the Agency for International Development as part of a restructuring of Washington's cold war apparatus.

Future of Security Assistance

The principal cold war justification for foreign aid vanished by at least 1991. Hence, it was understandable that aid levels would fall. There is still a rationale for SA, however. Post–cold war administrations thus far have found SA (and commercial arms sales) important for strengthening U.S. defense presence overseas, assisting newly democratic nations, maintaining ties with key friends and allies, supporting Middle East peace, and countering nuclear proliferation, terrorism, and illicit drugs. There will be changes, of course. Base rights loans to Greece and Turkey might end; aid to the NIS could decline; and peace between Arabs and Israelis could decrease (or increase) aid levels. Yet some form of SA, by whatever name, will likely be used as long as the United States plays a leading role in a conflict-prone international system.

This is not a paean for SA. Since 1946 the program has supported both commendable and questionable policy objectives, from helping South Korea move toward a secure, self-confident, dynamic society and inhibiting global nuclear proliferation, to funding the Vietnam War and bolstering repressive regimes in Central America. Few cold war or post–cold war goals and rationales for SA are unchallengeable. The program has always been a two-edged sword for the United States, and often for aid recipients. SA may advance national and regional security, but it does not invariably encourage internal political or economic stability. Human rights and promotion of democracy took a backseat to containing communism during the cold war in Iran, Guatemala, the Philippines, and elsewhere. Likewise, there is no assurance that historians will judge that aiding Russia bolstered democracy. Moreover, the correlation between aid and influence is exceedingly imperfect. While SA affords levers for affecting the policies and practices of governments, it may breed a sense of resentment and dependence, as in Greece and the Philippines. Military aid may also either fuel regional instability or contribute to a more stable deterrence.

There are other problems, including shoddy oversight of aid programs and ineffective international narcotics control efforts. Particularly daunting is the albatross of Israel-Egypt aid that consumes the SA budget, distorts the larger foreign aid program, and thwarts fundamental reform. While reasonable U.S. financial support for an Arab-Israeli peace process is advisable, the notion that the United States must annually subsidize Israel and Egypt in excess of $5 billion in a post–cold war era is spurious. Israel and Egypt view these subsidies, compliments of the American taxpayer, as entitlements.

In a classic case of aid misexpenditure, many farmers in Egypt have fed their cattle bread from American grain. That aid once served the U.S. strategic objective of solidifying peace with Israel. Now, however, the time is long past for the United States to stop rewarding Cairo for doing what is in its own best interests. This level of dependency is unhealthy. Perhaps domestic fiscal and political factors and competing priorities may eventually combine to force Washington to look past the fear that its interests cannot be realized *without* continual massive aid to Egypt (see Zimmerman 1993, 85–106, 180). Contrary to declaratory U.S. policy, most of those within the national security bureaucracy agree with Bernard Reich, a vigorous champion of Israel, that "Israel is of limited military or economic importance to the United States. . . . It is not a strategically vital state" (Reich 1995, 123). Yet a former Israeli deputy minister of finance has been proven correct in his 1981 assertion that U.S. "aid is a narcotic and we [Israelis] are hooked. . . . This [aid] elevator will go down when we tell you. You won't tell us" (quoted in Zimmerman 1993, 150). Notable public support for large-scale aid to Israel plummeted by the late 1980s (Ginsberg 1993, 220; Kull 1995, 11–12), but a supportive Congress, prodded by the Israel lobby, has maintained the flow. Yet an avowedly pro-Israeli group of past and present U.S. government officials warned in 1993 that public support for this aid could wane even further. That group advised considering the reduction of ESF aid (Report 1993, 25–27, 52).

Aid to Israel and Egypt illustrates why an attempt such as that of the Clinton administration to rationalize or harmonize foreign aid programs with broad national goals and interests will inevitably fall short. Foreign aid is infused with domestic political and economic considerations. It straddles one of the busiest intersections of executive-legislative relations, where partisan, institutional, interest group, and individual preferences meet and regularly collide. Foreign assistance also affords Congress a unique lever for affecting U.S. foreign policy. Unless Congress opts out of the foreign policy business, an unlikely prospect, foreign aid is here to stay. Aid, including SA, will be adjusted, if haltingly and imperfectly, to a new international environment.

Pietro S. Nivola

10. Commercializing Foreign Affairs?

American Trade Policy After the Cold War

A newly established council convenes at the White House. Its charge is to oversee and coordinate international and domestic economic policy. Within four months the council issues a report entitled "The United States in a Changing World Economy." Many of the report's 132 pages bewail America's waning competitiveness. A decline in the U.S. share of world wealth is said to be "striking and disturbing." "Our economic leadership in many fields is being challenged" by foreign competitors. Policy makers have not placed sufficiently "high priority on our planning now to increase the strength of our position in technology-intensive products." "Establishing a more equitable relationship with Japan is an immediate problem." From now on, U.S. commercial policy "must command major attention" in order to create "jobs" ("The Peterson Report" 1971; "White House Report" 1971).

The president is much taken with these themes. He reads the report three times and soon prepares a series of aggressive measures, some of which reportedly leave the Japanese, among others, "angry, resentful and determined to retaliate sooner or later" (Meier 1973, 153). One of his aides explains: "In the past, economic interests were sacrificed when they came into conflict with diplomatic interests." Those days are over. Henceforth, declares a key cabinet officer, "Santa Claus is dead."

The script reads like an opening scene from the Clinton presidency—except that the year is 1971, the president is Richard Nixon, and the report is the work of his Council on International Economic Policy, not to be confused with Clinton's National Economic Council established more recently ("The Peterson Report" 1971; "White House Report" 1971). The considerable similarity between the activities then and now raises questions about how, if at all, U.S. trade policy has changed after the cold war.

The Clinton administration's eagerness to "raise the prominence of economic issues" in foreign affairs is not especially novel ("NEC Seeks to Highlight Trade" 1993, 2). In truth, the U.S. government was busy raising the prominence of those issues long before the current administration's keen preoccupation with them. True, the foreign policy of the first of the post–cold war presidencies frequently lacked clarity with respect to other international priorities, particularly at the outset. Whereas U.S. policy during most of the years following World War II moved synergistically on the dual tracks of commerce and security, policy in 1993 and 1994 often seemed to ride on a commerce-driven monorail. After that, however, some rebalancing got under way. By 1996, geostrategic concerns had regained more of their traditional claim on U.S. international relations, even for a president predisposed to dwell on other matters.

These observations have important implications. The emphasis in the early 1990s on the hot pursuit of commercial goals abroad was premised in part on the false impression that the nation had routinely sacrificed its economic welfare to security objectives in the past, and that the American economy was suffering as a consequence. Setting the record straight casts doubt on the notion, prevalent at the beginning of the Clinton administration, that the supposed self-denials of an earlier time called for compensation. The lessons of history suggest, moreover, that the imperatives of the cold war years and those of their aftermath have elements in common. In today's still perilous world Americans have to continue reconciling their economic wants with wider strategic interests, much as we did earlier in the postwar period. There seems to be better recognition of that reality now than four years ago, at least in the executive branch. How stable American global leadership is likely to be in the years ahead, however, remains unclear. Discomfort with globalism persists.

Commercial Martyrdom?

During a nationally televised debate about the North American Free Trade Agreement (NAFTA) in November 1993, Ross Perot told viewers that the United States had burdened itself with unfavorable trade treaties. "Our problem," said Perot, "is we do the world's dumbest trade agreements. You go back to the agreements we've done all over the world, you'd be amazed that adults did them" (CNN 1993). Perot's assertion was not original; he was only the latest in a long line of populist politicians to claim that U.S. negotiators regularly gave away more than they received. The response of Perot's opponent, Vice President Albert Gore, was more surprising. Gore spent little time challenging the "dumb deals" premise; he stressed instead that NAFTA represented an exception.

The incident illustrated a curious phenomenon. Evidently, perceiving this country as a long-suffering trade "wimp" or "sucker" had become the received wisdom. Indeed, even sophisticated observers have accepted the notion. Although no serious scholar would characterize any stage of American commercial history in the same simplistic fashion, some of the best have perhaps been too quick to conclude that U.S. policy frequently abnegated the national economic interest in the years of the Pax Americana (Nye 1990).

But what actually happened during those years?

Nixon's Economic Bombshells

Let us return to President Nixon's initiatives more than two decades ago. His trade advisers felt they "needed to get the attention of the world and make it realize we are in a new era" ("White House Report" 1971, 2238). That they did—in spades. In August 1971 the president threatened to impose mandatory quotas on Asian textiles, levied an across-the-board surcharge on imports, and abandoned unilaterally the Bretton Woods monetary system. (On the domestic front, Nixon took the draconian step of imposing wage and price controls on the entire economy.)

Nor did the government's forceful remediation of commercial grievances stop there. At the other end of Pennsylvania Avenue, lawmakers had been lamenting the way "the rest of the world hides behind variable levies, export subsidies, import equalization fees, border taxes, cartels, government procurement practices, dumping, import quotas, and a host of other practices which effectively bar our products" (U.S. Congress, Senate Committee on Finance 1974, 2). By 1974, with the administration's cooperation, a massive trade bill addressing these woes was wending its way through Congress.

Although not everyone appreciated it at the time, the Trade Act of 1974 was a consequential statute. At least two parts of it armed U.S. trade warriors with weapons that would unsettle trading partners throughout the rest of the century. One was the law's section 301, which extended the government's authority to retaliate against countries deemed to be hindering U.S. businesses "unreasonably." (Prior to 1974, the authority was limited to cases where a country's trade practices were "unjustified"—that is, in direct violation of articles in the General Agreement on Tariffs and Trade). The other, even more momentous change pertained to protection from "unfairly" priced imports. Foreign traders selling their products "below cost" could now be charged with price discrimination ("dumping"), even if the domestic and foreign prices were identical (Boltuck and Litan 1991).

These technicalities proved to be bolder than any piece of trade legislation since the Smoot-Hawley tariff of 1930, and, in the case of the antidumping language, more protectionist than any of the provisions in subsequent laws, including the controversial Omnibus Trade and Competitiveness Act of 1988. Although the full force of the new regulations was not felt for some time, their trajectory soon became discernible. In its first year of operation, the 1974 law quadrupled the volume of trade actions against foreigners accused of selling subsidized and underpriced exports (Pastor 1980). From 1975 to 1979, the number of antidumping cases nearly doubled again (U.S. Congress, House Committee on Ways and Means 1978,8). The countries of origin, moreover, were often close allies, some in the front lines of the East-West conflict.

The Reagan Years

Interventionist precedents set in the 1970s expanded in the following decade under the unlikely auspices of Ronald Reagan. While Reagan professed confidence in the ability of markets to take care of themselves—and while he was urging the free world to close ranks against "the evil empire"—his administration presided over a profusion of U.S. trade restrictions. Exploiting to good advantage the legal remedies introduced in 1974 and refined through additional legislation in 1979 and 1984, various U.S. industries showered the government with petitions for relief from foreign competition in the first half of the 1980s. Trade officials worked double time. Quotas were first arranged for imports of Japanese automobiles, and then for steel imports from virtually every European producer. Protection was later extended to three more major industries: machine tools, lumber, and computer memory devices.

The president had vowed to defend "unceasingly" American firms and workers that were "victims" of pernicious trading practices abroad (Reagan 1988, 1129). By 1988, some form of trade sanction covered almost a quarter of the $550 billion a year the United States spent on imported goods, up from 12 percent in 1980 (Hufbauer 1989). A World Bank study of fifteen countries in the Organization for Economic Cooperation and Development (OECD) found that, between 1981 and 1986, "hard-core" nontariff barriers increased so sharply in the United States that the share of total U.S. imports subject to these barriers now seemed to approximate the OECD's average level (Laird and Yeats 1988).[1]

In sum, well before the Berlin Wall came down, the extent, if not always the severity, of defensive U.S. trade measures had begun to resemble that of other industrial nations. Few postwar presidents took the Soviet menace more seriously than did President Reagan. Yet, at the risk of rattling some of the mainstays of the West's anticommunist alliance, Reagan's trade regime also confronted Europe, Canada, and Japan with more protection for American industry than any of his predecessors had imposed in more than half a century (Baker 1987).

Glory Days

The many interventions on behalf of domestic trade victims during the Reagan years—or, for that matter, the plans to police unfair foreign textiles, glass, steel, and numerous other imports in the 1970s—were more vigorous than earlier postwar efforts to press American commercial claims. But this is not to imply that the prior administrations or Congresses were in the habit of ignoring such claims.

In the immediate aftermath of World War II, the U.S. government adopted a relatively openhanded approach toward allies and former adversaries alike (Keohane 1984). They were offered major economic assistance, primarily in the form of grants, technical aid, and credits under the Marshall Plan. The altruism of those years needs to be placed in perspective, however. The U.S. stance reflected unique, and temporary, circumstances. Shell-shocked economies overseas had barely begun to recover. As an undisputed economic hegemon, the United States could readily afford to be generous without the quid pro quo of prompt repayment. Indeed, so dominant was the American economy that there was not much difference between doing favors for others and doing them for oneself; the incentives to provide public goods (financial assistance, currency stabilization, liberal trade) for the outside world were strong at a time when a preponderant share of the gains from economic growth overseas would ultimately redound to the United States (Paarlberg 1995).

Contrary to much contemporary mythology, the Americans did not as a matter of course go around lowering U.S. tariffs unilaterally. Tariffs were reduced, but on a two-way basis. Presidents did not have much choice; they were explicitly required, under the extant enabling legislation (the Reciprocal Trade Agreements Act of 1934), to negotiate *reciprocal* concessions. It is true that the United States took the lead in liberalizing world trade and did not always insist on leveling the playing field right away. Japanese access to the American market, for instance, was eased before Japan entered the General Agreement on Tariffs and Trade in 1953. In the meantime, other countries continued to discriminate against Japanese exports while the U.S. economy absorbed them. U.S. policy makers were not endlessly complacent about the flagrant free riding, however. They pushed Japan's admission into the GATT and demanded nondiscriminatory treatment of that country by other GATT members, not just for the benefit of Japan but also to relieve the strain of trade adjustment in the United States (Keohane 1982). Then, beginning in the late 1950s, Japan itself became increasingly a target of U.S. commercial complaints.

Congress often made the U.S. commitment to free trade conditional on the protection of powerful constituencies. In exchange for renewing presidential authority to negotiate tariff cuts, the lawmakers required Harry Truman to heed a peril-point provision and an escape clause limiting the cuts to levels that would not impair domestic producers (Baldwin 1979). Congress extended the executive's negotiating authority through the 1950s, but President Eisenhower had to order limitations on imports of cotton fibers and of crude oil. On his watch, despite an increasingly favorable trade balance in the agricultural sector, Congress secured quantitative restrictions on the importation of goods such as sugar and dairy products. Also, the legislators insisted on waiving U.S. obligations to remove these restrictions and to discipline U.S. crop production programs under the GATT (Hathaway 1987). Eisenhower had limited success in overturning stringent Buy American procurement rules that had been (and remain) in effect since 1933.

Similarly, to obtain passage of the Trade Expansion Act of 1962, which authorized another round of multilateral negotiations, President Kennedy widened the use of import quotas on cottons. Lyndon Johnson, in turn, agreed to restrain an influx of Japanese steel, and he failed to gain congressional support for ending the so-called American Selling Price system with its special duties on chemicals (Destler 1995). Further, Johnson was unable to lift quotas on imports of beef, thereby partially undercutting a program of trade preferences (the Alliance for Progress) intended to assist various Latin American countries.

Not all these safeguards for domestic interests signified grave departures from the generally liberal world economic order the United States was promoting. But neither were they trivial. Under Nixon, the "short-term" restraints on imported cottons grew into the Multifiber Arrangement—an enduring apparatus for managing worldwide commerce in almost all textiles and apparel.

By 1990 more than one thousand quotas had been arranged with thirty-eight nations, covering three-quarters of all imports. For the United States, the MFA has provided the equivalent of a 50 percent tariff, costing American consumers an extra $20 billion a year for the clothes they buy (William R. Cline's estimates, cited in Passell 1990).

Likewise, the early attempts to regulate trade in steel eventually expanded into far more complex operations such as the Carter administration's steel trigger-price mechanism and Reagan's comprehensive quotas. The GATT waiver for agriculture, enshrined by Congress in 1955, long complicated international efforts to curb disruptive farm subsidies and trade restraints elsewhere.

The point here is not to portray American economic leadership as hypocrites preaching open trade while practicing protectionism. From Bretton Woods to Punta del Este, no other country's leaders ordinarily championed with greater conviction the idea that collective well-being and security would be enhanced by lowering barriers to commerce and investment among nations. By the same token, much political rhetoric and punditry in the 1990s seemed to embrace a fiction: that American international economic policy during the cold war was faintly naive, selflessly passing handouts to the rest of the world, forsaking domestic groups, and getting little in return.

In reality, this country, like any other, minded its national economic interests, often tenaciously. When they served the nation's purposes—reinforcing the anticommunist fire wall, but also improving the balance of payments, diverting imports to other markets, or enabling other economies to become potential customers for U.S. exports—the United States advanced multilateral tariff reductions.[2] When the flow of freer trade was injurious or unjust to native industries, we frequently sheltered them. And when emerging international institutions threatened to encroach on sovereign economic rights, such as U.S. antidumping laws or farm price supports, we negotiated exemptions.[3] This nuanced pattern of give-and-take, moreover, was evident almost from the start, not just in recent years when cold war tensions had waned.[4]

Enter the Clinton Administration

In most respects, American trade policy in recent years has been more of the same.

Granted, it has not always sounded the same. Early in his term, President Clinton's public utterances on the trade issue were sometimes jarring. Shortly after his inauguration, for instance, he dismayed the European Community by seeming to suggest that a bilateral agreement on commercial aircraft subsidies, concluded by President Bush only a year before, ought to be scratched and redrawn. Then, at a press conference that spring, the new president suddenly expressed astonishment that the previous administration had declined to order a tenfold increase in duties on imported minivans. He reckoned emphatically that this decision, which he called "a $300 million-a-year freebie to the Japanese," was for "no apparent reason" (quoted in Sterngold 1993).[5] Proclamations like these had few parallels in the preceding twelve years of Republican rule.

If we judge it by its deeds instead of its words, however, the new administration did not bring on a fundamental revolution in the conduct of commercial policy.

Settlements

Clinton's trade team showed more continuity than contrast with the Bush administration's pragmatic approach in a series of early skirmishes. Almost all the trade cases that the new administration had inherited in 1993 were dispatched, without trashing existing accords or resorting to reprisals.

In reasonably short order, the errant trial balloon proposing to revise the European Airbus pact was lowered. Quarrels with the Europeans over public procurement practices for telecommunications equipment, and with Canada about imports of beer, were also resolved uneventfully. Interim settlements were reached on the long-festering matter of American participation in Japanese public works contracts, and on penetration of the Japanese market by vendors of American apples. In June 1993, the Commerce Department did slap new penalties on imports of steel in response to another wave of complaints by U.S. producers about foreign dumping and unfair subsidies, but the U.S. International Trade Commission promptly voided most of these duties. At the beginning of 1994, only one country faced any new constraint in the U.S. market: imports of silks and other fabric from China were further limited under an arrangement announced in January. But Sino-U.S. trade overall was scarcely disrupted. According to Clinton in 1992, in light of human rights abuses, Bush had erred by treating China as a most-favored nation (Clinton and Gore 1992). But four years later Beijing's MFN trade status remained intact and seemed likely to stay that way, despite China's brazen transgressions of intellectual property agreements, provocative military exercises, and violations of nuclear nonproliferation norms and of human rights.

Initial worries that the first Democratic administration in a dozen years would lurch reflexively toward the protectionist proclivities of a bedrock constituency—organized labor—proved unfounded. The litmus test was the North American Free Trade Agreement. Clinton had sought to straddle the question of NAFTA during the campaign, lending lukewarm support to the prospective treaty so as not to alienate labor support. Some of this ambivalence seemed to persist until the fall of 1993. However, in the last decisive stages of the debate, the president strove energetically for ratification. Final passage of NAFTA in the House of Representatives required bipartisan backing built around a solid bloc of Republican votes. Clinton managed to cobble this winning coalition together at least as well as Bush would have done.

Likewise, the administration might have, but did not, succumb to the spirited attacks of liberal factions (some vociferous environmental groups, for instance, and various unions) on the Uruguay Round's pending trade pact. Congressional consent for this sweeping multilateral accord was needlessly delayed by the administration's attempt to request authorization for a new round of negotiations, replete with fast-track procedures, to take up divisive questions of labor rights and environmental standards. Attaching these immensely complicated items to the GATT's subsequent agenda before the ink was dry on the existing treaty gave pause even to its proponents on Congress's gatekeeping panels, in particular the Senate Finance Committee. Thus, debate dragged through the second legislative session, with a final vote put off until late in 1994. Nevertheless, with a strong tug from the president and the usual flurry of last-minute bargaining, legislation implementing the Uruguay Round collected substantial bipartisan support and finally cleared Congress at the end of the year.

Battling Japan

Many observers believed that the commercial plans unfolding in Washington during 1993 would diverge markedly from those of preceding administrations in one place: Japan.

Clinton's trade strategists lost little time pressing the government of Japan to negotiate more consignments of automobiles, auto parts, supercomputers, medical equipment, and insurance services—and to measure "tangible progress" in each of the sectors with "objective criteria" (U.S. Trade Representative 1993, 3, 8). The elliptical terminology may have sounded flexible and innocuous; nonetheless, the Japanese interpreted the U.S. position as a demand for specific sales figures or designated market shares.

The reason was that U.S. trade officials had sought to set import targets in some earlier disputes with Japan. In 1986, for example, the Americans had insisted on a quantitative trajectory for sales of semiconductors (Anderson 1994). A decision regarding frequency standards for cellular phones in 1987 appeared to alter a service area in Japan to suit one American company, Motorola (Latham 1994). In 1992, a numerical goal of $15 billion was set for Japanese purchases of imported automotive equipment over the next two years (Irwin 1994). Thus, the Japanese side now suspected the Clinton administration not of taking an unfamiliar tack but of drawing too closely on nettlesome precedents.

The suspicion was not without basis. While billing their approach as a big change from "business as usual," administration officials frequently pointed to the semiconductor deal as a model for rectifying imbalances in trade with Japan (Mickey Kantor, quoted in Harbrecht and Ullmann 1994, 26). And though Clinton's negotiators sought to allay Japanese fears of acquiescing to a system of sectoral managed trade under the threat of U.S. sanctions, the fact remained that the United States and Japan had slid down that slippery slope before: In 1987, when orders of computer chips fell short of an "expected" interim target, the Japanese were met with retaliatory duties on approximately $300 million worth of electronics products (Auerbach 1987). The reality of Clinton's trade tactics with Japan was not that they were "a clean break from the past," as U.S. Trade Representative Mickey Kantor asserted, but, on the contrary, that they were an extension of the past.

A major showdown, which seemed imaginable at first, never materialized. Instead, through 1994 the two sides gradually settled back into a customary pattern of bickering over sectoral items, resolving or finessing some while continuing to argue about others (Armacost 1996). The squabble over automobiles and auto parts was dramatic for a while; an agreement was finally reached at the end of June 1995, but only hours before the United States planned to impose 100 percent tariffs on luxury car imports. By the time of the Tokyo summit the following April, however, this and other old thorns in U.S.-Japan trade relations were no longer high profile. Japan's bilateral trade surplus had declined, U.S. auto exports were up, and Clinton instead chose to solidify security arrangements with Prime Minister Ryutaro Hashimoto amid greater worries about other tensions in Asia.

Commercial Promotionalism

Another realm in which the first post–cold war presidency was said to depart from past practice was in its active promotion of export programs and of commercial technologies.

In September 1993 the president announced that a somewhat larger share of the dwindling U.S. foreign aid account would be tied to purchases of U.S. products by the recipient countries. Secretary of the Treasury Lloyd Bentsen made it seem as if this was a shift of historic proportions: "I'm tired of a level playing field. We should tilt the playing field for U.S. business. We should have done it 20 years ago" (quoted in Frisby 1993b). In fact, the shift had been going on for some time. To counteract countries such as France and Japan, whose volume of export credits surpassed those of the United States in the early 1980s, the Trade and Development Enhancement Act of 1983 had authorized the Export-Import Bank and the Agency for International Development (AID) to begin arranging tied-aid credit packages. Three years later, these exertions were supplemented by an Export-Import Bank "war chest." In 1990, its resources, blended with grants from AID, were deployed in a concerted effort to recapture "spoiled" markets in Indonesia, Pakistan, the Philippines, and Thailand. Clinton's subsequent steps did not break much new ground.

What about the administration's industrial policy? Initially, a noticeable effort was made to torque up the Commerce Department's Advanced Technology Program (ATP, which boosts research and development of new civilian technologies), the Manufacturing Extension Partnership (MEP, which funds technical assistance to state industrial extension services), and the laboratories of the National Institute of Standards and Technology. The Clinton agenda also called for more spending by the Department of Energy on a host of development programs, and by the Department of Defense on conversion assistance and technological base support through the Advanced Research Projects Agency, or ARPA (specifically its so-called Technology Reinvestment Program, TRP). For many of these projects, the Clinton administration believed public-private consortia would enhance the competitiveness of U.S. firms.

But most of this activity was just old wine in new, or somewhat bigger, bottles. Several of the programs—the ATP and the MEP, for instance—predated Clinton's election; only their budgets improved, though not for long. By the spring of 1996, facing a Republican-controlled Congress that had proposed to eliminate the Commerce Department entirely, the president accepted budgetary reductions in his administration's favored technology initiatives.[6] As for the various research consortia, there were few new strides there either. Some additional partnerships were tried, but all were clearly modeled on earlier ventures, such as the chip-making equipment consortium (SEMATECH) launched in 1987 under ARPA's aegis.

For years, the role of government in helping U.S. industries meet, beat, or avoid international competition had been more pronounced than academic industrial policy mavens recognized or admitted (Nivola 1991). Semiconductors, computers, supercomputers, automated machine tools, aeronautics, communications satellites, biotechnology—all these fields and more had been nurtured by a silent partner, operating chiefly through defense-related contracts, preferential procurement, and R&D subsidies. The modernization of shipyards was one of President Clinton's highest industrial priorities—just as it had been for George Washington in 1789 (Clinton 1993c; Heine 1980). Although Clinton tried to pay more than the usual attention to an explicit and proactive deployment of trade and technology-base programs in the Department of Commerce and other government agencies, tighter constraints on discretionary spending by the mid-1990s inevitably downsized these ventures (Tolchin 1996).

Understanding the Steady State

If today's management of commercial affairs is not all that different from yesterday's, the explanation has to with a combination of historical and institutional constants that have been, if anything, reinforced by globalization.

The historical given is still the lingering legacy of the Smoot-Hawley Act, the misadventure in U.S. tariff legislation that set off worldwide trade warfare and deepened the Great Depression. Long after that catastrophe, policy makers remain bound by the time-honored imperative of expanding global business opportunities while continuing to shield or boost salient domestic economic interests—and of performing this juggling act without incurring unacceptable risks. Put another way, trade policy makers have to keep pedaling toward a congenial trading system, lest, like a bicycle coming to a halt, it should topple back to closed, segmented markets reminiscent of the 1930s. But virtually every administration must also countenance the succoring of important constituents, even as it remains skittish about provoking retaliation against U.S. exporters and investors abroad.

The result is the perennial three-part exercise of pushing—vigorously but not recklessly—more trade and investment into some relatively impenetrable foreign markets, pumping the government's own considerable share of industrial support programs, and extending trade relief to an assortment of domestic producers through technical import regulations such as those against dumping. The economic conditions, statutory rules, and political incentives underlying this process have varied somewhat from time to time, but most have been of long duration. Here, the passing of the cold war has altered little; it has permitted somewhat less forbearance toward trading partners, but current policies still fall far short of rupturing important relationships.

The institutional constant is quite simply the U.S. Constitution, which explicitly charges Congress with the responsibility "to regulate commerce with foreign nations." Although Congress began delegating routine administration of the trade laws to the executive branch long ago, the legislators retain extensive influence over everything from broad presidential negotiating authority to the fine details of administrative procedures and even the disposition of some specific trade cases (Nivola 1993). The principal consequence of this arrangement is clear: compared to the commercial ministries of America's main competitors, the various U.S. trade bureaucracies have lacked (and will almost certainly continue to lack) great autonomy. The Office of the U.S. Trade Representative and the Department of Commerce may be acquiring a somewhat higher profile in the post–cold war years, but no trade agency's power in Washington is likely to resemble that of, say, the Ministry of International Trade and Industry in Tokyo.

Extensive congressional involvement in trade decisions inevitably means that a good deal of the agenda is driven by a disjointed collection of private or particularistic concerns. Administrators spend most of their time responding to these pressures ("putting out fires") rather than formulating independent executive strategies or long-range plans. This fact of bureaucratic life renders much trade policy making repetitious. Many of the pressures tend to be recurrent and familiar: every few years integrated steel producers can be counted on to protest unfair competition; the textile manufacturers will petition for tighter quotas; the lumber industry will assail Canadian timber subsidies; the makers of automotive equipment will complain about their meager sales in Japan; the dairy farmers will demand preferential treatment; and so on (Yoffie 1989). Thus, old problems are seldom wholly depleted. On a day-to-day basis, the job of commercial officials at present usually resembles their tasks five, ten, or even twenty years ago.

Global economic integration has not altered the basic patterns. On the contrary, it keeps giving greater meaning to the lessons of Smoot-Hawley and prevents congressional clientelism from reverting to raw protectionism or to overly aggressive unilateralism in trade policy. Big errors now would involve enormous stakes. Today's international financial markets transact more than a trillion dollars of business *every day* (Herring and Litan 1994). When perturbations on the trade front rattle those markets, multiple billions in wealth can change hands in a matter of minutes. More than $800 billion in exports of U.S. goods and services would be on the line in a full-fledged trade conflagration (Council of Economic Advisers 1996).

Some saber rattling still occurs, of course, but when push comes to shove in a global marketplace, heavy-handed tactics almost always lack credibility. Recently, officials contemplated commercial sanctions against China in light of that country's continuing piracy of U.S. copyrights and trademarks. But sanctions on China, with its gigantic emerging market for U.S. products, are highly implausible. In a world where several major trading rivals are competing head-to-head for such a market, unilateral trade sanctions that could trigger counterretaliation suffer a free rider problem: America's self-imposed loss is someone else's commercial gain. In the spring of 1996, would-be trade hawks in the United States were again reminded of how the global economic game is played; the Chinese government served notice that it would place a $1.5 billion order for new airliners—with Europe's Airbus.

Whither Foreign Policy?

At first, the election of Bill Clinton looked as if it might mark the end of history in one very big sense: his young administration appeared in essence to be redefining American foreign policy. The paradigm shift in 1993 seemed to go something like this: With the cold war behind us, the principal conflicts of relevance to major powers would be over "economic issues."[7] Traditional missions—those dealing with the clear and present danger of armed aggression wracking the international community—seemed largely antiquated in a world safely rid of the Soviet Union. Having paid dearly in lives and treasure as the world's policeman over nearly half a century, America had lost ground economically; the nation was no longer in a position to be continually taking the lead in maintaining international order. In the words of the U.S. Trade Representative, "The days when we could afford to subordinate our economic interests to foreign policy or defense concerns are long past" (quoted in "Cool Winds from the White House" 1993, 58).

In this view of the world, commercial policy would inevitably gain primacy, if not by design then by default. Commercialism in foreign relations was nothing new, but it would now protrude conspicuously as attention to classical security interests receded.

Turning Inward

It did not take long for the new paradigm to prove largely unconvincing. The post–cold war world has not been benign. Its dangers, to name only a few, include: China, an emerging industrial powerhouse with a repressive regime; other trouble-making dictatorships in Iraq, Iran, Libya, Syria, and North Korea; turmoil and perhaps resurgent irredentism in Russia; ingredients for weapons of mass destruction spreading from several of these places; a nuclear arms race between India and Pakistan; vast tribal massacres in Africa; and a genocidal Balkan war that, by mid-1995, had gravely challenged the credibility of the North Atlantic Treaty Organization. Could all these developments be considered "economic" conflicts in any meaningful sense of the word?

The multipolar environment, at least in the first half of the 1990s, featured local bullies marauding with impunity on the doorstep of Europe and elsewhere frightening neighbors, orchestrating international terrorism, trafficking freely in high-tech weaponry, and sending waves of refugees streaming across borders. Was such a world always more serene than the earlier bipolar balance in which the dominant powers exerted a measure of control over their clients?

America was now the sole superpower. With its $7 trillion economy growing more robustly than Germany's and Japan's, how could this colossus be regarded as anything less than primus inter pares in global geopolitics (Nau 1995)?

Nevertheless, in the Clinton administration's first months, there was no mistaking the revisionist outlook. The Clintonites came to town convinced that huge parts of the U.S. economy needed radical surgery, and that while this operation was going on, international issues (other than commercial ones) could be for the most part marginalized. Now and then, pesky external events—such as a late-twentieth-century reprise of ethnic cleansing and national dismemberment in Europe's backyard—interrupted the administration's deliberations on domestic matters. But during its first couple of years, the flash points overseas usually seemed to elicit lengthy ruminations, numerous pronouncements, and some spasmodic initiatives from Washington, but rarely a sustained, credible response. There were exceptions. In the Middle East, the administration persevered with the Arab-Israeli peace process, and remained prepared to meet Saddam Hussein's provocations. But in a series of other trouble spots—Somalia, Bosnia, Korea, and for a time, Haiti—foreign policy wobbled.

The Ascent of Declinism

Clinton was not the first postwar American president to invoke an electoral mandate to concentrate on internal economic problems, but his administration started out belaboring those problems, seemingly to the point of resisting, if not begrudging, leadership in international venues (such as NATO) that the United States had traditionally dominated.

In fairness, an inclination to rule as if America were too beleaguered to lead has to be placed in context. The end of the cold war weakened domestic political support for internationalism almost everywhere. Surely, by their own dithering and confusion, western European governments scarcely responded effectively to the crisis in the former Yugoslavia. Americans had grown understandably weary of policing the world. They insisted that more of the burden be shared. Neoisolationist murmurs had become audible among Republicans as well as Democrats. When, after hesitating for nearly eighteen months, the president finally readied an invasion force to oust a defiant Haitian junta that threatened to fill the Caribbean with refugees, his decision met with bipartisan consternation in Congress. The Bosnian debacle, the North Korean nuclear program, the mess in Somalia—these troubles and others began well before Clinton's victory at the polls.

Perhaps the drift of U.S. policy could also be traced in part to undercurrents in Democratic party politics since the early 1970s (Wolfowitz 1994). The party's standard-bearer in 1972, we may recall, proposed slashing the U.S. defense budget by one-third. The next year the Democratic majority leader in the Senate was the author of a legislative proposal calling for drastic reductions of U.S. forces in Europe. In 1983, while the Reagan administration was struggling to counterbalance a new deployment of Soviet intermediate-range missiles by placing Pershing missiles in Europe, Democratic majorities in the House of Representatives were adopting resolutions supporting a nuclear freeze. Then, seven years ago, when Iraq's conquests in the Persian Gulf threatened to sever the world's oil lifeline, Democratic members of Congress were for the most part opposed to authorizing the use of force against the aggressor.

Awkwardly positioned in the international arena and sidelined in presidential politics for twenty of the previous twenty-four years, the Democrats groped for an electoral strategy. Increasingly, they fastened on what Tony Coelho, a former chairman of the Democratic Congressional Campaign Committee, dubbed the "Democratic macho issue," economic nationalism (*Congressional Quarterly Almanac* 1985, 253). Democratic candidates would rally to the defense of a supposedly vulnerable and declining U.S. economy and would finally call a halt to America's "freebies" for trade adversaries. The issue did not resonate in 1984, when Walter Mondale warned that Americans faced "a lifetime serving MacDonald's hamburgers" or "sweeping up around Japanese computers" (quoted in Schlossstein 1984, 3–4). But by 1992, amid temporarily sluggish economic conditions, American decline and visions of the government riding to the rescue were themes that may have finally helped a Democratic presidential aspirant get elected.

Even by the permissive standards of partisan oratory, however, the Clinton campaign's perception of U.S. economic frailty was sometimes startling. In 1992 the country was described, for example, as suffering its "worst economic performance since the Great Depression," even inviting comparisons with "Sri Lanka" (Barnes 1992; Clinton 1992b). The campaign literature celebrated "a strong 'Super 301'" (an abrasive, lapsed provision of the 1988 trade act) because in years past "we" had received "plenty of empty promises" from our trading partners but not "results" (Clinton and Gore 1992, 156).

With the nation so embattled, policy makers drew predictable inferences. "It is necessary to make the point that our economic interests are paramount," declared the undersecretary of state for political affairs in the spring of 1993 (quoted in Williams and Goshko 1993). The United States still faced threats from "middleweight powers," he added, but deterring them would be hard, given the lack of national resources and will: "We don't have the money to bring positive results any time soon" (quoted in Williams and Goshko 1993).

Salesman-in-Chief

One implication of this worldview was that priorities at home would tend to take precedence over strong stewardship abroad. But a second was that, in forays beyond the water's edge, the business of America might turn out to be mostly business. This was not because Clinton's trade activism deviated sharply from, say, Reagan's or Nixon's. Rather, the difference was that cold war presidents almost always worried about the balance of power as well as the balance of trade. The helmsmen inside the Beltway in the aftermath of the 1992 election seemed to acknowledge only belatedly that the two were not necessarily synonymous.

Thus, statecraft in the early 1990s sometimes smacked unabashedly of a public sales pitch for private interests. Scorekeeping of specific merchandise imported and exported became a focus of two bilateral summits with

Japan, in July 1993 and February 1994. A few months later the president of the United States personally lobbied the president of Indonesia to improve the market share of U.S. firms in that country. Lest it be thought that high-level diplomacy with Saudi Arabia is all about containing Iraq, Iran, or the spread of Islamic fundamentalism, the White House intervened personally to head off Europe's Airbus vendors and close a deal for Boeing and McDonnell-Douglas, ensuring that the Saudi national airline would buy almost its entire complement of new planes from the American companies (Barnes 1994).

Stories such as these could be told about prior U.S. administrations (not to mention French presidents, German chancellors, and Japanese prime ministers). Not infrequently during the Reagan years, the foreign offices, even the heads of state, of the United States and its allies met to converse about matters such as softwood lumber exports and airport construction contracts. Early in 1992, President Bush transformed a long-awaited state visit to Japan into a trade mission, departing with a retinue of corporate executives. The Tokyo summit that year included much haggling over auto sales, auto parts, and paper products. Even so, somehow commercial boosterism now appeared more lopsided than before, not because there was necessarily a great deal more of it, but because the ballast of a higher purpose in foreign policy was missing.

Restoring Equilibrium

If the leader of the Western world found himself acting like a kind of "glorified secretary of commerce" (Judis 1993, 20) earlier in the decade, more was surely expected of him by July 1995.

That was the month when Serbian forces overran the UN "safe heaven" of Srebrenica in eastern Bosnia. Watching the slaughter of Muslim civilians by the thousands, the NATO allies, led by the United States, were at last shamed into forcing a halt to fighting in the region. Two years earlier the American president had regarded the unfolding fiasco in Bosnia as a distraction; in his words, "I felt really badly because I don't want to have to spend more time on [Bosnia] than is absolutely necessary because what I got elected to do was to get America to look at our own problems" (quoted in Judis 1993, 18). Now this stance had begun to look like an abdication and loomed as a potential liability in the upcoming presidential election year. Having vacillated long enough, the president was finally persuaded that the time had come for a decisive combination of NATO airpower and vigorous diplomacy to bear down on the situation. By November, the heads of the warring Balkan factions were made to convene at a U.S. base in Dayton, Ohio, where they were prodded into signing an armistice. In due course, Clinton dispatched almost twenty thousand U.S. troops as part of a large NATO peacekeeping operation to enforce the Dayton accords through 1996.

In the end, the Dayton treaty could easily unravel. No one really knows what will transpire after the NATO peacekeepers decamp. Even now, basic objectives of their mission—such as bringing the principal perpetrators of war crimes to justice and securing the right of refugees to return to their homes—have faded. (With painful irony, on the fiftieth anniversary of the Nuremberg trials, the worst of Europe's new war criminals were still at large.) Nonetheless, Dayton seemed to signify an adjustment in Clinton's foreign policy. An initial emphasis on trade issues gave way to a phase in which renewed importance was attached to stabilizing a wider assortment of corrosive foreign conflicts and to meeting emergent security threats with a more credible military deterrent.

In the fall of 1994, a rapid deployment of U.S. forces to the Persian Gulf had been ordered to reinforce Kuwaiti defenses against Iraq. But by the spring of 1996, American power was displayed in more theaters. A U.S. division had taken up positions in Bosnia. The Seventh Fleet steamed into the South China Sea when Chinese military exercises in the Formosa Strait menaced Taiwan. In the face of China's rising power in Asia, hints of a Sino-Russian détente, and a dangerously unstable regime in Pyongyang, mutual defense precautions dominated the 1996 U.S.-Japan summit. When hostilities escalated alarmingly along Israel's border with Lebanon, concerted U.S. diplomatic pressure on Damascus and on Jerusalem imposed a firm cease-fire.

Will this apparent reassertion of American leadership hold up? The answer depends on a host of circumstances—the continuing strength of the U.S. economy, the might of the nation's armed forces, the relative gravity of foreign crises, the cohesion of our alliances, the president's convictions, and so on. But not least among the determinants will be the number of internationalists left in Congress. Here, too, the picture has become murky. The Republican 104th Congress showed signs of retreating from the GOP's traditional postwar consensus. In part, the change has reflected popular sentiment that has not only soured on political institutions in Washington but has also grown increasingly skeptical of international obligations vaguely suspected of impinging on national sovereignty or on economic self-interest.

The mistrustful mood has manifested itself in both a loss of enthusiasm for new trade-expanding initiatives and growing unease with new foreign policy entanglements. Accordingly, accession of Chile and other Latin American countries to a hemispheric free trade zone is on hold. A fierce congressional backlash early in 1995 nearly blocked all U.S. efforts to rescue Mexico (hence also the North American Free Trade Agreement) from financial collapse. Even deference to the very foundations of an orderly multilateral trading system—specifically the adjudicative role of its new governing body, the World Trade Organization—has been called into question.[8] Appropriate military interventions have also drawn much noisy criticism on Capitol Hill. Just as George Bush had to overcome Democratic opposition to Operation Desert Storm, Bill Clinton had to contend with Republican resistance to the use of ground forces, first in Haiti and then in Bosnia.

Concluding Reflections

In the 1990s, it became clear that a policy fixated on commercial competition between nations risked being blindsided by other international challenges. Ancient problems, such as local hostilities born of virulent ethnocentric nationalism, surfaced with the passing of the cold war. So did new and profoundly disturbing uncertainties such as the spread of material and technology for nuclear and chemical weapons. Most of the threats to global stability—and ultimately to the security and integrity of American civilization—have had less to do with the intricacies of "geo-economics" than with a primal fact of international politics, namely, states and peoples intimidating one another by force of arms.[9] Sooner or later, the United States would have to confront this reality resolutely, much as it faced down the Soviet empire. At the White House, the realization did not seem to sink in until the middle of the decade; among many members of Congress, it has yet to penetrate at all.

Still, more of the customary U.S. role in the world now seems reasonably intact. Certainly the dynamics of U.S. trade politics and policy have remained more or less consistent for at least the past quarter century. And though narrow commercial considerations often appeared to eclipse broader concerns in foreign relations earlier in the 1990s, efforts have been made since then to correct the imbalance.

A Question of Balance

Are there lessons in all this for policy makers looking to the next century? No past president or Congress impaired national prosperity for the sake of magnanimous statesmanship or global policing, and none is likely to do so in the future. America's influence abroad has always depended in no small part on its strength at home. Depicting U.S. diplomacy of earlier decades as an exercise in unreciprocated philanthropy may be a convenient myth for special interests queuing up for an affirmative action program (so to speak) to redress an alleged backlog of trade inequities. But the fact is, the nation's economic fortunes, or those of particular firms and workers, were seldom very far from the minds of politicians, even during the darkest days of the cold war, and surely no realistic observer can expect them to be "subordinated" today. What can be urged, however, is that the competing demands of geoeconomics and of conventional security requirements remain properly balanced.

In a sophisticated democracy such as the United States, a good deal of that balance eventually occurs spontaneously. As it entered the 1996 election season, the Clinton administration was somewhat less consumed with economics. Campaign operatives were hardly going to suggest, as they did in 1992, that the American economy was so wretched that other problems had to be peripheral (or "stupid") by comparison. Instead, there was a natural inclination to take credit for the solid performance since 1993 and a desire not to spook financial markets with rash trade actions against Japan, China, or anyone else. Meanwhile, an ever chaotic world keeps encroaching, forcing the president to deliver more of the "foreign policy of engagement" that had been promised in 1992.

Demystifying the Trade Issue

But some of the balancing also requires an intellectual adjustment that is only partly under way. For starters, the importance of commerce—what U.S. consumers and firms buy and sell in world markets—needs to be put in perspective. About 88 percent of the goods and services Americans use is still produced by Americans (Bosworth and Lawrence 1989). The difference, made up by imports, remains relatively modest in relation to the economy's total output. To be sure, import competition has affected employment and wages in particular industries, but electoral campaign perorations have tended to blow way out of proportion the consequences for American workers as a whole (Lawrence and Slaughter 1993).

On the export side, it is true that export industries constitute an appreciable source of new employment, but there, too, only about 11 percent of the U.S. economy is involved—barely more than the share in 1980, and a relatively small one compared to many other industrial economies (Nothdruft 1993). These figures ought to give pause to politicians who insist, year after year, that "trade is the most important issue we face" (Nivola

1993, xiv). For at these levels, "trade" cannot have a profound impact on the bottom line, America's living standards, because it simply does not make or break enough jobs and incomes.[10]

Commercial issues have always had a place on America's international agenda. They always will, and often should. But cluttering foreign policy with too many business calculations can expend a great deal of diplomatic capital, often in return for disappointingly marginal material gains to the United States. Even if the trade deficit is a grave predicament (a big "if"), going to the mat to get rid of it might, in Paul Krugman's estimate, lift the share of manufacturing employment in the U.S. economy from 17 percent to 17.5 percent (Krugman 1994).[11] Knocking down all of Japan's known barriers to U.S. products seems long overdue, but even under utopian conditions (with no offsetting exchange rate effects and no displacement of productive resources), the Herculean feat would at best lift U.S. exports by the equivalent of one-fifth of 1 percent of GDP.[12]

Prizes of that magnitude may still be worth pursuing doggedly, but not at the cost of neglecting a larger strategic architecture, painstakingly built over half a century, to protect us and others from the world's ever present thugs and tyrants.

David P. Forsythe

11. Human Rights Policy

Change and Continuity

Has the end of the cold war fundamentally altered U.S. foreign policy and the process of making that policy? While some changes are obvious, we should not leap to the conclusion that everything has changed. Some observers might think that with the demise of the Soviet Union and of European communism in general, the United States would be freed from geostrategic struggles and could concentrate on subjects such as human rights. But some aspects of an anarchic international society without a world government may remain the same. Furthermore, some aspects of American politics may show considerable continuity.

John Shattuck (1993), assistant secretary of state for human rights and humanitarian affairs (his department was later renamed Human Rights, Democracy, and Labor) in the Clinton administration, said in 1993: "With the passing of the cold war, all of [its negative impact] has changed. The basic principles of human rights and democracy must no longer be debased with impunity. Nor should they be blinked at for the sake of some larger geostrategic goal. Rather, they must be restored to their rightful primary place in the relationship among nations."

The State Department articulated a similar but broader argument at the end of the Bush administration. In a forward-looking official report, "Managing Foreign Affairs," the study group's head, Undersecretary James Rogers, wrote: "The foreign policy of the United States and the machinery for its formulation and execution must change in order to meet the challenges presented by a dramatically altered international environment" (U.S. Department of State 1992).

Change in U.S. foreign policy, certainly that pertaining to human rights, may turn out to be less significant than anticipated. Even new officials and an apparently new process may produce the same policy. Just as U.S. human rights policy during the second Reagan administration, despite new personnel and procedures, looked very similar to Jimmy Carter's record (Forsythe 1990), so Bill Clinton's human rights policy may turn out to look very similar to George Bush's or Carter's.

While it is too early to say anything definitive about Clinton's record (that point should be emphasized in everything that follows), Clinton started out by adopting Bush's policy concerning the treatment of Haitian "boat people." They were intercepted outside U.S. territorial waters and forcibly returned to Haiti, despite the opposition of the UN high commissioner for refugees and of American private human rights groups. While Clinton made numerous changes in Haitian policy thereafter, the initial policy toward boat people should give pause for thought. The absence of the Soviet Union and the cold war at first made no difference in U.S. policy concerning the rights of Haitian asylum seekers. Nor did new personnel in Washington offices using a new bureaucratic process.

One important continuity is that, whereas European communist repression has ended, there is within a larger perspective no "problem depletion" concerning international human rights. The end of European repressive communism produced various conditions after 1989–1991. In places such as the Czech Republic, Hungary, and Poland, genuine rights progress has been made (though serious problems are not lacking). In other areas of former communist control, wartime atrocities, systematic rape, anti-Semitism, and even holocausts are among the violations of human rights. It is not as if the end of the Soviet empire meant the end of human rights violations.

Beyond Europe, places such as Somalia and Rwanda remind those who have not been paying close attention that gross violations of internationally recognized human rights are still pervasive around the world. In the first human rights reports compiled by the Clinton administration, covering 1993, a generic "armed conflict" was named as the chief threat to human rights (U.S. Department of State 1994, xiii).

Therefore, while inquiring into the nature of U.S. foreign policy and human rights after the cold war, we should not assume that raising the question prejudges the answer. Some fundamental aspects of the global environment have not changed. And some things that have changed, such as personnel and bureaucratic procedure in Washington, may or may not result in important differences in policy.

Cold War Presidents

Debates about morality and the national interest in U.S. foreign policy date back to the founding of the republic (Graebner 1987; Schlesinger 1978). It was not until 1945, however, that states in general dealt extensively with human rights issues per se in their foreign policies (Burgers 1992). Some argue that the Truman administration took the lead on human rights issues after World War II and that even the Eisenhower administration, despite congressional pressures, tried to continue that leadership role (e.g., Nolan 1993). Most scholars agree that because of McCarthyite and Brickerite pressures in Congress, combined with an agreement to give priority to containing communism, human rights did not receive broad and specific consideration in U.S. foreign policy until the mid-1970s. During much of the cold war, containment of communism in the name of defending freedom reduced U.S. attention to specific human rights issues abroad.

Carter

The conventional wisdom is that Jimmy Carter entered office with a vague and naive view of the place of human rights in foreign policy. He supposedly left office never having developed a "big picture" about the place of human rights in world affairs and never having understood the negative consequences of his good intentions (Kaufman 1991; see also Hoffmann 1978). This interpretation should not be very controversial; Carter issued a mea culpa in his memoirs by saying, "I did not fully grasp all the ramifications of our new [human rights] policy" (Carter 1982, 44). Key players on the Carter team admitted they set few priorities (Brzezinski 1983b).

It became increasingly clear that human rights could not be the promised "cornerstone" and "soul" of Carter foreign policy during the cold war; security policy "trumped" human rights repeatedly. Carter apparently never appreciated the inconsistency in boldly preaching human rights but practicing business as usual with communist Poland, with the dictatorial and corrupt Philippines, or with reactionary Saudi Arabia. He apparently also never appreciated the inconsistency between preaching universal human rights but practicing rights pressures primarily against relatively weak Latin American states possessing neither valued resources nor perceived geostrategic position. Moreover, Carter never resolved the contradiction between his commitment to human rights abroad and his reluctance to interfere with economic processes. This contradiction helps explain his reluctance to use economic sanctions on Idi Amin's brutal rule in Uganda (finally voted in by Congress), and his early resistance to a congressional effort to link human rights to World Bank and other multilateral loans.

Another piece of conventional wisdom is that Carter, while a hands-on president in foreign policy who took great interest in the details of Middle East geography and the workings of the Panama Canal, never saw the need to institute a coherent foreign policy process—in general or for human rights in particular. Two publications have documented how human rights policy was made under Carter (Maynard 1988, 1989). But Carter never resolved the differences between National Security Adviser Zbigniew Brzezinski and Secretary of State Cyrus Vance. While Brzezinski saw human rights primarily as a weapon with which to attack the Soviet Union and its communist allies, Vance saw them in more cosmopolitan terms and was as much interested in protecting rights under friendly tyrants as under communist adversaries (Brzezinski 1983b; Vance 1983). The twin crises of Afghanistan (1979) and Iran (1980) pushed Carter toward an emphasis on traditional security concerns and away from human rights, which meant that Brzezinski eventually won out while Vance resigned over the aborted rescue attempt in Iran.

There was even more chaos in the Carter bureaucratic process concerning human rights than the Brzezinski-Vance competition would suggest. It is well established now that the first assistant secretary for human rights and humanitarian affairs, Patricia Derian, and her politically appointed assistants in that bureau were not warmly received by the foreign service officers who made up the core of the State Department's working professionals. HA staff were sometimes cut out of cable traffic. HA had constant clashes, particularly with the geographical bureaus and above all with those dealing in Asian and Latin American affairs (Rossiter 1984; Maynard 1989). Vance did not consistently resolve these bitter arguments in his department in favor of HA. Many times he was not directly involved. Sometimes his deputy, Warren Christopher, refereed those human rights disputes touching upon foreign assistance, and sometimes the disputes were resolved in other ways. HA and others helped persuade Christopher to reduce U.S. foreign assistance to about a dozen countries, at least partially on human rights grounds (Cohen 1982), but the entire process remained murky, especially since Christopher never articulated the reasons for the reductions.[1]

It was under Carter, and by devolution under Derian and one of her assistants, Frank Sieverts, that the State Department began to take the human rights reporting requirements seriously. Kissinger had in effect violated the law by refusing to carry out Congress's instructions to compile and allow to be published a serious human rights report on those receiving U.S. security assistance. The Carter team took the law seriously and began to give Congress detailed reports. These were then critiqued vigorously by Congress, especially on the House side, in tandem with private human rights groups, who had their own sources of information. The result was the beginning of a process in which every embassy was made responsible for serious reporting on human rights questions, and in which human rights concerns gradually became more accepted by FSOs, and by their politically appointed colleagues and superiors, as a legitimate part of the U.S. foreign policy agenda.

The annual reports did not guarantee high-level attention to human rights, except of course at the time of publication, each January or February, when some diplomatic feathers had to be smoothed. There was always a gap between the reporting of facts and the "proper" adjustment of policy to accord with those facts. During the Carter period some of the country reports were widely seen as biased or politicized—euphemistically, one could say they were heavily edited prior to release. But by 1994 most observers, whether Democrat or Republican, realist or liberal, believed that the reporting procedure required by Congress and implemented seriously by the Carter team had led to a change in the U.S. foreign policy agenda. Human rights were put on the agenda in part because of the annual reports. In my judgment, Congress should get most of the credit (or blame), but Carter's HA and State Department also share responsibility.

The Carter team, especially in HA but also at the lower levels of the NSC, were for the most part sympathetic to private human rights groups. Derian herself, while having no foreign policy experience, had been a civil rights activist in the south. She appointed a staff member, Roberta Cohen, to be in charge of liaison with the private human rights groups. Information was exchanged rather freely, though of course there were differences of opinion on various issues. For example, Amnesty International pushed Derian hard over Indonesia and East Timor, but with little success. Another Derian staffer had long experience with Red Cross agencies, and hence they did not lack for access either. In other parts of the Carter bureaucratic process, however, the private human rights groups were sometimes viewed as unwelcome. Some assistant secretaries regarded them as woefully naive politically and would have virtually nothing to do with them. Thus private groups had some special access, but inconsistently and without demonstrable success in affecting policy broadly. The private groups consistently thought they had better access to Congress than to Carter's administration (Forsythe 1989b, chap. 6).

How significant a role did the Carter bureaucratic process play in the matter of human rights? It is noteworthy that the president himself did not send clear and consistent signals about the place of human rights in his foreign policy. It is significant that he never imposed order on the Brzezinski-Vance differences and that he did not use their differing approaches and opinions to come up with a more creative and effective policy. It is important that none of his lieutenants impressed upon Carter the need to look at the consequences of his early rhetoric about human rights in the Soviet Union, the drift toward a punitive focus on friendly tyrants in Latin America, and the damage done to his rights policy by blatant and unexplained inconsistencies. Apparently, no one told Carter that his rhetoric had raised expectations so high that disappointments were bound to set in.

But beyond these points, I rather doubt that the bureaucratic process per se was a factor of primary importance. What damaged the Carter record on human rights was, first, that the president himself did not treat them as seriously in fact as his rhetoric had led many to believe. Carter himself never took human rights seriously in many places of the world, such as Mobutu's Zaire, where gross violations of human rights occurred daily. In a typical instance of presidential action, Carter signed three human rights treaties and submitted them to the Senate. But he did not lobby for them and he allowed lawyers at State and Justice to add crippling reservations. Carter did not insist that either Brzezinski or Vance follow up his presidential initiative.

Second, the Soviet invasion of Afghanistan and the Iranian takeover of the embassy in Tehran changed the whole mood of the country about foreign policy, especially when the Reagan team began criticizing Carter for being soft on national security issues. Given other setbacks, such as intemperate statements by the Sandinistas and unwise policies that fed into the Reagan focus on American weakness, no president could have maintained human rights as a high priority in foreign policy.

Third, in an era of stagflation, with low rates of economic growth and high rates of inflation, it was impossible to sell at home a consistent foreign policy that demanded economic sacrifices from American business in the name of protecting the rights of foreigners—especially if foreign competitors got the profits denied to American business. Carter never understood that if human rights were truly assigned the primary value in foreign policy, private pursuit of profit would be secondary. Needless to say, there were powerful elements in American society opposed to that orientation. If the Carter team was unable to maintain a policy that denied U.S.

Export-Import Bank loans to Argentina because of human rights violations, it was not because of bureaucratic incompetence; it was because Allis-Chalmers and probusiness congressional elements overcame the policy initiative (Forsythe 1989a; Schoultz 1981).

Thus, it was not the bureaucratic process that most hurt Carter's rights policies abroad, though there were more than enough deficiencies to go around. Rather, presidential values and commitment, the nature of international relations, and the domestic mood were the primary factors affecting the fate of human rights abroad during the Carter years. As required by Congress, the human rights bureaucracy did begin serious reporting on human rights abroad. This was to have considerable impact on routine foreign policy issues but not on salient ones.

Reagan, 1980–1984

One observer who was genuinely concerned about internationally recognized human rights wrote that the problem with Carter was that he did not do what he said he was going to do, and that the problem with the first Reagan administration was that the president did exactly what he said he was going to do (Heaps 1984). That is to say, Reagan in his first incarnation said he was going to use human rights as a weapon in the cold war, that he was going to focus his human rights policy on communist violators, and that friendly authoritarians would not bear the brunt of U.S. human rights policy. Reagan did indeed adopt the view of Jeane Kirkpatrick, namely, that friendly dictators could be gradually reformed via friendly persuasion and constructive engagement, whereas communist totalitarians could never reform and thus should be attacked with various weapons, including human rights diplomacy (Kirkpatrick 1979). But the friendly persuasion of friendly tyrants became a quiet diplomacy that was so quiet it was almost nonexistent.

There are several reasons why Reagan was eventually able to set a firm course on human rights and to get his bureaucratic process to enforce it.[2] First, Reagan—or at least his inner circle of advisers—was careful in his first administration to place in key positions people who shared his views on human rights. However much they might disagree on other matters, Alexander Haig, Caspar Weinberger, William Casey, and other top foreign policy advisers all agreed to direct human rights criticisms at communist adversaries. In the beginning, James Baker, chief of the White House staff, avoided the public confusion and bickering on this issue that had characterized the Carter top echelon.

Haig began at State, Kirkpatrick as ambassador at the UN; John Bolton eventually landed at the International Organization Bureau and Richard Allen was first NSC adviser. Throughout the first Reagan administration, individuals were sometimes placed in positions not so much for their expertise at the job but for their loyalty to Reagan and his policies. They could be relied on to report to Reagan's advisers if professional staff acted to undercut the president's policies. The chief example of this was Judge William Clark, who was sent to State despite his ignorance of foreign affairs. His principal job was to keep an eye on those, including Haig, whose loyalty might be suspect. Various ideologues were thus sprinkled throughout this administration. (This was also true in HA, though in that case the measure was unnecessary.) It was an effective bureaucratic strategy if measured in terms of coherence, consistency, and loyalty.

The president moved Elliott Abrams from the head of the International Organization Bureau in State, where he had already been confirmed, over to HA, where he easily obtained confirmation. Abrams was a smart and aggressive Washington insider. Arrogant and abrasive, he enjoyed turf battles and won his share of them. Abrams's wife of six years, Rachel, was quoted in a friendly newspaper as saying, "The truth about Elliott is that he really isn't meant to work for other people" (quoted in West 1986). As a neoconservative and convert to the radical right, he totally supported the preoccupation of the Reagan team with Soviet-led communism.

Second, Abrams, and eventually George Shultz when he replaced Haig, used the language of universal human rights and evenhandedness, and this somewhat reduced the criticism in Congress and elsewhere that Reagan's human rights policies blatantly embraced a double standard. Abrams wrote a memo for Haig stressing a balanced approach to human rights, one of two that were intentionally leaked to the press, and Shultz may have even believed he was being evenhanded. The trend continued when Reagan made a balanced speech on human rights, freedom, and democracy to the House of Commons in the UK—though the British prime minister noted in her memoirs that the speech was designed to put the Soviet Union on the defensive (Thatcher 1993, 258). Thus the rhetoric championed a universal crusade, but the practice was to remain closer to Kirkpatrick's advice.

That is, the first Reagan administration systematically practiced a double standard (Jacoby 1986; Maechling 1983; Tonelson 1983). Interviews made clear that, like the president, Abrams, Kirkpatrick, and others had the Soviet Union and communism in mind when they spoke about human rights (Maechling 1983). Reagan went out of his way to invite to the

White House, and display prominently to the Washington press corps and society, friendly authoritarians from South Korea, Zaire, Liberia, etc.—all of whom had been given the diplomatic cold shoulder by Carter. The most difficult decision Reagan had to make was to pressure cold war friends such as Marcos in the Philippines (Bonner 1988; Shultz 1993). The president was not inclined to pressure friendly tyrants and the Reagan team knew it. Abrams fully shared the view that in places such as El Salvador nothing could be worse than a leftist rebel victory, and therefore gross violations of human rights in association with the government should be played down—even if that meant lying to Congress. At the UN, Reagan's team focused almost exclusively on Cuba and other communist states, while attempting to block diplomatic pressure on friendly authoritarians in El Salvador and Guatemala.

Typical of the Washington climate of the times were the secret grants that the supposedly independent National Endowment for Democracy, led by Reagan supporters, made to both rightist parties in France and to an army-backed politician in Panama. Congress acted to stop such practices.

Abrams at HA, in a position mandated by Congress, actually carried out at least one balanced policy that had a long-term impact. He continued and expanded the Carter policy of serious annual reporting to Congress on human rights. The introduction to the reports supervised by Abrams contained a controversial philosophy, rejecting the international definition of human rights and endorsing the traditional American version—namely, that human rights encompass only civil and political, not social and economic, rights. But beyond the introduction, which became progressively blander under congressional pressure, the annual reports were widely viewed as about as honest and balanced as they had been during the Carter years. Some countries were treated more leniently than congressional critics and human rights groups thought proper. But the general opinion was, and is, that the annual reports under Abrams and his Republican successors did much to solidify human rights as a legitimate foreign policy concern in the State Department and FSO community. After all, if Reagan, like Carter, took the reporting requirement seriously, human rights as a legitimate issue was probably here to stay. Abrams should get part of the credit for this development. He helped make human rights a bipartisan subject at State.

However, HA under Abrams had for the most part terrible relations with private human rights groups. The two sides openly exchanged brickbats, and Abrams eventually tried to discredit the reports of the groups—

especially concerning Central America (Kinzer 1984; Mohr 1984; Omang 1984). Later disclosures tended to validate NGO human rights reporting on El Salvador in particular. But during the first Reagan administration most private human rights groups despaired of receiving a warm welcome in HA or indeed in most offices in the executive branch. Their input was certainly not encouraged by HA or any other office, since the groups were generally critical of Reagan's orientation toward human rights—for example, his rejection of the International Bill of Rights as a foundation and guideline, and his heavy emphasis on communist violations. The private groups teamed with congressional critics to give Reagan officials a very hard time indeed when they testified on human rights matters before congressional committees and subcommittees.

As for coordination matters, both within and outside State, they declined in importance. Inside State, the Christopher Committee was disbanded; there was no high-level attempt to integrate human rights and U.S. foreign assistance. Abrams was quoted as saying he did not spend his time thinking about such matters. At lower levels in State there was some coordination, and some states were denied consideration of small amounts of development assistance because of their human rights records (Poe et al. 1994). HA and AID officials met and made routine decisions. Most U.S. security and political foreign assistance flowed as usual, regardless of human rights performance. Reagan wanted to increase political and security assistance to friendly countries. It would have been counterproductive to reduce that assistance on human rights grounds, and in general, the Reagan team did not do so—regardless of legislation mandating a linkage. This is why Congress moved from general to country specific legislation on human rights; Reagan would not implement the general legislation as intended by Congress.[3]

Other possible tools for linking human rights to U.S. foreign policy during 1981–1984 were simply not used and thus did not need coordination or supervision. The Export-Import Bank and OPIC were not linked to human rights by the Reagan team, for two reasons. First, no credits or insurance went to close Soviet allies; and second, the administration strongly opposed interference with private economic transactions unless linked to communist governments.

Overall, the first Reagan administration represents an almost perfect textbook example of how to set clear priorities and goals for a human rights policy and how to put together a bureaucratic team to implement them. Unfortunately for Reagan and his ultraconservative supporters, this human rights orientation was supported neither by many members of

Congress nor by many politically active elements in American society. Nor was it entirely appropriate to many foreign situations. Hence considerable change was about to occur.

Reagan, 1984–1988

In the second Reagan administration there may not exactly have been a "turnaround" on human rights (Jacoby 1986), but there were significant changes. The reasons for this are complex.

First, the overall White House management changed, with a related loss of control and direction. When Reagan put Baker at Treasury and named Regan chief of the White House staff, White House management suffered. Infighting and indeed chaos increased. This was especially true of foreign policy. Reagan, who was always less a hands-on president than Carter, and who may have even been removed from many foreign policy issues, now had Shultz, Casey, Weinberger, Poindexter, North, and possibly others fighting for control of the overall policy. Clear signals from the White House declined, for human rights as well as for other issues.

Second, many of the more ideological officials in the first administration were not present in the second. Haig was gone, Allen was forced out, Kirkpatrick resigned, as did Judge Clark. Casey fell ill and died. Poindexter and North continued into the second administration, but eventually they were gone too. Shultz was far more pragmatic than Haig; professional diplomats took over at the UN; and Howard Baker and Colin Powell eventually brought more order and pragmatism to the White House and NSC.

Third, Shultz moved Abrams from HA to the Latin American bureau (ARA) and put Richard Schifter in as assistant secretary of state for human rights and humanitarian affairs. Abrams had considerable influence, especially on Central American affairs, as a strong champion of both the contras and the Salvadoran government. But he had less impact on human rights in general, especially when he became persona non grata in Congress. Schifter, too, was a neoconservative whose real preoccupation was with communist violations of human rights. But he was not the aggressive infighter Abrams was, and thus had less impact on U.S. human rights policy overall. Schifter was essentially a behind-the-scenes tactical manager. He was not a major shaper of policy in the second Reagan administration. At the UN Human Rights Commission, for example, he agreed to the appointment of Armando Valladares as head of delegation. Valladares did not speak English, had a fixation on Cuban violations of human rights to the exclusion of most other issues, and was widely disliked and ineffectual in Geneva. On this and other issues, decisions were taken either in the White House or in the IO bureau. Schifter and HA tagged along, though Schifter and others in the administration eventually tried to repair relations with human rights groups. Under Schifter the practice was begun of using retired FSOs to comment on the accuracy of the annual human rights reports. This was a beneficial change.

In this context of shifting personnel and declining central control, a number of pragmatists in the second Reagan administration made the judgment that certain "friendly" authoritarians were inimical to U.S. national interests. This was decidedly not a complete housecleaning; rather, it was a case-by-case decision-making process in which some repressive allies were jettisoned and others were embraced even more closely. Shultz and others struggled against Reagan's rigidity and anticommunist impulses to get rid of Marcos in the Philippines. Ambassador Harry Barnes Jr. did much to ease Pinochet from the presidency in Chile. Congress added its clout by overriding a Reagan veto to vote in economic sanctions on racist South Africa. At approximately the same time, Shultz made the tragic mistake of embracing an incompetently repressive Samuel Doe in Liberia, which contributed to a vicious civil war and anarchy there. Mobutu in Zaire continued his repression without U.S. interference.

Rather than a "turnaround on human rights" per se, this evolution in 1985–1988 signaled a more pragmatic look at U.S. security interests, with human rights still an appendage to that more dominant issue. What the United States especially feared in Chile was a resurgence of the radical left if Pinochet stayed too long; thus criticism on human rights grounds served the larger U.S. national interest. What the United States especially feared in the Philippines was so much repression and corruption under Marcos that there would be another Iran; U.S. influence would be thrown out along with the old regime—which at that time was seen as very costly to the U.S. military presence there. (Ironically, shortly after the demise of Marcos, the United States terminated its military presence in the Philippines, which was unnecessary after the cold war.)

These pragmatic judgments did not issue from the White House, however. They trickled up from the State Department and other places, as Shultz and others fought for the ear of a consistently unengaged president who was consumed by the emerging scandal that resulted after the United States traded arms for hostages in the Middle East, then diverted some of the payoff to the contras in Central America. The confusion of the Reagan White House in 1985–1988, the chaotic nature of the policy process, and the inconsistencies of policy outputs were almost enough to make observers long for the days of the Carter administration.

If Shultz's memoirs are accurate, U.S. foreign policy making during this period was an utter snake pit of clashing views without consistent or considered presidential direction (Shultz 1993). One observer has concluded there were two Reagans—one ideological and one pragmatic (Tucker 1993). In 1981–1985 most presidential advisers appealed to his ideology, and it predominated. In 1985–1988, Shultz appealed above all to his pragmatism, and at the very end this dimension predominated.

These high-level developments, more than the effect of any bureaucratic process (which in any case may not have consistently existed), affected the fate of human rights policy in the second Reagan administration. The disintegration of the NSC and the lack of dynamic leadership at HA are worthy of mention but were not decisive for human rights policy. However, a pragmatic secretary of state, knowledgeable about Washington infighting, could be considered an important "bureaucratic" element.

Congress and the human rights groups fought the more ideological approaches, insisting on at least the appearance of balance, and that contributed to the shift as well. In 1985–1987 the Soviet Union under Gorbachev also changed. When Reagan finally concluded—as Margaret Thatcher had earlier done—that Gorbachev was a man with whom he could do business, Reagan's first (ideological and unbalanced) approach to human rights was dead. The second Reagan team knew that the first approach was not always consistent with U.S. national interest.

Post–Cold War Presidents

The end of the cold war cannot be measured with a stopwatch. Just as attention to international human rights had been building since 1945 and especially since about 1970, so the cold war had been winding down since the Cuban missile crisis in 1962 and the official beginning of détente in 1969. Even Reagan's harsh rhetoric during the early 1980s did not completely reverse historical trends.

George Bush's administration was transitional and is thus difficult to analyze with bold strokes. President Bush's pragmatic nature, and a certain chameleon quality, add to the difficulties of analysis. He held office during the collapse of communism in both eastern Europe (1989) and the Soviet Union (1991). He articulated a "new world order" but was in office only one year after the collapse of the USSR. Bill Clinton was the first of the truly post–cold war presidents. But as of this writing, his record on human rights has been both fuzzy and incomplete.

Bush

Historians may eventually pin a lasting label on George Bush's administration. No such label has yet emerged concerning his foreign policy in general or its human rights dimension. The "vision problem" persists. Eschewing grand labels, some observers have described his overall foreign policy as a mixture of different elements (Deibel 1991). The conventional wisdom is that Bush was good at pragmatic reactions to crises but poor at long-range planning and creative thought. Even though I closely followed human rights events during the Bush years, I have been unable to produce a synthetic description. Few clear, high-level, and consistent signals were sent by the president about human rights to those responsible for the policy in 1989–1992.

Bush, experienced and interested in foreign policy, was a hands-on president in the Carter mode. He also had great confidence in James Baker as secretary of state. The two, along with NSC Adviser Brent Scowcroft, worked well together and with Defense Secretary Dick Cheney. Baker tended to operate with a small group of confidants on the seventh floor of State, thus reducing the importance of the rest of the State bureaucracy—as during the days when Kissinger was secretary of state.

In some ways Bush sought to establish continuity with the Reagan legacy, without necessarily specifying whether it was the ideological or the pragmatic Reagan he was seeking to emulate. There continued to be no explicit human rights officer in the NSC. NSC Adviser Scrowcroft occasionally met with human rights groups, as did others at the NSC, but there was no focal point in NSC for human rights matters.

Bush kept Schifter as assistant secretary of state for human rights and humanitarian affairs, despite his low-profile performance. It is somewhat ironic that Schifter later resigned and campaigned for Clinton, ostensibly on the grounds that Bush was the one president since Carter who was insufficiently interested in human rights. In Schifter's view, Carter, Reagan, and Clinton all represented continuity on human rights in U.S. foreign policy; Bush was odd man out. Some others share this view: one interviewee said that after the demise of the Soviet Union and its empire, "human rights fell off the table" in the Bush administration. It is difficult to verify this view, but that does not mean Schifter did not genuinely believe it. Thus far it is impossible to say what might be other reasons for his resignation. Was Schifter increasingly irritated that the Bush-Baker team voiced strong criticism of Israel's human rights record in the occupied territories? Was Schifter increasingly ignored by Secretary Baker?

Schifter oversaw the required annual reports, and whether because of him or despite him, those reports did continue to be essentially accurate. The general consensus is that reporting was much more objective about Israeli practices in the territories than it had been before. Cold war reasons for softening reports about Israel no longer held; without a Soviet Union, there was less need for Israel as a strategic ally in the Middle East. A number of rumors circulated about why the annual report on Israel had become more candid, but these proved impossible to verify. It is clear that congressional pressures did not account for the change, since the pro-Israel bloc in Congress remained strong.

HA, like other functional bureaus at State, continued to be viewed as a career backwater or secondary choice. FSOs have always preferred the geographical bureaus, particularly the European one, as stepping stones to advancement. Occasionally a dynamic assistant secretary and shrewd operator, such as Joe Sisco, was able to transform a functional bureau (in Sisco's case, IO during the late 1960s) into a key player in policy making. But such transformations have been rare. Under Derian and Schifter, this traditional problem was evident for HA, though Derian was far more assertive than Schifter. Even the increasing acceptance of human rights as part of the U.S. foreign policy agenda did not lead FSOs to prefer HA over a geographical bureau. They could, and did, report on human rights and handle human rights issues from the geographical bureaus. Abrams came the closest to making HA more of a central player, but Abrams was so ideological and abrasive that many FSOs did not want to hitch their star to his wagon; his style did not fit well with the FSO penchant for button-down, pin-striped, case-by-case understatement and accommodation (Clarke 1987, 135–36).

Valladares continued to head the U.S. delegation to the UN Human Rights Commission in Geneva, and U.S. foreign policy in the UN continued with its fixation on Cuban violations of human rights, so much so that there was friction between the U.S. and the UN secretary-general over how to treat Cuba (Lewis 1990). With the exception of the Cuban focus, U.S. human rights policy at the UN broadened during the Bush era, but this had more to do with the demise of European communism than with any grand human rights strategy. Bush, Baker, Schifter et al. were simply not given to grand strategizing.

Bush foreign policy also continued to treat China essentially as before, that is, as a strategic ally and a huge potential market for exports. This was not unlike U.S. policy to Indonesia, Saudi Arabia, etc. After Tiananmen Square, Bush responded to domestic pressure to do something, but his back-channel secret diplomacy by National Security Adviser Scowcroft and others made clear to the Chinese leadership that Bush was not going to let the massacre upset shared political and economic interests. The Bush administration issued public statements about human rights in China, and the administration tried to engage China in a dialogue about rights. But once Bush had sent secret envoys to China after Tiananmen, the public process must have been viewed in Beijing as more show than substance. The overall policy toward China was made at the highest levels of the Bush administration, and the human rights bureaucracy contributed only slightly. Bush had been ambassador to China and thought he knew the situation well.

The Bush policy toward Iraq prior to August 1990 was typical of a series of foreign situations. Elements in Congress wanted to use economic levers to pressure Saddam Hussein about his repressive policies (among other things), including the use of poison gas against Iraqi Kurds. The Bush administration resisted this effort, seeing Hussein as a buffer against Iranian expansionism. Ambassador April Gallespie's notorious meeting with Hussein, just prior to his invasion of Kuwait, was less a blunder by the ambassador than a reflection of Bush policy. Hussein was to be treated gingerly, as a useful if brutal strategic partner; he was not to be firmly opposed or overtly pressured.

On the other hand, Bush made changes in U.S. policy toward Central America, away from Reagan's ideological approach and in favor of pragmatic support for national reconciliation in El Salvador and Nicaragua (Pastor 1992). Part of this shift involved increased pressure on the Salvadoran government and military to control right-wing death squads engaged in gross violations of human rights. Again we see that both the policy process and policy outputs varied from issue to issue. East Asia was not Central America. Neither area was the Middle East. The process, the players, and the attention to human rights all varied.

There were other changes beyond Central America concerning internationally recognized human rights during the Bush era, but some did not originate strictly with the U.S., and some can only be explained by idiosyncratic factors. At the World Bank, for example, after 1989 there was a greater willingness to link bank loans to issues of "good government." Some of these issues involved certain human rights, such as political participation and "transparency" in government process. While the Bush officials at the bank supported these trends, they did not initiate them (Gillies 1993). And, just as Reagan's ambassador to Chile, Harry Barnes Jr., had earlier aided the opposition to Pinochet (Boeninger 1986), so Ambassador Smith Hempstone in Kenya pressed President Daniel Arap Moi to ease the repression there and accept multiparty democracy (Norowjee 1992, 141).

But a "Bush push" for human rights in Kenya, however inconsistent and ineffective in the view of private human rights groups, did not imply a similar push for human rights in places such as Kuwait (Lewis 1991). And while the World Bank briefly delayed loans to China after Tiananmen Square, it continued loans to some other governments with poor human rights records. India, for example, though a democracy, increasingly manifested serious human rights problems without losing its bank funding on rights grounds (Gargan 1992).

Bush also made new and interesting decisions in favor of "humanitarian intervention" in both Iraq during the spring of 1991 and Somalia during the fall and winter of 1992. The decision to use force in support of Kurds in northern Iraq beginning in March 1991 was an ad hoc decision that stemmed from media coverage and European pressures. It was taken at the highest levels of the U.S. government, with the bureaucratic process playing a rather insignificant role. The president's military and political advisers told him that limited military involvement would not lead to another Vietnam. By using existing UN resolutions already adopted, the United States could do what it wanted without great problems from a diplomatic or legal standpoint. Other states were ready to join the intrusive venture.

As for the presidential decision to commit about thirty thousand troops to Somalia, this too was essentially an ad hoc decision. One should not read it as a new, systematic, broad policy (Pease and Forsythe 1993). In the face of extensive media coverage and pressures from the UN secretary-general, the president acted from genuinely humanitarian motivations to create order for the delivery of humanitarian assistance in a situation of anarchy. There was not only international support through the UN, but also local consent from the various "warlords" contesting power in Somalia. The intervention was short-term and essentially American. It did not address the structural problems of the situation, did not attempt national reconciliation and the creation of a functioning, humane national government that could maintain humanitarian if not democratic order after the withdrawal of U.S. forces. It was only minimally linked to the UN.

The U.S. bureaucratic politics supportive of this intervention were somewhat serendipitous. After Schifter resigned at HA to work for candidate Clinton, James Bishop, an FSO, was named acting assistant secretary of state human rights and humanitarian affairs. Bishop had extensive experience in Africa, including Somalia. He knew the situation there as well as anyone in Washington, and he strongly favored U.S. involvement to relieve disorder and starvation. So did other parts of the State Department, such as the African bureau and the Office of Refugee Affairs. Early in 1992, when the International Committee of the Red Cross and other private groups were reporting disastrous conditions in Somalia, much of the Bush administration, including Secretary of State Baker and the high levels of the Pentagon, were opposed to involvement. As media coverage of the situation increased, and as UN Secretary-General Boutros Boutros-Ghali spoke openly both of Somalia and of new UN uses of force, those favoring involvement gradually persuaded Baker and Cheney—and the president—to consider it more seriously.

The elements leading to a shift in U.S. policy on Somalia, however, were primarily external—stemming from the international media and the UN secretary-general. The bureaucratic process was issue-specific; its functioning was greatly affected by these external factors. Normally Bishop, like Schifter, did not have great influence on policy. Schifter had had poorer relations with Baker than with Shultz. It was only in the context created by the media and the UN that the views of people such as Bishop took on increased importance.

The Bush record on human rights is still amorphous. The private group Human Rights Watch was extremely critical of that record (Howe 1991), but overall it seems to be similar to that of other administrations (except Reagan's first). Bush's policies lacked the lofty rhetoric of the Carter era, but also the ideological imbalance of the first Reagan administration. In practice there was real support for an improved human rights situation in places such as Somalia and El Salvador. At one point the Bush administration recalled the U.S. ambassador in Bulgaria to protest repression of Turkish Bulgarians. There was also a real lack of support for an improved human rights situation in places such as Indonesia and Kuwait.

These actions did not depend very much on a particular bureaucratic process. Rather, they were linked more to the nature of international relations: as before, states with resources or geostrategic importance avoided human rights pressures; smaller, weaker, and poorer states became laboratories for efforts to link U.S. foreign policy to human rights performance. When the media and foreign parties directed a great deal of attention to human rights, they sometimes generated important support for new policies. The overall record on human rights was certainly shaped by the pragmatic nature of Bush, Baker, Scowcroft, and Cheney. This pragmatism, while a clear change from the first Reagan administration (but not the second), did not solve the problem of inconsistency or arbitrariness in human rights policy abroad any better than the Carter or second Reagan administrations had done.

The end of the cold war meant that Bush could afford deeper "humanitarian" involvement in places such as Iraq without fear of offsetting action by a competing superpower. The end of the cold war also meant that Bush could commit tens of thousands of troops to a place such as Somalia without having to conserve resources for geostrategic competition. But the end of the cold war also meant that if a country such as Liberia no longer mattered in East-West relations, then its severe human rights problems might be left to others, such as Nigeria and the Economic Community of West African States (ECOWAS), to manage or mismanage.

During the Bush administration—after the cold war as before—it was not the nature of the bureaucratic process that mattered for human rights policy, especially in salient countries such as Iraq and Somalia. Rather, what mattered was media coverage and international pressure—whether from European states and their public opinion (e.g., Iraq in the spring of 1991) or from the UN secretary-general (Somalia in late 1992).

Clinton

Bill Clinton seems to be a classic, pragmatic American politician—certainly as far as human rights are concerned. He used the rhetoric of human rights in campaigning against the Bush record. He repeatedly criticized Bush for insufficient attention to human rights. Upon assuming office, however, he immediately confronted the complexity of world affairs. (Similarly, candidate Reagan had spoken strongly on the need for a two-China policy; President Reagan continued the one-China policy of his predecessors, although with slight tinkering). Clinton was to eventually take risks for human rights in places such as Haiti and Bosnia. But his early inclination was to back away from human rights issues when they raised, as they almost always did, major complications. In places such as Bosnia, China, and Haiti, early Clinton policy looked so much like Bush policy that one wag said Clinton was Bush with angst.

The president himself seemed at first overwhelmingly oriented toward domestic issues, whether out of personal preference or political calculation. Clinton reportedly said at one point that he wanted to resolve the issues in the former Yugoslavia as quickly as possible because he was not elected to spend a lot of time on foreign affairs. He did not spend very much time with his foreign policy advisers, at least during his first years as president. From mid-1994, suffering from intense criticism about his foreign policies, he obviously tried to give the appearance of more (and more decisive) foreign policy involvement. When a crisis occurred, as when there was a backlash against U.S. involvement in Somalia in the wake of eighteen American deaths there, Clinton became engaged in foreign policy but in a way to abruptly reduce commitment. Early on, drift was combined with frequent changes of course.

Probably no other situation received as much media attention about human rights as China. There the Clinton administration engaged in a high-profile dialogue on human rights, against the background of a possible loss of MFN status for China. But in the last analysis, the Clinton administration continued MFN status. American business and labor groups had deluged Washington with self-interested lobbying. (The AFL-CIO, however, lobbied for a loss of MFN status, largely because of the plight of Chinese labor, which led to cheap competition for American-made goods.) China was too important a market, and its regional and global political role too important, for Clinton to sacrifice it on the altar of human rights. In this respect, too, there was more similarity than difference between Bush and Clinton.

The faces in the bureaucracy were different, but the nature of international relations and of American domestic politics were fundamentally the same as before. Congressional Democrats, however, were less inclined to criticize Clinton over human rights in China. By 1994, Clinton had not only severed the link between human rights and MFN status for China; he had also relegated human rights to a relatively low position in the dialogue with China. In the last analysis, the end of the cold war and the decline of the importance of "the China card" in Soviet-American relations made little difference for U.S. human rights policy toward China. Other foreign and domestic factors impeded a focus on rights.

As for Clinton's early process of making and implementing foreign policy, there was no consistent or coherent pattern (Hoagland 1993). U.S. foreign policy in general was so ill defined and confused that Secretary of Defense Les Aspin was eased out, National Security Adviser Anthony Lake offered to resign, the number two man at State, Wharton, was pressured out, and criticism of Secretary of State Warren Christopher abounded. Beyond individuals, the entire process seemed unsettled, and that is being kind. The White House and the State Department supported Father Aristide in Haiti, while the CIA continued to circulate derogatory reports about him. The head of HA, John Shattuck, called publicly for a policy review on Haiti, and shortly thereafter his superiors said publicly there would not be any such review.

All was not chaos. In June 1993 at the UN World Conference on Human Rights at Vienna, the Clinton team fielded an organized delegation with a coherent and largely successful strategy of reaffirming universal human rights. But this performance tended to be the exception rather than the rule during Clinton's early years.

Clinton, through his foreign policy appointments and paper organization, seemed favorably predisposed to human rights, though it cannot be stressed too much that these factors do not guarantee policy outputs. Shattuck at HA was a former head of the Washington office of the ACLU. Morton Halperin, first nominated to head the new Office of Democracy and Peacekeeping in the Department of Defense, had held the same ACLU position. Eventually, Halperin's nomination was blocked by a number of conservative senators, but not because of the new DOD office per se. Secretary of State Christopher had been responsible for coordinating many human rights issues during the Carter years. Schifter was rewarded for abandoning the Bush ship by becoming NSC counselor and special assistant to the president. It is difficult to see how this position could have generated much influence on human rights, compared to the role of speech maker and diplomatic troubleshooter.

The new DOD post for democracy was scuttled by Clinton's second secretary of defense, William Perry; it could have been a base from which to inject more education on human rights and democracy into military training. But at State, a new Office of Global Issues was created at a high level. Former Colorado senator Timothy Wirth headed that office, and he brought considerable enthusiasm to the position. While Wirth showed some interest in human rights per se, he was widely regarded as more interested in other "global issues," such as population control. The NSC resumed the practice, dormant since the Carter years, of having a human rights officer. Halperin was placed in charge of the new NSC Office of Democracy, Human Rights, and Humanitarian Affairs. When he resigned the position in 1996, Halperin was replaced by Eric Schwartz. One of the organizations that Schwartz had previously worked for was Asia Watch, part of the complex making up Human Rights Watch.

The Clinton team renamed HA the Bureau for Human Rights, Democracy, and Labor. This displeased several circles of opinion in Washington, who feared a downgrading of internationally recognized human rights concerns (Carothers 1994). Some observers saw a "human rights group" and a "democracy group" jousting for bureaucratic turf, though others did not see any substantive importance in the semantic differences being discussed. To the critics of the "prodemocracy crowd," Clinton's proposed approach suggested American nationalism and unilateral action rather than international standards and multilateral action. The first annual human rights report under Clinton showed more attention to women's and labor issues, regardless of the name change for the bureau. Within HA there was a new coordinator for women's rights, but few if any observers thought this bureaucratic change was important.

Late in 1993 the Clinton administration proposed to Congress a radical overhaul of U.S. foreign assistance. In scrapping the 1961 Foreign Assistance Act as amended, the Clinton team wanted to proceed thematically rather than country by country. One of the proposed themes was promoting democracy. There was no explicit mention of human rights (Lippman 1993b). "Enlarging" the democratic community was supposed to be one of the three basic pillars of Clinton's foreign policy.

In addition to moving Halperin over to the NSC and making Schifter a special troubleshooter for central Europe, the Clinton administration created an interagency, interdepartment working group on democracy in 1994. Already, U.S. foreign policy was interjecting democratic considerations into foreign assistance through several consultative mechanisms: the World Bank Consultative Group, the UN Development Program Round Tables, and the Development Assistance Committee of the Organization for Economic Cooperation and Development (Nelson and Eglinton 1993). The U.S. Agency for International Development had several democratic projects under way; its Western Hemispheres division employed a complicated matrix in an effort to measure democratic progress and adjust country assistance accordingly (Nelson and Eglinton 1993).

Contrary to popular mythology, no modern president has made promoting democracy a serious part of U.S. foreign policy, despite the fact that such a program would make a cost-effective contribution to U.S. national security (Diamond 1992). Clinton's emphasis on democracy, while echoing Reagan's House of Commons speech in particular, was obviously an effort to develop a new "pillar" of U.S. foreign policy after the cold war. Several observers (including Robert Tucker and David Hendrickson) doubt whether the United States has the persistence to take on successfully all such foreign policies, which are complex and require sustained commitment.

Clinton did, in fact, come to take considerable risks for human rights in Haiti and Bosnia. In both countries, he put a relatively large number of American troops in harm's way without solid backing from the Congress and public. Had either turned into another Somalia (or Lebanon under Reagan), Clinton's presidency would have been tarnished. In both cases, factors somewhat apart from human rights affected key decisions. In Haiti, the congressional black caucus, whose support Clinton needed on a variety of issues, demanded decisive U.S. involvement. In Bosnia, concerns about America's leadership seemed to fuel the decision to deploy NATO troops in the form of IFOR (International Implementation Force under the Dayton Accords of 1995). For whatever combination of reasons, Clinton did act decisively to restore an elected president in Haiti and to first mediate, then enforce, a peace agreement in the former Yugoslavia. Questions of long-term commitment and staying power persist. (Most U.S. troops were withdrawn from Haiti by spring 1996).

Clinton has also been a supporter of the UN tribunal for the prosecution of serious violations of humanitarian law in the former Yugoslavia. The United States teamed with a few other states to create and then support a second "war crimes" tribunal to deal with the aftermath of genocide in Rwanda. In both cases the creation of a tribunal by the UN Security Council, under U.S. leadership, was in large part a move to assuage the bad conscience that resulted from a lack of timely intervention to stop atrocities. Nevertheless, the United States was the strongest supporter of these proceedings on behalf of individual criminal prosecutions, even though both processes were replete with controversy.

The private human rights groups believed almost uniformly that the Clinton administration was more sympathetic to human rights issues than the Bush administration. One interviewee put the comparison this way: neither the Bush nor the Clinton team had a grand strategy or big picture concerning human rights, but while neither had vision, at least the Clinton team had interest. The private groups probably did have more access to HA, and were more warmly received, than when Schifter headed that bureau. But access and reception are not the same as influence. Winston Lord, assistant secretary of state for Asian affairs, met with the groups, but that does not mean he followed their advice concerning China, Indonesia, or other areas. It is fairly clear that Shattuck, while he might have had good access to Christopher, was not going to be able to push human rights at the expense of major expediential considerations.

Conclusion

The end of the cold war did indeed cause major changes in U.S. foreign policy, though those changes have yet to distill into consistently clear policies. The U.S. foreign policy process also changed, but perhaps as much because the Democrats won control of the White House in 1992 as because the Soviet empire collapsed. Republican control of Congress after the 1994 elections created further changes. Thus, the actual nature of the bureaucratic process, while important from time to time, is not a factor of the highest importance most of the time—at least for the issue of human rights. Only an exceedingly broad conception of the bureaucratic process, including presidential values and power, would lead one to conclude that the fate of human rights policy was greatly and consistently affected by bureaucratic structure. U.S. human rights policy abroad was consistently more affected by high-level executive decisions, Congress, the media, domestic public opinion, and foreign pressures than by the bureaucratic process in Washington, at least insofar as that process can be separated from the other factors.

The end of the traditional, geostrategic security threat from Soviet-led communism left the United States with no clear conception of security threats and security policy. This situation led the Bush and Clinton administrations to adopt the view that certain human rights violations, including denial of democracy, could be conceived as security threats. It was not always clear what was a strictly American security threat and what was an international security threat meriting U.S. military participation in a multilateral effort—even when U.S. "vital interests" were not necessarily involved.

The Bush administration first articulated a sweeping definition of security threats as general policy through the UN Security Council in early 1992 (Weiss, Forsythe, and Coate 1994). Not only human rights violations but also environmental degradation and economic disaster could, in this view, be seen as security problems. The Clinton administration adopted the same view in 1994 when it successfully argued in the Security Council that the overthrow of democracy in Haiti represented a threat to international peace and security. A debate then followed, at home and abroad, as to whether the United States should use military force in Haiti, even if approved by the UN Security Council. Clinton argued that U.S. security, in the form of the social stability of Florida and the sanctity of borders, was indeed threatened by the arrival of Haitian boat people—and slightly later by Cuban boat people. Others argued that since there was no traditional international aggression by the Haitian military, the situation was not a security threat and military force was inappropriate.

Not only was it the case that human rights violations continued after the cold war, they actually increased in scope and severity in numerous places—both in areas of former European communism and beyond. The scale of suffering in Iraq, combined with political pressures generated by media coverage and European politics, led the Bush administration to endorse the view in 1991 that the situation, especially in Iraqi Kurdistan, was a threat to international peace and merited a military response. In late 1992 the situation in Somalia, combined with political pressures generated by media coverage and UN officials, led Bush to a similar view. Especially in the latter case, domestic pressures were intense, and pressure groups were ultimately successful in arguing that the human rights situation in Somalia was not a security threat and did not involve U.S. vital interests.

Thus, absent traditional security threats from other great powers, the United States after the cold war sometimes elevated human rights violations into a security issue meriting military action. But after American deaths in Somalia, and during genocide in Rwanda in 1994, the Clinton administration manifested shifting views on this question. Denial of democracy and brutal repression in Haiti was a security threat; genocide in Rwanda was not. Gross violations of human rights in Bosnia did not generate decisive foreign intervention at first; later they did.

The question of the linkage between security and human rights aside, even before the end of the cold war it had not proven easy to establish the exact place of human rights on the U.S. foreign policy agenda. It was increasingly clear that for reasons of both domestic and international politics, for American opinion and international law and organization, modern U.S. administrations would have to address human rights in foreign policy. But how, specifically, would they do so (Forsythe 1995)?

Carter never found a general answer to this question. Reagan offered an answer in his first administration, which actually built on Brzezinski's views: use human rights as a weapon in the cold war, directing human rights pressures primarily toward communist adversaries. But in Reagan's second administration, this orientation, persistently if inconsistently challenged by Congress, increasingly yielded to the same case-by-case decision making and inconsistency that had plagued Reagan's predecessor.

Likewise, the Bush administration seemed to illustrate the maxim that the only broad generalization about U.S. foreign policy and human rights was that if a country is perceived as of great strategic or economic interest, it will escape serious and sustained attention to its human rights record. Bulgaria was targeted but not Zaire, Kenya but not Kuwait. A second, more limited generalization also emerged during the Bush period: If an administration has no clear strategy and set of priorities in its foreign policy, it will be whipsawed by the communications media. Media reports were a large part of the reason why Bush committed military force in behalf of the Iraqi Kurds and Somalis, even though these reports were filtered through European peoples and states (in the case of Iraq) and the UN (for Somalia).

Just as the early Clinton period closely resembled the Bush antecedent, so too did its record on human rights policy abroad. China's human rights situation first merited close scrutiny and threats of sanctions by the Clinton team; then it did not. Somalia merited U.S. military forces; then it did not. Bosnia did not merit a costly U.S. involvement; then it did. Expansion of democracy abroad was to be one of the three basic pillars of Clinton foreign policy. But a major allocation of resources was not directed to this objective.

Since 1977 different presidents have tried different ways of organizing the executive branch to integrate their version of human rights into foreign policy. Reagan in his first administration was the only one to have success in this regard, and he did this more through personnel appointments than through administrative reshuffling. Because of clear leadership from the White House, combined with dedicated personnel throughout State, Defense, and the CIA especially, the first Reagan administration was able to make human rights an adjunct to its cold war attacks on the Soviet Union and its allies. But even this "success" proved short-lived; the second Reagan administration, with essentially the same bureaucratic scheme but different personnel, and most important, a different evaluation of some foreign situations, had a distinctly different record on human rights.

The Clinton administration was positioned to carry out an interesting experiment. Presidential rhetoric, a very broad working group cutting across U.S. departments, and international coordinating mechanisms at the World Bank, United Nations, and OECD seemed to signal a push to advance democracy. But it remains to be seen whether the president will indeed exercise significant leadership in this regard, and whether these bureaucratic arrangements (some new and some old) will make any real difference. Given the difficulties of advancing democracy in many foreign countries, especially if other G-7 and OECD countries do not coordinate policy in an unprecedented way, it is unlikely that a strictly U.S. interagency or interdepartment group will be all that important.

In general, of all the factors that might explain the importance (or lack thereof) of human rights in U.S. foreign policy, bureaucratic politics narrowly defined ranks relatively low on this list. The nature of international relations, presidential interest in the subject, and congressional pressures against the background of American political culture and public opinion—with the media thrown in—all explain more than bureaucratic politics. Certain administrative arrangements might make some difference on some issues. Having a group of retired FSOs oversee the writing of the annual human rights reports might in fact increase the reports' objectivity. When important strategic and economic interests were out of the picture, the reports may have encouraged FSOs and other career policy makers to interject human rights considerations into routine foreign assistance decisions. But salient and significant human rights policies are to be explained for the most part by other, extrabureaucratic factors.

Richard K. Herrmann and Shannon Peterson

12. American Public Opinion and the Use of Force

Change or Continuity in the Post–Cold War World?

How will the end of the cold war affect U.S. decisions to use force in world affairs? Will the collapse of the Soviet Union and the end of the perceived global threat from communism lead to a reduction in the size and use of the standing military? Or will the collapse of countervailing Soviet power and the deterrent effect of potential nuclear escalation unleash U.S. military action, as Washington builds a world order based on its own preferences? To decide how the end of the cold war will affect U.S. decision making about the use of force, we need to understand the perceptions and circumstances that led Washington to use force in the past. We can then speculate on which of these causal factors, some inside the United States and others in the international environment, will be affected by the end of the cold war and the collapse of the Soviet Union.

The decision to use force is a function of three factors: first, the interests and priorities defined by the political process in Washington; second, the perceived threats to these interests and the perceived opportunities to advance them that prevailing leaders in Washington see; and third, the ideas regarding the utility, effectiveness, efficiency, acceptability at home and abroad, and morality of using force. Before we can identify change in these factors, we need to establish a clear baseline regarding the use of force during the cold war, based on public opinion data on mass and elite attitudes.

Presidential decision making and leadership may affect public and elite opinion, perhaps even more than this opinion affects presidential decisions. Our purpose, however, is not to test a causal decision-making model that begins with public opinion, but to take data regarding attitudes as a reflection of the priorities and ideas regarding the use of force that compete in the political process. The baseline on the three factors may shift depending on the strategic and situational context: it may look different for Washington's use of force in central Europe and its use of force in Vietnam. We therefore divide the empirical study into two parts.

The first part examines attitudes about the use of force in the context of strategic nuclear arms, NATO, and Japan, while the second focuses on the U.S. use of force in all other situations. We establish a baseline for these factors beginning in 1975 and then look for change through 1994. We then speculate on the implications of the empirical patterns for both the construction of domestic political coalitions in favor of the use of force and for Washington's military involvement in world affairs after the cold war.

The Use of Force: What, When, and Why?

In this chapter three uses of force are considered relevant. The first is the deployment of conventional troops into ongoing combat. The second is the deployment of force to deter or compel, even if there is no active fighting. Because it is difficult to tell which forward deployments will escalate into combat and which may succeed without having to fight, we will treat all forward deployments as uses of force. For instance, Desert Shield, the deterrent phase of the crisis over Kuwait, would have counted as a use of force even if Desert Storm, the active combat phase, had not occurred. A third use of force is the development and maintenance of U.S. strategic nuclear weapons, presumably more to deter and compel than to use on the battlefield.

The scope of our definition of the use of force is broader than several other common conceptions. In Blechman and Kaplan's classic study of the U.S. use of force, for instance, "major uses of force" were limited to those occasions of "non-routine military operations involving a strategic nuclear unit, two or more aircraft carrier task groups, at least one air combat wing, or more than a battalion of ground forces" (Blechman and Kaplan 1978, 50–51). For our purposes, this more narrow scope would exclude the most expensive and large-scale commitments of U.S. force during the cold war, such as those in NATO. These routine U.S. commitments, of course, directly targeted the Soviet Union and would be the most likely to change with the end of the cold war.

The interpretations of the U.S. use of force most popular in the United States stress the importance of perceived threat and the priority given to defense against the Soviet Union. Of course, defense from communism was not the only interest that drove U.S. cold war policy. Washington's economic and messianic interests and elite perceptions not of threat but of the opportunity for preponderance also played a role (Leffler 1992). So did the institutional vested interests—bureaucratic, military, and commercial—that shaped domestic coalition politics (Cumings 1990). Motivational attributions, of course, are at the core of competing interpretations. They are not mutually exclusive and have fueled historical debates throughout the cold war. We cannot resolve these issues here, but we will consider three questions: (1) Has the end of the cold war reduced perceived threat and in turn undermined support for the use of force? (2) Has the end of the cold war produced perceptions of opportunity and support for the use of force to acquire preponderance? (3) Has the end of the cold war led the traditional elites with vested interests in the use of force to identify new threats or to form new coalitions that now advance different reasons for using force?

Bruce Jentleson has argued that public support for the U.S. use of force since Vietnam has been a function of the objectives sought (Jentleson 1992; see also Jentleson and Britton 1996). In cases of intervention to stop civil wars, support has been harder to mobilize than in situations that involved interstate war. In neither situation has it been easy to convince a majority of Americans that the use of force was the best idea, until after the president had already committed troops to combat. The domestic or international character of conflict was not the only factor affecting U.S. decision making. After all, there are a multitude of conflicts in the world and in only a small fraction of them does the United States become involved. In 1994, for instance, U.S. airpower and sea power played a role in Bosnia, and U.S. troops went ashore in Haiti—the first case was a mix of civil and international war, the second an internal contest—while violent conflicts that Washington was not involved in raged in Sudan, Afghanistan, Angola, Azerbaijan, Kashmir, and Tajikistan. Clearly, the political identification of national interests plays an important role in discriminating between the host of occasions where force might be used and those cases where it actually is.

The bottom-up review issued by Secretary of Defense Aspin in 1993 argued that the United States must be prepared to use force in "those areas of the world that are critical to U.S. interests" (Aspin 1993, 5–6). Western Europe and Japan are two areas that have been deemed vital since the end of World War II. Originally, they may have been simply instrumental interests, needed to contain the Soviet Union, but over the last forty years the huge economic, cultural, and security developments in these two areas have made them intrinsically vital to the United States. Other areas of the world were also deemed vital during the cold war, but often the interests involved were instrumental and symbolic (Jervis 1989, 174–225). Pakistan and the Philippines, for instance, played important roles in containing communism and facilitating the defense of sea and land routes. Vietnam and Bangladesh were perceived as important tests of U.S. credibility and were symbolically linked to European and Japanese confidence in U.S. defense or to Moscow's estimate of American resolve. The end of the cold war should affect the definition of instrumental and symbolic interests, though inertia and vested institutional interests may slow down policy change.

The Use of Force in Europe and the Pacific

Perhaps the most clear and least surprising change in U.S. elite opinion about foreign affairs that came with the end of the cold war was the decline of the perceived threat from the Soviet Union. Since 1975 the Chicago Council on Foreign Relations (CCFR) has commissioned surveys to measure elite and mass U.S. opinion (Chicago Council on Foreign Relations [hereafter CCFR] 1975, 1979, 1982, 1986, 1990, 1994). Table 12.1 presents the responses to two questions that have been asked more or less consistently since surveys began in 1975. The first deals with the importance the respondent attaches to the goal of containing communism and the second asks about the importance of matching Soviet military power. In both cases the change in the elite sample is striking. In 1990 less than 11 percent of the elite surveyed felt containing communism was very important, while more than 46 percent felt it was not important at all. Just four years earlier, in response to the same questions, fewer than 10 percent thought containment was not important and more than 43 percent felt it was very important. By 1994 the threat had apparently declined so significantly that the question was dropped from the survey.

With regard to the importance of matching Soviet military power, an even more dramatic change is evident. Among elites, the proportion of those feeling it was very important dropped from more than 58 percent in 1986 to just over 20 percent in 1990. A significant but less dramatic change was apparent in mass opinion. By 1990, those feeling it was very important had fallen from the previous high of 55 percent to 41 percent. In 1994,

Table 12.1 Public Opinion on Foreign Policy Goals

I am going to read a list of possible foreign policy goals that the United States might have. For each one please say whether you think that it should be a very important foreign policy goal of the United States, a somewhat important foreign policy goal, or not an important goal at all? How important a foreign policy goal should *containing communism* be?

	Elite					*Mass*				
	1975	*1979*	*1982*	*1986*	*1990*	*1975*	*1979*	*1982*	*1986*	*1990*
Very important	34.6	45.2	44.9	43.2	10.4	58.0	65.1	61.3	59.6	43.3
Somewhat important	48.9	47.1	47.0	48.2	43.2	28.3	25.5	30.0	31.3	38.1
Not important	16.5	7.7	8.0	8.8	46.4	13.7	9.4	8.7	9.1	18.7

How important a foreign policy goal should *matching Soviet military power* be?

	Elite				*Mass*			
	1982	*1986*	*1990*	*1994a*	*1982*	*1896*	*1990*	*1994a*
Very important	52.1	58.6	20.2	15.7	51.7	54.9	41.3	33.2
Somewhat important	40.8	33.8	48.4	52.2	35.3	35.5	41.9	50.9
Not important	7.1	7.6	31.5	31.9	12.9	9.6	16.8	15.9

Sources: CCFR 1975, 1979, 1982, 1986, 1990, 1994.

a. 1997 CCFR dropped the question of matching Soviet military power. We have substituted a similar question regarding the degree of perceived threat (critical, important but not critical, not important at all) to American vital interests posed by the military power of Russia.

when both groups were asked a similar question about whether Russian military power posed a critical threat to U.S. vital interests, the degree of perceived threat had declined even further.

Interpreters of American foreign policy who stress the importance of the Soviet threat as a key motivating factor behind containment strategies ought to expect very significant policy change to accompany the collapse of the perceived threat from Moscow. To some degree, the expected change is evident in elite and mass attitudes about different policy options. In table 12.2, for instance, we find that 1990 responses shifted dramatically on the often asked question about whether spending on national defense ought to be expanded, cut back, or kept the same. The proportion of elites ready to expand spending dropped to a low of 2.4 percent, while those ready to cut defense spending nearly doubled from just four years earlier—jumping from 38.6 percent to 77.1 percent. Similar but less dramatic change is evident in general public opinion. It appears that by 1994 the desire for increased cuts in defense spending had more or less leveled off. In that year, more than 50 percent of both groups agreed that spending on national defense should be kept the same, while those argu-

Table 12.2 Public Opinion on National Defense Spending

Do you think that we should expand our spending on national defense, keep it the same, or cut back?

	Elite					*Mass*				
	1979	*1982*	*1986*	*1990*	*1994*	*1979*	*1982*	*1986*	*1990*	*1994*
Expand	31.2	20.8	11.7	2.4	16.6	34.6	22.1	20.5	11.5	18.4
Same	40.1	37.0	49.7	20.5	50.3	48.2	52.4	56.2	55.0	55.1
Cut	28.7	42.2	38.6	77.1	33.2	17.1	25.5	23.3	33.5	26.5

Sources: CCFR 1979, 1982, 1986, 1990, 1994.

ing for deeper cuts dropped from 77 percent to 33 percent among the elite, and from 33.5 percent to 26.5 percent among the general public.

Arms Control

There was also a change in attitudes about arms control. The end of the cold war, however, did not produce new interest in arms control. From 1975 to 1990, both elite and mass opinion consistently rated arms control as an important foreign policy goal, with more than 80 percent of the elite and typically 70 percent of the masses rating it as very important. Even in 1982, more than 80 percent of the elite and more than half the general public preferred to accept a nuclear weapons freeze if the USSR agreed to do so. Only 5.8 percent of the general public wanted to build weapons regardless of what Moscow agreed to do and only 14 percent made their support for the freeze conditional upon the United States building more weapons first (CCFR 1975, 1979, 1982, 1986, and 1990).

What changed most in 1990 was not the interest in arms control but the trust Americans put in Moscow to keep its part of an agreed-upon bargain. Table 12.3 presents general public responses to the trust question over time. The trend toward increasing trust is clear. Although we do not have cross-time data on elite attitudes, when the CCFR asked their elite sample in 1990 if they agreed or disagreed with the statement, "The Cold War is not really over and you cannot really trust the Russians," 74.7 percent disagreed. While a president may have enjoyed public support for the idea of arms control throughout the 1970s and 1980s, in the 1990s trust in Moscow and support for concrete arms control deals such as INF, START, and START II made it easier politically for the president to move in this direction.

Table 12.3 Public Opinion on Nuclear Arms Reductions

In reaching agreements on nuclear arms reductions, do you think the Soviet Union can be trusted to keep its part of the bargain or not?[a]

	ATI	*NBC*[b]	*ATS*	*LA Times*	*LA Times*	*LA Times*
	Nov. '91	*Aug. '91*	*Jan. '88*	*Nov. '85*	*Jan. '85*	*March '82*
Can be trusted	44	51	35	24	23	17
Cannot be trusted	49	43	55	66	68	66
Don't know/refused	7	6	9	10	9	17

Source: Americans Talk Issues survey 17 (March 1991), 33.

a. Question wording approximately the same across prior surveys. Past surveys used the word "control" where the current survey uses "reductions."

b. NBC–*Wall Street Journal*, August 9, 1991. The question read: "The United States and the Soviet Union have just agreed to reduce the overall number of nuclear weapons in their arsenals by 25 to 35%. Do you believe we can or cannot trust the Soviets to live up to this agreement?"

NATO and Japan

For forty years, the largest deployment of U.S. military forces directly arrayed against the Soviet Union was in central Europe. As might be expected, attitudes about this situation also changed at the end of the cold war. Perceiving a less threatening environment, Americans, elite and public alike, were ready to reduce U.S. commitments to NATO. As seen in table 12.4, the elite support for the policy of keeping the U.S. commitment to NATO at the current level fell by roughly half from 1986 to 1990, dropping from 77.6 percent to 35.6 percent. The proportion of elites who favored cutting back the commitment across this same time period increased more than fourfold, from 13.5 percent to 57.8 percent. The movement in public attitudes was in the same direction but far more modest. Nearly 65 percent of the general public was ready to keep the same commitment and not quite 25 percent was ready to cut back. As with defense spending, by 1994 attitudes toward decreasing the U.S. commitment had leveled off, with almost 58 percent of the elites agreeing that the commitment should be kept as it is, moving up twenty-two percentage points from its previous low of nearly 36 percent four years earlier. Attitudes among the general public stayed more or less constant, with over two-thirds agreeing that U.S. commitments should remain the same.

In October 1991, a CBS poll asking a similar question about NATO found that more than 75 percent of the general public felt it was still necessary for the United States to maintain the military alliance with NATO.[1] They wanted to do so with fewer U.S. troops, but this had been a desire for some time. In 1975, for example, 93 percent of the elite and 85.5 percent of the general public wanted to reduce the number of U.S. troops in Europe.[2]

Table 12.4 Public Opinion on Support for NATO

Some people feel that NATO, the military organization of Western Europe and the United States, has outlived its usefulness, and that the United States should withdraw its military from NATO. Others say that NATO has discouraged the Russians from trying a military takeover in Western Europe. Do you feel we should increase our commitment to NATO, keep our commitment what it is now, decrease our commitment but still remain in NATO, or withdraw from NATO entirely?

	Elite						*Mass*					
	1975	*1979*	*1982*	*1986*	*1990*	*1994*	*1975*	*1979*	*1982*	*1986*	*1990*	*1994*
Increase	4.7	21.5	7.1	7.6	2.7	5.5	5.8	12.1	11.3	9.4	4.9	5.8
Same	63.6	65.6	79.6	77.6	35.6	57.6	67.7	71.2	70.7	72.3	64.5	64.1
Cut	29.1	12.4	12.4	13.5	57.8	34.0	17.4	11.8	13.7	12.5	24.9	23.5
Withdraw	2.5	.6	.9	1.2	4.0	2.9	9.1	4.9	4.2	5.9	5.7	6.5

Sources: CCFR 1975, 1979, 1982, 1986, 1990, 1994.

Table 12.5 Public Opinion on the Use of Troops

There has been some discussion about the circumstances that might justify using U.S. troops in other parts of the world. I'd like to ask your opinion about several situations. First, would you favor or oppose the use of U. S. troops?

	Elite											
	1975a		*1979*		*1982*		*1986*		*1990*		*1994b*	
	Favor	*Opp*	*Favor*	*Opp*	*Favor*	*Opp*	*Favor*	*Opp*	*Favor*	*Opp*	*Favor*	*Opp*
If Soviet troops invaded western Europe	84.6	15.4	93.1	7.0	92.1	7.9	94.6	5.4	89.3	10.7	92.1	7.9
If Japan were invaded by the Soviet Union			82.2	17.7	78.0	22.0	87.0	13.0	76.1	23.9		

	Mass											
	1975a		*1979*		*1982*		*1986*		*1990*		*1994b*	
	Favor	*Opp*	*Favor*	*Opp*	*Favor*	*Opp*	*Favor*	*Opp*	*Favor*	*Opp*	*Favor*	*Opp*
If Soviet troops invaded western Europe	49.9	50.1	63.8	36.3	66.1	33.9	73.9	26.1	66.1	33.9	61.3	38.7
If Japan were invaded by the Soviet Union			48.9	51.2	50.7	49.3	59.5	40.5	76.1	23.9		

Sources: CCFR 1975, 1979, 1982, 1986, 1990, 1994.

a. 1975 question omitted the word "USSR" in conjuction with invasion.

b. In 1994, the word "USSR" was replaced with "Russia."

This desire, however, did not translate into significant change in the professed willingness to defend NATO allies. As table 12.5 shows, in every survey since 1975, nearly 90 percent of elites consistently said they would support the use of U.S. military force, including troops in combat, to defend western Europe against a Soviet or Russian invasion. Similar continuity was evident in general public attitudes. Since 1979, more than two-thirds of the general public have favored the use of force to defend western Europe. One interesting difference that did appear in the 1990 survey among the general public was the increased willingness to use troops to defend Japan. While more than three-quarters of elite respondents had since 1979 consistently favored the use of troops to defend Japan, only in 1990 did more than half the general public agree with the traditional elite perspective. Unfortunately, we are unable to determine if this increase in support of Japanese defense was an anomaly or part of a new trend in attitudes, since the CCFR omitted the question in 1994.

Opportunity for Preponderance?

Although the perceived threat from Moscow has been considerably reduced, Americans display a continued willingness to use force in defense of traditional allies. Has this declining threat given way to an increased sense of security and rising perceptions of opportunity? When in 1991 CBS asked a national sample if they felt more secure now that the Soviet Union had broken up into many different republics, 54 percent said yes.[3] Likewise, when asked about the likelihood of the United States becoming involved in a nuclear war in the next ten years, only 27 percent thought this was likely, compared to 47 percent ten years earlier. Those who felt nuclear war was unlikely or very unlikely increased from 49 percent to 70 percent during this same period.[4]

This increased sense of security may stem in part from relative perceptions of U.S. strength. Table 12.6 presents the elite and mass reaction over an eight-year period to the question of whether the United States or Soviet Union was perceived stronger militarily. Responses were constant in the 1980s, with more than 60 percent judging the two superpowers equal in strength. In 1990 the change in elite attitudes was dramatic: more than 71 percent of elite respondents felt the United States was now stronger militarily, while only 25 percent still perceived equality in military capability. Less than 4 percent of the elites thought the Russians had an edge. In contrast, by 1990 the public showed no significant change in perceptions of relative power. Most likely, lower levels of attentiveness and knowledge explain the lack of change in public attitudes.

Table 12.6 Public Opinion on the Strength of the Soviet Union

At the present time, which nation do you feel is stronger in terms of military power, the United States or the Soviet Union—or do you think they are about equal militarily?

	Elite			*Mass*		
	1982	*1986*	*1990*	*1982*	*1986*	*1990*
United States	20.2	28.6	71.1	23.3	30.3	34.2
Soviet Union	15.7	11.3	3.4	30.8	18.0	15.9
About equal	64.0	60.1	25.5	45.9	51.7	49.9

Sources: CCFR 1982, 1986, 1990.

Table 12.7 Public Opinion on Military Strength

As of now, do you think the United States is stronger militarily than the Soviet Union, do you think the Soviet Union is stronger than the United States, or are both countries about equal in military strength?[a]

	June 1991	*Oct. 1986*	*Nov. 1985*	*May 1982*	*March 1982*	*Dec. 1981*	*Sept. 1981*	*Feb. 1981*	*July 1980*	*May 1980*	*April 1979*	*June 1978*
United States is stronger	44	25	25	11	14	13	34	10	6	15	17	17
Soviet Union is stronger	9	22	24	41	38	38	36	33	57	45	37	37
Equal in strength	43	45	44	40	38	39	41	49	28	31	39	35
Not sure	4	8	11	8	10	10	9	8	9	9	7	11

Source: NBC–*Wall Steet Journal,* July 9, 1991.

a. All results prior to 1991 are among adults, not registered voters. Prior to December 1981, this question referred to the Soviet Union as "Russia."

In table 12.7 we see that by 1991 the general public was exhibiting a similar pattern of perceived U.S. advantage. In July 1980, for instance, only 6 percent saw the United States as stronger than the USSR, and 57 percent saw the USSR as having the advantage. By June 1991, 44 percent said the United States was stronger militarily, while only 9 percent still felt that way about the Soviet Union. When in March 1992 CBS asked a national sample of the U.S. general public if the United States should share power with other nations now that the Soviet Union no longer existed or should use its power to ensure that no other nations could challenge its dominance in world affairs, 43 percent preferred to use power to insure there would be no challengers.[5]

Evidently, Americans feel their nation is both stronger and more secure. Whether this translates into support for internationalist or isolationist policies, however, is debatable. In spite of a relative sense of U.S. superiority, the elite and general public still perceive a variety of critical threats to U.S. power and vital interests. Primary among them is the threat of nuclear proliferation. According to the 1994 CCFR survey, nuclear proliferation was the number one policy concern among elites, with nearly 90 percent agreeing that preventing the spread of nuclear weapons should be a very important foreign policy goal of the United States. More than 84 percent of the general public agreed with the statement, making it the number two foreign policy concern, just behind stopping the inflow of illegal drugs. Moreover, both groups viewed the possibility of unfriendly countries becoming nuclear powers as the most salient threat to the vital interests of the United States over the next ten years, with nearly 61 percent of the elite and more than 75 percent of the general public perceiving the threat as "critically important."

Embedded within the threat of nuclear proliferation are rising levels of concern and distrust toward possible challengers to U.S. power and global interests. The most salient threats emanate from relatively weaker adversaries such as North Korea, Iraq, and China. In 1994, when the CCFR asked if the United States should secretly spy on the Iraqi government, nearly 93 percent of the elite said yes. Likewise, 91 percent of the elite and 72 percent of the general public felt that the United States should spy on North Korea, while 84 percent of the elite and 71 percent of the general public were as distrustful of, or threatened by, China. The 1994 CCFR data also revealed an increasing concern with international terrorism and Islamic fundamentalism, two issues that could easily be linked to the rising threat and distrust of these potential nuclear challengers and adversaries.

The saliency of these new threats could translate into increased support for preventive international action. In other words, with the end of the cold war and the diminished Russian threat, Americans may feel more inclined to use force in pursuit of opportunity and in the preservation of U.S. security and preponderance. As the 1994 CCFR data revealed, a solid majority of both the elite and mass public see maintaining superior military power worldwide as a very important goal of U.S. foreign policy. It is important to note, however, that any enthusiasm for launching preventive measures is balanced by strong public sentiment for reducing U.S. international exposure and acting through cooperative multilateral institutions.

For instance, in October 1991, a CBS news poll revealed stark public disagreement when it asked if the United States should assert itself more in international affairs now that relations with the Soviet Union had improved. Of those responding, 31 percent said yes, it should assert itself more, 32 percent said no, the United States should assert itself less, while another 32 percent said the level of assertion should remain the same. When the question wording was slightly changed to read: *would* the United States assert itself more, rather than *should* it do so, the predictions were also divided, with 43 percent expecting it to assert itself more, 43 percent expecting it to retain its current level of assertion, and only 9 percent expecting it to assert itself less.[6] At nearly the same time, however, a *Time*-CNN poll found that only 19 percent of Americans wanted the United States to use its leadership position in world affairs to settle international disputes—74 percent favored a reduction in Washington's involvement in world politics in order to concentrate on problems at home.[7] In March 1991 the *Los Angeles Times* found a parallel result. When it asked a national sample if the United States should be more active in using military force to defend key U.S. interests and to combat terrorism, or if it should be more cautious, 15 percent favored a more active posture and 80 percent favored a more cautious approach.[8] When the *New York Times* asked respondents in June 1992 whether they felt that the United States had a responsibility to intervene in trouble spots around the world, sharp division was again evident, with 41 percent responding that the U.S. does have such a responsibility and 49 percent saying it does not.[9]

The Use of Force in the Third World

While the end of the cold war affected attitudes about the use of force in the areas where Soviet power was directly involved, the pattern in the rest of the world is more complicated. In some cases, where the main U.S. interests were derived from their instrumental connection to containing communism, the end of the cold war apparently had an effect. For instance, in the CCFR sample of 1990 and 1994, U.S. elite support for military aid to other countries declined substantially from its 1980s average, as shown in table 12.8. Mass attitudes also declined sharply by 1994. In addition, when asked if the United States might have to support some military dictators because they are friendly toward us and opposed to the communists, both mass and elite support dropped quite noticeably from 1986 to 1990. In 1979, 1982, and 1986 about two-thirds of those asked in both elite and mass samples made the instrumental trade-off to back dictators in order to stop communists (see table 12.9). In 1990, however, only slightly more than 40 percent of respondents would make this choice and those opposed to it rose in number from about a third to over half.

It is possible that the perception of some countries as important to U.S. interests may have also changed, but the available evidence is difficult to

Table 12.8 Public Opinion on Military Aid

On the whole do you favor or oppose our giving military aid to other nations? By military aid I mean arms and equipment, but not troops.

	Elite						*Mass*					
	1975	*1979*	*1982*	*1986*	*1990*	*1994a*	*1975*	*1979*	*1982*	*1986*	*1990*	*1994a*
Favor	43.8	64.8	65.5	78.3	40.8	47.3	26.0	34.5	32.2	36.2	31.0	16.5
Oppose	56.2	35.2	34.5	21.7	59.2	52.7	74.0	65.5	67.8	63.8	69.0	83.5

Sources: CCFR 1975, 1979, 1982, 1986, 1990, 1994.

a. 1994 question wording substituted "selling" for "giving."

Table 12.9 Public Opinion on Support for Military Dictators

I am going to read some statements about international affairs and U.S. foreign policy. For each tell me if you tend to agree strongly, agree somewhat, disagree somewhat, or disagree strongly with the statement: The United States may have to suport some military dictators because they are friendly toward us and opposed to the Communists.

	Elite				*Mass*			
	1979	*1982*	*1986*	*1990*	*1979*	*1982*	*1986*	*1990*
Strongly agree	16.3	13.9	9.4	3.2	19.8	19.6	19.5	6.9
Agree some	51.4	51.3	52.2	40.5	47.5	50.0	45.6	35.3
Disagree some	19.4	22.8	24.6	31.4	17.8	17.6	20.9	32.6
Strongly disagree	12.9	11.9	13.8	24.9	14.8	12.9	14.1	25.2

Sources: CCFR 1979, 1982, 1986, 1990.

interpret. In 1986, 83.7 percent of the CCFR's elite sample thought that a communist takeover in the Philippines would be a great threat to U.S. interests. Nearly 80 percent of the general public felt the same way. When asked in 1990 if they would favor or oppose U.S. military involvement, including troops in the Philippines should it fall to leftist revolution, 93.2 percent of the elite and 67.9 percent of the public said no. It is possible that the perceived instrumental value of the Philippines declined with the collapse of Soviet power and the need for containment. The 1990 response would then reflect the rapidly changing calculation of interest. Unfortunately, across these four years other things changed as well, including the American perception of the institutionalization of democratic processes in Manila and the wording of the questions CCFR asked. The CCFR did not ask about the threat of communist takeover in 1990 or in 1994 and it did not ask about the use of force in 1986.[10]

In other cases, where the CCFR did ask both questions together, even during the cold war the relationship between perceived threat and support for the use of force was not impressive. For instance, in 1982 the CCFR asked Americans how threatening they thought it would be if communists came to power in Taiwan, another country whose importance to the United States may have been largely instrumental and related to containment. Of those surveyed, 93 percent of the elite thought it would be a serious threat and 87.3 percent of the general public agreed. At the same time, when asked if they would support the use of force, including troops, to defend Taiwan against Chinese invasion, 84.8 percent of the elite and 77.5 percent of the general public opposed the idea. Likewise, in 1986, more than two-thirds of the public (66.6 percent) thought a communist takeover in El Salvador would threaten the United States, yet 69.6 percent opposed the use of force. In the case of Saudi Arabia, in both 1982 and 1986, more than 80 percent of the public thought a communist takeover would be a threat, but in neither year did support for the use of troops to defend Saudi Arabia against foreign invasion by Iran exceed 31 percent. In 1982, 73.4 percent of the public were opposed to using troops to defend the kingdom in Riyadh, and in 1986, 69.9 percent were opposed.

Bruce Jentleson has argued that public support for the use of force is easier to mobilize when the situation at hand involves foreign invasion rather than internal civil war (Jentleson 1992; see also Jentleson and Britton 1996). In the Saudi case, strong opposition to the use of force was evident even in the invasion scenario, despite widespread agreement that internal change could be a great threat. Apparently, the use of force is affected by more than simply the perceived interests at stake and the character of the local conflict. While it is true that opposition to the use of force was overwhelming in all the internal revolution scenarios the CCFR asked about in 1975, 1979, 1982, 1986, 1990, and 1994, opposition to the use of force was also overwhelming in many invasion scenarios. For instance, in the elite sample in 1982, 93.5 percent opposed using force to defend Poland against the USSR. In 1979, about 90 percent of the elite opposed the use of force to defend Yugoslavia from a Soviet invasion, Rhodesia from a Cuban-USSR invasion, or Arabs from an Israeli invasion. Defending Taiwan from China was equally unpopular in both 1979 and 1982 and, in 1994, almost 78 percent opposed defending the Ukraine from an invasion by Russia. In the case of Taiwan, Yugoslavia, and the Ukraine, perceived cost and the effectiveness of using force may explain the opposition. In Rhodesia, it may be more the product of perceived interests at stake, while in the case of an Israeli invasion of Arab states, opponents to the use of force might not question that interests are at stake but might doubt that the invasion threatens those interests. The complexity of specific decisions to use force and the variation in past patterns of U.S. military action make generalizations about the baseline that existed during the cold war problematic. Of course, without a baseline, we cannot identify change. Consequently, before we turn to the cases where Washington has recently used force, we need to make two general observations about the use of force in the last two decades of the cold war.

First, since 1975 there has not been strong elite- or mass-based support for the use of force outside Europe and Japan. In the scenarios that generated the strongest support over time—defending Israel against an Arab invasion and defending South Korea against a North Korean invasion—opposition among the masses remained consistently 50 percent or higher. Only since 1986 have more than 50 percent of the elite favored the use of force even in these cases, though support in 1994 appears to be on the rise. Also, in 1994, there continued to be substantial elite and mass support for the defense of Saudi Arabia against an invasion by Iraq. In other cases during the cold war, a substantial majority typically opposed the use of force, as can be seen in tables 12.10 and 12.11. When the Soviet military threat was portrayed as direct, such as in the scenario involving Soviet missiles in Nicaragua presented to respondents in 1986, support rose substantially. In most other cases, neither the indirect threat from Moscow nor other threats or opportunities intrinsic to the region induced widespread public enthusiasm for the use of force.

Second, the Vietnam War played an important role in shaping beliefs about the connection between regional conflicts and the Soviet threat, the utility of using U.S. force in civil wars, and the possible costs of military engagement. Fading and changing memories of the Vietnam experience, as much as the end of the cold war, may affect American attitudes about the use of force. Whether the demise of the Soviet Union will affect memories of Vietnam is a complicated question. For many Americans, one of the lessons of Vietnam was that interpreting complex regional conflicts in strict bipolar East-West terms led to serious distortion and policy error. When in 1975 the CCFR asked respondents about nine possible lessons of Vietnam, the only two on which there was widespread agreement in both the elite and mass samples were that we should not commit our troops to other peoples' civil wars and that we should not commit U.S. lives to the defense of corrupt foreign governments. Almost 80 percent of the elite and 73.3 percent of the public agreed with the first lesson, and 68 percent of the elite and 77 percent of the masses agreed with the second. In table 12.12, we see that when Americans were asked in 1979, 1982, 1986, 1990, and

Table 12.10 Public Opinion on the Use of Troops

There has been some discussion about the circumstances that might justify using U.S. troops in other parts of the world. I'd like to ask your opinion about several situations. First, would you favor the use of U.S. troops:

	Elite											
	1975		*1979*		*1982*		*1986*		*1990*		*1994*	
	Favor	*Opp*	*Favor*	*Opp*	*Favor*	*Opp*	*Favor*	*Opp*	*Favor*	*Opp*	*Favor*	*Opp*
If North Vietnam attacked Saigon	6.0	94.0	—	—	—	—	—	—	—	—	—	—
If Arab forces invaded Israel[a]	48.0	52.0	31.8	68.2	47.5	52.5	59.8	40.2	71.2	28.8	73.5	26.5
If the People's Republic of China invaded Taiwan[b]	12.4	87.6	18.5	81.5	15.2	84.8	—	—	—	—	—	—
If North Korea invaded South Korea	22.1	77.9	47.1	52.8	50.1	49.9	66.8	33.2	59.1	40.9	84.0	16.0
If Communist China attacked India	19.9	80.1	—	—	—	—	—	—	—	—	—	—
If the Arabs cut off oil shipments to United States	—	—	30.5	69.5	36.1	63.9	—	—	—	—	—	—
If Soviet troops invaded Yugoslavia[c]	9.2	90	.8	15.9	84.1	—	—	—	—	—	—	—
If the government of El Salvador were about to be defeated by leftist rebels	—	—	—	—	9.7	90.3	—	—	13.4	86.6	—	—
If Panama refused to let the U.S. use the Canal	—	—	50.4	49.5	—	—	—	—	—	—	—	—
If Rhodesia were invaded by Cuban troops supplied by the Soviet Union	—	—	10.5	89.4	—	—	—	—	—	—	—	—
If the Nicaraguan government allowed the Soviet Union to set up a missile base in Nicaragua	—	—	—	—	—	—	70.9	29.1	—	—	—	—
If Nicaragua invaded Honduras in order to destroy contra rebels' bases there	—	—	—	—	—	—	19.0	81.0	—	—	—	—
If Iraq invaded Saudi Arabia	—	—	—	—	—	—	—	—	—	—	85.7	14.3
If civil war broke out in South Africa	—	—	—	—	—	—	—	—	—	—	5.9	94.1
If people in Cuba attempted to over-throw the Castro dictatorship	—	—	—	—	—	—	—	—	—	—	18.9	81.1

Sources: CCFR 1975, 1979, 1982, 1986, 1990, 1994.

a. 1975 survey asked: "If Israel were being defeated by Arabs."

b. 1975 used "Communist China" rather than PRC; 1979 survey asked "if mainland China invaded nationalist China (the island of Taiwan).

c. 1975 survey asked "if the Soviet Union invaded Yugoslavia after Tito's death."

Table 12.11 Public Opinion on the Use of Troops

There has been some discussion about the circumstances that might justify using U.S. troops in other parts of the world. I'd like to ask your opinion about several situations. First, would you favor or oppose the use of U.S. troops:

	Mass											
	1975		*1979*		*1982*		*1986*		*1990*		*1994*	
	Favor	*Opp*	*Favor*	*Opp*	*Favor*	*Opp*	*Favor*	*Opp*	*Favor*	*Opp*	*Favor*	*Opp*
If North Vietnam attacked Saigon	12.8	87.2	—	—	—	—	—	—	—	—	—	—
If Arab forces invaded Israel[a]	35.5	64.5	20.9	79.0	30.0	70.0	37.7	62.3	51.0	49.0	50.2	49.8
If the People's Republic of China invaded Taiwan[b]	22.7	77.3	23.7	76.3	18.7	81.3	22.5	77.5	—	—	—	—
If North Korea invaded South Korea	18.5	81.5	26.0	74.0	23.0	77.0	27.5	72.5	29.7	70.3	45.1	54.9
If Communist China attacked India	22.2	77.8	—	—	—	—	—	—	—	—	—	—
If the Arabs cut off oil shipments to the United States	—	—	40.7	59.3	38.5	61.5	41.3	58.7	—	—	—	—
If Soviet troops invaded Yugoslavia[c]	14.2	85.8	22.1	77.9	—	—	—	—	—	—	—	—
If the government of El Salvador were about to be defeated by leftist rebels	—	—	—	—	18.8	81.2	30.4	69.6	30.2	69.8	—	—
If Panama refused to let the U.S. use the canal	—	—	66.2	33.9	—	—	—	—	—	—	—	—
If Rhodesia were invaded by Cuban troops supplied by the Soviet Union	—	—	29.6	70.4	—	—	—	—	—	—	—	—
If the Nicaraguan government allowed the Soviet Union to set up a missile base in Nicaragua	—	—	—	—	—	—	52.1	47.9	—	—	—	—
If Nicaragua invaded Honduras in order to destroy contra rebels' bases there	—	—	—	—	—	—	28.7	71.3	—	—	—	—
If Iraq invaded Saudi Arabia	—	—	—	—	—	—	—	—	—	—	57.8	42.2
If civil war broke out in South Africa	—	—	—	—	—	—	—	—	—	—	21.1	78.9
If people in Cuba attempted to overthrow the Castro dictatorship	—	—	—	—	—	—	—	—	—	—	49.7	50.3

Sources: CCFR 1975, 1979, 1982, 1986, 1990, 1994.

a. 1975 survey asked: "If Israel were being defeated by Arabs."

b. 1975 used "Communist China" rather than PRC; 1979 survey asked "if mainland China invaded nationalist China (the island of Taiwan)."

c. 1975 survey asked: "if the Soviet Union invaded Yugoslavia after Tito's death."

Table 12.12 Public Opinion on the Vietnam War

I am going to read some statements about international affairs and U.S. foreign policy. For each tell me if you tend to agree strongly, agree somewhat, disagree somewhat, or disagree strongly with the statement: the Vietnam war was more than a mistake, it was fundamentally wrong and immoral.

	Elite					*Mass*				
	1979	*1982*	*1986*	*1990*	*1994*	*1979*	*1982*	*1986*	*1990*	*1994*
Strongly agree	31.1	21.6	22.6	27.5	25.8	50.1	48.3	45.5	42.4	36.7
Agree somewhat	20.1	24.6	19.9	30.7	25.8	26.8	26.9	25.4	31.4	29.4
Disagree somewhat	26.8	25.7	28.7	23.3	25.8	14.9	16.1	18.1	17.0	21.4
Strongly disagree	22.0	28.1	28.7	18.4	22.5	8.2	8.7	11.0	9.2	12.5

Sources: CCFR 1979, 1982, 1986, 1990, 1994.

1994 whether the Vietnam War was not just a mistake but also fundamentally wrong and immoral, more than 50 percent of the elite and about 70 percent of the general public consistently agreed.

Since 1990, the United States has engaged its military forces in a number of conflicts, including the Gulf War, Bosnia, Somalia, North Korea, Rwanda, and Haiti. These six cases are of course diverse, ranging across different regions of the world. They also include cases of interstate war (the Gulf and Bosnia), civil war (parts of Bosnia, Somalia, and Rwanda), conflicts stemming from United Nations and International Atomic Energy Agency (IAEA) pressure to allow inspections (North Korea), and an intervention to change a regime (Haiti). Adding to the difficulties in generalizing from these cases is the complexity within each of them. Washington's use of force was surely motivated in all these cases by a combination of factors, making it hard to determine the role that specific concerns may have played. (In Haiti, for instance, National Security Adviser Anthony Lake argued that a "compelling mix of interests made the use of force necessary" [quoted in Williams and Devroy 1994]). For the Gulf War, ABC– *Washington Post* polls in November 1990, and in January and March 1991, asked respondents to judge whether the United States had sent troops to defend moral principle or American oil supplies. In November 48 percent said oil and 41 percent said principle. By March, moral principle appeared to be a more popular explanation for the war, with 56 percent listing it over economic concerns.[11] However, when Gallup asked respondents simply to identify the various goals that Washington should be pursuing in the conflict, the vast majority saw many important interests at stake, none of which were mutually exclusive. For instance, 92 percent of respondents were concerned about rescuing hostages, 84 percent wanted to force Iraq to leave Kuwait, 78 percent were interested in destroying Iraq's nuclear capability, and 73 percent wanted to see Saddam Hussein removed from power.[12] The decision to use force was most likely a product of the convergence of many interests, not the motivating power of one interest or the other.

It is difficult to generalize about how the U.S. public will define interests and perceive threats and opportunities from the cases in which the United States used force, because these cases are complicated and because the cases in which the United States decided not to use force are also complicated. Washington intervened in Somalia's civil war and food crisis, but not in nearby Sudan's. It became involved in the ethnic struggle over statehood in Bosnia, but not in Kashmir. It defended Saudi Arabia from invasion and liberated Kuwait, but did not liberate Nagorno-Karabakh or defend either Armenia or Azerbaijan. Washington intervened in Haiti to restore democracy but abandoned the civil war in Afghanistan it had contributed to throughout the 1980s, and it ignored almost completely the Russian intervention in Tajikistan and the ensuing border war. Moreover, in the various cases in which U.S. force was used, there was relatively little variation in the total amount of public support and there was consistently strong domestic opposition. In fact, in none of the cases is there strong evidence that more than half the public supported the use of force before the president made the decision to send troops.

We do not have data on how people felt about the United States defending Saudi Arabia from Iraq before Iraq invaded Kuwait in 1990, but only 18 percent favored the use of troops to defend Saudi Arabia from Iran in 1988 and 34 percent favored staying out of such a conflict altogether (Mueller 1994, 49). In 1990, as the president increased the number of U.S. troops in the Gulf and hence the apparent prospects for war, some polls reflected growing public support for using force. As John Mueller demonstrates in *Policy and Opinion in the Gulf War,* however, the phrasing of questions produced important differences. For instance, if a question was phrased: "Should the U.S. initiate war?" 28 percent were in favor; when phrased: "Should the U.S. go to war?" 38 percent approved; and when asked: "Should the U.S. engage in combat?" 46 percent approved. Meanwhile, when asked if the United States should be willing to use force, 65 percent approved (Mueller 1994, 30). It is not clear from these polls whether we should conclude that two-thirds of the public favored the use of force or that nearly two-thirds opposed it. In any case, once the war began in January 1991, a strong rally-round-the-flag effect boosted support to more than 70 percent (Mueller 1994, 208, 219).

Similarly, when asked whether the United States should participate in air strikes over Bosnia, about 50 percent of the public said yes in 1992, and again in 1994.[13] Predictably, when asked if they would support air strikes if the president had already ordered them, 65 percent rallied to support.[14] In December 1995, after the president's commitment of twenty thousand U.S. peacekeeping troops to the region, a poll conducted by NBC and the *Wall Street Journal* again provided some evidence of a rallying effect. When asked if Congress should support the president's decision to send troops to Bosnia, 43 percent of those surveyed said it should, while 49 percent said it should not. Although these data suggest a divided public, they also reveal a substantial change in support: when the public was asked the same question a few months earlier, in October, 65 percent had opposed sending troops (Pine 1995). Meanwhile, questions about the purpose and objectives of the use of force continued to provoke sharp divisions. In the late summer of 1992, for instance, 43 percent favored the use of ground troops to provide humanitarian relief in Bosnia, while 44 percent were opposed. When asked if the ground troops should also be used to stop the war and violence, barely one-quarter of the sample said yes and nearly two-thirds said no.[15]

We do not have data on public opinion before President Bush announced his decision to initiate an airlift to Somalia in August 1992 and then to initiate Operation Restore Hope on December 4, 1992. By the second week of December 1992, perhaps reflecting a rallying effect, 75 percent of respondents to a Harris poll voiced their approval.[16] However, divisions remained obvious on the issue of how long and what missions the troops should undertake: 48 percent felt the United States should be prepared to stay only as long as it took to provide stable relief supply lines, while 44 percent favored staying until the situation was more peaceful and a new government was established.[17]

When asked a series of questions about the missions that might use force, 71 percent supported deployment for the distribution of humanitarian relief, 48 percent supported the use of force to restore order, and 46 percent felt the United States had a responsibility to use force when asked to help settle conflict.[18] Nearly 60 percent supported the principle of contributing troops to a UN mission to keep peace, but at the same time, more than one-third opposed even this multilateral use.[19] In 1994, when the United States was considering using the U.S. military to restore order in Haiti, two different polls, one conducted by the *Wall Street Journal,* the other by the *Boston Globe,* showed that about two-thirds of the respondents opposed using force in Haiti.[20]

Although it is risky to generalize from diverse cases, four propositions are worth considering. They are reflected in Presidential Decision Directive 25 (PDD 25), issued in May 1994, which identified the conditions under which Washington should use force.[21] First, as Somalia illustrates, there is public support for the use of troops to perform humanitarian relief missions as long as the expectation of combat is low. As objectives become more ambitious or the risks of combat more apparent, support declines substantially, but can be rallied for a time if U.S. troops are already engaged. Second, there is a strong preference for UN legitimacy and multilateral participation in the use of force. A substantial majority of Americans feels a responsibility to send troops to enforce peace plans in trouble spots around the world. They do not see it as their exclusive responsibility, however. In Bosnia, for instance, more than 80 percent of those polled by *Time*-CNN felt that the United Nations and the European countries had the main responsibility for peacekeeping. At the same time, while 80 percent of those polled by Harris felt that the United States should be willing to send troops to Bosnia as part of a UN peacekeeping mission, only 50 percent were ready to see these troops engage in combat to repel the aggressor. Only 30 percent were ready to deploy U.S. troops independent of their role in a UN mission.[22] For Rwanda, an ABC-Nightline news poll conducted on May 4, 1994, found that 80 percent of the public approved of the use of U.S. military planes to airlift relief supplies to the refugees, but a majority of those polled felt it was up to African nations and the UN to stop the fighting.[23]

Third, although supportive of humanitarian missions, the public is generally not interested in using force as part of a "nation-building" project. It is also wary of using force to construct or maintain political order in a foreign country. This is true both because the risks of combat increase and because political objectives expand, lengthening the time of deployment. In Somalia, for instance, when the operation was viewed as simply humanitarian, three-quarters of those polled by Harris in December 1992 favored the intervention. At the same time, 71 percent of the respondents expected that U.S. troops would be out of Somalia within a year and nearly half expected them to be home in six months (Harris poll, December 12, 1992).[24] Eleven months later, after the aims of the mission expanded to include more politically ambitious objectives, Gallup asked a national sample what they thought the United States should do in Somalia. Nearly 70 percent favored either immediate or gradual withdrawal. Only 18 percent of the respondents were ready to escalate at that point. More than half the respondents had concluded that the mission was a mistake and a failure. Even with a rallying effect, only 55 percent of those polled favored

President Clinton's decision to increase troop strength before withdrawing.[25]

This public wariness in using force to construct or maintain peace in other countries is evident in attitudes toward Bosnia. For instance, in Gallup polls asking national samples whether they approved of the presence of U.S. troops in Bosnia, public support dropped from 41 percent to 36 percent between December 1995 and January 1996 ("Opinion Outlook" 1996). As with Somalia, the drop in approval appears related to public perceptions of length of stay, the degree to which national interests are engaged, and the possibility of casualties. In June and July 1995, 58 percent and 59 percent of Americans surveyed by ABC and the *Washington Post* believed that America's vital interests were not at stake in Bosnia ("Opinion Outlook" 1995b). Americans were also pessimistic about the timely withdrawal of U.S. troops. When ABC asked a national sample in November 1995 whether U.S. troops would leave Bosnia within a year as the president promised, 68 percent believed U.S. troops would end up staying longer ("Opinion Outlook" 1995c). Meanwhile, 57 percent of a national sample surveyed by Gallup in December 1995 lacked confidence that the United States would be able to accomplish its goals in Bosnia with few or no casualties ("Opinion Outlook" 1995c).

Fourth, if the mission is framed from the outset as directly related to U.S. national security, then, while support for the use of force may still be hard to mobilize, once troops are engaged the American public will expect the threat to be eliminated. The Gulf War is the only recent case that substantial sectors of the public perceived to be directly related to U.S. national security. In this conflict, Washington returned to the demands for unconditional victory, which were among the memories of World War II and the frustrated U.S. aspirations in both Korea and Vietnam. Throughout much of the cold war, regional conflicts produced negotiated outcomes as escalation on both sides was limited by fears of countervailing power, and ultimately, by the fear of nuclear war. In the Gulf War, however, a large asymmetry in power allowed the United States, through the UN, to demand unconditional surrender. While too many interests were at stake in the Gulf contest for us to be able to identify those that are most responsible for the decision to use force, we can examine the bases on which Americans thought war was justified. In fact, a series of polls conducted by Gallup provides evidence that one consequence of the Gulf War was to remind many Americans that war is sometimes necessary. As shown in table 12.13, in 1991, after twenty years of fairly stable and divided opinion on the question of whether or not war was outmoded, 80 percent decided it was not.

Table 12.13 Public Opinion on War

Some people feel that war is an outmoded way of settling differences between nations. Others feel that wars are sometimes necessary to settle differences. With which point of view do you agree?

	1971	*1975*	*1981*	*1990*	*1991*
War is outmoded	46	45	50	48	17
War is sometimes necessary	43	46	43	49	80
Don't know	11	9	7	3	3

Source: Gallup Poll Monthly, February 1991, 19; from Mueller 1994, 323.

In November 1990, the *Los Angeles Times* gave respondents seven reasons that might explain why the United States was involved in the Middle East crisis. It then asked the respondents which reasons justified a major war, a limited military engagement, or no military involvement at all. Three of the reasons cited had to do with a defensive war: the protection of oil supplies, the defense of Saudi Arabia, and the protection of the lives of U.S. hostages. Three other reasons had to do with a preventive war: Saddam Hussein's removal from power, the neutralization of Iraq's army, and the destruction of Iraq's nuclear and chemical weapons facilities. Between 70 and 75 percent of the respondents felt that both the defensive and the preventive reasons justified either major or limited war. In contrast, nearly 40 percent felt that restoring the Kuwaiti government to power did not justify any military involvement at all.[26] The support for preventive war persisted after Iraq was defeated and evolved into strong support for the use of force to ensure Iraqi compliance with UN restrictions on military acquisitions and the UN inspection and destruction of Iraq's nuclear, chemical, and missile facilities.[27] Of course, after the war, Americans could be relatively sure that the costs of preventive military strikes against Iraq would be limited and that Iraq had little ability to threaten countermilitary action.

Related to the desire for preventive war was support for using force to remove Saddam Hussein from power. Although President Bush had never made this an explicit objective, many among the general public came to see it as a central goal of the Gulf conflict. When ABC and the *Washington Post* asked a national sample of Americans in February 1991 what Washington's final objective should be, only 28 percent said it should be to force Iraq out of Kuwait; 71 percent felt it should be to force Saddam out of power.[28] Even as late as August 1992, 56 percent of respondents to a *Time*-CNN poll said they felt that Washington should still use force to remove Saddam Hussein from power.[29] President Clinton's decision in October

1994 to send 35,000 troops to the Persian Gulf in response to Iraq's movement of forces toward Kuwait also enjoyed public support. An October 12, 1994, poll conducted by *USA Today*–CNN and Gallup found that 74 percent of the Americans surveyed supported the president's decision, 84 percent were ready to have U.S. troops engage in military action if Iraqi troops attacked, and 72 percent favored the use of military force to oust Saddam Hussein from power. Of course, those high levels of professed support include a rally-round-the-flag effect and reflect the prior demonization of Saddam Hussein. Just the same, they suggest that only the removal of Saddam Hussein from power would fulfill what many Americans saw as both a primary objective of the war and a precondition for regional stability.

In March 1991, a news poll conducted by *Time*-CNN asked Americans what lessons were learned from the Gulf War. As shown in table 12.14, 86 percent felt that one major lesson was that "the U.S. is a great military power"; 65 percent felt that another lesson was that we ought "to do more to settle the unrest in the Middle East." Outside these two very general conclusions, there was little consensus. Although Americans can agree on generalizations, such as wanting the United States to "do something" to help achieve peace in the Middle East, reaching a consensus on concrete solutions or policies is more difficult. For instance, in the Arab-Israeli conflict, Americans do not agree on which side is the biggest obstacle to peace.

In 1991, polls put out by NBC and the *Wall Street Journal* found that one-third of their respondents saw the Arab nations as the biggest obstacle, another third felt that Israel was to blame, and a final third either did not know or felt both sides were equally at fault.[30] When asked about specific solutions, divisions were again substantial. Half the respondents felt that Israel should give up control of the occupied territories in exchange for peace, while a third felt it should not.[31] Meanwhile, in May 1991, two-thirds of the respondents to a *Time*-CNN poll thought the United States should not take the lead in forging a Middle East peace process and 37 percent answered that it "was none of our business."[32] Opinions were also split over the wisdom of maintaining a larger military presence in the Middle East than the United States deployed prior to the Gulf War: 43–46 percent were in favor, while 47–48 percent were opposed.[33] Evidently, even in a region where many Americans see interests at stake, there remains substantial disagreement over the nature of the threats to these interests and the best way to deal with them.

Although attitudes about national interests may vary and disagree-

Table 12.14 Public Opinion on War with Iraq

Which of these, if any, do you think are the lessons from the war with Iraq?

	A lesson	*Not a lesson*	*Don't know*
The U.S. is a great military power	86	11	3
The U.S. should do more to settle unrest in the Middle East	65	28	7
The U.S. should not hesitate to use force in the world	58	34	8
Only the U.S. can take a lead in protecting democracy in the world	43	50	7

Source: Time/CNN, March 1991; from Mueller 1994, p. 322.

ments regarding threats and solutions in regional contexts may persist, reluctance to use force in preventive wars for other reasons—especially those related to nuclear proliferation—can be potent motivators in some circumstances. It is clear from the public sentiment recorded in the 1994 CCFR data that the threat of nuclear proliferation is highly salient. Other opinion polls give support to this finding. In March 1994, the North Korean government announced its withdrawal from the nonproliferation treaty and refused to allow IAEA inspections of two nuclear facilities. When asked about this in June 1994, roughly 75 percent of respondents to a *Washington Post*–ABC poll said they would support committing U.S. forces to North Korea to prevent it from obtaining nuclear weapons (Morin 1994). This high level of support for a preventive war against a nuclear proliferator, however, was not consistent across polls. Two polls taken several weeks earlier by *Time*-CNN and ABC found only 46–48 percent of the American public in favor of allied military action against North Korean nuclear facilities, and 40–44 percent opposed (Pine 1994b).[34] Given the limited evidence in the Gulf and North Korean cases, it is clear that preventive war arguments justify the use of force for many Americans (Mueller 1996, 13). Whether they will actually provoke the use of force is, of course, a more complicated question, which undoubtedly also involves the expected cost and regional context.

Conclusion

The end of the cold war has affected American attitudes about the use of force. The decline in a perceived threat from the Soviet Union led to a reduction in public support for traditional strategic nuclear policies and troop commitments in central Europe. At the same time, the collapse of

Soviet power opened the way for new American perceptions of opportunity for both preponderance and security. The public recognition of the United States's power advantages, however, has not translated into consistent popular support for the use of force in the Third World, nor has it overcome long-standing disagreements over the morality and utility of using force in complicated regional settings. Finally, the end of the cold war has eliminated the primary "just war" scenario that lent strategic coherence to U.S. global policies. Without the umbrella of a global containment mission, the integration of cross-situational attitudes about the use of force has eroded, as have the traditional domestic coalitions in favor of using force.

A just war scenario is a mental construction of the situation in which the use of force is legitimate. During the cold war, the perceived global threat from the Soviet Union provided many Americans with a number of "just war" scenarios that not only justified the use of force but also provided cross-situational connections between various policy decisions. The result was a sense of cross-theater strategic coherence and purpose that was captured with the metaphor of containment. The organizing power of this metaphor and its political power in Washington began to break down in the 1970s. The Vietnam War produced sharp differences of opinion about the wisdom of interpreting Third World conflicts as part of a global containment mission. Throughout the 1970s and 1980s, this resulted in substantial public opposition to the use of force in most theaters outside Europe and Japan. While perhaps 30 to 40 percent of the public continued to support a hard-line East versus West interpretation of global affairs, in the last two decades of the cold war more than half the public consistently doubted this perspective and opposed the use of force. When presidents decided to use force, they could depend on a rally-round-the flag response, but from our data it is not clear whether this rallying effect revealed either strong perceptions of threat from Moscow or commitments to the logic of global containment. While the perceived Soviet threat may have been withering in public perceptions for some time, it collapsed almost completely in the early 1990s. Change in attitudes about the use of force in the Third World accelerated, and support for the hard core of containment, that is, for strategic nuclear deterrence and forward-based forces in NATO, declined.

The collapse of the Soviet Union reduced the primary threat Americans saw to Europe and Japan and undermined the instrumental value they saw in containment. It did not, however, reduce the perception that vital U.S. interests were intrinsic to these theaters. Other threats became more salient, and while the public willingness to support the deployment of troops eroded, the basic support for alliance relationships continued. In other theaters, the collapse of the Soviet containment–based "just war" scenario heightened domestic debate over the importance of regional allies and Washington's commitment. The value attached to instrumental interests had been declining for some time, and the intrinsic importance of the regions vis-à-vis American interests had become the subject of sharp debate. Although Americans continued to see many areas of the world as important to American interests, they were split both over the relative importance of these areas, as measured by the willingness to have the United States send troops and risk lives, and over how best to protect U.S. interests in the regions that were at stake.

Forging public consensus on the use of force outside Europe and Japan was difficult during the cold war. It is likely to become even harder in the post–cold war environment. Without an overarching "just war" scenario, case-specific arguments compete for attention and resources. Rather than appealing to a general containment and credibility argument, advocates in favor of using force make their case in terms of region-specific interests, on which there is not widespread agreement. Lacking political consensus on the interests and threats involved in specific cases, advocates for the use of force may appeal to moral duty and the importance of exercising global leadership (Mandelbaum 1994; Haass 1994). These traditional imperial justifications for the use of force, however, enjoy only limited appeal among the U.S. public or elite. While many Americans may sympathize with them in the abstract, as seen in a number of the polls discussed above, they do not translate into popular and compelling arguments for the use of force. A preventive war scenario, especially if it involves the risk of nuclear proliferation to states ruled by reckless leaders, may become an effective mobilizing argument. This appears to be the case in Iraq and North Korea, but in Iraq the perceived costs of action remained low and in North Korea the confrontation did not escalate to combat and was defused by diplomatic compromise.

Domestic coalitions in favor of using force in Third World regions have always included members concerned about different interests and regional threats. Some may have joined the coalition because they saw specific material interests in the region. Others may have supported the policy because they had vested institutional interests at home, or perhaps because they shared an ethnic identity with allies in the region. Despite the various reasons for supporting the use of force, the disparate elements of the coalition were able to find common cause and agree upon moral justification in the containment metaphor. In the post–cold war situation, the dynamics of building coalitions is more complicated. With no overarching "just war" claim, Americans remain divided over how specific conflicts should be resolved and what role if any Washington should play. Traditional advocates of the use of force for instrumental cold war reasons may now not see a reason to use force, while traditional opponents of intervention may support forceful action in the name of human rights. The reversal of roles in the Haiti case was particularly interesting, as traditional voices in favor of intervention in El Salvador and Nicaragua opposed military action, while the Congressional Black Caucus and other traditionally anti-intervention voices strongly endorsed the military option. It is unlikely that this episode reveals a shift in general attitudes; rather it reveals the case- and region-specific nature of contemporary public opinion and decision making.

Americans still appear to be sorting out the implications of the end of the cold war. Public opinion, like the opinion of most elites in the political process, has not agreed on a clear set of post–cold war priorities and interests. There is also substantial debate over the threats and opportunities in the new environment that may affect these interests. Without consensus or even a clear winning coalition with regard to these fundamental questions of value and perception in foreign policy, it is not surprising that sharp debate continues to characterize discussions pertaining to the use of force. Barring the emergence of a compelling foreign threat, the priority given to domestic concerns is likely only to further reduce the resources available for foreign policy and in turn intensify the debate over which interests abroad should be protected or advanced by force. Presidents can rely on a rally-round-the-flag effect when American troops are put in harm's way, but the American public has not yet accepted a clear and shared definition of post–cold war U.S. interests, nor has it decided on the wisdom of using force to defend or advance these causes. While we cannot predict the future from our data, we have tried to identify some of the major fault lines that are likely to characterize the ongoing debate and to highlight the important interaction between definitions of interests, perceptions of regional situations, and public opinions about the use of force.

PART IV

CONCLUSION

Randall B. Ripley and James M. Lindsay

13. Promise Versus Reality

Continuity and Change After the Cold War

The collapse of the Berlin Wall and the demise of the Soviet Union prompted much talk of refashioning U.S. foreign policy to meet the demands of a new era. Politicians from both political parties spoke openly of the need to free government institutions and policies from the mind-sets of the past. Liberals debated how to spend the coming "peace dividend," while conservatives debated whether the collapse of the Soviet Union signaled the "end of history" (Fukuyama 1989, 1992). Meanwhile, private foundations sponsored conferences and workshops so that scholars could "rethink" and "reconceptualize" U.S. foreign policy.

As a reading of the chapters in this volume show, these expectations of rapid and dramatic change in the structure and substance of U.S. foreign policy proved to be greatly exaggerated. Five years after Mikhail Gorbachev stepped down as the last Soviet leader, the organizational flowchart of the U.S. foreign policy bureaucracy looked much as it did ten, twenty, and even thirty years earlier. While some programs were canceled and others downsized (or "rightsized" in the parlance of corporate consultants), much of this organizational change appeared to be a case of "old wine in new bottles." Likewise, while U.S. policies in areas such as trade, security assistance, and human rights were cloaked in a new rhetoric—few political speechwriters missed the opportunity to note that the world had entered a new era—they had far greater continuity with the past than one might gather from public speeches and press releases.

In this chapter we offer some comments that, in effect, help explain why the amount of post–cold war change—whether in processes, structures, or policies—has been so small.

Foreign Policy Structures and Policies After the Cold War

We noted in chapter 1 that most observers believed that the end of the cold war presented the United States with a classic case of "problem depletion." Much of the foreign policy bureaucracy had been constructed in the wake of World War II to contain the Soviet threat. When the Soviet Union disappeared, much of that bureaucracy was presumably rendered obsolete because many of its assigned tasks no longer needed to be performed, or at least, they required major changes to make sense. Moreover, the end of the cold war came at a time of growing "environmental entropy," as the American public became less willing (at least in the abstract) to bear the costs of big government. With many foreign policy programs made obsolete and many Americans eager to rein in federal spending, all signs pointed to a substantial restructuring of the U.S. foreign policy bureaucracy and a dramatic reordering of U.S. foreign policy priorities.

Yet, despite problem depletion and environmental entropy, U.S. foreign policy witnessed nowhere near the level or extent of change that many had predicted in the first half of the 1990s. In 1993, Secretary of State Warren Christopher (1993a, 137) remarked that "our foreign policy institutions continue in large measure to mirror the Cold War imperatives. . . . Budgets and bureaucracies still reflect the reality of a world that's passed." Three years later, Christopher's observation remained largely accurate.

The lack of fundamental change in the agencies that make up the U.S. foreign policy bureaucracy is perhaps clearest in the case of the State Department. As James Lindsay shows, despite Christopher's early pledge to remake State to reflect the realities of the post–cold war world, very little changed during his four years at Foggy Bottom. The Clinton administration initially floated proposals to abolish the Arms Control and Disarmament Agency (ACDA) and to kill Radio Liberty and Radio Free Europe, but it abandoned both proposals when confronted with congressional opposition. Elsewhere the administration pushed for the creation of the post of undersecretary for global affairs and made a series of long-overdue management changes at the Agency for International Development (AID), but it failed to redirect substantial funds to global affairs and its proposal to rewrite the legislation underpinning U.S. foreign assistance died on Capitol Hill. Moreover, by 1995 the administration had abandoned its earlier reform efforts and instead fought vigorously to defeat a proposal by congressional Republicans to merge AID, ACDA, and the U.S. Information Agency (USIA) into the State Department.

The lack of substantial change was even more pronounced at the Central Intelligence Agency. As Loch Johnson and Kimberly Zisk show, under Robert Gates, the director of central intelligence during the Bush administration, the agency made some steps toward recognizing the changes that had occurred in the international environment (while still preserving its budget). These changes came to a halt under Gates's successor, R. James Woolsey, who defended traditional intelligence missions and roles and even argued for budget increases in a context of general economic retrenchment. Woolsey's attachment to the status quo eventually led Congress to create an independent commission to review the operations and budgets of the intelligence services, but the commission, which got off to a very slow start, was further hobbled in its work when its chairman, Les Aspin, died suddenly. Woolsey resigned as DCI in December 1994, and his successor, John Deutch, testified at his confirmation hearing that the agency had failed to adapt to a changed world. Nevertheless, when the commission (now chaired by Harold Brown) reported in March 1996, it basically endorsed the existing structure of the CIA and other intelligence agencies. It provided no serious critique.

The one exception to the relative lack of change in the foreign policy bureaucracy seems to be the Defense Department. Paul Stockton and Kimberly Zisk both argue that the Defense Department experienced a great deal of change in its budget and personnel levels. In 1991, President Bush and Congress agreed to cut defense spending by 22 percent and military personnel by 26 percent over five years. In 1993, President Clinton even proposed slightly deeper cuts in defense spending and military personnel. (Clinton subsequently reversed course and argued for adding to the defense budget.) Yet, as both Peter Hahn and Stockton remind us, those budget cuts were not accompanied by a rethinking of the roles and missions of the individual services. Indeed, military leaders bitterly resisted efforts to redefine roles and missions by defining the threats to U.S. security in the post–cold war era in terms equally dire as those used during the cold war. Thus, even in the case of Defense, the pattern has been a retrenchment around traditional goals and operations more than a restructuring that introduces new goals and operations.

The lack of fundamental change in the structure of the foreign policy bureaucracy has been accompanied by a similar lack of fundamental change in the content of U.S. foreign policy. In their chapter on security assistance, Duncan Clarke and Daniel O'Connor show that neither the executive branch nor Congress rethought the need for security assistance in the wake of the Soviet Union's demise. The amount of aid fell, but the priority list remained unchanged, with most of the aid going to Israel and Egypt. Neither the executive branch nor Congress seemed willing to question the accommodations and priorities reached in an earlier era.

Similar continuity can be seen in the realm of trade policy. As Pietro Nivola argues, such policy certainly received much more media play during the Clinton years than before them. Yet if we leave rhetoric aside, Clinton's approach to trade issues looked much like that of his predecessors. Whereas he pointed to the passage of NAFTA and GATT as the shining achievements of his administration, the substance of both agreements was negotiated largely by the preceding administration. His political contribution, by no means trivial, was engineering congressional approval.

In dealing with complaints of unfair trading practices by Japan, the Clinton trade team followed the customary practice of quarreling over sectoral items while stopping well short of initiating a trade war. And while Commerce Secretary Ron Brown was highly visible in promoting U.S. exports, commercial "boosterism" has a long history in the United States.

Finally, David Forsythe shows that the Clinton administration did little to elevate human rights policy as a foreign policy priority. Like his predecessors, Bill Clinton spoke out about human rights abuses abroad when doing so appeared to be politically attractive. Yet he showed no signs of having a particular vision about the place of human rights in American policy. And because there is no entrenched bureaucracy to push human rights, the issue remained on the periphery of the foreign policy agenda.

Leadership and Nonleadership in the Post–Cold War Era

Why was U.S. foreign policy so slow to change in the face of dramatic change in the international arena? The authors in this volume all suggest that the answer to this question lies in the lack of political leadership. While perceptions of problem depletion and environmental entropy may create opportunities for dramatic changes in structures and policies, they by no means guarantee change. What is needed to translate the opportunity for change into actual change is leadership. Yet in the first half of the 1990s, no source provided such leadership.

The President

Bert Rockman argues persuasively that the conventional wisdom is correct: the main engine for change in U.S. foreign policy has to be the president. As Rockman shows, presidents can lead in three ways: first, by providing "directional clarity"; second, by centralizing control over foreign policy; and third, by delegating to officials who can be trusted to implement presidential wishes. Of these three, the most important by far is directional clarity. Much of the benefit of centralized control over policy is lost when presidents do not know which direction they wish to go. Key administration officials cannot implement presidential wishes when the president does not know or fails to make clear those wishes.

The picture that emerges from the chapters in this volume is of two presidents unable to chart a course for the United States in the post–cold war era. George Bush was president when the dramatic events that signaled the end of the cold war occurred. He was very much a figure from the cold war: a longtime public servant inured to the cold war mentality by virtue of his service and experience. A man who openly acknowledged his problem with the "vision thing," he became president precisely at a time when world events called for a new vision. While he spoke earnestly about creating a "new world order," neither he nor his advisers succeeded in breathing any specifics into his vision for the post–cold war era.

In contrast to George Bush, Bill Clinton campaigned in 1992 as the candidate of vision and change. Yet once in office, he gave little evidence of understanding the nature of the challenge to U.S. foreign policy, and engaged in or directed little activity designed to address that challenge. As Vincent Auger points out in his review of the National Security Council, Bill Clinton did not provide strong leadership for the NSC staff, nor did he surround himself with advisers skilled at presenting the administration's policies to either Capitol Hill or the American public. Nor, as Lindsay, Stockton, Johnson, and Zisk indicate in their chapters, did Clinton weigh in on the debates going on within his own administration over whether and how to restructure the foreign policy bureaucracy. Aside from his showing up on the White House lawn in September 1993 to endorse the findings of Vice President Al Gore's national performance review, little was heard from the president on how to redesign foreign policy structures and programs to meet U.S. interests in the post–cold war era.

In short, Bill Clinton campaigned in part on a promise to respond to the changes brought about by the end of the cold war, but he provided neither directional clarity nor centralized control over a foreign policy that could then be placed in the hands of one or a few key subordinates. He filled the principal positions in the foreign and defense policy bureaucratic establishment, but did not seem to know what he wanted or expected of those people, except that they keep him out of trouble. The result was a foreign and defense policy that often wobbled.

One can only speculate why Clinton failed to provide directional clarity. At root, his problems were probably a mix of lack of experience, relative lack of interest, and a political character that seems to shrink from stating clear policies about anything and sticking with them. No doubt these personal characteristics were reinforced by the lack of political benefits to be gained from engineering change in foreign policy institutions and substantive policy. After all, it is a rare voter who will credit a president for revamping the CIA, closing down AID, or reallocating missions at the Defense Department.

Congress

A spate of recently published research has pointed to the growing importance of the congressional role in foreign policy (see Lindsay 1991, 1994a; Peterson 1994; Ripley and Lindsay 1993; Rosner 1995; Smist 1994; for dissenting views, see Hinckley 1994; Weissman 1995). The authors in this book repeatedly offer evidence of the centrality of Congress. Beginning with the fall of the Berlin Wall and continuing unabated to the present, Congress has made its views on foreign policy matters felt in a variety of ways. In some instances, it pushed the administration to cut programs and spending. This was the case, for example, with spending for the CIA and the Department of Defense before the 104th Congress that began in 1995. Then Congress—controlled by a new Republican majority—shifted gears and added money for defense and for core intelligence functions for fiscal year 1996 (when compared to fiscal year 1995), though it continued to cut spending for other international programs. In other instances, it blocked administration efforts to eliminate or downsize agencies, at times going so far as to broaden the mandate of an agency, as with ACDA in 1993.

In some important ways constitutional structure, precedent, and the simple fact that the executive branch, in contrast to Congress, is headed by a single individual—the president—mean that Congress is always less important in the broad realm of foreign affairs than is the executive branch. That assertion, however, is a long way from the claim that Congress is unimportant, that it is subservient to the executive branch and president, or that its activities have no substantive impact. None of these claims is true.

Congress's influence over how policy is made flows directly from its power of the purse and its power to create, modify, and abolish executive branch agencies. In his chapter on defense reform in the post–cold war era, Stockton nicely lays out the four consequences of these powers:

> First, fear of congressional activism can encourage Pentagon officials to adjust their proposals to forestall or co-opt congressional efforts to change U.S. defense spending and force structure. Second, Congress can shape the patterns of conflict and coalition building within the Pentagon, rewarding end runs by the services or (as in the base force) serving as the tacit ally of Pentagon reformers. Third, Congress can use its power of the purse to legislate changes in force structure and modify efforts by military or civilian officials to reshape the armed services. Fourth, by enacting legislation such as Goldwater-Nichols, Congress can alter the authorities granted to defense policy makers and shift the power relationships between them.

Given the wide-ranging nature of its powers, then, Congress is likely to continue to be central to the process of deciding how to change U.S. foreign policy to meet the needs of the post–cold war era.

Yet to indicate that Congress had a say in the debate over the future of U.S. foreign policy is not to claim that Congress provided the sort of directional clarity that was missing in both the Bush and Clinton White Houses. As observers have pointed out almost since the founding of the republic, the ideological, institutional, partisan, and regional divisions that beset Capitol Hill make it hard for Congress to endorse consistent policies, let alone display leadership. Indeed, while the chapters in this volume offer evidence that the 103d Congress (1993–1994) weighed in on a variety of foreign policy issues, its often unrelated actions did not amount to a consistent or coherent vision of the future of U.S. foreign policy.

Did the 104th Congress prove to be the exception to the rule? History tells us that periods of clearly identifiable policy preferences and wide-ranging action occur rarely in Congress and almost always in concert with presidential leadership, not as a substitute for it. In the twentieth century only the years 1913–1914, 1933–1934, 1964–1965, and 1981 fit this description, and those cases involved domestic policy almost exclusively. In January 1995 the Republicans took control of Congress with ambitious plans in both the domestic and foreign realms. In the latter arena, they stated their intent to remake the State Department Complex and to revamp spending on international affairs. By mid-1996, it was clear that the Republicans could not deliver on their early promises. While the House of Representatives acted quickly on its new agenda for U.S. foreign policy, the Senate showed much greater reluctance to challenge the status quo. And, of course, President Clinton did not agree with much of what the House majority proposed. Eventually, little happened substantively in the foreign policy realm, as quarrels between Congress and President Clinton over foreign policy became adjuncts to the overall 1996 campaign strategies of both Clinton and the Republicans.

The Public

Unsurprisingly, the American public provided no clearer guide to the future of U.S. foreign policy in the post–cold war 1990s than did either the president or Congress. What stands out in many of the chapters in this volume is the relative absence of the public from much of the debate over the future of U.S. foreign policy structures and policies. While narrowly based interest groups weighed in at times on proposals to restructure foreign policy agencies—the effort to save Radio Liberty and Radio Free Europe is perhaps the most pointed example—these issues never engaged the broader public. Indeed, the near total absence of specific foreign policy issues from the 1992 presidential election campaign suggests that most Americans simply preferred not to think about such matters. The 1994 congressional campaign—which had more issue coherence nationally than most congressional elections—was fought almost entirely on domestic issues. Neither party sought to inject significant discussion of foreign policy into the 1996 presidential campaign. Public interest in foreign policy was at low ebb. When a July 1996 *Wall Street Journal*–NBC News poll asked voters to rank sixteen issues that might help them decide how to vote in the presidential race, foreign policy was ranked last (Seib 1996).

As Richard Herrmann and Shannon Peterson show in their chapter, the ambivalence of the American public over the future of U.S. foreign policy is especially pronounced when it comes to the use of force. The end of the cold war removed the last clear justification for "just war." Ambivalence about the legitimate use of force in pursuit of American national interests became even more pronounced. Discussion in the run-up to the use of force in the Persian Gulf against Iraq displayed such ambiguity even though Saddam Hussein was clearly accepted as a villain. The paralysis over the use of American or even United Nations force in Bosnia, even though most Americans would agree that the Serbs were villains, was an even more dramatic illustration of the inability of leaders, foreign policy elites, and the mass public to agree on what made sense and was morally justified.

Of course, disagreements among American citizens over the future course of U.S. foreign policy are hardly surprising. "The people" rarely speak clearly without sustained prompting from political leaders (Zaller 1992). Yet the lack of anything approaching a foreign policy consensus among the American public in turn made it easier for both the president and Congress to put off having to grapple with the tough issues raised by the end of the cold war. Thus leaders content to drift with inherited policies could claim to reflect the public mood. In doing so, of course, they abdicated any responsibility to lead.

Bureaucratic Resistance to Change

Given the absence of strong presidential or congressional leadership, it is not surprising that, according to the authors in this volume, the agencies that make up the foreign policy bureaucracy displayed little interest in rethinking how they defined and pursued their missions. In chapter 1 we offered the hypothesis that organizations will resist changes that require them to forfeit missions and to accept smaller budgets. Thus, while almost every agency undertook what it claimed was a thoroughgoing review of the need for its programs in the post–cold war era, relatively little came of these reviews in terms of either structural or programmatic change.

The lack of political leadership, especially leadership from the White House and the president's principal advisers and appointees, hampered the few efforts that were made by lower-ranking officials (whether for reasons of good policy or from a desire for greater political influence) to shut down or expand existing programs. Thus, efforts by officials in the State Department to abolish ACDA and the radio services faltered because of Warren Christopher's lack of sustained interest in rethinking the structure of his agency. Without Christopher's political weight behind them, officials seeking to revamp the structure of the State Department could not overcome the forces of resistance at Foggy Bottom.

With the political leadership to a great extent sitting on the sidelines, bureaucracies, not surprisingly, turned much of their attention to foiling changes they believed were inimical to their interests. The specific strategies they employed varied from moment to moment and from agency to agency. At times, agencies sought to stonewall those pushing for change, in a straightforward test of political influence. At other times, however, agencies sought to co-opt the forces of change, either by redefining the nature of the problem in ways that served bureaucratic self-interest or by proposing their own, preemptive changes. Individual agencies behaved differently from one another, in part because of their different bureaucratic cultures.

Stonewalling

Agencies may resist change by seeking allies and confronting the forces pushing for change directly in a test of political will and, above all, political strength. An example of such behavior was the battle over the future of

Radio Liberty and Radio Free Europe. As Lindsay shows in his chapter on the State Department Complex, the radio services responded to proposals for their abolition by mobilizing political support both at home and abroad. The op-ed articles by former American officials and the testimonials of foreign heads of state paid off; although the budgets for Radio Liberty and Radio Free Europe were cut substantially, they both continued operation.

In 1995 there was a brief alliance of views between Secretary of State Warren Christopher and Republican leaders in Congress. They all wanted to consolidate AID, ACDA, and USIA into the State Department. The three smaller agencies all opposed the proposal and put pressure on the White House to change Christopher's mind and to oppose the initiatives of congressional Republicans, especially Sen. Jesse Helms (R-N.C.), the new chairman of the Senate Foreign Relations Committee. The administration succumbed to this pressure, Christopher complied, and the administration successfully stonewalled.

The CIA under James Woolsey took a similarly confrontational approach to dealing with Capitol Hill. The FY 1994 budget request that the agency submitted to Congress in February 1993 sought to add $1 billion to the intelligence budget, even though congressional sentiment favored deep cuts in spending on intelligence activities and even though Bill Clinton had promised during his presidential campaign that he would cut intelligence spending by $7 billion over four years. Eventually, Woolsey had to settle for an authorization that froze intelligence spending at fiscal year 1993 levels. Only an alliance between Democratic congressional leaders and Republican members of Congress staved off even deeper budget cuts. The following year, Woolsey again resisted congressional efforts to streamline the intelligence community. Irritated by his obstructionism, Congress essentially bypassed Woolsey by creating an independent commission to review U.S. intelligence operations.

Whereas the radio services and the CIA confronted proposals for budget cuts from the start, the Department of Defense began directly to resist budget cuts only after first accepting sizable reductions in its funding and personnel. By 1994, however, military officers began to complain loudly that the defense budget had been cut too deeply, thereby jeopardizing the ability of the services to carry out their missions. In particular, the military services and their allies on Capitol Hill began to warn that the United States faced a "readiness gap" in its ability to meet potential threats to ter of much dispute. Lawrence Korb (1995b), a former assistant secretary the nation. Whether military readiness was in fact in dire straits is a matter of defense in the Reagan administration, argues that the readiness gap was simply a ploy by the services to fend off budget reductions. Whatever the merits of the contending arguments, opposition among the uniformed military to deeper budget cuts convinced the Clinton administration to abandon proposals for further downsizing the Department of Defense.

Co-optation through Problem Redefinition

Although agencies from time to time tried to stare down efforts to slash their budgets or cut their programs, perhaps more common were efforts to co-opt the forces of change. One way agencies accomplished this was by trying to redefine the consequences of the end of the cold war. Whereas commentary on the end of the cold war tended to focus on the declining threat to the United States, agencies often argued that at least for them the collapse of the Soviet Union created more and not fewer problems. By arguing that the United States faced new and pressing problems that were central to their missions, agencies sought to redefine the situation as "problem expansion" rather than "problem depletion."

In some respects, the quintessential example of an agency attempting to co-opt change by redefining problem depletion as problem expansion was the CIA under James Woolsey. As Johnson discusses in his chapter, Woolsey pushed for a larger CIA budget on the grounds that the collapse of the Soviet Union meant that "we live now in a jungle filled with a bewildering variety of poisonous snakes" (Woolsey 1993b). The job of tracking all these new snakes would belong to the intelligence community. Thus, the end of the cold war did not make the intelligence agencies less important, as the conventional wisdom had it; rather, it made them all the more important and all the more deserving of government funding.

The Defense Department also sought to protect its roles and missions by redefining the threats facing the United States. Hahn, Stockton, and Zisk in their chapters all show that the Defense Department reacted to the end of the cold war by defining the new threat to its own advantage. In particular, the highly trumpeted "bottom-up review" was predicated on a seven-scenario assessment of the post–cold war foreign threat and required a force structure quite similar to the one the United States had built during the cold war. As one critic of the bottom-up review put it, the review "maintains the U.S. planning perspective that existed during the cold war: it focuses on the near-term future, and on the most *familiar* threats, as opposed to the *greatest* or *most likely* threats to the national security, which will probably appear in the next decade, at the earliest" (Krepinevich 1994, i).

The various agencies that make up the State Department Complex made similar arguments that the end of the cold war had made their work more important than ever. As Lindsay discusses in his chapter, Warren Christopher sought to increase the State Department's budget by $3 billion with the argument that the demise of the Soviet Union would put an even greater strain on diplomatic resources. Likewise, ACDA argued that the demise of the Soviet Union made the threat of nuclear proliferation more pronounced, and AID argued that its expertise was needed to help encourage democracy in eastern Europe and the former Soviet Union. Even Radio Free Europe and Radio Liberty, which had been founded specifically to undermine communism in the Soviet Union and eastern Europe, refused to declare victory and close up shop. Instead, the radio services argued they had a crucial role to play in helping democratic institutions and practices take root in what was once the Soviet empire.

Preemptive Changes

In chapter 1, we noted that bureaucracies may propose or even make changes on their own to ward off externally imposed changes that would be worse. By doing so, they hope to make changes they can live with and that do not threaten their core values or functions, thereby staving off more threatening changes imposed by "outsiders," such as the president or Congress.

Examples of such preemptive behavior dot the post–cold war landscape. Perhaps the best example is the work of Gen. Colin Powell during his tenure as chairman of the Joint Chiefs of Staff. As Stockton and Zisk argue, Powell recognized that cuts in defense spending were inevitable. He, in turn, acted to preempt truly threatening change by sacrificing the peripheral needs of the services while still protecting their core missions. In practice, this meant agreeing to accept sizable cuts in funding and personnel while preserving the traditional allocation of roles and missions among the four services. To judge by presidential and congressional efforts in 1995 to increase the defense budget—despite repeated public opinion polls showing that a majority of Americans favored deeper cuts in defense spending—Powell's willingness to seize the initiative on defense spending helped to inoculate the Defense Department against further cuts.

Other agency heads seemed less inclined to use or less adept at using the preemptive change strategy. In the State Department, Secretary Warren Christopher in January 1995 proposed absorbing AID, ACDA, and USIA into State. A subhead in the *New York Times* story covering Christopher's position caught the essence of the reason for the initiative: "Sweeping Before the Republican Broom Hits the Floor" (Sciolino 1995c). But he—unlike Powell—declined to fight for consolidation. As already mentioned, Secretary Christopher subsequently repudiated his proposal, primarily because of fierce opposition from the affected agencies, who successfully co-opted the White House.

Democrats in Congress continued to press Christopher for some preemptive action to fend off proposals they knew would be forthcoming from Republicans in Congress, particularly from Senator Helms. Christopher eventually responded with a plan to cut about five hundred jobs in the Department of State from a total workforce of about twenty-six thousand. Again, a *New York Times* subhead made the central point: "Effort Is Intended to Avert Overhaul" (Greenhouse 1995a).

Efforts to preempt change were equally fitful in the intelligence community. As Johnson details in his chapter, Robert Gates recognized that Congress would revamp the CIA if he totally ignored calls for change, and to that end he reallocated resources within the agency (again, while preserving the preexisting level of spending). While the practical import of this reallocation is subject to debate—Dan Glickman (D-Kans.), chair of the House Intelligence Committee, complained in 1994 that under Gates the CIA rushed to do any task "simply to preserve its infrastructure" (quoted in Engelberg 1994). Gates's willingness to talk about the need for change helped forestall efforts to cut the CIA's budget. In contrast, James Woolsey failed to respond to congressional demands that he streamline and reorient the intelligence community for the post–cold war era. As one White House adviser described Woolsey's tenure as DCI: "He had an opportunity to be a new broom, and instead he was a defender of the status quo" (quoted in Weiner 1994b).

While Woolsey chose to resist rather than preempt congressional pressure, his successor, John Deutch, showed himself to be much more attuned to sentiment on Capitol Hill. Upon succeeding Woolsey in May 1995, Deutch immediately made major changes in senior staff and promised he would revamp the workings of the agency. Presumably, he hoped these changes would be sufficient to prevent external forces—both legislative and executive—from making even more dramatic changes. The depth and pervasiveness of Deutch's proposed changes remain to be seen. It is worth remembering that in the 1970s the CIA successfully resisted change despite severe buffeting over illegal domestic activities. The instincts of the agency, despite the pledges of Deutch, remain the same. "Preemptive changes" could turn out to be purely cosmetic.

Change After the Cold War: Where Do We Stand?

This volume has addressed questions involving the presence and absence of both substantive and structural change in U.S. foreign policy and the foreign policy bureaucracy following the end of the cold war. What do the preceding chapters tell us about U.S. foreign policy in those years?

On balance, the authors suggest that the United States is confused and unsure of itself as it grapples with its place in the world. Despite a plethora of blue-ribbon reports and an abundance of political oratory on the need to adapt to a changed world, the structure and substance of U.S. foreign policy changed remarkably little between 1989 and 1996. This lack of change stemmed in large part from the fact that no clear and sustained guidance on goals or strategies came from any source: not from the White House, any individual bureaucracy, the bureaucracy collectively, Congress, or from the public. In fact, the signs of drift and confusion were present in all these entities. Such coherence as existed came primarily from the bureaucracy and that coherence opposed rather than supported significant changes.

When the Berlin Wall fell, when the eastern European Soviet satellite nations threw off both their communist governments and their subordination to the Soviet Union, and when the Soviet Union itself first weathered a coup and then vanished as a single entity, the cold war in classic form quickly became a thing of the past. Most commentators and public officials seemed to assume—and stated their assumptions aloud—that these changes simply compelled the United States to make major changes in its foreign policies and the bureaucratic structure engaged with those policies.

In fact, the collapse of the Soviet empire and the end of the cold war did not irresistibly produce change in U.S. policy and bureaucracy. Few external events compel either bureaucratic or policy change. The Japanese attack on Pearl Harbor was a compelling event. The United States could not ignore it and, in fact, it virtually guaranteed President Roosevelt's immediate call for war and total victory. But very few external events are like that; most do not compel change. They may create the opportunity for change. They may present constraints that rule out some specific changes or a total lack of response. Some external events may even be ignored altogether; they may provoke no U.S. response aimed at changing either bureaucratic organization or the content of policy.

Without a clear-cut external challenge or threat, it is very difficult for the American political system to generate an overall vision of foreign policy. There are too many distractions: different interests, different opinions, indifference, defensiveness in support of the status quo, and admittedly, an incredibly complex external world that does not change at the beck and call of the United States, no matter how powerful it is.

The end of the cold war presented and still presents the United States with opportunities for meaningful change. But the costs of little change do not appear unacceptably high to the president, to the foreign policy bureaucracy, to Congress, or to the concerned part of the public. Individual observers may predict dire consequences because of missed opportunities. But these arguments have not mobilized the political system to act.

American history has demonstrated again and again that only the president can produce a sustained, clear focus in U.S. foreign policy. Likewise, the president is ultimately the primary engine of a change in that focus. To be sure, he develops relationships with other players in the complex process that leads to the content of policy and also to the structure of the foreign policy bureaucracy. But none of the other players can successfully substitute for the president over the long term. They can provide momentary leadership and can certainly provide goads to and constraints on presidential action. Generally speaking, the reaction of foreign policy bureaucracies, Congress, and public opinion to presidential initiatives falls somewhere between hostility and support. Occasionally, these players can inject new issues or new ways of looking at familiar issues into the policy debate. But the fact remains that a relatively stable, clear focus on a global scale requires an articulate, interested, focused president.

In the absence of a broad presidential vision of overall U.S. foreign policy goals, the pieces of the foreign policy bureaucracy are almost inevitably led to pursue the survival of their core functions, personnel, and views, along the lines Halperin has delineated and chapter 1 of this volume summarizes. Sporadic challenges to that survival can usually be fended off in one way or another. Thus change—rarely initiated by the bureaucracy itself—is minimal.

The task of designing meaningful change is of course neither easy nor trivial. Gen. John Shalikashvili, chairman of the Joint Chiefs of Staff, points out that in his view the United States took ten years to settle on its major policies after World War II, even though everyone knew for the last year or two of the war that it would end in victory for the allies (Dreifus 1995). On the other hand, he says, no one expected the series of events that marked the end of the cold war, and therefore there was no advance planning for a postcommunist Europe and a post-Soviet world. The discussion started from scratch. His prognosis is that it will take at least as long to redirect policy now as it did after World War II.

With the demise of the cold war, more U.S. agencies beyond those traditionally involved in foreign and defense policy have an enhanced role to play. This fact might produce confusion in the short run but might also help reduce the power of the entrenched bureaucracies. For example, a variety of economic agencies—the Treasury, the Office of the Trade Representative, and the Department of Commerce—all have a more visible foreign policy role to play as economic and trade issues loom as large as military ones. This could create competition for policy leadership that, *if orchestrated by the president and his close staff,* might produce deep and pervasive changes within the bureaucracy and in the substance of policy. Without presidential leadership the increased importance of these new players might simply produce added confusion.

In seeking to provide policy leadership, presidents will no doubt face constraints on the courses of action they may choose. One such constraint is the environmental entropy that characterizes American politics at present. The new Republican majority in the 104th Congress both resulted from and contributed to a political climate hostile to government deficits, tax increases, and spending on international affairs. In their plan for balancing the federal budget by 2002, the Republicans proposed cutting international affairs spending by more than a third (before taking inflation into account) over seven years. Yet Congress approved the blueprint outlining these deep cuts in the international affairs budget in large part because President Clinton made almost no effort to protect international affairs spending.

In charting a new course for the United States in the post–cold war era, presidents also face the constraint created by public opinion. Yet even here presidents may enjoy more freedom to maneuver than is commonly acknowledged. Contrary to much recent commentary, a mood of isolationism has not gripped the American public. Americans are skeptical about risking the lives of American troops in far-off places, and they are still worried, but less so, about risking American capital in pursuit of foreign policy ends. But they do not want the United States to retreat within itself and ignore the world. In February 1995, for example, the Times Mirror Center reported that 65 percent of those surveyed agreed with the statement: "The United States should cooperate fully with the United Nations." Only 29 percent disagreed ("Opinion Outlook" 1995a, 642).

The 1994 survey sponsored by the Chicago Council on Foreign Relations (Rielly 1995b, 6) reported a similar finding. In response to the question: "Do you think it will be best for the future of the country if we take an active part in world affairs or if we stay out of world affairs?" 65 percent chose "active part" and 29 percent chose "stay out." Of those in a "leadership" sample, 98 percent chose "active part" and 1 percent chose "stay out." The proportion of the general public choosing "active part" has fluctuated between 54 percent and 66 percent in the six quadrennial Chicago Council on Foreign Relations surveys dating back to 1974. The 1994 response supporting an active U.S. role in the world was near the top of the twenty-year range. The leaders were consistently either 97 percent or 98 percent on the side of "active part."

In analyzing the results of the 1994 Chicago poll, Rielly (1995b, 40) offers the following summary:

> The overall results of this survey show that the American people are now confident about the present and future role of their country, despite the perceived absence of strong foreign policy leadership from their president. The end of the Cold War has not shaken America's fundamental commitment to maintaining an active role in world affairs, as recognition of global economic competition and interdependence has grown. Relief from the long competition with the Soviet Union and the lack of a clear external threat have made Americans more reluctant to use force abroad and become involved in the affairs of other countries. But they want to maintain current levels of defense in an uncertain world and are committed to diplomatic engagement through alliances and multilateral organizations.

In short, there is no popular mandate to dismantle either the U.S. role in the world or the agencies that conduct the business implied by that role. There is skepticism about some programs—foreign aid is a very good example—and great concern about protecting American jobs, factors that put some limits on acceptable policies. And the fear of U.S. casualties also inhibits policy makers. But the state of public opinion in the mid-1990s does not dramatically hamstring creative leaders who want to advance U.S. interests in the world arena.

In sum, while events overseas may create the opportunities for dramatic change in the structure and substance of U.S. foreign policy, they do not by themselves guarantee change. Whether U.S. foreign policy adapts to its new challenges or continues yearning for a past that is no more depends ultimately on a commitment by political leaders to fashion a new political blueprint for the United States. Above all, the president must have the will to change and the capacity to articulate a vision of change and to work to achieve it. He may not always succeed, but clear and purposeful change is surely unlikely at best—and perhaps impossible—without such presidential leadership. Indeed, only with forceful presidential leadership, some supporting conditions, and no doubt some good luck, does planned change become a possibility.

The United States has lived much of its collective life without a coherent and all-encompassing foreign policy. Before 1918 that made almost no difference to anyone in the United States or the rest of the world. From 1918 to 1939 it began to make a difference. Since 1945 the state of U.S. foreign policy makes considerable difference both to our own condition and to that of the rest of the world. The republic will not crumble without a coherent global policy, but the republic may well suffer embarrassments that could be avoided if we have such a policy. Nor would the world be better ordered just because the United States developed a coherent policy. On the other hand, the rest of the world would know what to expect, because our concrete actions would be derived from a few well-articulated, clear principles. Predictability of behavior—at least for rational players in the foreign policy arena—has its own virtues.

But such predictability has not emerged since the end of the cold war. American foreign policy has no new shape, nor do the institutions that develop and deliver it. Details will be debated, small changes will occur, blunders will be made, some successes will be had, but we will not be in a position to know if some general entity called "foreign policy" is in general succeeding or not. We can proclaim or analyze success in some ventures, failure in others, and mixed results in still others—but we will not know how to aggregate the overall record. Nor will we or anyone else know quite how to measure the overall impact of the United States in world affairs.

NOTES

REFERENCES

CONTRIBUTORS

INDEX

Notes

Chapter 3. The National Security Council System After the Cold War

I would like to thank the following individuals for their valuable comments about this analysis: Jim Lindsay, Rip Ripley, Paul Stockton, Pietro Nivola, Loch Johnson, Samuel Lewis, and Duncan Clarke, and the two reviewers for the University of Pittsburgh Press. Two former NSC officials who wish to remain anonymous also read the entire manuscript and offered valuable criticisms, and I thank them for their efforts. I also thank those current and former officials from the NSC, NEC, and State Department who so generously allowed me to interview them and who shared their knowledge and insights about the foreign policy–making process with me.

1. These issues are not "new" with the end of the cold war, of course; they have been staples of both academic analysis and political rhetoric for two decades. Rather, the end of the cold war eliminated the issue that dominated the U.S. foreign policy agenda since the late 1940s, thereby creating room for other issues to rise in priority and for debate about the very nature of the agenda itself.

2. In addition to published sources, my analysis draws on interviews with current and former officials of the National Security Council staff, National Economic Council staff, and State Department, conducted during 1994 and 1995. For obvious reasons, all interviewees requested anonymity, and I have honored those requests.

3. Technically, Congress could control at least the size of the staff by refusing to appropriate the funds necessary to pay their salaries. This power has never been used; in fact, between 1950 and 1987, Congress rarely conducted any meaningful oversight of the NSC budget request.

4. Philip Odeen reached very similar conclusions concerning what he termed the "institutional" and "staff" roles of the NSA and the NSC staff when he led an internal Carter administration study of national security policy integration (see Odeen 1980, 1985).

5. Given past State Department dissatisfaction with its relative subordination within the NSC system, this may seem surprising at first. However, some at State feared that a parallel structure would reduce even further the department's influence on a wide range of "new" foreign policy issues whose salience was rapidly growing, according to a former State Department official.

6. Some administrations had used economic or domestic policy councils, but the commission clearly envisioned that such groups would have a much more prominent and institutionalized role than had generally been the case in the past.

7. Some NSC staff indicated that these offices were not created primarily for substantive policy reasons, but to pave over personnel problems and create positions for individuals whose original appointments were not working out.

8. One Bush NSC staffer said he usually let an official from one of the agencies chair working groups in his area of policy. While that official was busy coordinating the paperwork for a meeting involving as many as thirty to thirty-five participants, the NSC aide would meet with a small group of trusted allies to plan their strategy for the meeting. He said this allowed him more time and flexibility both to shape the substantive agenda and to oversee the entire process.

9. Several NSC staffers were highly critical of the staff director. They viewed her as a gatekeeper whose job was to review their work for possible domestic political ramifications, and they believed she knew or cared very little about the substance of foreign policy issues. These staffers saw her office as a paperwork bottleneck, and attempted to circumvent her review of their work at every opportunity—which was apparently the source of some tension within the staff.

10. Several NSC staffers suggested that Lake had a strong personal distaste for conflict and confrontation. As an example, they discussed his reluctance to dismiss one senior director even though it was widely known among the staff that Lake had lost all confidence in that individual. More than six months passed before he finally asked the person to leave.

11. Especially striking was the conclusion offered by each of the NSC, NEC, and State Department officials interviewed that, except for the decision-making bottleneck at the NSC/DC level and the potential for conflict between the NEC and NSC principals, the basic structure and process of the Clinton NSC system was sound. They all suggested that the crucial issues were *who* was running the system and *how* they were running it. One individual who had served in the Bush NSC pointed out that that system had functioned much less effectively after Deputy NSA Robert Gates left the staff to go to the CIA.

Chapter 7. The Threat of Soviet Decline

The conference draft of this paper was completed while I was a visiting scholar at the Olin Institute for Strategic Studies, Harvard University; the final version has benefited from comments offered by members of that community, and I am especially grateful to director Samuel Huntington. I am also grateful to those current and former government officials (who wish to remain anonymous) who allowed me to interview them and generously gave of their time and expertise. In addition, many participants in the May 1994 conference that prepared for this volume offered valuable critiques and recommendations. Special thanks to Loch Johnson, Paul Stockton, and Don Lair for their suggestions about source materials and their willingness to help me arrange interviews. Obviously, the opinions expressed here and any remaining errors are mine alone.

Chapter 9. Security Assistance Policy After the Cold War

1. Funding for PKOs in the SA account is limited to *voluntary* U.S. contributions for UN PKOs. Funding of the much larger *assessed* contributions for UN PKOs is pro-

vided through annual Departments of Commerce, Justice and State Appropriation Acts.

2. Much of the information in this section comes from interviews conducted in 1993–1994 with past and present U.S. government officials. Unless otherwise indicated, names and titles for officials and offices are those of the Clinton administration.

3. Reagan administration secretary of state George Shultz reportedly told American-Israel Affairs Committee (AIPAC) Executive Director Tom Dine that he hoped to make it impossible for a future secretary of state who might be less supportive of Israel "to overcome the bureaucratic relationship between Israel and the U.S." created by the Reagan administration (Dine 1986, 8). That administration's two most senior backers of U.S.-Israeli strategic cooperation later regretted having supported core elements of such strategic cooperation (McFarlane 1994, 187–88; Shultz 1993, 143).

4. Earmarks are congressionally mandated set-asides for specified countries, regions, or programs. "Conditionality" refers to conditions or restrictions set by legislation or committee reports on recipient countries or by the executive branch.

Chapter 10. Commercializing Foreign Affairs

I am grateful to Peter Hahn, Lawrence J. Korb, Thomas E. Mann, Helmut Sonnenfeldt, and Susan L. Woodward for their comments and suggestions in preparing this chapter.

1. These comparisons of NTB "coverage" do not measure restrictiveness. The trade barriers in Japan and Europe were generally less penetrable than those of the United States. Still, the proliferation of U.S. "voluntary" restraint agreements, orderly marketing arrangements, and other nontariff restrictions—and their huge cost—during the 1980s was striking (see Hufbauer, Berliner, and Elliot 1986).

2. The urgency of correcting a large balance of payments deficit and the need to ensure access to European markets for U.S. exporters were central elements of President Kennedy's case for launching a new multilateral trade round in 1962 (see, for instance, Bauer, Pool, and Dexter 1972).

3. U.S. participation in the GATT's antidumping code, as part of the Kennedy Round, was challenged in Congress. In the end, the Johnson administration was forced to compromise, ensuring that U.S. law would have supremacy in any case where it and the international code were in conflict (Destler 1995).

4. In an epic survey of U.S. international relations over the first ten years of the postwar period, a group of Brookings scholars concluded in 1956: "United States foreign economic policy . . . had become so hedged about with restrictions and so inflexible that they created uncertainty and gave rise to a good deal of restiveness among allied and associated states. . . . Relations were further embittered as fears were generated in different parts of the free world by various domestic proposals for the disposal of American agricultural surpluses and for the protection of American industries" (Reitzel, Kaplan, Coblenz 1956).

5. The "reason" was quite simple. To impose a 1,000 percent tariff increase on minivans, U.S. Customs would have had to reclassify these vehicles as "trucks," which remained subject to punitive duties. The prohibitive truck duties, however, were the permanent result of a U.S. retaliation against imports from Europe in an ancient trade dispute over poultry exports (the fabled transatlantic "chicken war" of 1963).

There was little basis for expanding an anachronistic trade sanction originally aimed at Europe to a new, quite different product, passenger minivans that happened to come from Japan. Yet Clinton seemed to be reasoning that the Bush administration had somehow extended a gratuitous concession to the Japanese (one for which "we got *nothing*, and I emphasize *nothing* in return") by deciding against the customs reclassification.

6. Both the ATP and the MEP were established under the Omnibus Trade and Competitiveness Act of 1988. The TRP was initiated by the Defense Technology Conversion, Reinvestment, and Transition Assistance Act of 1992. The budget authority of various programs, particularly those of the Commerce Department, briefly increased under Clinton. Much of the change, however, reflected a shuffling of labels from defense-based to civilian-based R&D—often a distinction without a difference. Overall federal R&D support, which stood at almost $72.5 billion in 1993, did not exceed $73 billion in 1995 (White House Office of Science and Technology Policy 1994).

7. For a no-holds-barred exposition of this thesis, see Huntington 1993c. Elsewhere, however, Huntington argues that something much larger than "economic issues" will be the main source of international conflict, namely, clashing "civilizations" (Huntington 1993a).

8. Even internationalist Republican lawmakers have raised questions about U.S. adherence to the WTO. In 1995, for instance, Sen. Robert Dole (R-Kans.) introduced legislation that would impanel a special commission comprised of U.S. federal judges to oversee and possibly contest proceedings that were perceived to be contrary to U.S. interests.

9. These reflections may not agree with those of a burgeoning, and foreboding, literature on the dominance of geoeconomics. In this literature, international "struggles" for economic supremacy appear to be the order of the day. See Garten 1992a; Luttwak 1993; Sandholtz et al. 1992; Thurow 1992.

10. Krugman and Lawrence 1994 estimate that the likely wage loss from "deindustrialization" in the face of foreign competition has been on the order of less than 0.07 percent of national income.

11. In a world of fluid capital markets and transnational corporations enmeshed in global production strategies and complex interfirm alliances, it is not always clear what some conventional commercial calculations signify. As Peter Drucker and others have repeatedly stressed, merchandise trade statistics (which show a perennial U.S. deficit) do not adequately measure the full commercial linkages and trade flows among economies (Drucker 1994).

12. Bergsten and Noland 1993 estimate that Japan's closed markets deny U.S. exporters about $13.6 billion worth of business.

Chapter 11. Human Rights Policy

1. Beyond the State Department, other federal agencies such as Treasury and Commerce were involved in human rights matters. Treasury had to sign off on U.S. votes in multilateral banks. Congress had mandated that the United States would use its voice and vote in these international financial institutions to advance human rights. Commerce had to sign off on export licenses for sensitive items that could be used to violate human rights, products such as electric shock batons (cattle prods) sometimes

favored by torturers. Neither Treasury nor Commerce officials were very interested in human rights abroad, and both resisted coordination by the State Department. Congressional elements periodically joined the fray through oversight committees, and media reports sometimes galvanized Commerce to scrutinize more carefully exports to South Korea and South Africa.

There was an office in the NSC that dealt with human rights and other "global" issues. It was first held by Jessica Tuchmann Mathews and later by Lincoln Bloomfield. Particularly under Mathews it was an ineffectual office, held in disdain by Derian at HA, and it provided little coordination on human rights matters. Under both Mathews and Bloomfield, human rights policy was shaped by others whose decisions varied according to the geographical region addressed, the egos of the bureaucratic protagonists, and the involvement of higher-ups.

2. The early Reagan efforts in this direction were crude and ineffectual, but he finally succeeded in establishing this orientation in his first administration. His first nominee for assistant secretary of state for human rights, Ernest Lefever, was on record as favoring the repeal of congressional human rights legislation; he considered it unwise in the global struggle with communism. His research institute had also accepted money from South Africa to distribute material favorable to that racist (but anticommunist) state. He was forced to withdraw his name for the HA position in the face of widespread opposition in the Republican-controlled Senate Foreign Relations Committee. Secretary of State Alexander Haig said in his bumbling fashion that Carter's emphasis on human rights was going to be replaced in the Reagan years by a focus on antiterrorism; this also did not sit well with Congress, human rights groups, or the media.

3. U.S. security and political assistance also flowed to nongovernment or private armies under the Reagan Doctrine, regardless of human rights performance, unless Congress got involved. Thus U.S. foreign assistance, both overt and covert, went to the contras fighting the Sandinistas in Nicaragua, UNITA fighting the Dos Santos government and its Cuban supporters in Angola, and various "rebel" parties fighting the Nagib government and its Soviet backers in Afghanistan. None of these irregular fighters, including the contras, were clearly democratic and protective of human rights, administration rhetoric notwithstanding. All committed attacks on civilians, and other violations of human rights. Nevertheless, since they were trying to roll back weak "communist" governments, they merited support. We might also note that the sitting governments in question could not be characterized as generally protective of rights either, though the complexity of the situation resists easy generalization. I rather doubt that any person anywhere in the Reagan administration ever took an initiative to reduce U.S. assistance to these private armies because of their human rights record, barring action by Congress—and Congress became interested primarily in the contras. In 1989 the contras created a panel to review human rights violations by their fighters, but this was long after Congress, not the Reagan team, first pressured them to clean up their act (Pear 1989). The CIA had even provided a manual to the contras giving instruction on how to "neutralize" civilian leaders who opposed them. In 1992 the Bush administration put some pressure on UNITA concerning its human rights violations in Angola; this was after the cold war ended and after UNITA had fallen out of favor in Washington ("U.S. Asks Angola Rebel to Explain Rights Abuses" 1992). Beyond State, the Commerce Department, perhaps because of bureaucratic

routine or congressional oversight, continued to block the exportation of certain commodities on human rights grounds. The value of commodities so blocked during the first Reagan administration may have exceeded that recorded during the Carter years; public information is scarce and researchers have to rely on confidential interviews. Treasury, on the other hand, did not play a large role in U.S. votes in multilateral banks. The Reagan administration voted against loans to leftist governments of small, poor countries, but not to others; Treasury simply deferred to prevailing political directives. As during the Carter years, in no case was a loan application actually voted down on human rights grounds. Some states may have been deterred from making application because of their human rights performance, but this is impossible to research and was in any case unlikely during the first Reagan administration.

Chapter 12. American Public Opinion and the Use of Force

1. The question read: "In today's world, is it still necessary for the U.S. to maintain NATO or is this military alliance no longer necessary?" (CBS news poll, October 10, 1991, *New York Times*, October 11, 1991).

2. The CCFR question read: "Now let me read you some proposals which have been made for possible agreement between the United States and the Soviet Union. For each, tell me if you would favor or oppose such an agreement: reducing the number of American and Russian troops in Europe?" (CCFR 1975, *New York Times*, October 11, 1991).

3. The question read: "Is the U.S. more secure now that the Soviet Union has broken up in many different republics each with its own government or was the U.S. more secure when all the republics of the Soviet Union were under one central government?" (CBS news poll, October 10, 1991, *New York Yimes*, October 11, 1991).

4. The question read: "How likely do you think we are to get into a nuclear war within the next ten years—very likely, fairly likely, fairly unlikely, or very unlikely?" (*New York Times*–CBS news poll on the new world order, October 5–7, 1991, *New York Times*, October 11, 1991).

5. The question read: "Now that the Soviet Union no longer exists, do you think the U.S. should share world power with other nations, or should we use our power to ensure that no other nations can challenge our dominance in wor1d affairs?" (*Time*-CNN news poll, March 12, 1992).

6. The first question read: "Now that relations between the U.S. and the Soviet Union have improved, do you think the U.S. will assert itself more in international affairs, will assert itself less, or won't make much difference?" The second question changed the wording from "will" to "should" (CBS news poll, October 10, 1991).

7. The question read: "Which of these approaches to foreign policy do you think the U.S. should follow in the 1990s: (1) use its leadership position in the world to help settle international disputes and promote democracy, or (2) reduce its involvement in world politics in order to concentrate on problems at home?" (*Time*-CNN news poll, August 9, 1991).

8. The question read: "Some people say the U.S. should make more active use of its military forces overseas to defend key U.S. interests and to combat terrorism. Others say the U.S. should be more cautious in using military force, to make sure military goals are clearly defined and that actions are supported by the American people. Which comes closer to your view?" (*Los Angeles Times* news poll, March 11, 1991).

9. The question read: "In today's world does the United States have a responsibility to intervene militarily in trouble spots around the world or is that not a responsibility of the United States?" (*New York Times*–CBS news poll, June 1992).

10. In 1986, the CCFR question read: "I am going to read a list of countries. For each, tell me how much of a threat it would be to the U.S. if the Communists came to power. First, what if the Communist party came to power in the Philippines. Do you think this would be a great threat to the U.S., somewhat of a threat to the U.S., not very much of a threat to the U.S., or no threat at all to the U.S.?" In 1990 the CCFR asked, "Would you favor or oppose the use of U.S. troops . . . if the government of the Philippines were threatened by a revolution or civil war?" (CCFR 1986, question 24 and 1990, question 22).

11. The question read: "Which of these two views best describes yours: (A) The United States has sent troops to the Middle East (Persian Gulf) because of the moral principle that we cannot allow Iraq or any other country to invade another, or (B) The United States has sent troops to the Middle East (Persian Gulf) because of the economic reality that we cannot let Iraq or any other country gain too much control over the flow and price of Middle Eastern oil?" (ABC–*Washington Post,* November 30–December 2, 1990; January 20, 1991; March 1–4 1991; from Mueller 1994, 243).

12. The question read: "Which of the following should be among the goals for U.S. forces (in the Middle East crisis) and which should not: (a) rescuing as many hostages as possible, (b) forcing Iraq to leave Kuwait, (c) restoring the former government of Kuwait, (d) destroying Iraq's nuclear and chemical weapons and military capabilities, (e) removing Saddam Hussein's government from power in Iraq?" (Gallup poll, August 23–24, 1990; from Mueller 1994, 246).

13. In 1992 the question read: "Should the U.S. air units participate in U.N. backed air strikes?" (*Newsweek,* poll, September 17, 1992). In 1994, Americans were asked: "Currently, there is some discussion that President Clinton should order U.S. military planes to conduct air strikes against Serbian military positions in Bosnia, along with planes from some Western European countries. Would you favor or oppose such air strikes?" (Moore 1994, 14).

14. The question read: "Regardless of what your current feelings are, if President Clinton and Congress do order air strikes in Bosnia, would you be inclined to support the air strikes or not?" (Moore 1994, 14).

15. The questions were as follows: "Would you favor or oppose the use of U.S. ground troops in order to help keep humanitarian aid flowing to the civilian population in the besieged areas of Bosnia?" (*Los Angeles Times,* poll, August 14, 1992); "Should the U.S. send troops to end the violence in Sarajevo?" (*Time*-CNN, August 20, 1992); "Do you favor or oppose the U.S. sending troops to Yugoslavia to try to stop the civil war there?" (NBC, August 12, 1992).

16. The question read: "Do you favor or oppose sending 28,000 troops to Somalia to help distribute food and medicine?" (Harris poll, December 12, 1992).

17. The question read: "Do you think U.S. troops should stay in Somalia only as long as it takes to set up supply lines to make sure people don't starve, or do you think they should stay there as long as it takes to make sure Somalia will remain peaceful?" (*New York Times*–CBS news poll, December 7–9, 1992).

18. The question read: "In general, do you favor or oppose the U.S. sending troops overseas to save lives and help distribute food in countries where people are starving but where U.S. national security is not involved?" A follow-up question changed the

wording to read "to help restore order and save lives" (Harris poll, December 10, 1992). The other question read: "In today's world, does the United States have a responsibility to intervene militarily in trouble spots around the world or is this not a responsibility of the United States?" (*New York Times*–CBS news poll, October 1992).

19. The question read: "Do you think the U.S. has a responsibility to contribute military troops to enforce peace plans in trouble spots around the world when it is asked by the United Nations, or don't you think the U.S. has that responsibility?" (*Polls in Four Nations 1994*).

20. The *Wall Street Journal*–NBC poll showed that 65 percent of Americans were opposed to a military intervention in Haiti; the *Boston Globe* poll showed that 63 percent of Massachusetts voters were opposed ("Washington Wire" 1994; Pertman 1994).

21. Included among the conditions were whether the UN involvement advanced U.S. interests, whether there was a threat to peace, whether there were clear objectives and the means to accomplish them, whether the consequences of inaction had been considered and deemed unacceptable, and whether the operation's endpoint could be identified and tied to clear objectives. More demanding conditions for consideration included such factors as whether risks to American personnel were considered acceptable and whether domestic and congressional support existed or could be marshaled for the operation (Sloan 1994).

22. The question was as follows: "I will read you a series of suggestions for ways to react to situations like those which we now have in Serbia, Croatia, and Bosnia where, in effect, one country has invaded another. Please say for each if you oppose or support the U.S. to: (1) send UN peacekeeping troops to maintain peace but not fight the aggressor; (2) send UN forces to support the country which is the victim of aggression and to fight and repel the aggressor; (3) send U.S. troops to support the country which is the victim of aggression to fight and repel the aggressor" (Harris poll, August 11, 1992).

23. The question read: "Who is not doing enough in Rwanda?" The African countries? (83 percent responded yes); the United Nations? (68 percent); or the United States? (49 percent) (Reuters, May 4, 1994).

24. The question read: "How long do you think the U.S. troops will have to remain in Somalia—for just a month or two, for three to six months, for six months to one year, or will U.S. troops have to stay in Somalia for a year or more?" (*New York Times*–CBS news poll, December 7–9, 1992).

25. The questions were as follows: "In your view what should the United States do *now* in Somalia: withdraw all U.S. troops now; withdraw U.S. troops gradually; increase the U.S. military commitment, or continue our current policy as before?"; "Overall do you think it was a mistake for the United States to get involved in Somalia in the first place?" (Moore 1993, 24); "As you may know, President Clinton announced he is doubling the number of U.S. troops in Somalia, in order to protect American troops already there and complete the mission by March 31. Do you support the sending of more U.S. troops to Somalia?" (Wheeler and Moore 1993, 27).

26. The questions asked were as follows:

> I am going to mention several reasons that have been offered to explain why the United States should be involved in the Mideast crisis. For each of the following reasons, would you please tell me whether you think it justifies a major war, a limited military involvement but not a major war, or does it not justify U.S. military involvement at all? (1) . . . Do you think the U.S. is justified in get-

ting involved in a major war to protect our oil supplies in the Persian Gulf? . . . (2) . . . What about defending Saudi Arabia from attack by Iraq? . . . (3) . . . What about protecting the lives of American hostages in Kuwait and Iraq? . . . (4) . . . What about helping to restore the previous government of Kuwait? . . . (5) . . . What about the removal of Saddam Hussein from power? . . . (6) . . . Do you think the U.S. is justified in getting involved in a major war in order to neutralize Iraq's army? . . . (7) . . . Do you think the U.S. is justified in getting involved in a major war in order to destroy Iraq's nuclear and chemical weapons facilities does not justify a limited military involvement but not a major war, or wanting to destroy Iraq's nuclear and chemical weapons facilities does not justify a U.S. military involvement at all?" (*Los Angeles Times,* November 14, 1990; from Mueller 1994, 251–53).

27. The questions read as follows: "Would you favor or oppose the United States resuming miliary action against Iraq if Saddam Hussein continues to develop nuclear weapons?" (NBC news poll, July 26–29, 1991); "If Saddam Hussein again fails to comply with United Nations cease-fire resolutions, do you think the United States should . . . take no miliary action, or take military action to force Saddam to comply with the resolutions, or take military action to force Saddam to comply with the resolutions and remove him from power in Iraq?" (Gallup poll, July 31–August 2, 1992 and August 17, 1992); "As you may know, United Nations economic sanctions are in place against Iraq. Some say the economic sanctions should be lifted because they are preventing Iraq from taking care of its people. Others say Iraq can take care of its people well enough and the sanctions should not be lifted while Saddam Hussein remains in power. What do you think—should the sanctions be lifted while Saddam Hussein remains in power or should they be lifted only if he leaves power?" (ABC news poll, July 25–28, 1992; all polls taken from Mueller 1994, 274–75).

28. The question read: "What do you think should be the final objective of the United States in this war: forcing Iraq out of Kuwait, or forcing Iraqi President Saddam Hussein out of power?" (ABC–*Washington Post,* February 22, 1991; from Mueller 1994, 266).

29. The question read: "Do you favor or oppose using military force now to remove Saddam Hussein from power?" (*Time*-CNN poll, August 19–20, 1992; from Mueller 1994, 273).

30. The question read: "In general, who do you think is currently the biggest obstacle to finding a peace settlement in the Arab-Israeli dispute—the Arab nations or Israel?" (NBC–*Wall Street Journal,* July 26–29 and September 20–21, 1991).

31. The question read: "Do you think Israel should or should not give up control of land in the occupied territories of the West Bank, Gaza Strip, and Golan Heights in exchange for a peace agreement with the Arab nations?" (NBC–*Wall Street Journal,* October 10, 1991).

32. The question read: "In the wake of the Gulf War, do you think the U.S. should take the lead in trying to forge and maintain peace and stability in the Middle East or should we not be so involved in this part of the world?" (*Time*-CNN, May 8, 1991).

33. The question read: "Do you think the U.S. should maintain a larger military presence in the Middle East than before the war in order to protect friendly nations and safeguard vital U.S. interests such as oil?" (*Time*-CNN news poll, May 8, 1991).

34. The question read: "If North Korea keeps refusing inspections, should the U.S. take military action to destroy their nuclear facilities?" Forty-six percent responded yes, 40 percent no (*Hotline,* June 8, 1994).

References

ABC. 1994. "Nightline," May 3.

Aberbach, Joel D., and Bert A. Rockman. 1976. "Clashing Beliefs Within the Executive Branch: The Nixon Administration Bureaucracy." *American Political Science Review* 70: 456–68.

"ACDA on the Line." 1993. *The Bulletin of the Atomic Scientists* 49:6.

Allard, Kenneth. 1990. *Command, Control, and the Common Defense.* New Haven: Yale University Press.

Allison, Graham T. 1969. "Conceptual Models and the Cuban Missile Crisis." *American Political Science Review* 63: 689–718.

———. 1971. *Essence of Decision: Explaining the Cuban Missile Crisis.* Boston: Little, Brown.

Allison, Graham T., and Morton H. Halperin. 1972. "Bureaucratic Politics: A Paradigm and Some Policy Implications." In *Theory and Policy in International Relations,* edited by Raymond Tanter and Richard H. Ullman. Princeton: Princeton University Press.

Allison, Graham, and Peter Szanton. 1976. *Remaking Foreign Policy: The Organizational Connection.* New York: Basic Books.

Anderson, Stanton D. 1994. "Why Japan Hates Trade Targets." *Journal of Commerce,* February 28.

Andrew, Christopher. 1995. *For the President's Eyes Only: Secret Intelligence and the American Presidency from Washington to Bush.* New York: Harper Collins.

Angleton, James J. 1976. Interviews with author. Washington, D.C., February 21–22.

"Another Top Navy Official Questions the Merit of Aspin's Base Force Concept." 1992. *Inside the Navy,* March 30.

Apple, R. W. 1995. "Summit in Moscow: The Policy." *New York Times,* May 11.

"Are U.S. Forces Ready to Fight?" 1994. *New York Times,* December 27.

Armacost, Michael H. 1969. *The Politics of Weapons Innovation: The Thor-Jupiter Controversy.* New York: Columbia University Press.

———. 1996. *Friends or Rivals? The Insider's Account of U.S.-Japan Relations.* New York: Columbia University Press.

Art, Robert J. 1968. *The TFX Decision: McNamara and the Military.* Boston: Little, Brown.

———. 1974a. "Bureaucratic Politics and American Foreign Policy: A Critique." *Policy Sciences* 4:467–90.

———. 1974b. "Restructuring the Military-Industrial Complex: Arms Control in an Institutional Perspective." *Public Policy* 22:423–59.

———. 1985a. "Congress and the Defense Budget: Enhancing Policy Oversight." In *Reorganizing America's Defense: Leadership in War and Peace,* edited by Robert J. Art, Vincent Davis, and Samuel P. Huntington. Washington, D.C.: Pergamon-Brassey's.

———. 1985b. "Congress and the Defense Budget: New Procedures and Old Realities." In *Toward a More Effective Defense: Report of the Defense Organization Project,* edited by Barry M. Blechman and William J. Lynn. Cambridge, Mass.: Ballinger.

———. 1985c. "Pentagon Reform in Comparative and Historical Perspective." In *Reorganizing America's Defense: Leadership in War and Peace,* edited by Robert J. Art, Vincent Davis, and Samuel P. Huntington. Washington, D.C.: Pergamon-Brassey's.

———. 1992. *Strategy and Management in the Post–Cold War Pentagon.* Carlisle, Pa.: U.S. Army War College.

ASD/Public Affairs. 1993. "Bottom-Up Review Briefing by SECDEF Aspin and CJCS Powell," September 1.

Aspin, Les. 1973. "Games the Pentagon Plays." *Foreign Policy* 11: 80–92.

———. 1992a. *An Approach to Sizing American Conventional Forces for the Post–Cold War Era: Four Illustrative Options.* Washington, D.C.: House Armed Services Committee, February 25.

———. 1992b. *Continuing the Strategic Drawdown: A Bottom-Up Threat-driven Bill for the Post-Soviet World at the House Budget Level.* Washington, D.C.: House Armed Services Committee, June 1.

———. 1992c. Letter to Leon E. Panetta. February 26. Copy provided by House Armed Services Committee staff.

———. 1992d. *National Security for the 1990s: Defining a New Basis for U.S. Military Forces.* Washington, D.C.: House Armed Services Committee, January 6.

———. 1992e. *Seven Building Blocks of a Threat-based Defense: Supplemental Point Papers.* Washington, D.C.: House Armed Services Committee, June 1.

———. 1993. *Report on the Bottom-Up Review.* Washington, D.C.: U.S. Department of Defense (October).

———. 1994. Interview with author. Washington, D.C., July 8.

"Aspin Plan Would Cut Chance of Decisive Victory in War: Army Chief." 1992. *Aerospace Daily,* March 4.

Auerbach, Stuart. 1987. "Reagan Orders Penalties on Japanese Products." *Washington Post,* March 28.

Auger, Vincent A. 1995. *Human Rights and Trade: The Clinton Administration and China.* Washington, D.C.: Institute for the Study of Diplomacy, Georgetown University.

Bacchus, William I. 1994. *The Price of Policy: Money and Foreign Affairs,* unpublished manuscript.

Bacevich, A. J. 1993. "Clinton's Military Problem—and Ours." *National Review,* December 13.

Baker, James A. 1987. Remarks at a conference sponsored by the Institute for International Economics, Washington, D.C. *Treasury News,* no. B1118.

Baldwin, Robert E. 1979. "Protectionist Pressures in the United States." In *Challenges to a Liberal International Economic Order,* edited by Ryan C. Amacher, Gottfried Haberler, and Thomas D. Willett. Washington, D.C.: American Enterprise Institute.

Barnes, Fred. 1992. "What It Takes." *New Republic,* October 19.

———. 1994. "Saudi Doody." *New Republic,* March 14.

Barone, Michael, and Grant Ujifusa. 1993. *The Almanac of American Politics 1994.* Washington, D.C.: National Journal.

Bauer, Raymond, Ithiel Pool, and Lewis A. Dexter. 1972. *American Business and Public Policy: The Politics of Foreign Trade.* New York: Aldine-Atherton.

Bergsten, C. Fred, and Marcus Noland. 1993. *Reconcilable Differences: United States–Japan Economic Conflict.* Washington, D.C.: Institute for International Economics.

Berkowitz, Bruce D., and Allan E. Goodman. 1989. *Strategic Intelligence for American National Security.* Princeton: Princeton University Press.

Berman, Larry. 1982. *Planning a Tragedy: The Americanization of the War in Vietnam.* New York: Norton.

Berman, Larry, and Emily O. Goldman. 1996. "Clinton's Foreign Policy at Midterm." In *The Clinton Presidency: First Appraisals,* edited by Colin Campbell and Bert A. Rockman. Chatham, N.J.: Chatham House.

Black, Chris. 1991. "Red Army Goes Crimson at Harvard." *Boston Globe,* September 10.

Blackwell, James A., Jr., and Barry M. Blechman. 1990a. *Making Defense Reform Work.* Riverside, N.J.: Brassey's.

———. 1990b. "The Essence of Reform." In *Making Defense Reform Work,* edited by James A. Blackwell Jr. and Barry M. Blechman. Washington, D.C.: Brassey's.

Blechman, Barry M., and Stephen S. Kaplan. 1978. *Force Without War: U.S. Armed Forces as a Political Instrument.* Washington, D.C.: Brookings Institution.

Blechman, Barry M., et al. 1993. *Key West Revisited: Roles and Missions of the U.S. Armed Forces in the Twenty-first Century.* Washington, D.C.: Henry L. Stimson Center.

Boeninger, Edgardo. 1986. "The Chilean Road to Democracy." *Foreign Affairs* 64:812–32.

Bolton, John R. 1994. "Wrong Turn in Somalia." *Foreign Affairs* 73:56–66.

Boltuck, Richard, and Robert E. Litan, eds. 1991. *Down in the Dumps: Administration of the Unfair Trade Laws.* Washington, D.C.: Brookings Institution.

Bonner, Raymond. 1988. *Waltzing with a Dictator.* New York: Vintage.

Bosworth, Barry P., and Robert Z. Lawrence. 1989. "America's Global Role: From Dominance to Interdependence." In *Restructuring American Foreign Policy,* edited by John D. Steinbruner. Washington, D.C.: Brookings Institution.

Bradsher, Keith. 1993. "U.S.-Japan Chip Rift Deepens." *New York Times,* December 28.

Breckinridge, Scott D. 1986. *The CIA and the U.S. Intelligence System.* Boulder, Colo.: Westview Press.

Brugioni, Dino A. 1993. *From Balloons to Blackbirds.* The Intelligence Profession Series no. 9. McLean, Va.: Association of Former Intelligence Officers.

Brzezinski, Zbigniew. 1983a. "Deciding Who Makes Foreign Policy." *New York Times Magazine,* September 18.

———. 1983b. *Power and Principle: Memoirs of the National Security Adviser, 1977–1981.* New York: Farrar, Straus, Giroux.

———. 1987–1988. "NSC's Midlife Crisis." *Foreign Policy* 69: 80–99.

Builder, Carl H. 1989. *Masks of War.* Baltimore: Johns Hopkins University Press.

Burgers, Jan Herman. 1992. "The Road to San Francisco: The Revival of the Human Rights Idea in the Twentieth Century." *Human Rights Quarterly* 14:447–77.

Burke, Joseph. 1990. "U.S. Arms Sales to the Middle East: How and Why." In *Military Assistance and Foreign Policy,* edited by Craig M. Brandt. Wright-Patterson Air Force Base, Ohio: Air Force Institute of Technology.

Burrows, William E. 1986. *Deep Space: Space Espionage and National Security.* New York: Random House.

Bush, George. 1991a. "In Defense of Defense (1990)." In *Annual Report to the President and Congress.* Washington, D.C.: GPO (January).

———. 1991b. *National Security Strategy of the United States.* Washington, D.C.: The White House.

———. 1991c. *Public Papers of the Presidents of the United States: George Bush, 1991.* Book 1. Washington, D.C.: GPO.

———. 1993. *National Security Strategy of the United States.* Washington, D.C.: GPO.

———. 1994. Letter to author. January 23.

Callahan, David. 1992. "The Honest Broker: Brent Scowcroft in the Bush White House." *Foreign Service Journal* 69:27–32.

———. 1993. "The Green Portfolio." *Foreign Service Journal* 70:41–43.

———. 1994. "Reforming Foreign Aid: Will a Revamped AID be Recognizable?" *Foreign Service Journal* 71:18–25.

Calvert, Randy L., Mathew D. McCubbins, and Barry R. Weingast. 1989. "A Theory of Political Control and Agency Discretion." *American Journal of Political Science* 33:588–611.

Campbell, Colin. 1996. "Management in a Sandbox: Why the Clinton White House Failed to Cope With Gridlock." In *The Clinton Presidency: First Appraisals,* edited by Colin Campbell and Bert A. Rockman. Chatham, N.J.: Chatham House.

Campbell, Colin, and Bert A. Rockman, eds. 1991. *The Bush Presidency: First Appraisals.* Chatham, N.J.: Chatham House.

———. 1996. *The Clinton Presidency: First Appraisals.* Chatham, N.J.: Chatham House.

Campbell, Kurt M. 1991. "All Rise for Chairman Powell." *National Interest* 23:51–60.

Cannon, Lou. 1991. *President Reagan: The Role of a Lifetime.* New York: Simon and Schuster.

"Capability Enhancements Key to Win-Win Strategy—Aspin." 1993. *Defense Daily,* September 28.

Caraley, Demetrios. 1962. *The Politics of Military Unification.* New York: Columbia University Press.

Carnegie Endowment for International Peace, and the Institute for International Economics. 1992–1993. "Special Report: Policymaking for a New Era." *Foreign Affairs* 72:175–89.

Carothers, Thomas. 1994. "The NED at 10." *Foreign Policy* 95: 123–38.

Carter, Jimmy. 1982. *Keeping Faith: Memoirs of a President.* Toronto: Bantam Books.

———. 1995. "Open Season on AID." *Washington Post,* January 22.

Cassata, Donna. 1995. "Clinton Accepts Defense Bill in Bid for Bosnia Funds." *Congressional Quarterly Weekly Report* 53: 3672.

Chandler, Clay. 1994. "Clinton's Japan Team Schooled in Hard Knocks." *Washington Post,* February 22.

———. 1995. "Record Sanctions Against Japan Recommended." *Washington Post,* May 7.

"Changes Draw Protests from Pentagon Brass." 1986. *Congressional Quarterly Weekly Report.* 44:573.

Chicago Council on Foreign Relations. 1975. *American Public Opinion and U.S. Foreign Policy.* ICPSR 5808. Ann Arbor: Inter-University Consortium for Political and Social Research.

———. 1979. *American Public Opinion and U.S. Foreign Policy.* General public ICPSR 7748; national leaders ICPSR 7786. Ann Arbor: Inter-University Consortium for Political and Social Research.

———. 1982. *American Public Opinion and U.S. Foreign Policy.* ICPSR 8130. Ann Arbor: Inter-University Consortium for Political and Social Research.

———. 1986. *American Public Opinion and U.S. Foreign Policy.* ICPSR 8712. Ann Arbor: Inter-University Consortium for Political and Social Research.

———. 1990. *American Public Opinion and U.S. Foreign Policy.* ICPSR 9564. Ann Arbor: Inter-University Consortium for Political and Social Research.

———. 1994. *American Public Opinion and U.S. Foreign Policy.* ICPSR 6561. Ann Arbor: Inter-University Consortium for Political and Social Research.

Christopher, Warren. 1993a. "Budget Priorities for Shaping a New Foreign Policy." *U.S. Department of State Dispatch* 4:137–40.

———. 1993b. "Department of State Reorganization." *U.S. Department of State Dispatch* 4:69–73.

———. 1993c. "Statement at Senate Confirmation Hearing." *U.S. Department of State Dispatch* 4:45–49.

CIA deputy director for congressional affairs. 1994. Briefing to the author. April 1.

CIA Officials. 1995. Interviews with author. Langley, Va., July 21.

Clapper, Lt. Gen. James R., Jr. 1995. Luncheon remarks, Association of Former Intelligence Officers (AFIO), reported in John Macartney, "RUMINT and Tidbits." *Intelligencer* (an AFIO newsletter), October 3.

Clarke, Duncan L. 1979. *Politics of Arms Control: The Role and Effectiveness of the U.S. Arms Control and Disarmament Agency.* New York: Free Press.

———. 1987. "Why State Can't Lead." *Foreign Policy* 66: 128–42.

———. 1989. *American Defense and Foreign Policy Institutions: Toward a Sound Foundation.* Cambridge, Mass.: Ballinger.

———. 1994. "The Arrow Missile: The United States, Israel, and Strategic Cooperation." *Middle East Journal* 45:475–91.

Clarke, Duncan L., and Daniel O'Connor. 1993. "U.S. Base-Rights Payments After the Cold War." *Orbis* 37:441–57.

Clarke, Duncan L., and Steven Woehrel. 1991. "Reforming United States Security Assistance." *American University Journal of International Law and Policy* 6:217–49.

Cline, Ray S. 1976. *Secrets, Spies and Scholars.* Washington, D.C.: Acropolis.

Clinton, Bill. 1992a. Address at Georgetown University, excerpted in "Secretary Aspin Announces Bottom Up Review Results," *DOD News Release.* Washington, D.C.: Department of Defense, September 1.

———. 1992b. "In Their Own Words: Transcript of Speech by Clinton Accepting Democratic Nomination." *New York Times,* July 17.

———. 1993a. "Executive Order 12835—Establishment of the National Economic Council." *Weekly Compilation of Presidential Documents* 29:95–96.

———. 1993b. "Organization of the National Security Council." Presidential Decision Document 2, January 20.

———. 1993c. "Strengthening America's Shipyards: A Plan for Competing in the International Market." October 1.

———. 1994. *A National Security Strategy of Engagement and Enlargement.* Washington, D.C.: GPO.

———. 1995. *A National Security Strategy of Engagement and Enlargement.* Washington, D.C.: The White House.

Clinton, Bill, and Al Gore. 1992. *Putting People First: How We Can All Change America.* New York: Times Books.

CNN. 1993. "Larry King Live: A Larry King Special—Perot Debates Gore on NAFTA," November 9.

Cogan, Charles G. 1993a. "The In-Culture of the DO." *Intelligence and National Security* 8:78–86.

———. 1993b. "The New American Intelligence: An Epiphany." Working Paper 3 of the John M. Olin Institute for Strategic Studies Project on the Changing Security Environment and American National Interests. Cambridge: Harvard University Press.

Cohen, Michael D., James G. March, and Johan P. Olsen. 1972. "A Garbage Can Model of Organizational Choice." *Administrative Science Quarterly* 17:1–25.

Cohen, Stephen B. 1982. "Conditioning U.S. Security Assistance on Human Rights Practices." *American Journal on International Law* 76:246–79.

Colby, William E., and Peter Forbath. 1978. *Honorable Men: My Life in the CIA.* New York: Simon and Schuster.

Combest, Larry. 1995. "HPSCI Chairman Combest Outlines Vision for the Future of Intelligence." *What's News at CIA* (CIA internal newsletter), November 13: 1–6 (unclassified).

Commission on Government Renewal. 1992–1993. *Report of the Commission on Government Renewal.* Carnegie Endowment for International Peace.

Commission on the Roles and Capabilities of the United States Intelligence Community (Aspin-Brown Commission). 1996. *Preparing for the 21st Century: An Appraisal of U.S. Intelligence.* Washington, D.C.: GPO.

Condit, Kenneth W. 1979. *The History of the Joint Chiefs of Staff,* vol. 2: *The Joint Chiefs of Staff and National Policy, 1947–1949.* Wilmington, Del.: Glazier.

Congressional Quarterly Almanac. 1985. Washington, D.C.: Congressional Quarterly.

Congressional Record. 1995. December 14.

Conner, William E. 1993. *Intelligence Oversight: The Controversy Behind the FY 1991 Intelligence Authorization Act.* The Intelligence Profession Series, no. 11. McLean, Va.: Association of Former Intelligence Officers.

"Cool Winds from the White House." 1993. *Economist,* March 27.

Cottam, Richard W., and Bert A. Rockman. 1984. "In the Shadow of Substance: Presidents as Foreign Policy Makers." In *American Foreign Policy in an Uncertain World,* edited by David P. Forsythe. Lincoln: University of Nebraska Press.

Council of Economic Advisers. 1996. *Economic Report of the President.* Washington, D.C.: GPO.

Crossette, Barbara. 1992. "NATO Eyes Military Role to Halt Azerbaijani Feud." *New York Times,* March 11.

C-SPAN. 1994. "American Profile: Anthony Lake," June 26.

Cumings, Bruce. 1990. *The Origins of the Korean War.* Vol. 2: *The Roaring of the Cataract, 1947–1950.* Princeton: Princeton University Press.

Cushman, John H., Jr. 1988. "Beyond the Campaign, More Tests Await 'Star Wars.'" *New York Times*, October 16.

———. 1990. "The Planning, Command and Conduct of Military Operations: An Assessment of DoD Performance, 1986–88." In *Making Defense Reform Work*, edited by James A. Blackwell Jr. and Barry M. Blechman. Washington, D.C.: Brassey's.

Cyert, Richard M., and James G. March. 1963. *A Behavioral Theory of the Firm*. Englewood Cliffs, N.J.: Prentice-Hall.

Daalder, Ivo. 1994. "The Clinton Administration and Multilateral Peace Operations." *Pew Case Studies in International Affairs*, no. 462.

Darling, Arthur B. 1990. *The Central Intelligence Agency: An Instrument of Government to 1950*. University Park: Pennsylvania State University Press.

Davies, Lawrence F. 1953. "Security Is Fiscal, Humphrey Asserts." *New York Times*, October 21.

Davis, Bob. 1994. "White House Maintains Its Hard-Line Approach to Japan, Despite Ongoing Political Turmoil." *Wall Street Journal*, April 14.

Davis, Vincent. 1966–1967. *The Politics of Innovation: Patterns in Navy Cases*. Vol. 4. Monograph 3 of the Social Science Foundation and Graduate School of International Studies Monograph Series in World Affairs. Denver: University of Denver.

———. 1967. *The Admiral's Lobby*. Chapel Hill: University of North Carolina Press.

———. 1985. "The Evolution of Central U.S. Defense Management." In *Reorganizing America's Defense: Leadership In War and Peace*, edited by Robert J. Art, Vincent Davis, and Samuel P. Huntington. Washington, D.C.: Pergamon-Brassey's.

———. 1991. "Defense Reorganization and National Security." In *New Direction in U.S. Defense Policy; Annals of the American Academy of Political and Social Science*, edited by Robert L. Pfaltzgraff Jr. 517:157–73.

Deibel, Terry L. 1991. "Bush's Foreign Policy: Mastery and Inaction." *Foreign Policy* 84:3–23.

DeParle, Jason. 1995. "The Man Inside Bill Clinton's Foreign Policy." *New York Times Magazine*, August 20.

Destler, I. M. 1972. *Presidents, Bureaucrats, and Foreign Policy*. Princeton: Princeton University Press.

———. 1980. "A Job That Doesn't Work." *Foreign Policy* 39: 80–88.

———. 1994. "A Government Divided: The Security Complex and the Economic Complex." In *The New Politics of American Foreign Policy*, edited by David A. Deese. New York: St. Martin's.

———. 1995. *American Trade Politics*, 3d ed. Washington, D.C.: Institute for International Economics.

Destler, I. M., Leslie H. Gelb, and Anthony Lake. 1984. *Our Own Worst Enemy*. New York: Simon and Schuster.

Deutch, John M. 1995. Speech, National Press Club, Washington, September 12.

———. 1996a. Memorandum for the President (April 5).

———. 1996b. "C.I.A., Bunker Free, Is Declassifying Secrets." Letter to the Editor, *New York Times*, May 3.

Devroy, Ann. 1993. "Latest White House Reorganization Plan Leaves Some Insiders Skeptical." *Washington Post*, December 12.

———. 1994. "Clinton Seen as Missing an Opportunity on Bosnia." *Washington Post*, February 17.

Dewar, Helen. 1990. "GOP Senators Propose Doubling Bush's Defense Cuts." *Washington Post,* April 6.

Diamond, Larry. 1992. "Promoting Democracy." *Foreign Policy* 87: 25–46.

Dine, Thomas A. 1986. "The Revolution in U.S.-Israel Relations." Typescript.

Directions for Defense: Report of the Commission on Roles and Missions of the Armed Forces. 1995. Washington, D.C.: Department of Defense.

Divine, Robert A. 1981. *Eisenhower and the Cold War.* New York: Oxford University Press.

Dogan, Mattei, ed. 1989. *Pathways to Power: Selecting Rulers in Pluralist Democracies.* Boulder, Colo.: Westview Press.

Doherty, Carroll J. 1993a. "AID Gets Task Force's Support in Long-Delayed Draft Report." *Congressional Quarterly Weekly Report* 51:1892.

———. 1993b. "Tempers Flare Over Plan to Revamp Overseas Broadcasting Programs." *Congressional Quarterly Weekly Report* 51:1890–91.

———. 1994a. "Authorization Bill Urges Clinton to Arm Bosnian Muslims." *Congressional Quarterly Weekly Report* 52: 1011–12.

———. 1994b. "GOP Sharpens Budgetary Knife Over International Programs." *Congressional Quarterly Weekly Report* 52: 3566–69.

———. 1994c. "International Affairs." *Congressional Quarterly Weekly Report* 52:307–08.

———. 1994d. "New Drive to Overhaul Aid Faces Perennial Obstacle." *Congressional Quarterly Weekly Report* 52: 74–76.

———. 1994e. "Stalemate Stalls President's Overhaul of Foreign Aid." *Congressional Quarterly Weekly Report* 52:807–08.

———. 1995a. "Helms Puts His Own Stamp on Cuts Gore Rejected." *Congressional Quarterly Weekly Report* 53:540.

———. 1995b. "Helms Seeks to Cut 3 Agencies, Revamp Aid Redistribution." *Congressional Quarterly Weekly Report* 53: 828.

———. 1995c. "Helms's Reorganization Plan Stymied by Democrats." *Congressional Quarterly Weekly Report* 53:2388.

———. 1995d. "Democratic Unity Stalls GOP Juggernaut." *Congressional Quarterly Weekly Report* 53:1513–16.

———. 1995e. "Panel Adopts Helms' Plan to Kill Three Agencies." *Congressional Quarterly Weekly Report* 53:1437–39.

———. 1995f. "Panel Approves Overhaul Bill." *Congressional Quarterly Weekly Report* 53:1439.

———. 1995g. "Republicans Poised to Slash International Programs." *Congressional Quarterly Weekly Report* 53: 1334–36.

———. 1995h. "Senate Slashes Agency Budgets, Confirms 18 Ambassadors." *Congressional Quarterly Weekly Report* 53: 3821–22.

———. 1996a. "Clinton, with Veto Pen Poised, Gets Agency-Cutback Bill." *Congressional Quarterly Weekly Report* 54: 895.

———. 1996b. "Conferees Agree on Bill to Abolish an Agency." *Congressional Quarterly Weekly Report* 54:634.

———. 1996c. "GOP Not Giving Up on Agency Cuts." *Congressional Quarterly Weekly Report* 54:1059.

Dowd, Maureen. 1990. "Backing Pentagon, Bush Says Military Can Be Cut 25% in 5 Years." *New York Times,* August 3.

Dreifus, Claudia. 1995. "Who's the Enemy Now?" *New York Times Magazine,* May 21.
Drew, Elizabeth. 1994. *On the Edge: The Clinton Presidency.* New York: Simon and Schuster.
Drucker, Peter. 1994. "Trade Lessons from the World Economy." *Foreign Affairs* 71:99–108.
Eisenhower, Dwight D. 1953. *Public Papers of the Presidents of the United States: Dwight D. Eisenhower, 1953.* Washington, D.C.: GPO.
Engelberg, Stephen. 1990. "Pentagon Looks for Ways to Stave Off Budget Cuts." *New York Times,* January 9.
———. 1994. "Spy Agency Under Siege." *New York Times,* December 29.
———. 1995. "How Events Drew U.S. Into Balkans." *New York Times,* August 19.
Engelberg, Stephen, and Alison Mitchell. 1995. "A Seesaw Week for U.S. Policy in the Balkans." *New York Times,* June 5.
Engelberg, Stephen, and Susan F. Rasky. 1988. "Briefing: Secretary's Award." *New York Times,* September 20.
Erlanger, Steven. 1993. "Russia Warns NATO on Expanding East." *New York Times,* November 26.
———. 1994a. "Anti-Western Winds Gain Force in Russia." *New York Times,* April 17.
———. 1994b. "Gore Upbeat After Talks with Top Russian Leaders." *New York Times,* December 17.
———. 1995. "Russia to Activate Role in NATO Partnership." *New York Times,* June 2.
———. 1996a. "Christopher Cautions the Russians on Isolation." *New York Times,* March 21.
———. 1996b. "For Christopher, It's Foreign Policy, Not Politics." *New York Times,* January 8.
———. 1996c. "Russia Wants No Return to Cold War, Offical Says." *New York Times,* February 11.
———. 1996d. "U.S. Won't Punish China Over Sale of Nuclear Gear." *New York Times,* May 11.
"Europe Freed, Radio Signs Off?" 1993. *Economist,* February 27.
Falk, Stanley L. 1988. "The NSC Under Truman and Eisenhower." In *Decisions of the Highest Order,* edited by Karl F. Inderfurth and Loch K. Johnson. Pacific Grove, Calif.: Brooks/Cole.
Fallows, James. 1989. "Containing Japan." *Atlantic Monthly* 263:40–54.
Finnegan, Philip. 1994. "'95 Budget Nears End of Procurement Cuts." *Defense News,* February 14.
Fiorina, Morris P. 1986. "Legislator Uncertainty, Legislative Control, and the Delegation of Legislative Power." *Journal of Law, Economics, and Organization* 2:33–51.
Fisher, Louis. 1988. "The President, the Congress, and Foreign Policy" (book review). *California Law Review* 76:939–60.
Fisher, Marc. 1993. "From Communism to Clinton: U.S. Radio Free Europe Switches to New Focus." *Washington Post,* April 3.
Forbes, Malcolm S., Jr. 1993a. "Murderous Myopia." *Forbes,* June 7.
———. 1993b. "RFE/RL—More Important than Ever." *Forbes,* March 15.
Ford, Harold P. 1993. *Estimative Intelligence,* rev. ed. New York: University Press of America.
"Foreign Aid Spending." 1995a. *Congressional Quarterly Weekly Report* 53:1761.
———. 1995b. *Congressional Quarterly Weekly Report* 53:3316.

"Foreign Aid: Under Siege in the Budget Wars." 1995. *New York Times*, April 30.

Forsythe, David P. 1987. "Congress and Human Rights in U.S. Foreign Policy: The Fate of General Legislation." *Human Rights Quarterly* 9:382–404.

———. 1988. *Human Rights and U.S. Foreign Policy: Congress Reconsidered.* Gainesville: University of Florida Press.

———. 1989a. *Human Rights and U.S. Foreign Policy: Congress Reconsidered.* Gainesville: University of Florida Press.

———. 1989b. *Human Rights and World Politics*, 2nd ed. Lincoln: University of Nebraska Press.

———. 1990. "Human Rights in U.S. Foreign Policy." *Political Science Quarterly* 105:435–54.

———. 1995. "Human Rights and U.S. Foreign Policy: Two Levels, Two Worlds." *Political Studies* 43:111–30.

Fox, J. Ronald. 1974. *Arming America: How the U.S. Buys Weapons.* Cambridge: Harvard University Press.

Friedman, Thomas L. 1993a. "Clinton Keeping Foreign Policy on a Back Burner." *New York Times*, February 8.

———. 1993b. "Clinton Rebuffs Bosnian Leader in Plea for Help." *New York Times*, September 9.

———. 1993c. "Clinton's Foreign Policy: Top Adviser Speaks Up." *New York Times*, October 31.

Frisby, Michael K. 1993a. "At the White House, Titles Offer Few Clues About Real Influence." *Wall Street Journal*, March 26.

———. 1993b. "Clinton Weighs Linking Exports to Foreign Aid." *Wall Street Journal*, September 29.

FRUS, 1948. 1973. See U.S. Department of State. *Papers Relating to the Foreign Relations of the United States, 1948.* Washington, D.C.: GPO.

FRUS, 1952–1954. 1984. See U.S. Department of State. *Papers Relating to the Foreign Relations of the United States, 1952–1954.* Washington, D.C.: GPO.

Fukuyama, Frances. 1989. "The End of History." *National Interest* 16:3–18.

———. 1992. *The End of History and the Last Man.* New York: Free Press.

FY 1995 Defense Budget. 1994. Washington, D.C.: Office of Assistant Secretary of Defense for Public Affairs, February 7.

Gaddis, John Lewis. 1982. *Strategies of Containment: A Critical Appraisal of Postwar American National Security Policy.* New York: Oxford University Press.

———. 1992. "The Cold War, the Long Peace, and the Future." In *The End of the Cold War: Its Meanings and Implications*, ed. Michael J. Hogan. New York: Cambridge University Press.

Gargan, Edward A. 1992. "India Rights Groups Cry: Police Rape and Torture." *New York Times*, October 14.

Garten, Jeffrey E. 1992a. *A Cold Peace: America, Japan, Germany, and the Struggle for Supremacy.* New York: Times Books.

———. 1992b. "White House Renovation." *International Economy* 6:45–47.

Garthoff, Raymond L. 1994. *The Great Transition: American-Soviet Relations and the End of the Cold War.* Washington, D.C.: Brookings Institution.

Gates, Robert M. 1992. Remarks Before the Economic Club of Detroit, Michigan, April 13.

———. 1994. Interview with author. Washington, D.C., March 28.

Gelbspan, Ross, and Jerry Ackerman. 1987. "CIA Waives Secrecy Rule for $1M Harvard Study." *Boston Globe,* December 5.

Gellman, Barton. 1993a. "Defense Budget Passes Despite Warnings of Reduced Readiness." *Washington Post,* November 18.

———. 1993b. "Services Moving to Protect Turf: Powell to Rebuff Call to Streamline." *Washington Post,* January 28.

Gentry, John A. 1993. *Lost Promise: How CIA Analysis Misserves the Nation.* Lanham, Md.: University Press of America.

Gertz, Bill. 1993a. "Gay Ban 'Revolt' Feared." *Washington Times,* January 25.

———. 1993b. "Military Proposal Called Retread." *Washington Times,* September 3.

Gigot, Paul A. 1993. "Clinton Abroad Resembles Bush at Home." *Wall Street Journal,* October 8.

Gillespie, Ed, and Bob Schellhas. 1994. *Contract with America: The Bold Plan by Rep. Newt Gingrich, Rep. Dick Armey and the House Republicans to Change the Nation.* New York: Times Books/Random House.

Gillies, David. 1993. "Human Rights, Governance, and Democracy: The World Bank's Problem Frontiers." *Netherlands Quarterly of Human Rights* 11:3–24.

Ginsberg, Benjamin. 1993. *The Fatal Embrace: Jews and the State.* Chicago: University of Chicago Press.

"GOP Lawmakers Air Their Readiness Concerns in New Newsletter." 1994. *Inside the Army,* 11 April.

Gorbachev, Mikhail S. 1996. "NATO's Plans Threaten Start II." *New York Times,* February 10.

Gordon, Michael R. 1986. "Reagan, the Joint Chiefs of Staff, and Arms Control." *New York Times,* November 3.

———. 1987. "At Foreign Policy Helm: Shultz vs. White House." *New York Times,* August 26.

———. 1988. "U.S. and Soviets to Seek Ways to Avoid Fighting by Mistake." *New York Times,* July 12.

———. 1989. "Bush Is Criticized on Capitol Hill over NATO Dispute." *New York Times,* May 4.

———. 1990. "Pentagon Drafts Strategy for Post-Cold War World." *New York Times,* August 2.

———. 1991a. "Despite Detailed Pentagon Blueprint, Questions on Spending Remain." *New York Times,* February 5.

———. 1991b. "Despite War, Pentagon Plans Big Cuts." *New York Times,* February 3.

———. 1992a. "Report by Powell Challenges Calls to Revise Military." *New York Times,* December 31.

———. 1992b. "Report by Powell Challenges Call to Revise Military." *New York Times,* December 31.

———. 1993a. "Joint Chiefs Curtail Plans for Reducing Duplication." *New York Times,* January 29.

———. 1993b. "Joint Chiefs Warn Congress Against More Military Cuts." *New York Times,* May 20.

———. 1993c. "Military's Plan to Cut Back Is Short of Clinton's Vision." *New York Times,* February 13.

———. 1993d. "A Needless Gift to the Pentagon." *New York Times,* December 27.

———. 1993e. "Pentagon Fights Budget Officials Over $50 Billion." *New York Times,* December 10.

———. 1993f. "Pentagon Seeking to Cut Military But Equip It for 2 Regional Wars." *New York Times,* September 2.

———. 1993g. "Pentagon's Budget Gap Is Narrowed to $31 Billion." *New York Times,* December 18.

———. 1994a. "Navy's Top Admiral Strives to Preserve Size of Fleet." *New York Times,* November 15.

———. 1994b. "U.S. and Bosnia: How a Policy Changed." *New York Times,* December 4.

Gore, Al. 1995. *Common Sense Government.* New York: Random House.

Gorman, Paul F. 1984. "Toward a Stronger Defense Establishment." In *The Defense Reform Debate: Issues and Analysis,* edited by Asa Clark IV, Peter W. Chiarelli, Jeffrey S. McKitrick, and James W. Reed. Baltimore: Johns Hopkins University Press.

Goshko, John M. 1993. "State Department Reorganizes Ranks." *Washington Post,* February 6.

———. 1994a. "Foreign Aid May Be Early Test of New Hill Order." *Washington Post,* November 21.

———. 1994b. "Panel Urges U.S. to Keep Funding Radio, TV Marti Signals to Cuba." *Washington Post,* April 1.

———. 1994c. "USIA: 'I Bureau' Is Recasting the Story for a New Era." *Washington Post,* November 10.

———. 1995. "'Super State Department' May Absorb Other Agencies; Clinton Considers Consolidating AID, ACDA, and USIA." *Washington Post,* January 11.

Graebner, Norman A. 1987. "Tradition, the Founding Fathers, and Foreign Affairs." In *Rhetoric and the Founders,* edited by Dumas Malone et al. Tucson: University Press of Arizona.

Graham, Bradley. 1996. "Panels Challenge Clinton on Defense." *Washington Post,* May 3.

Gray, Jerry. 1996. "State Dept. Budget Is Vetoed; Clinton Protests Planned Cuts." *New York Times,* April 13.

Greenberger, Robert S. 1994. "Cacophony of Voices Drowns Out Message From U.S. to China." *Wall Street Journal,* March 22.

Greenhouse, Steven. 1994a. "Foreign Aid and G.O.P.: Deep Cuts." *New York Times,* December 21.

———. 1994b. "Russia and NATO Agree to Closer Military Links." *New York Times,* June 23.

———. 1994c. "U.S. Seeking to Lift Cloud Over Rapport with Moscow." *New York Times,* December 8.

———. 1995a. "Christopher to Cut Jobs at State Department." *New York Times,* May 7.

———. 1995b. "Clinton to Tell Yeltsin That NATO Is Not Anti-Russian." *New York Times,* March 14.

———. 1995c. "Gore Rules Against Merger of A.I.D. and Others Into State Department." *New York Times,* January 26.

———. 1995d. "Helms Seeks to Merge Foreign Policy Agencies." *New York Times,* March 16.

———. 1995e. "NATO and Russian Officials Meet to Try to Forge Closer Link." *New York Times*, June 1.

Grimmett, Richard F. 1985. "The Role of Security Assistance in Historical Perspective." In *U.S. Security Assistance: The Political Process*, edited by Ernest Graves and Steven A. Hildreth. Lexington, Mass.: Lexington Books.

———. 1995. "Conventional Arms Transfers: President Clinton's Policy Directive." *CRS Report to Congress*. Washington, D.C.: Congressional Research Service.

Grossman, Larry. 1992. "Base Force." *Government Executive*, May.

Gugliotta, Guy. 1994. "Competing Signals Generate Static at Post–Cold War Radio Marti." *Washington Post*, March 23.

Haass, Richard N. 1994. "Military Force: A User's Guide." *Foreign Policy* 96:21–37.

Hadley, Arthur T. 1988. "In Command." *New York Times Magazine*, August 7.

Halloran, Richard. 1986. "Joint Chiefs of Staff Shifting Gears." *New York Times*, December 11.

———. 1987a. "A Russian Marshal Marches into the Pentagon for a Visit." *New York Times*, December 10.

———. 1987b. "Steering an Uncharted Course." *New York Times*, March 2.

Halperin, Morton H. 1974. *Bureaucratic Politics and Foreign Policy*. Washington, D.C.: Brookings Institution.

Halperin, Morton, and Arnold Kanter, eds. 1973. *Readings in American Foreign Policy: A Bureaucratic Perspective*. Boston: Little, Brown.

Hammond, Paul Y. 1961. *Organizing for Defense*. Princeton: Princeton University Press.

———. 1990. "Fulfilling the Promise of the Goldwater-Nichols Act in Operational Planning and Command." In *Making Defense Reform Work*, edited by James A. Blackwell and Barry M. Blechman. Riverside, N.J.: Macmillan-Brassey's.

———. 1992. *L.B.J. and the Presidential Management of Foreign Relations*. Austin: University of Texas Press.

Hansen, Allen C. 1989. *USIA: Public Diplomacy in the Computer Age*, 2nd ed. New York: Praeger.

Harbrecht, Douglas, and Owen Ullmann. 1994. "Tough Talk: Are the U.S. and Japan Headed for a Trade War?" *Business Week* 3360: 26–28.

Harris, Allen G. 1995. "Letter to the Editor." *New York Times*, February 1.

Harris, F. A. "Tex." 1995a. "President's Views: Moving Beyond Stalemate." *Foreign Service Journal* 72:5.

———. 1995b. "President's Views: Navigating on the Road to Nowhere." *Foreign Service Journal* 72:5.

———. 1995c. "President's Views: A Year's Worth of Lessons Learned." *Foreign Service Journal* 72:5.

Harris, John F., and Steven Pearlstein. 1995. "Clinton Chooses Adviser Tyson to Chair National Economic Council." *Washington Post*, February 22.

Harrison, Selig S., and Clyde V. Prestowitz Jr. 1990. "Pacific Agenda: Defense or Economics." *Foreign Policy* 79:56–76.

Hastedt, Glenn P. 1986–1987. "Controlling Intelligence: The Role of the D.C.I." *International Journal of Intelligence and Counterintelligence* 1:25–40.

Hathaway, Dale E. 1987. *Agriculture and the GATT: Rewriting the Rules*. Washington, D.C.: Institute for International Economics.

Havemann, Judith. 1990. "At USIA, The Beef Over the Chief." *Washington Post,* June 8.

Havemann, Judith, and Ann Devroy. 1990. "Two Visit White House Woodshed." *Washington Post,* February 14.

Heaps, David. 1984. *Human Rights and US Foreign Policy: The First Decade 1973–1983.* Report prepared for the American Association for the International Commission of Jurists.

Hedley, John Hollister. 1994. "The CIA's New Openness." *International Journal of Intelligence and Counter-intelligence* 7:129–42.

Heginbotham, Stanley J., and Larry Q. Nowels. 1988. *An Overview of U.S. Foreign Aid Programs.* Washington, D.C.: Congressional Research Service.

Heine, Irwin M. 1980. *The U.S. Maritime Industry: In the National Interest.* Washington, D.C.: National Maritime Council.

Hellinger, Stephen, Douglas Hellinger, and Fred M. O'Regen. 1988. *Aid for Just Development: The Development Gap.* Boulder, Colo.: Lynne Rienner.

Helms, Jesse. 1995. "Christopher Is Right." *Washington Post,* February 14.

Hendrickson, David C. 1988. *Reforming Defense: the State of American Civil-Military Relations.* Baltimore: Johns Hopkins University Press.

———. 1994. "The Recovery of Internationalism." *Foreign Affairs* 73:26–43.

Herring, Richard J., and Robert E. Litan. 1994. *Financial Regulation in the Global Economy.* Washington, D.C.: Brookings Institution.

Hersh, Seymour M. 1994. "Spy vs. Spy." *New Yorker,* August 8.

Heymann, Hans. 1985. "Intelligence/Policy Relationships." In *Intelligence: Policy and Process,* edited by Alfred C. Maurer, Marion D. Tunstall, and James M. Keagle. Boulder, Colo.: Westview Press.

Hilsman, Roger. 1971. *The Politics of Policy Making in Defense and Foreign Affairs.* New York: Harper and Row.

Hilton, Robert P. 1990. "The Role of Joint Military Institutions in Defense Resource Planning." In *Making Defense Reform Work,* edited by James A. Blackwell and Barry M. Blechman. Riverside, N.J.: Macmillan-Brassey's.

Hinckley, Barbara. 1994. *Less Than Meets the Eye: Foreign Policy Making and the Myth of the Assertive Congress.* Chicago: University of Chicago Press.

Hoagland, Jim. 1993. "Flaws and Fissures in Foreign Policy." *Washington Post,* October 31.

Hoffmann, Stanley. 1978. "The Hell of Good Intentions." *Foreign Policy* 29:3–26.

Hogan, Michael J. 1987. *The Marshall Plan: America, Britain, and the Reconstruction of Western Europe, 1947–1952.* New York: Cambridge University Press.

"Holding Up the Process." 1995. *Congressional Quarterly Weekly Report* 53:3552.

Holmes, Steven A. 1993. "State Department Seeks Funds of Other Agencies." *New York Times,* November 11.

Holzer, Robert, and Stephen C. LeSueur. 1994a. "JCS Chairman's Rising Clout Threatens Civilian Leaders." *Defense News,* June 13–19.

———. 1994b. "JCS Quietly Gathers Up Reins of Power." *Defense News,* June 13–19.

Horan, Hume. 1993. "Corporate Cultures in Conflict." *Foreign Service Journal* 70:17–19.

Horne, A. D. 1993. "U.S. to Close 21 Foreign Aid Missions." *Washington Post,* November 20.

Howe, Marvine. 1991. "Group Accuses U.S. of Devaluing Rights in Its Foreign Policy." *New York Times,* December 30.

Hufbauer, Gary C. 1989. "Introduction: Two Challenges." In *The Free Trade Debate: Report of the Twentieth Century Fund Task Force on the Future of American Trade Policy.* New York: Priority Press Publications.

Hufbauer, Gary C., Diane T. Berlinger, and Kimberly A. Elliott. 1986. *Trade Protection in the United States.* Washington, D.C.: Institute for International Economics.

"Huge Defense Cut Rolling in Congress Despite Bush, Pentagon Opposition." 1992. *Journal of Commerce,* March 4.

Hughes, Emmet John. 1963. *The Ordeal of Power: A Political Memoir of the Eisenhower Years.* New York: Atheneum.

Hulnick, Arthur S. 1991. "Controlling Intelligence Estimates." In *Controlling Intelligence,* edited by Glenn P. Hastedt. Portland, Ore.: Frank Cass.

Hunter, Robert E. 1982. *Presidential Control of Foreign Policy.* The Washington Papers, 91. New York: Praeger.

Huntington, Samuel P. 1988. "Defense Organization and Military Strategy." In *Bureaucratic Politics and National Security,* edited by David C. Kozak and James M. Keagle. Boulder, Colo.: Lynne Rienner.

———. 1993a. "The Clash of Civilizations?" *Foreign Affairs* 72:22–49.

———. 1993b. "New Contingencies, Old Roles." *Joint Force Quarterly* 1:2.

———. 1993c. "Why International Primacy Matters." *International Security* 17:68–83.

———. 1994. In "An Exchange on Civil-Military Relations,"*National Interest,* 36:27-29.

Ifill, Gwen. 1992. "Clinton to Summon Economic Leaders to Set Priorities." *New York Times,* November 9.

———. 1993a. "The Economic Czar Behind the Economic Czars." *New York Times,* March 7.

———. 1993b. "Security Official Guides U.S. Aims at Conference." *New York Times,* July 5.

Ignatius, David. 1994. "The Curse of the Merit Class." *Washington Post,* February 27.

Inderfurth, Karl F., and Loch K. Johnson. 1988. *Decisions of the Highest Order: Perspectives on the National Security Council.* Pacific Grove, Calif.: Brooks Cole.

Irwin, Douglas A. 1994. *Managed Trade: The Case Against Import Targets.* Washington, D.C.: American Enterprise Institute.

Jacoby, Tamar. 1986. "Reagan's Turnaround on Human Rights." *Foreign Affairs* 64:1066–86.

Jaffe, Lorna S. 1993. *The Development of the Base Force 1989–1992.* Office of the Chairman of the Joint Chiefs of Staff, Joint History Office. Washington, D.C.: GPO.

"The Jane's Interview." 1993. *Jane's Defense Weekly,* July 23.

Jeffreys-Jones, Rhodri. 1989. *The CIA and American Democracy.* New Haven: Yale University Press.

Jehl, Douglas. 1993. "C.I.A. Nominee Wary of Budget Cuts." *New York Times,* February 3.

———. 1995. "Summit Meeting in Moscow." *New York Times,* May 6.

Jentleson, Bruce W. 1990. "American Diplomacy: Around the World and Along Pennsylvania Avenue." In *A Question of Balance: The President, the Congress, and Foreign Policy,* edited by Thomas E. Mann. Washington, D.C.: Brookings Institution.

———. 1992. "The Pretty Prudent Public: Post Post-Vietnam American Opinion on the Use of Military Force." *International Studies Quarterly* 36:49–74.

Jentleson, Bruce, and Rebecca Britton. 1996. "Still Pretty Prudent: Post-Cold War

American Public Opinion on the Use of Military Force." Paper presented at the National Convention of the International Studies Association in San Diego.

Jervis, Robert. 1989. *The Meaning of the Nuclear Revolution: Statecraft and the Prospect of Armageddon.* Ithaca: Cornell University Press.

Johnson, Loch K. 1980. "Congress and the CIA: Monitoring the Dark Side of Government." *Legislative Studies Quarterly* 5: 477–99.

———. 1985. *A Season of Inquiry: Congress and Intelligence.* Lexington: University Press of Kentucky.

———. 1989. *America's Secret Power: The CIA in a Democratic Society.* New York: Oxford University Press.

———. 1992. "On Drawing a Bright Line for Covert Operations." *American Journal of International Law* 86:284–309.

———. 1992–1993. "Smart Intelligence." *Foreign Policy* 89: 53–79.

———. 1996. *Secret Agencies: U.S. Intelligence in a Hostile World.* New Haven: Yale University Press.

Jones, David C. 1984. "What's Wrong with the Defense Establishment." In *The Defense Reform Debate: Issues and Analysis,* edited by Asa A. Clark IV, Peter W. Chiarelli, Jeffery S. McKitrick, and James W. Reed. Baltimore: Johns Hopkins University Press.

Judis, John B. 1993. "The Foreign Unpolicy." *New Republic,* July 12.

Kaiser, Frederick M. 1994. "Impact and Implications of the Iran-Contra Affair on Congressional Oversight of Covert Action." *International Journal of Intelligence and Counterintelligence* 7:205–34.

Kamen, Al. 1993a. "The New Regime: Arms Control Agency Languishes in Limbo." *Washington Post,* February 11.

———. 1993b. "Quayle Takes to the Reporter's Life." *Washington Post,* October 4.

———. 1993c. "Recycling Begins on Administration Jobs." *Washington Post,* November 12.

———. 1994a. "In the Loop." *Washington Post,* June 1.

———. 1994b. "In the Loop: Accord Near on Stationery Control." *Washington Post,* July 12.

———. 1994c. "In the Loop: Pete Wilson Rides the River." *Washington Post,* May 2.

Kamen, Al, and Thomas Lippman. 1993. "Task Force Favors Restructuring and Refocusing Troubled AID." *Washington Post,* July 3.

Kanter, Arnold. 1979. *Defense Politics.* Chicago: University of Chicago Press.

Kaplan, Lawrence S. 1988. *NATO and the United States: The Enduring Alliance.* Boston: Twayne.

Karalekas, Anne. 1976. "History of the Central Intelligence Agency." In *Supplementary Detailed Staff Reports on Foreign and Military Intelligence,* U.S. Senate Select Committee to Study Governmental Operations with Respect to Intelligence Activities (Church Committee), Final Report, Book 4 (Senate Rept. no. 94–755), 94th Cong., 2nd sess.

Karatnycky, Adrian. 1994. "Russia's Nuclear Grasp." *New York Times,* August 30.

Kaufman, Burton I. 1991. *The Presidency of James Earl Carter, Jr.* Lawrence: University of Kansas Press.

Kehoe, Mark T. 1996a. "Brown Commission Shies Away from Radical Suggestions." *Congressional Quarterly Weekly Report* 54: 1477.

———. 1996b. "House Passes Bill to Protect Spy Agencies from Cuts." *Congressional Quarterly Weekly Report* 54:1477.

Kempe, Lawrence. 1991. "NATO Leaders Prepare to Expand Ties to Ex-Warsaw Pact Countries." *Wall Street Journal,* November 4.

Kennedy, Paul. 1991. "Grand Strategy in War and Peace: Toward a Broader Definition." In *Grand Strategies in War and Peace,* edited by Paul Kennedy. New Haven: Yale University Press.

Keohane, Robert O. 1982. "Hegemonic Leadership and U.S. Foreign Economic Policy in the 'Long Decade' of the 1950s." In *America in a Changing World Political Economy,* edited by William P. Avery and David P. Rapkin. White Plains, N.Y.: Longman.

———. 1984. *After Hegemony: Cooperation and Discord in the World Political Economy.* Princeton: Princeton University Press.

"The Keys to the Spy Kingdom." 1996. *New York Times,* May 19.

Kinzer, Stephen. 1984. "Sandinistas' Foes Give Up a Demand." *New York Times,* August 16.

Kirkpatrick, Jeane J. 1979. "Dictatorships and Double Standards." *Commentary* 68:34–45.

———. 1993. "Needed Then, Needed Now." *Washington Post,* March 8.

Kirschten, Dick. 1993a. "Overhaul Overdue!" *National Journal* 25: 1165–68.

———. 1993b. "Radio Wars." *National Journal* 25:865–67.

———. 1993c. "Rescuing AID." *National Journal* 25:2369–72.

———. 1993d. "To Arms!" *National Journal* 25:1016.

———. 1994a. "Arms and the Man." *National Journal* 26: 235–37.

———. 1994b. "Martyr or Misfit." *National Journal* 26:2502–06.

———. 1994c. "Mensch on the Move." *National Journal* 26: 2971–73.

———. 1994d. "Mitch, Dick Want to Be Heard, Too." *National Journal* 26:2974–75.

———. 1995a. "Helms's Helpers." *National Journal* 27:952.

———. 1995b. "Restive Relic." *National Journal* 27:976–80.

———. 1995c. "USS Foggy Bottom's No Happy Ship." *National Journal* 27:197.

———. 1995d. "Where's the Bite?" *National Journal* 27: 739–42.

Kohler, Robert. 1994. "The Intelligence Industrial Base: Doomed to Extinction?" Monograph. Working Group on Intelligence Reform, Washington: 1–22.

Kohn, Richard H. 1994. "Out of Control: The Crisis in Civil-Military Relations." *National Interest* 35:3–17.

Komer, Robert W. 1985. "Strategymaking in the Pentagon." In *Reorganizing America's Defense: Leadership in War and Peace,* edited by Robert J. Art, Vincent Davis, and Samuel P. Huntington. Washington, D.C.: Pergamon-Brassey's.

Korb, Lawrence J. 1994. "Shock Therapy for the Pentagon." *New York Times,* February 15.

———. 1995a. "The Cold War Ended, But the Spending Didn't." *Baltimore Sun,* July 20.

———. 1995b. "The Readiness Gap. What Gap?" *New York Times Magazine,* February 16.

———. 1995c. "The Two-War Fantasy." *New York Times,* February 5.

———. 1996. "Our Overstuffed Armed Forces." *Foreign Affairs* 74:22–34.

Korologos, Tom C. 1992. "Getting the Message to China." *Washington Post,* July 25.

Krebsbach, Karen. 1995. "The Consolidation Game." *Foreign Service Journal* 72:36–45.

Krepinevich, Andrew F. 1994. *The Bottom-Up Review: An Assessment.* Washington, D.C.: Defense Budget Project.

Krepon, Michael, Amey E. Smithson, and James A. Schear. 1992. *The U.S. Arms Control and Disarmament Agency: Restructuring for the Post–Cold War Era.* Washington, D.C.: Henry L. Stimson Center.

Kristof, Nicholas D. 1993. "Clinton Aide Ends China Trip With No Sign of Accord." *New York Times,* May 13.

Krugman, Paul R. 1994. *Peddling Prosperity: Economic Sense and Nonsense in the Age of Diminished Expectations.* New York: W. W. Norton.

Krugman, Paul R., and Robert Z. Lawrence. 1994. "Trade, Jobs and Wages." *Scientific American* 270, 4:44–49.

Kull, Steven. 1995. *Americans and Foreign Aid: A Study of American Public Attitudes.* Program on International Policy Attitudes. College Park: University of Maryland.

———. 1995–1996. "What the Public Knows That Washington Doesn't." *Foreign Policy* 101:102–15.

Laird, Sam, and Alexander Yeats. 1988. *Quantitative Methods for Trade Barrier Analysis.* World Bank.

Lake, Anthony. 1993. "From Containment to Enlargement." *U.S. State Department Dispatch* 4:658–64.

———. 1994. "The Reach of Democracy; Tying Power to Diplomacy." *New York Times,* September 23.

———. 1995a. Address before the National Press Club. Washington, D.C. Typescript.

———. 1995b. "The Price of Leadership." *U.S. State Department Dispatch* 6:388–91.

———. 1996. "Defining Missions, Setting Deadlines: Meeting New Security Challenges in the Post–Cold War World." *U.S. State Department Dispatch* 7:127–30.

Lancaster, John. 1993a. "Army Challenges Clinton Defense Cuts as Security Threat." *Washington Post,* March 9.

———. 1993b. "Aspin Opts for Winning 2 Wars—1 1/2—At Once." *Washington Post,* June 25.

———. 1993c. "Military Plan Is Short of Clinton Goals." *Washington Post,* February 13.

Lancaster, John, and Barton Gellman. 1994. "National Security Strategy Paper Arouses Pentagon, State Dept. Debate." *Washington Post,* March 3.

Laqueur, Walter. 1994. "Save Public Diplomacy." *Foreign Affairs* 73:19–24.

Latham, Scott. 1994. "Poor, Poor Motorola." *Wall Street Journal,* March 3.

Lawrence, Robert Z., and Mathew J. Slaughter. 1993. "International Trade and American Wages in the 1980s: Giant Sucking Sound or Small Hiccup?" *Brookings Papers on Economic Activity.* Washington, D.C.: Brookings Institution.

Leffler, Melvyn P. 1992. *A Preponderance of Power: National Security, the Truman Administration, and the Cold War.* Stanford: Stanford University Press.

Lehman, John. 1994. "An Exchange on Civil-Military Relations." *National Interest* 36:23–31.

Levine, Charles H. 1978. "Organizational Decline and Cutback Management." *Public Administration Review* 38:316–25.

———. 1980. "Organizational Decline and Cutback Management." In *Managing Fiscal Stress: The Crisis in the Public Sector,* edited by Charles H. Levine. Chatham, N.J.: Chatham House.

Levy, Amir. 1986. "Second Order Planned Change: Definition and Conceptualization." *Organizational Dynamics* 15:5–23.

Lewis, Anthony. 1996. "Abroad at Home: The Defense Anomaly." *New York Times*, January 22.

Lewis, Neil A. 1995. "Helms, After Winning Leaner Foreign Policy, Clears Way to Approve Ambassadors." *New York Times*, December 9.

Lewis, Paul. 1990. "Move by UN Chief on Cuba Irks U.S." *New York Times*, January 30.

———. 1991. "Iraq's Moves to Meet Conditions for Truce Termed Insufficient." *New York Times*, March 6.

Liddell Hart, B. H. 1967. *Strategy*, 2nd rev. ed. New York: Praeger.

Lindsay, James M. 1991. *Congress and Nuclear Weapons*. Baltimore: Johns Hopkins University Press.

———. 1994a. *Congress and the Politics of U.S. Foreign Policy*. Baltimore: Johns Hopkins University Press.

———. 1994b. "Congress, Foreign Policy, and the New Institutionalism." *International Studies Quarterly* 38: 281–304.

Lippman, Thomas W. 1993a. "Christopher Lobbying for $3 Billion More in Foreign Aid." *Washington Post*, December 17.

———. 1993b. "U.S. Foreign Aid Overhaul Urged; Goals, Not Nations, Would Be Funded." *Washington Post*, September 18.

———. 1994a. "One Year After Starting Work, Wirth Close to Getting the Job." *Washington Post*, April 26.

———. 1994b. "State—With Wirth in Position, Old Lines Lose Weight." *Washington Post*, June 30.

———. 1995. "Entrenched Constituencies Help Kill Merger." *Washington Post*, February 3.

———. 1995. *U.S. Intelligence Community: A Bibliography*. New York: Garland.

Lowenthal, Mark M. 1992. "Tribal Tongues: Intelligence Consumers, Intelligence Producers." *Washington Quarterly* 15:157–72.

———. 1994. *U.S. Intelligence Community: A Bibliography*. New York: Garland.

Lowi, Theodore. 1967. "Making Democracy Safe for the World: National Politics and Foreign Policy." In *Domestic Sources of Foreign Policy*, edited by James N. Rosenau. New York: The Free Press.

Lucas, William A., and Raymond H. Dawson. 1974. *The Organizational Politics of Defense*. Pittsburgh, Pa.: International Studies Association.

Lumpe, Lora. 1995. "Clinton's Conventional Arms Export Policy: So Little Change." *Arms Control Today* 25:9–14.

Lundberg, Kirsten. 1994. "CIA and the Fall of the Soviet Empire: The Politics of 'Getting It Right.'" Kennedy School of Government Case Program C16-94-1251-0. Cambridge: Harvard University.

Luttwak, Edward N. 1993. *The Endangered American Dream*. New York: Simon and Schuster.

McAllister, Bill. 1991. "Turning Down the Volume on USIA." *Washington Post*, June 13.

McCubbins, Mathew, Roger Noll, and Barry Weingast. 1987. "Administrative Procedures as Instruments of Political Control." *Journal of Law, Economics, and Organization* 3: 243–77.

———. 1989. "Structure and Process, Politics and Policy: Administrative Arrangements and Political Control of Agencies." *Virginia Law Review* 75:431–82.

MacEachin, Douglas J. 1994. "The Tradecraft of Analysis: Challenge and Change in the CIA." Working Group on Intelligence Reform Papers. Washington, D.C.: Consortium for the Study of Intelligence.

McFarlane, Robert C. 1994. *Special Trust.* New York: Cadell and Davies.

Madison, Christopher. 1992a. "Agency in Agony." *National Journal* 24:2667–71.

———. 1992b. "Help for AID May Have to Wait a Bit." *National Journal* 24: 1001–02.

Maechling, Charles, Jr. 1983. "Human Rights Dehumanized." *Foreign Policy* 52:118–35.

Mandelbaum, Michael. 1994. "The Reluctance to Intervene." *Foreign Policy* 95:3–18.

Manget, Frederick F. 1995. "Intelligence and the Rise of Judicial Intervention." *Conflict Quarterly.*

Mangold, Tom. 1991. *Cold Warrior.* New York: Simon and Schuster.

March, James G. 1981. "Footnotes to Organizational Change." *Administrative Science Quarterly* 26:563–77.

March, James G., and Johan P. Olsen. 1984. "The New Institutionalism: Organizational Factors in Political Life." *American Political Science Review* 78:734–49.

———. 1989. *Rediscovering Institutions: The Organizational Basis of Politics.* New York: Free Press.

Marchetti, Victor L., and John D. Marks. 1974. *The CIA and the Cult of Intelligence.* New York: Knopf.

Mark, Clyde R. 1995. "Israel: U.S. Foreign Assistance Facts." Washington, D.C.: Congressional Research Service.

May, Ernest. 1992. "The U.S. Government, a Legacy of the Cold War." In *The End of the Cold War,* edited by Michael J. Hogan. New York: Cambridge University Press.

Maynard, Edwin S. 1988. *Bureaucracy and Diplomacy.* Project Series on Human Rights and U.S. Foreign Policy no. 4, published by the Lawyers Committee for Human Rights.

———. 1989. "The Bureaucracy and Implementation of US Human Rights Policy." *Human Rights Quarterly* 11:175–248.

Maze, Rick. 1992. "DoD: Personnel Would Take Brunt of Cuts." *Air Force Times,* March 23.

Means, Howard. 1992. *Colin Powell: A Biography.* New York: Ballantine.

Meier, Gerald. 1973. *Problems of Trade Policy.* New York: Oxford University Press.

Mendelsohn, Jack. 1992. "Studies Offer Alternative Futures for U.S. Arms Control Agency." *Arms Control Today* 22:23, 29.

Meyer, Alan D., James B. Goes, and Geoffrey R. Brooks. 1993. "Organizations Reacting to Hyperturbulence." In *Organizational Change and Redesign,* edited by George P. Huber and William H. Glick. New York: Oxford University Press.

Migranyan, Andranik. 1994. "Unequal Partnership." *New York Times,* June 23.

Mintz, John. 1995. "Lockheed Martin Works to Save Its Older Spies in the Skies." *Washington Post,* November 28.

Mitchell, Alison. 1995. "Panetta's Sure Step in High-Wire Job." *New York Times,* August 17.

Moe, Terry M. 1993. "Presidents, Institutions, and Theory." In *Researching the Presidency: Vital Questions, New Approaches,* edited by George C. Edwards III, John H. Kessel, and Bert A. Rockman. Pittsburgh: University of Pittsburgh Press.

Mohr, Charles. 1984. "U.S. Says Uganda Rights Abuses Are Among Most Grave in World." *New York Times,* August 10.

Mohrman, Allan M., Jr., Susan Albers Mohrman, Gerald E. Ledford Jr., Thomas G. Cummings, Edward E. Lawler III, and Associates. 1989. *Large-Scale Organizational Change.* San Francisco: Jossey-Bass.

Moore, David W. 1993. "Public: 'Get Out of Somalia.'" *Gallup Poll Monthly* 337:23–24.

———. 1994. "Americans Split Over Air Strikes in Bosnia." *Gallup Poll Monthly* 341:13–15.

"More Is the Pity at the Pentagon." 1994. *New York Times,* February 9.

Morin, Richard. 1994. "Support for Sending GIs to Haiti May Be Increasing Polls Show." *Washington Post,* June 29.

Morrison, David C. 1995. "Fending Off Bureaucratic Sniper Fire." *National Journal* 27:698.

Moynihan, Daniel P. 1991. "Do We Still Need the CIA? The State Department Can Do the Job." *New York Times,* May 19.

Mueller, John. 1994. *Policy and Opinion in the Gulf War.* Chicago: University of Chicago Press.

———. 1996. "Fifteen Propositions About American Foreign Policy and Public Opinion in an Era Free of Compelling Threats." Paper presented at the National Convention of the International Studies Association, San Diego.

Murdock, Clark. 1974. *Defense Policy Formation: A Comparative Analysis of the McNamara Era.* Albany: State University of New York Press.

National Public Radio. 1994. "All Things Considered," September 22.

Nau, Henry R. 1995. *Trade and Security: U.S. Policies at Cross-Purposes.* Washington, D.C.: AEI Press.

"NEC Seeks to Highlight Trade in U.S. Foreign Policy, Official Says." 1993. *Inside U.S. Trade,* April 30.

Nelson, Joan M., and Stephanie J. Eglinton. 1993. "The International Donor Community: Conditioned Aid and the Promotion and Defence of Democracy." Photocopy, read by permission.

Neustadt, Richard E. 1990. *Presidential Power and the Modern Presidents: The Politics of Leadership from Roosevelt to Reagan.* New York: Free Press.

Newsom, David D. 1993. "The Clinton Administration and the Foreign Service." *Foreign Service Journal* 70:24–27.

Nivola, Pietro S. 1991. "More Like Them? The Political Feasibility of Strategic Trade Policy." *Brookings Review* 9:14–21.

———. 1993. *Regulating Unfair Trade.* Washington, D.C.: Brookings Institution.

Nixon, Richard M. 1970. "U.S. Foreign Policy for the 1970s: Strategy for Peace." *Department of State Bulletin* 62: 292–96.

Nolan, Cathal J. 1993. *Principled Diplomacy: Security and Rights in U.S. Foreign Policy.* Westport, Conn.: Greenwood.

Norowjee, Eruch. 1992. "Kenya: Political Pluralism, Government Resistance, and United Nations Responses." *Harvard Human Rights Journal* 5:149–62.

Nothdruft, William E. 1993. *Going Global: How Europe Helps Small Firms Export.* Washington, D.C.: Brookings Institution.

Novak, Michael. 1993a. "The Prague Option." *Forbes,* December 20.

———. 1993b. "The Truth Weapon." *Forbes,* March 15.

Nowels, Larry Q. 1987. "Economic Security Assistance as a Tool of American Foreign Policy." Research Report. Washington, D.C.: National War College.

———. 1989. "An Overview of the Economic Support Fund." In *Background Materials on Foreign Assistance.* U.S. Congress, House Committee on Foreign Affairs, 101st Cong., 1st sess. Rpt. 94-080.

———. 1990. *Foreign Assistance: Congressional Initiatives to Reform U.S. Foreign Aid in 1989.* Washington, D.C.: Congressional Research Service.

———. 1992. *Foreign Assistance and Congressional Debate: International Challenges, Domestic Concerns, Decisions Deferred.* Washington, D.C.: Congressional Research Service.

———. 1993. "Foreign Aid: Clinton Administration's Policy and Budget Reform Proposals." *CRS Issue Brief.* Washington, D.C.: Congressional Research Service.

———. 1994. *Foreign Aid Reform Legislation: Background, Contents and Issues.* Washington, D.C.: Congressional Research Service.

———. 1995. "Foreign Aid Budget and Policy Issues for the 104th Congress." Washington, D.C.: Congressioal Research Service.

Nowels, Larry Q., and Ellen Collier. 1991. *Foreign Policy Budget: Issues and Priorities for the 1990s.* Washington, D.C.: Congressional Research Service.

Nowels, Larry Q., and Clyde R. Mark. 1994. "Israel's Request for U.S. Loan Guarantees." *CRS Issue Brief.* Washington, D.C.: Congressional Research Service.

Nunn, Sam. 1990a. "The Changed Threat Environment of the 1990's." *Congressional Record,* March 29, S3444–51.

———. 1990b. "Defense Budget Blanks." *Congressional Record,* March 22, S2965–70.

———. 1990c. "A New Military Strategy." *Congressional Record,* April 19, S4449–45.

———. 1993a. *Domestic Missions for the Armed Forces.* Carlisle, Pa.: U.S. Army War College.

———. 1993b. "NATO and the Successors of the Soviet Empire." *Washington Post,* December 26.

Nye, Joseph S., Jr. 1990. *Bound to Lead: The Changing Nature of American Power.* New York: Basic Books.

Oberdorfer, Don. 1992. "'Isolated AID Should Be Merged with State Department, Study Panel Say." *Washington Post,* March 3.

Oberdorfer, Don, and Bill McAllister. 1992. "SWAT Team Formed to Study AID." *Washington Post,* January 28.

Obey, David, and Carol Lancaster. 1988. "Funding Foreign Aid." *Foreign Policy* 71:141–55.

Odeen, Philip A. 1980. "Organizing for National Security." *International Security* 5:111–29.

———. 1985. "The Role of the National Security Council in Coordinating and Integrating U.S. Defense and Foreign Policy." In *Public Policy and Political Institutions: United States Defense and Foreign Policy—Policy Coordination and Integration,* edited by Duncan L. Clarke. Greenwich, Conn.: Jai Press.

Olmsted, Kathryn S. 1996. *Challenging the Secret Government: The Post-Watergate Investigations of the CIA and FBI.* Chapel Hill: University of North Carolina Press.

Omang, Joanne. 1984. "U.S. Offical Charges 'Apologists' Are Ignoring Cuba's Rights Abuses." *Washington Post,* August 24.

"Opinion Outlook." 1995a. *National Journal* 27:642.

"Opinion Outlook." 1995b. *National Journal* 27:2121.

"Opinion Outlook." 1995c. *National Journal* 27:3174.

"Opinion Outlook." 1996. *National Journal* 28:220.

Ott, Marvin. 1993–1994. "Shaking Up the CIA." *Foreign Policy* 93:132–51.

Owens, William A. 1994. "JROC: Harnessing the Revolution in Military Affairs." *Joint Forces Quarterly* 4:55–58.

Paarlberg, Robert L. 1995. *Leadership Abroad Begins at Home: U.S. Foreign Economic Policy After the Cold War.* Washington, D.C.: Brookings Institution.

Palmer, Elizabeth. 1994. "Detente Sought in Senators' War Over Radio Services' Future." *Congressional Quarterly Weekly Report* 52:127–29.

Passell, Peter. 1990. "Apparel Makers' Last Stand?" *New York Times,* September 26.

Pastor, Robert A. 1980. *Congress and the Politics of U.S. Foreign Economic Policy, 1929–1976.* Berkeley: University of California Press.

———. 1992. "George Bush and Latin America." In *Eagle in a New World,* edited by Robert Oye et al. New York: Harper Collins.

Pear, Robert. 1989. "Contra Tribunal Says 6 Guerrillas Committed Serious Rights Abuses." *New York Times,* March 27.

———. 1995. "Imperiled Agencies Mount Life-Saving Efforts." *New York Times,* May 21.

Pease, Kelly Kate, and David P. Forsythe. 1993. "Human Rights, Humanitarian Intervention, and World Politics." *Human Rights Quarterly* 15:290–314.

"The Pentagon Jackpot." 1995. *New York Times,* July 10.

Perry, Mark. 1992. *Eclipse: The Last Days of the CIA.* New York: William Morrow.

Pertman, Adam. 1994. "Survey of Massachusetts Voters Finds 63 Percent Reject Military Action in Haiti." *Boston Globe,* May 15.

Peterson, Paul E., ed. 1994. *The President, the Congress, and the Making of Foreign Policy.* Norman: University of Oklahoma Press.

"The Peterson Report: Rationale of the New Economic Policy." 1971. *National Journal,* November 13.

Pincus, Walter. 1996. "Relaxed CA Covert Action Rules Urged." *Washington Post,* January 30.

Pine, Art. 1994a. "Clinton Unveils Long-Awaited Security Strategy." *Los Angeles Times,* July 22.

———. 1994b. "U.S. Dilemma: Is Korea Dispute Reason for War?" *Los Angeles Times,* June 12.

———. 1995. "Wishing for a War Without Blood." *Los Angeles Times,* December 13.

"Plan Would Shuffle Broadcast Services." 1993. *Congressional Quarterly Weekly Report* 51:1588.

Poe, Steven, et al. 1994. "Human Rights and US Foreign Aid Revisited: The Latin American Region." *Human Rights Quarterly* 16:539–58.

Pollack, Andrew. 1995. "U.S. Trade Negotiator Urges Shift in Approach on Japan." *New York Times,* August 1.

Posz, Gary, Bruce Janigian, and Jong Jun. 1994. "Redesigning U.S. Foreign Aid." *SAIS Review* 14:159–69.

Powell, Colin L. 1990. *Remarks to the Armed Forces Communications and Electronics Association.* Washington, D.C.: Department of Defense.

———. 1993a. *Report on the Roles, Missions, and Functions of the Armed Forces of the United States.* Washington, D.C.: Joint Chiefs of Staff.

———. 1993b. "U.S. Forces: Challenges Ahead." *Foreign Affairs* 72:32–45.

———. 1995. *My American Journey.* New York: Random House.

Powell, Colin, John Lehman, William Odom, Samuel Huntington, and Richard Kohn. 1994. "An Exchange on Civil-Military Relations." *National Interest* 36:21–31.

Powers, Thomas. 1979. *The Man Who Kept the Secrets: Richard Helms and the CIA.* New York: Knopf.

Prados, John. 1986. *President's Secret Wars: CIA and Pentagon Covert Operations Since World War II.* New York: William Morrow.

Priest, Dana. 1992a. "For Voice of America, a Benchmark and a Changing World." *Washington Post,* February 24.

———. 1992b. "Major Revamping of AID Urged by Presidential Commission." *Washington Post,* April 17.

Pringle, Robert. 1977–1978. "Creeping Irrelevance at Foggy Bottom." *Foreign Policy* 29:128–39.

Puschel, Karen L. 1992. *US-Israeli Strategic Cooperation in the Post–Cold War Era: An American Perspective.* Boulder, Colo.: Westview Press.

Quinn-Judge, Paul. 1993. "Pentagon's Bottom-Up Review Builds on Bush Ideas." *Boston Globe,* September 5.

Rainey, Hal G. 1996. *Understanding and Managing Public Organizations.* 2nd ed. San Francisco: Jossey-Bass.

Ranelagh, John. 1987. *The Agency: The Rise and Decline of the CIA.* Rev. ed. New York: Simon and Schuster.

Ransom, Harry Howe. 1970. *The Intelligence Establishment.* Cambridge: Harvard University Press.

Reagan, Ronald. 1988. "Remarks at a White House Meeting with Business and Trade Leaders." In *Public Papers of the Presidents of the United States, 1985.* Book 2: *June 29 to December 31, 1985.* Washington, D.C.: GPO.

Reich, Bernard. 1995. *Securing the Covenant: United States–Israel Relations After the Cold War.* Westport, Conn.: Praeger.

Reisman, W. Michael, and James E. Baker. 1992. *Regulating Covert Action.* New Haven: Yale University Press.

Reitzel, William, Morton A. Kaplan, and Constance G. Coblenz. 1956. *United States Foreign Policy, 1945–1955.* Washington, D.C.: Brookings Institution.

Report of the Commission on U.S.-Israel Relations. 1993. *Enduring Partnership.* Washington, D.C.: Washington Institute for Near East Policy.

———. 1990. *America's Secret Eyes in Space: The U.S. Keyhole Spy Satellite Program.* New York: Harper and Row.

Richelson, Jeffrey T. 1990. *America's Secret Eyes in Space: The U.S. Keyhole Spy Satellite Program.* New York: Harper and Row.

Ricks, Thomas. 1994. "A Post–Cold War Defense Plan Maps a Smaller But Ready Force." *Wall Street Journal,* February 8.

Rielly, John E. 1991. "Public Opinion: The Pulse of the '90s." *Foreign Policy* 82:79–96.

———. 1995a. "The Public Mood at Mid-Decade." *Foreign Policy* 98:70–93.

Rielly, John E., ed. 1995b. *American Public Opinion and U.S. Foreign Policy 1995.* Chicago: Chicago Council on Foreign Relations.

Ripley, Randall B., and James M. Lindsay, eds. 1993. *Congress Resurgent: Foreign and Defense Policy on Capitol Hill.* Ann Arbor: University of Michigan Press.

Risen, James. 1995. "Building a Better CIA." *Los Angeles Times,* October 8.

Robbins, Carla Anne. 1993a. "A Failure to Define Foreign Policy Plans Is Dogging Clinton." *Wall Street Journal,* August 25.

———. 1993b. "Gore's Success in Foreign Policy Role Depends on Commitment From Clinton." *Wall Street Journal,* December 13.

Rockman, Bert A. 1981. "America's Departments of State: Irregular and Regular Syndromes of Policy Making." *American Political Science Review* 75:911–27.

———. 1994a. "Leadership in the Post–Cold War World." A discussion paper prepared for The Council on Foreign Relations Study Group on "Problems of Governance and Democracy in the West," Session 3, New York.

———. 1994b. "Presidents, Opinion, and Institutional Leadership." In *The New Politics of American Foreign Policy,* edited by David A. Deese. New York: St. Martin's.

———. 1996. "Der Praesident nach dem Kalten Krieg." In *Das amerikanische Dilemma: Die Vereinigten Staaten nach dem Ende des Ost-West-Konflikts,* edited by Herbert Dittgen and Michael Minkenberg. Paderborn, Germany: Ferdinand Schoeningh.

Rosati, Jerel A. 1993. *The Politics of U.S. Foreign Policy.* New York: Harcourt Brace.

Rosati, Jerel A., Joe D. Hagan, and Martin W. Sampson III, eds. 1994. *Foreign Policy Restructuring: How Governments Respond to Global Change* Columbia: University of South Carolina.

Rosecrance, Richard, and Arthur A. Stein. 1993. "Beyond Realism: The Study of Grand Strategy." In *The Domestic Bases of Strategy,* edited by Richard Rosecrance and Arthur A. Stein. Ithaca: Cornell University Press.

Rosen, Stephen Peter. 1991. *Winning the Next War: Innovation and the Modern Military.* Ithaca: Cornell University Press.

Rosenau, James N. 1986. "Before Cooperation: Hegemons, Regimes, and Habit-Driven Actors in World Politcs." *International Organization* 40:849–94.

Rosenthal, Andrew. 1989. "Will New Helmsman at Joint Chiefs Weather Tricky Policy Crossroads?" *New York Times,* August 15.

———. 1990. "Congress Is Warned by Bush Not to Cut Pentagon Budget." *New York Times,* January 13.

Rosner, Jeremy D. 1995. *The New Tug-of-War: Congress, the Executive Branch, and National Security.* Washington, D.C.: Carnegie Endowment for International Peace.

———. 1996. "The Know-Nothings Know Something." *Foreign Policy* 101:116–29.

Rossiter, Caleb. 1984. *Human Rights: The Carter Record, the Reagan Reaction.* Washington, D.C.: Center for International Policy.

Rubin, Barry. 1987. *Secrets of State: The State Department and the Struggle Over U.S. Foreign Policy.* New York: Oxford University Press.

Rudavsky, Shari. 1992. "Panel Would Pull Plug on TV Marti." *Washington Post,* August 4.

Sandholtz, Wayne, et al. 1992. *The Highest Stakes: The Economic Foundations of the Next Security System.* New York: Oxford University Press.

Sanger, David E. 1995a. "At the End, U.S. Blunted Its Big Stick." *New York Times,* June 30.

———. 1995b. "Trade's Bottom Line: Business Over Politics." *New York Times,* July 30.

———. 1996a. "Clinton Approves Plan for Sanctions Against China Over Piracy." *New York Times,* May 9.

———. 1996b. "In Trade Rift, U.S. Outlines Penalties, and So Does China." *New York Times,* May 16.

Sanger, David E., with Steven Erlanger. 1996. "U.S. Warns China Over Violations of Trade Accord." *New York Times,* February 4.

Scarborough, Rowan. 1991. "Cheney Can't Ground Osprey." *Washington Times,* May 24.

Schilling, Warner R. 1962. "The Politics of National Defense: Fiscal 1950." In *Strategy, Politics, and Defense Budgets,* edited by Warner R. Schilling, Paul Y. Hammond, and Glenn H. Snyder. New York: Columbia University Press.

Schlesinger, Arthur M., Jr. 1978. "Human Rights and the American Tradition." *Foreign Affairs* 57:503–26.

Schlesinger, James P. 1994. Interview with author. Washington, D.C., June 16.

Schlossstein, Steven. 1984. *Trade War: Greed, Power and Industrial Policy on Opposite Sides of the Pacific.* New York: Congdon and Weed.

Schmidt, William E. 1994. "Russian Clarifies Hopes for a Link with NATO." *New York Times,* May 26.

Schmitt, Eric. 1992a. "Military Planning Deep Budget Cuts." *New York Times,* August 30.

———. 1992b. "New Battle Ahead for Powell: Budget in Congress." *New York Times,* January 17.

———. 1992c. "Pentagon Offers Some Deep Cuts But Stops There." *New York Times,* January 30.

———. 1992d. "Pentagon Warns Panel Against More Budget Cuts." *New York Times,* February 1.

———. 1993. "Aspin Resigns From Cabinet; President Lost Confidence in Defense Chief, Aides Say." *New York Times,* December 16.

———. 1994a. "Change in Direction for Pentagon." *New York Times,* January 26.

———. 1994b. "Closing the Pentagon Budget Gap." *New York Times,* September 15.

———. 1994c. "Lawmakers of Both Parties Challenge 2-War Strategy." *New York Times,* March 10.

———. 1994d. "2 Pentagon Leaders Oppose Amendment To Balance Budget." *New York Times,* February 9.

———. 1995a. "GOP Would Give Pentagon Money It Didn't Request." *New York Times,* July 5.

———. 1995b. "The Pentagon Jackpot." *New York Times,* July 10.

———. 1995c. "Worries About Military Readiness Grow." *New York Times,* April 3.

Schoultz, Lars. 1981. *Human Rights and U.S. Policy Toward Latin America.* Princeton: Princeton University Press.

Sciolino, Elaine. 1993a. "3 Players Seek a Director For Foreign Policy Story." *New York Times,* November 8.

———. 1993b. "U.S. Ends Bosnia Effort; Blames Europe for Crisis." *New York Times,* July 22.

———. 1994a. "Christopher Spreads Limelight Around." *New York Times,* January 2.

———. 1994b. "NATO Rebuffs the Russians on Role in Decision-Making." *New York Times,* June 10.

———. 1994c. "Russia's Comment on NATO Contradicted." *New York Times,* April 2.

———. 1994d. "2 Key Advisers in a Bitter Duel on U.S. Policy." *New York Times,* September 23.

———. 1994e. "U.S. Moves to Ease Beijing Sanctions." *New York Times,* March 8.

———. 1994f. "U.S. to Try a Conciliatory Tack with China." *New York Times,* March 23.

———. 1994g. "Yeltsin Says NATO Is Trying to Split Continent." *New York Times,* December 6.

———. 1995a. "Awaiting Call, Helms Puts Foreign Policy on Hold." *New York Times,* September 24.

———. 1995b. "Helms Again Blocks Senate Action on Envoys." *New York Times,* October 20.

———. 1995c. "State Dept. May Absorb 3 Independent Agencies." *New York Times,* January 11.

"Security Assistance and Commercial Arms Sales." 1991. *DISAM Journal* 13:1–7.

Seib, Gerald F. 1996. "Lamm Inspires a Fresh Look at Voters' Mood." *Wall Street Journal,* July 10.

Senior CIA Official. 1991. Letter to author. September 21.

Sestanovich, Stephen. 1994a. "At the Summit, It's All Uphill." *New York Times,* September 27.

———. 1994b. "Clinton, Yeltsin Make Arms Reduction Deal." *Columbus Dispatch (Ohio),* September 29.

Shattuck, John. 1993. *Vienna and Beyond: US Human Rights and Diplomacy in the Post–Cold War World.* Speech to the Union Internationale des Avocats, San Francisco, August 29. Photocopy.

Shoemaker, Christopher C. 1991. *The NSC Staff.* Boulder, Colo.: Westview Press.

Shultz, George P. 1993. *Turmoil and Triumph: My Years as Secretary of State.* New York: Charles Scribner's Sons.

Simon, Herbert A. 1964. "On the Concept of Organizational Goal." *Administrative Science Quarterly* 9:1–22.

Skelton, Ike. 1992. "Taking Stock of the New Joint Era." *Joint Forces Quarterly* 3:15–21.

Sloan, Stanley R. 1994. "The United States and the Use of Force in the Post–Cold War World: Toward Self-Deterrence?" *CRS Report for Congress,* July 20.

Smist, Frank J., Jr. 1990. *Congress Oversees the United States Intelligence Community, 1947–1989.* Knoxville: University of Tennessee Press.

———. 1994. *Congress Oversees the United States Intelligence Community,* 2nd ed. Knoxville: University of Tennessee Press.

Smith, Gerard, and Michael Krepon. 1993. "Keep Arms Control a Separate Agency." *New York Times,* May 3.

Smith, Hedrick. 1988. *The Power Game: How Washington Works.* New York: Random House.

Smith, R. Jeffrey. 1991. "Task Force Urges Creation of Radio for a Free Asia." *Washington Post,* December 17.

———. 1996. "Making Connections with Dots to Decipher U.S. Spy Spending." *Washington Post,* March 12.

Snow, Donald M., and Eugene Brown. 1994. *Puzzle Palaces and Foggy Bottom.* New York: St. Martin's.

Snyder, Jack. 1984. *The Ideology of the Offensive.* Ithaca: Cornell University Press.

Solomon, Burt. 1994. "Despite A Take-Charge Conductor . . . the Orchestra Is Still Off Key." *National Journal* 26:2298–99.

Sorenson, Theodore C. 1987–1988. "The President and the Secretary of State." *Foreign Affairs* 66:231–48.

Spence, Floyd. 1995. "Letter to the Editor." *New York Times,* January 5.
"The State of the Union." 1994. *Congressional Quarterly Weekly Report* 52:194–98.
Steigman, David. 1993. "O'Keefe Shakes Up Navy." *Navy Times,* August 3.
Sterngold, James. 1993. "Angry Japanese Deplore Clinton's Remarks." *New York Times,* March 25.
"Stick With Pentagon Downswing Plan or Risk Casualties in War: Cheney." 1992. *Aerospace Daily,* March 5.
Stockman, David A. 1986. *The Triumph of Politics.* New York: Harper and Row.
Stockton, Paul. 1993. "Congress and Defense Policy–Making for the Post–Cold War Era." In *Congress Resurgent: Foreign and Defense Policy on Capitol Hill,* edited by Randall B. Ripley and James M. Lindsay. Ann Arbor: University of Michigan Press.
Stokes, Bruce. 1992–1993. "Organizing to Trade." *Foreign Policy* 89:36–52.
———. 1994. "A Get-Tough U.S. Trade Negotiator." *National Journal* 26:199.
Stubbing, Richard. 1986. *The Defense Game.* New York: Harper and Row.
Tarnoff, Curt. 1995. "U.S. and International Assistance to the Former Soviet Union." *CRS Issue Brief.* Washington, D.C.: Congressional Research Service.
Thatcher, Margaret. 1993. *The Downing Street Years.* New York: Harper Collins.
Thurow, Lester. 1992. *Head to Head: The Coming Economic Battle Among Japan, Europe, and America.* New York: Morrow.
Tolchin, Susan J. 1996. "The Globalist from Nowhere: Making Governance Competitive in the International Environment." *Public Administration Review* 56:1–8.
Tonelson, Alan. 1983. "Human Rights: The Bias We Need." *Foreign Policy* 49:52–74.
Towell, Pat. 1996. "Senate Clears Compromise Bill: Clinton Expected to Sign." *Congressional Quarterly Weekly Report* 54:225–26.
Tower Commission. 1987. *The Tower Commission Report.* New York: Bantam/Times Books.
"Tower Report Assumes Biblical Status at NSC." 1987. *Washington Times,* March 10.
Trainor, Bernard E. 1986. "Defense Reorganization: New Bill Centralizes Authority at the Joint Chiefs." *New York Times,* September 19.
———. 1989. "Report Accuses Pentagon of Stalling on Changes." *New York Times,* April 9.
Treverton, Gregory F. 1987. *Covert Action.* New York: Basic Books.
Tucker, Robert W. 1993. "Book Review: Shultz: Playing a Good Hand." *Foreign Affairs* 72:138–43.
Tupfer, Timothy T. 1984. "The Challenge of Military Reform." In *The Defense Reform Debate,* edited by Asa A. Clark, Peter W. Chiarelli, Jeffrey S. McKitrick, and James W. Reed. Baltimore: Johns Hopkins University Press.
Turner, Stansfield. 1985. *Secrecy and Democracy: The CIA in Transition.* Boston: Houghton Mifflin.
———. 1987. Foreword to *The Soviet Brigade in Cuba: A Study in Political Diplomacy,* edited by David D. Newsom. Bloomington: Indiana University Press.
Twentieth Century Fund. 1992. *The Need to Know: The Report of the Twentieth Century Fund Task Force on Covert Action and American Democracy.* New York: Twentieth Century Fund.
Tyler, Patrick E. 1992a. "Pentagon Imagines New Enemies to Fight in Post–Cold War Era." *New York Times,* February 17.
———. 1992b. "War in 1990s? Doubt on Hill." *New York Times,* February 19.

U.S. Agency for International Development. 1991. *U.S. Overseas Loans and Grants.* Vol. 3: *East Asia—Obligations and Authorizations, FY 1946–1990.* Washington, D.C.: GPO.

———. 1994. *U.S. Overseas Loans and Grants, Obligations and Authorizations, July 1, 1945–September 30, 1993.* Washington, D.C.: GPO.

———. 1995. *U.S. Overseas Loans and Grants, Obligations and Authorizations, July 1, 1945–September 30, 1994.* Washington, D.C.: GPO.

U.S. Arms Control and Disarmament Agency. 1992. *New Purposes and Priorities for Arms Control.* A report to Sherman M. Funk, Inspector General of ACDA, December.

"U.S. Asks Angola Rebel to Explain Rights Abuses." 1992. *New York Times,* March 31.

U.S. Congress, Congressional Budget Office. 1994. *Congressional Budget Office Memorandum: Planning for Defense—Affordability and Capability of the Administration's Program.* Washington, D.C.: Congressional Budget Office (March).

U.S. Congress, House. 1993a. *International Relations Act of 1993.* 103d Cong., 1st sess., H. Rept. 126.

———. 1993b. *Making Appropriations for Foreign Operations, Export Financing, and Related Programs for the Fiscal Year Ending September 30, 1994, and Making Supplemental Appropriations for Such Programs for the Fiscal Year Ending September 30, 1993, and for Other Purposes.* 103d Cong., 1st sess., H. Rept. 267.

———. 1993c. *Making Appropriations for the Departments of Commerce, Justice, and State, the Judiciary and Related Agencies for the Fiscal Year Ending September 30, 1994, and for Other Purposes.* 103d Cong., 1st sess., H. Rept. 293.

———. 1994. *Foreign Relations Authorization Act, Fiscal Years 1994 and 1995.* 103d Cong., 2nd sess., H. Rept. 482.

U.S. Congress, House Committee on Appropriations. 1993. *Treasury, Postal Service and General Government Appropriations for Fiscal Year 1994, Part 3.* 103d Cong., 1st sess.

———. 1994a. *Foreign Operations, Export Financing, and Related Programs Appropriations Bills, 1994.* 103d Cong., 1st sess. Rpt. 103-125.

———. 1994b. *Treasury, Postal Service, and General Government Appropriations for Fiscal Year 1995, Part 3.* 103d Cong., 2nd sess.

———. 1995. *Treasury, Postal Service, and General Government Appropriations for Fiscal Year 1996, Part 2.* 104th Cong., 1st sess.

U.S. Congress, House Committee on Armed Services. 1982. "Reorganization Proposal for the Joint Chiefs of Staff." Hearings of the Investigations Subcommittee, April–August.

———. 1992a. *Defense for a New Era: Lessons of the Persian Gulf War.* Washington, D.C.: GPO.

———. 1992b. *Support the Committee's New "Lose Nukes" SDI Program.* Washington, D.C.: GPO.

U.S. Congress, House Committee on Energy and Commerce, Subcommittee on Oversight and Investigations. 1992. *Hearing: Illegal Military Assistance to Israel.* 102nd Cong., 2nd sess.

———. 1993. *Hearing: Illegal Military Assistance to Israel.* 103d Cong., 1st sess.

U.S. Congress, House Committee on Foreign Affairs. 1978. *International Security and Development Assistance Act of 1978.* 95th Cong., 2nd sess. Conf. Rpt. 95-1546.

———. 1989a. *Background Materials on Foreign Assistance.* 101st Cong., 1st sess. H. Rpt. 94-080.

———. 1989b. *Report of the Task Force on Foreign Assistance.* 101st Cong., 1st sess. H. Rpt. 94-080.

U.S. Congress, House Committee on Ways and Means, Subcommittee on Trade. 1978. *Hearing, Administration of the Antidumping Act of 1921.* 95th Cong., 2nd sess. Washington, D.C.: GPO.

U.S. Congress, House Select Committee to Investigate Intelligence Activities (the Pike Committee, chaired by Otis Pike, D-N.Y.). 1976. Final Report (excerpts), still classified and printed without authorization in "The CIA Report the President Doesn't Want You to Read: The Pike Papers," *Village Voice,* February 16, 69–92.

U.S. Congress, Senate. 1993. *U.S. Arms Control Disarmament Agency Authorization and Consideration of the Agency's Future Status and Responsibilities.* 103d Cong., 1st sess., S. Hrg. 351.

U.S. Congress, Senate Committee on Armed Services. 1985. *Defense Organization: The Need for Change.* Staff Report, 99th Cong., 1st sess., Committee Print 99-86: 139–57.

U.S. Congress, Senate Committee on Finance. 1974. *Hearings, The Trade Reform Act of 1973.* 93d Cong., 2nd sess. Washington, D.C.: GPO.

U.S. Congress, Senate Select Committee on Intelligence. 1991. Nomination of Robert M. Gates to Be Director of Central Intelligence. Executive Report 102-19.

U.S. Congress, Senate Select Committee to Study Governmental Operations with Respect to Intelligence Activities (Church Committee, chaired by Senator Frank Church, D-Idaho). 1976. *Foreign and Military Intelligence.* Final Report, Book 1 (Senate Rept. no. 94-755), 94th Cong., 2nd sess.

U.S. Department of Defense FY 1995 Defense Budget. 1994. Washington, D.C.: Office of Assistant Secretary of Defense for Public Affairs, February 7.

U.S. Department of Energy. 1993. *Partnership for Global Competitiveness: A Draft Strategic Plan.* Washington, D.C.: GPO.

U.S. Department of State. 1953. *Bulletin.*

———. 1973. *Papers Relating to the Foreign Relations of the United States, 1948 [FRUS, 1948].* Washington, D.C.: GPO.

———. 1984. *Papers Relating to the Foreign Relations of the United States, 1952–1954 [FRUS, 1952–1954].* Washington, D.C.: GPO.

———. 1992. *State 2000: A New Model for Managing Foreign Affairs.* Report of the U.S. Department of State Management Task Force. Washington, D.C.: U.S. Department of State Publication 10029.

———. 1993. *Congressional Presentation for Security Assistance Programs, Fiscal Year 1994.* Washington, D.C.: GPO.

———. 1994. *Country Reports on Human Rights Practices for 1993.* Washington, D.C.: US GPO.

———. 1995. *Congressional Presentation, Foreign Operations: Fiscal Year 1996.* Washington, D.C.: GPO.

U.S. General Accounting Office. 1992. *Foreign Assistance: A Profile of the Agency for International Development.* GAO/NSIAD-92-148. Washington, D.C.: GPO, April.

———. 1993a. *Foreign Assistance: AID Strategic Direction and Continued Management Improvement Needed.* GAO/NSIAD-93-106. Washington, D.C.: GPO.

———. 1993b. *Foreign Military Aid to Israel: Diversion of U.S. Funds and Circumvention of U.S. Program Restrictions.* GAO/T-O5I-94-9. Washington, D.C.: GPO.

———. 1995. *Weapons of Mass Destruction: Reducing the Threat from the Former Soviet Union: An Update.* GAO/NSIAD-95-165. Washington, D.C.: GPO.

United States Government Manual 1994–1995. 1994. Washington, D.C.: GPO.

U.S. Office of Management and Budget. 1993. *Budget of the United States Government: Fiscal Year 1994.* Washington, D.C.: GPO.

"U.S. Spy Satellite Photos Go Public." 1995. *New York Times,* February 25.

U.S. Trade Representative, Executive Office of the President. 1993. "Joint Statement of the United States–Japan Framework for a New Economic Partnership." Carlisle, Pa.: U.S. Army War College, July 10.

Vance, Cyrus. 1983. *Hard Choices: Critical Years in America's Foreign Policy.* New York: Simon and Schuster.

Wagner, John. 1992. "AID Chief Pledges Prompt Action to Fix Management Problems." *Washington Post,* July 17.

Walker, Jack L. 1981. "The Diffusion of Knowledge, Policy Communities, and Agenda Setting." In *New Strategic Perspectives on Social Policy,* edited by John E. Tropman, Milan J. Dluhy, and Roger M. Lind. New York: Pergamon.

Walker, Martin. 1992–1993. "The Establishment Reports." *Foreign Policy* 89:82–95.

Warburg, Gerald Felix. 1989. *Conflict and Consensus: The Struggle Between Congress and the President over Foreign Policymaking.* New York: Harper and Row.

Warner, Michael, ed. 1994. *CIA Cold War Records: The CIA Under Harry Truman.* Washington, D.C.: Center for the Study of Intelligence, Central Intelligence Agency.

"Washington Wire." 1993a. *Wall Street Journal,* October 8.

———. 1993b. *Wall Street Journal,* October 22.

———. 1994. *Wall Street Journal,* June 17.

Webster, William H. 1991. Interview with author. Langley, Va., May 2.

Weiner, Tim. 1994a. "C.I.A. Is Working to Overcome Sex and Race Bias, Chiefs Says." *New York Times,* September 21.

———. 1994b. "Director of C.I.A. to Leave, Ending Troubled Tenure." *New York Times,* December 29.

———. 1995a. "A Guatemala Officer and the C.I.A." *New York Times,* March 26.

———. 1995b. "The Mole's Ghost: The CIA Admits Feeding Suspect Data to Washington." *New York Times,* November 5.

———. 1996a. "CIA Chief Defends Secrecy, in Spending and Spying, to Senate." *New York Times,* February 27.

———. 1996b. "Military Chiefs Trying to Gain Extra Billions." *New York Times,* April 10.

Weiss, Thomas G., David P. Forsythe, and Roger A. Coate. 1994. *The United Nations and Changing World Politics.* Boulder, Colo.: Westview Press.

Weissman, Steven R. 1995. *A Culture of Deference: Congress' Failure of Leadership in Foreign Policy.* New York: Basic Books.

Wells, Samuel F., Jr. 1992. "Nuclear Weapons and European Security During the Cold War." In *The End of the Cold War: Its Meanings and Implications,* edited by Michael J. Hogan. New York: Cambridge University Press.

Wessel, David. 1992. "Economic Security Council Stirs Debate." *Wall Street Journal,* November 10.

West, Diana. 1986. "Presidential Man for Contras." *Washington Times,* April 10.
Westerfield, H. Bradford, ed. 1995. *Inside CIA's Private World.* New Haven: Yale University Press.
Wharton, Clifford R. 1993. "USAID and Foreign Aid Reform." *U.S. Department of State Dispatch* 4:526–31.
Wheeler, C. Gray, and David W. Moore. 1993. "Clinton's Foreign Policy Ratings Plunge." *Gallup Poll Monthly* 337:25–28.
The White House Office of Science and Technology Policy. 1994. *Science and Technology Budget Briefing.* February 8.
"White House Report: Peterson Unit Helps Shape Tough International Economic Policy." 1971. *National Journal,* November 13.
Whitney, Craig R. 1994a. "NATO Bends to Russia to Allow It a Broader Relationship." *New York Times,* May 19.
———. 1994b. "NATO Plight: Coping with Applicants." *New York Times,* January 4.
———. 1994c. "Treading Gently: Clinton and Europe Face Their Fears." *New York Times,* January 16.
———. 1995a. Depite Russian Objections, NATO Plans to Add Members." *New York Times,* September 21.
———. 1995b. "Russia Warns Against Haste in Adding NATO Members." *New York Times,* March 21.
Wildavsky, Aaron. 1988. "President Reagan as a Political Strategist." In *The Reagan Legacy,* edited by Charles O. Jones. Chatham, N.J.: Chatham House.
———. 1992. *The New Politics of the Budgetary Process.* New York: Harper Collins.
Williams, Daniel. 1994a. "China's Hard-Nosed Rights Stance Working Against Trade Status." *Washington Post,* March 5.
———. 1994b. "Christopher Sets Somber Mood for Human Rights Talks in China." *Washington Post,* March 12.
———. 1994c. "Duffey Urges Status Quo for Television Marti." *Washington Post,* July 9.
Williams, Daniel, and Ann Devroy. 1994. "U.S. Applies Two-Pronged Force Policy." *Washington Post,* October 16.
Williams, Daniel, and John M. Goshko. 1993. "Reduced U.S. World Role Outlined but Soon Altered." *Washington Post,* May 26.
Wilson, James Q. 1989. *Bureaucracy.* New York: Basic Books.
Winks, Robin W. 1987. *Cloak and Gown: Scholars in the Secret War, 1939–1961.* New York: Morrow.
Wise, David. 1992. *Molehunt.* New York: Random House.
Wisner, Frank G. 1993. *Memorandum to the Secretary of Defense: Bottom-Up Review of Defense Needs and Programs.* Undated memorandum from the U.S. Office of the Secretary of Defense.
Wittkopf, Eugene R. 1990. *Faces of Internationalism: Public Opinion and American Foreign Policy.* Durham, N.C.: Duke University Press.
Wolfowitz, Paul D. 1994. "Clinton's First Year: Harding or Truman?" *Foreign Affairs* 73:28–43.
Woolsey, R. James. 1993a. Interview with author. Langley, Va., September 29.
———. 1993b. Testimony, U.S. Senate Select Committee on Intelligence. 103d Cong., 2nd sess., March 6.

———. 1994. "National Security and the Future Direction of the CIA." Address to the Center for Strategic and International Studies, Washington, July 18.

WuDunn, Sheryl. 1996. "In Summit Silences, a Truce In U.S.-Japanese Trade Wars." *New York Times*, April 18.

Yoffie, David B. 1989. "American Trade Policy: An Obsolete Bargain?" In *Can the Government Govern?* edited by John E. Chubb and Paul E. Peterson. Washington, D.C.: Brookings Institution.

Zaller, John R. 1992. *The Nature and Origins of Mass Opinion.* New York: Cambridge University Press.

Zimmerman, Robert F. 1993. *Dollars, Diplomacy, and Dependency: Dilemmas of U.S. Economic Aid.* Boulder, Colo.: Lynne Rienner.

Zisk, Kimberly Marten. 1993. *Engaging the Enemy: Organization Theory and Soviet Military Innovation, 1955–1991.* Princeton: Princeton University Press.

Zuckerman, Stanley A. 1994. "USIA Revamps Its Image in the Post–Cold War Era." *Foreign Service Journal* 71:36–37.

Zuehlke, Arthur A., Jr. 1980. "What Is Counterintelligence?" In *Intelligence Requirements for the 1980s: Counterintelligence,* edited by Roy Godson. Washington, D.C.: National Strategic Information Center.

Contributors

Vincent A. Auger is assistant professor of government at Hamilton College.

Duncan L. Clarke is professor in the School of International Service at American University.

David P. Forsythe is professor and chairperson of the Department of Political Science at the University of Nebraska, Lincoln.

Peter Hahn is associate professor of history at Ohio State University.

Richard K. Herrmann is professor of political science and faculty associate of the Mershon Center at Ohio State University.

Loch K. Johnson is Regents Professor of Political Science at the University of Georgia.

James M. Lindsay is professor of political science at the University of Iowa. In 1996–1997 he served as director for global issues and multilateral affairs, National Security Council, The White House.

Pietro S. Nivola is a senior fellow in the Governmental Studies Program at the Brookings Institution.

Daniel O'Connor is a doctoral candidate in the School of International Service at American University.

Shannon Peterson is a doctoral candidate in political science at Ohio State University.

Randall B. Ripley is professor of political science and dean of the College of Social and Behavioral Sciences at Ohio State University.

Bert A. Rockman is university professor of political science and research professor of the University Center for International Studies at the University of Pittsburgh.

Paul N. Stockton is associate professor of national security affairs at the Naval Postgraduate School.

Kimberly Marten Zisk is assistant professor of political science and faculty associate of the Mershon Center at Ohio State University.

Index